Managing
Employee
Rights
and Responsibilities

Recent Titles from Quorum Books

The Privilege to Keep and Bear Arms: The Second Amendment and Its Interpretation
Warren Freedman

The Tort of Discovery Abuse
Warren Freedman

Classic Failures in Product Marketing: Marketing Principle Violations and How to Avoid Them
Donald W. Hendon

The Management of International Advertising: A Handbook and Guide for Professionals
Erdener Kaynak

Public Sector Privatization: Alternative Approaches to Service Delivery
Lawrence K. Finley, editor

The Work/Life Dichotomy: Prospects for Reintegrating People and Jobs
Martin Morf

Financial Management for Health Care Administrators
Ronald John Hy

Computer Simulation in Business Decision Making: A Guide for Managers, Planners, and MIS Professionals
Roy L. Nersesian

A Stakeholder Approach to Corporate Governance: Managing in a Dynamic Environment
Abbass F. Alkhafaji

The Impact of Intergovernmental Grants on the Aggregate Public Sector
Daniel P. Schwallie

MANAGING
EMPLOYEE
RIGHTS
AND RESPONSIBILITIES

EDITED BY
Chimezie A. B. Osigweh, Yg.

Q QUORUM BOOKS

NEW YORK • WESTPORT, CONNECTICUT • LONDON

Library of Congress Cataloging-in-Publication Data

Managing employee rights and responsibilities / edited by Chimezie
A.B. Osigweh, Yg.
    p.   cm.
    Bibliography: p.
    Includes index.
    ISBN 0–89930–336–6 (lib. bdg. : alk. paper)
    1. Labor laws and legislation—United States.   2. Employee rights—
United States.   3. Personnel management—United States.
I. Osigweh, Chimezie A. B.
KF3455.M36   1989
344.73'01—dc19
[347.3041]   88–38310

British Library Cataloguing in Publication Data is available.

Library of Congress Catalog Card Number: 88–38310
ISBN: 0–89930–336–6

First published in 1989 by Quorum Books

Greenwood Press, Inc.
88 Post Road West, Westport, Connecticut   06881

Printed in the United States of America

The paper used in this book complies with the
Permanent Paper Standard issued by the National
Information Standards Organization (Z39.48–1984).

10 9 8 7 6 5 4 3 2 1

To
mom and dad

The first teachers
Whose academy
Subtly, but tirelessly
Imparted to me
The reciprocal tenets
of human interrelationships
and the obligatory character
of rights:
Lucy Mgbokwere Ogbonna Osuigwe
Joseph Anyahuru Alexis Osuigwe
(In his living memory)

And to the little one:
Ndidi Mgbokwere-Lucy Osigweh

Who always silently wondered
What tomorrow might bring

Contents

APPENDIXES   xi

FIGURES AND TABLES   xiii

PREFACE   xv

Part I.   Introduction   1

1. The Challenge of Employee Rights and
   Responsibilities in Organizations
   Chimezie A. B. Osigweh, Yg. and Marcia P. Miceli   3

2. A Perspective on Workplace Justice for
   Organized and Unorganized Workers
   Michael E. Gordon and Robert Coulson   21

Part II. Legal Perspectives   49

3. Legislation as the Best Protection Against Unjust
   Discharge
   Jack Stieber   51

4. The Terrain of Wrongful Dismissal Legislation
   Henry H. Perritt, Jr.   59

5. Trends in Title VII Discrimination Legal Theories:
   The Future of Disparate Treatment and Disparate
   Impact
   Rebecca A. (Baysinger) Thacker and Stuart A.
   Youngblood   83

Part III. Human Resources and Management Education
Perspectives   97

6. Positive Discipline: A Nonpunitive Approach to
   Managing Human Resources
   William R. Hutchison and Chimezie A. B. Osigweh,
   Yg.   99

7. Positive Discipline from the Worker's Perspective
   Richard W. Humphreys, Frederick A. Zeller, and
   Sarah S. Etherton   117

8. Internal Mechanisms for Resolving Employee
   Complaints in Nonunion Organizations
   Alan F. Westin   151

9. Reactive and Proactive Resolution of Employee
   Responsibilities and Rights Staff Issues via the
   Ombudsman Concept
   Merle Waxman   161

10. How'm I Doin'? I Have a Need and a Right to
    Know
    Michael J. Kavanagh   175

11. The Communicative Act of Whistleblowing
    J. Vernon Jensen   187

12. The Responsibilities of the Management
    Professoriate in the Administrative State
    William G. Scott   199

Part IV. Conclusion   209

   13. Employee Rights: Required versus Desired
        Paul F. Salipante, Jr., and Bruce Fortado   211

   14. A Social Constructionist and Political Economic
        Perspective of Employee Rights
        Walter R. Nord   229

   BIBLIOGRAPHY   253

   INDEX   281

   CONTRIBUTORS   289

Appendixes

5.1   The Legal Cases Studied   93
7.1(a) In Capsule: Positive Discipline   139
7.1(b) Positive Discipline—Group I   140
7.2   Progressive Discipline—Group II   146

Figures and Tables

FIGURES

9.1	Interactive Relationships within the Academic Community	164
9.2	The Relationship of the Ombudsman to the Academic Hierarchy	167
12.1	Management's Triad of Orthodoxy	202
12.2	The Inner and Outer Circles of Management Thought	204
13.1	Actual Employer Practices and the Zone of Unfulfilled Expectations	228

TABLES

1.1	Some Examples of Rights and Corresponding Responsibilities	6
1.2	A Framework for Examining Employee Rights and Responsibilities	19
5.1	Outcomes of Content Analysis of Eighty-One Discrimination Cases	87
7.1	Forms of Conduct for which Severe Discipline Is Generally Conceded	121
7.2	More Usual Grounds for Industrial Discipline	122

7.3 Conditions under which Punishment Can Be Effective   125

7.4 Possible Advantages of Positive Discipline Compared to
     Other Disciplinary Arrangements   130

7.5 Possible Benefits from Present Discipline System (i.e.,
     Progressive) versus Any Other Discipline System   135

10.1 Employee Rights in Performance Appraisal   179

13.1 Incidence of Denied Employee Rights   219

Preface

"What exciting times we live in!" Frequently we are reminding ourselves of this statement, as if it were an immutable truth of our organizational society. Or, are we simply attempting to give ourselves courage? Of course courage is needed to launch bold attacks on the many stubborn problems confronting today's workplaces in the form of seemingly insolvable perturbations. To the daring, the challenge of possibly seeking out ways to effectively confront any of the difficult challenges of modern organization is quite exciting and perhaps further offers a sense of practical and intellectual adventure. The underlying maxim perhaps is that shying away from action, or a flirtation with a behavioral excess, if allowed to infiltrate the human character becomes a contagion. Nevertheless, the problems themselves, especially those that appear to be most insoluble, are quite complex. Complexity itself is viewed here as a euphemism for organizational perturbations that are encountered within environments of tremendous knowledge gap and uncertainty; hardened by long years of orthodox, if slightly questionable, practices; and enmeshed within (theoretical) myths that symbolize our (especially management's) traditional constructions of, and visions for, the corporate world. (On orthodoxy and mythical constructions, see Osigweh, 1989, 1988b; Scott, Chapter 12, infra). This book focuses on one such complex area of "perturbation," by exploring issues and approaches for dealing with employee/employer responsibilities and rights in a managerial context.

Employee responsibilities and rights have become considerably more important as a set of factors to be considered by management in the last decade. Among other reasons, this has been due to legal changes designed to redress organizational and individual relationships. In addition, there has been increased organizational recognition that failure to make moral, legal, and practical changes in the light of emerging individual and societal attitudes and expectations leads to imbalances that can, in turn, produce costly losses in organizational performance. Whatever the reasons, emergent employee responsibilities and rights comprise an important new management problem and challenge.

The magnitude of the phenomena encompassed by the subject of managing employee and employer responsibilities and rights is enormous and at times bewildering. As a result, the multiplicity of points from which the subject can be examined is quite impressive. It is not surprising, therefore, that contributions to organizational practice and theory in this area have spanned many traditional disciplines, even if merely confined to them. Indeed, much of the available conceptual and applied knowledge in the employee responsibilities and rights area have not only been generated by individuals in the traditional disciplines, but have also remained there—being applied only within the confines of the specific discipline by persons with backgrounds in those particular disciplines. Examples are in the fields of law, philosophy, collective bargaining, and communication. Thus, although the multiplicity of viewpoints from which the subject can be approached is very impressive, the volume of literature on employee responsibilities and rights per se (as a distinct and unique interdisciplinary area of knowledge) is unimpressive. Again, this is hardly surprising since organizational concern with employee rights and responsibilities challenges only reached salience in the mid- to late 1980s.

This book therefore charts a course that has been predominantly neglected in the past. First, it summarizes the current knowledge of employee responsibilities and rights issues and points out directions for future research and practice. Second, it suggests the need for a shift in paradigm, from the discipline-specific orientations to the development of a paradigm that is distinctive and yet interdisciplinary. Third, the book emphasizes the dual areas of (1) management, and (2) employee/employer responsibilities and rights. Fourth, it underscores the need to approach rights and responsibilities issues from a broader management context, while calling attention to the significance of managing the various issues in today's workplaces.

Works by various scholars and practitioners are used to present specific, but complementary, perspectives and insights for dealing with employee/employer responsibilities and rights within a management context. Detailed actual case explorations of programs that have worked well in other organizational settings (e.g., Chapters 6 and 9), short case examples, and court case decisions, as well as the provision of some hard evidence, or presentation of quantified data (e.g., Chapters 5, 6, 7, 8, 9, and 13) are used to document specific ideas all through the book. In the few instances where the language is laboriously technical and the data methodologically daunting, it is hoped that the professional, or lay reader, can read around the specific material or chapter, or sections thereof, without much loss of substance. Overall then, the language and style of data presentation contained in this volume are fashioned to be meaningful, and of significant appeal, to both practitioners and scholars in private and public-sector businesses and industries, as well as colleges and universities.

The book proceeds in four parts that help fulfill the above description. In Part I, "Introduction," Chimezie A. B. Osigweh, Yg. and Marcia P. Miceli take as their point of departure the increasing salience of rights and responsibilities issues in the management of contemporary organizations (Chapter 1). Here, at the onset, it is necessary to grasp the notions of "rights" and "responsibilities." Osigweh and Miceli lead the way, defining the concepts based on a "do no harm" principle. They further offer an analysis of factors that may have influenced the transformation of traditional employee-employer relationships and, in addition, provide a framework for understanding various manifestations of employee rights and responsibilities.

Organizational justice, viewed in terms of fairness broadly defined, from a management perspective is a major underlying focus of rights and responsibilities issues (see, e.g., Chapter 1). Management can effectively address various organizational justice concerns by drawing on the various strategies (philosophical, collective action, legal, human resources, and managerial education) proposed by Osigweh and Miceli. Michael E. Gordon and Robert Coulson (Chapter 2) underscore that the issue of justice for union and nonunion workers can be approached in management from behavioral and legal perspectives, even while reflecting other orientations or perspectives such as the collective action or the philosophical. On the legal side, the authors detail the problems arising when justice-related employee and employer behavioral problems are allowed to develop, thereby warranting the possible external involvement of some lawyers who have the tendency to be litigious. On the behavioral side, employee and employer expectations *and* potential and actual reactions when there are perceptions of breach in what is considered just or fair are explored. Of course, the latter (i.e., potential reactions) includes litigation, a reaction so widespread that Part III of the book is underscored by it, and most chapters of the book draw from its existence. Gordon and Coulson further argue that a nonunion worker may be just as secure as a union member depending upon the health of the enterprise, the good faith of management, the degree of sensitivity to employees that has been institutionalized as part of the organizational culture, and the prevailing legal framework within which managers and employees must interrelate.

Not many observers will disagree that justice in the workplace exists in the shadow of the law. If nowhere else, Osigweh and Miceli, and Gordon and Coulson (Chapters 1 and 2) substantiate this position. Nevertheless the law, regardless of its merits or demerits is one, and only one, way to address organizational justice and other rights and responsibilities concerns. It is partly based on that backdrop that Part II of the book, on the "Legal Perspectives," approaches issues of employee and employer responsibilities and rights of interest to management scholars and practitioners, by exploring various relevant notions and intricacies of the law.

Our government seems less pervasively involved in worker protection when compared to certain other countries of the world (see also Blades, 1967; Osigweh, 1988a; Summers, 1976). Indeed, evidence suggests that the extent to which recent court decisions have eroded the employment-at-will (EAW) doctrine (the notion that the employer has the right to fire any employee for good reason, for reason morally wrong, or even for no reason at all) has been greatly exaggerated. The public policy and implied contract exceptions to EAW have been interpreted narrowly by most courts and provide only limited protection to most of the 2 million nonunionized employees who are discharged for cause each year. Increased unionization, voluntary employer action, and reliance on the judiciary are found wanting as protections against unjust discharge. It is consistent with this state of affairs that Jack Stieber's conclusion in Chapter 3 proposes legislation, at either the federal or state level, as the best solution to the problem of at-will employment. The detailed exploration by Henry Perritt, Jr. (Chapter 4) examines the current wrongful dismissal legislation that will serve the interests of various concerned groups such as employers (e.g., protecting organizations from wrongful dismissal suits), employees, and others. Perritt presents and analyzes the prominent legislative models, discussing substantive and procedural fairness. His review and analysis would lead us to conclude that the more desirable legislation is one that clearly defines substantive rights, while establishing inexpensive and yet conclusive procedures for making and reviewing decisions that affect organizations and their workers.

There is a temptation to view the legal approach as the most effective perspective for addressing employer and employee responsibilities and rights issues within a management context. Rebecca A. (Baysinger) Thacker and Stuart A. Youngblood (Chapter 5), however, suggest that this tendency should be viewed with caution. They examine and provide data on how "disparate treatment" and "disparate impact" legal theories are used to address the problem of discrimination in organizations. Among other things, their conclusions point to instances when the legal philosophies cannot effectively address the problem of discrimination at work. Thus, Baysinger and Youngblood document, in specific empirical terms, that there are situations when the legal perspective is not effective for approaching workers' dispositions in the contemporary workplace. Similar suggestions have also been made by Gordon and Coulson in Chapter 2. Part III of this book, on "Human Resources and Management Education Perspectives," flows from these premises, extending the arguments by Osigweh and Miceli and the themes underpinned by Baysinger and Youngbood, and Gordon and Coulson. It emphasizes, illustrates, examines or, in parts, introduces in more detail the human resource management and managerial education components of the paradigmatic groundwork outlined in Chapter 1 by Osigweh and Miceli.

Consistent with the less legal and more behavioral human resources thinking (see Osigweh, 1985a, for a good treatment of the human resources philosophy), William R. Hutchison and Chimezie A. B. Osigweh, Yg. (Chapter 6) propose that the traditional approaches to discipline in organizations ignore the great majority of employees who are performing well. In response to employee problems, many organizations use punishment, instead of an emphasis on the notion of responsibility and the commitment to goals that derives therefrom. Further, the authors offer a nonpunitive performance management model called positive discipline. *Positive discipline*, as an approach to managing human resources without the dysfunctional aura of punishment, emphasizes commitment, individual responsibility, and the recognition of good performance. One of the innovative characteristics of this approach is that it allows the employee to receive a "decision-making leave," in the form of a one-day disciplinary "suspension" *with pay*. On this day, the employee must decide either to resolve the immediate problem and commit to totally acceptable performance in the future, or decide to quit and find more satisfying work elsewhere. While providing a detailed case description of how the approach has worked well at Union Carbide Corporation, Hutchison and Osigweh also examine the role of management development and training (executive or supervisory education) in implementing a new, innovative change, or management system such as positive discipline.

Any detailed examination of the employment-at-will doctrine (and its legal ramifications) as it bears upon industrial relations in general (see, e.g., Perritt, 1984a), and industrial discipline in particular (see, e.g., Humphreys, Zeller, and Etherton, Chapter 7), would reveal that although EAW has had a profound effect upon the characteristics of our industrial relations system, organizational behavior literature provides little guidance for practitioners seeking guidance regarding the form and substance of an effective discipline system that addresses or checks the organizational problems resulting from the doctrine. Richard W. Humphreys, Frederick A. Zeller, and Sarah S. Etherton (Chapter 7) make a timely effort toward filling this gap. Their chapter examines the progressive and positive systems of discipline from the perspective of two groups of workers, one group working under positive discipline, the other under a traditional progressive system. Their empirical data, obtained through questionnaires and structured interviews, suggest that the type of discipline system is less important than how it is administered. Both groups of workers found fault with the way in which discipline was administered in their respective workplaces. In addition, the data strongly suggest that employee discipline systems may have a perverse effect—to the extent that in the course of eliminating and/or minimizing deviant behavior, the discipline system may indeed evoke inefficient behavior. Thus, while Hutchison and Osigweh adopt the conceptual, exploratory, and exposé traditions in terms of methodology, making theoretical proposals, practical arguments, and providing actual case illustrations, Humphreys, Zeller, and Etherton employ the exploratory and empirical routes to provide additional concrete data to shed more light on the idea of positive discipline from a worker perspective.

Perhaps the most important development that will guide the outcome of the emerging rights and responsibilities issues of concern to management is how well employers in the years ahead install new employee relations practices, including new internal dispute resolution mechanisms. Based on the real-world experience of many employers and employees, Alan F. Westin (Chapter 8) strongly argues for designing and developing such dispute resolution frameworks. He points to the existence of excellent models of internal complaint systems that can be adopted and expanded elsewhere in the corporate world. His chapter also provides characteristics or elements to bear in mind while constructing a dispute resolution system that is based on fair processes mechanisms. Merle Waxman (Chapter 9) provides one example of how new "innovative" and "fair process" systems may be developed for the internal resolution of conflicts that pertain to employee and employer responsibilities and rights in modern organizations. Waxman accomplishes this by illustrating how one organization implemented an internal conflict resolution model at the individual level based on the concept of the corporate ombudsman. Her chapter suggests that under the ombudsman framework within large institutions, redundancy of problem-solving mechanisms is produced giving employees an important sense of multiple options. The complexity of Waxman's organization, a large medical center, and its unique hierarchical structure, together with the stress of medical training and care for patients, isolation, and historically enforced, gender-related stereotypes, all create a fertile environment for conflict within such an organizational milieu. The ombudsman concept provides a useful vehicle for nonlitigational conflict resolution. The om-

budsman office also serves an important proactive role, identifying in-
cipient problems or trends.

Concern over the performance evaluation process in organizations is
shared equally by management and employees. Since the results of the
performance evaluation process indicate the productivity level of the
organization and the individual, they are central and crucial to the operation of the organization. Michael J. Kavanagh (Chapter 10) details
the rights of employees in the performance appraisal process based on
a consideration of (1) the conceptual and empirical literature on the role
of performance appraisal and feedback on employee motivation and
efficiency, and (2) case law regarding proper practices in performance
appraisal. The implications of employee rights in performance appraisal
are then used to indicate specific design features that management practitioners should consider as guides in developing or revising current
performance appraisal programs. The redesign of performance appraisal
programs advocated in the chapter is consistent with the call for innovative and fair process systems by Alan F. Westin in Chapter 8 and the
positive discipline approach discussed by William R. Hutchison and
Chimezie A. B. Osigweh, Yg. in Chapter 6. Like Waxman's idea of the
ombudsman (Chapter 9), which among other things recognizes the role
of effective communication in managing rights and responsibilities, Kavanagh underscores the significance of effective feedback of workers'
performance on their job responsibilities, while examining the centrality
of communication to the performance appraisal process.

It is commonplace to discuss whistleblowing as episodes within the
contexts of business, industry, government, or the law. But whistleblowing has not been carefully analyzed as a dynamic phenomenon in
communication and within an organizational rights-responsibilities context. Indeed, the communicative act of whistleblowing is very complex.
It involves intentional, responsive, accusatory interactions. It is public
and refutational, uses varying media, and may linger over a long period
of time. It seeks support for one's claims, strains a contractual arrangement, and struggles with many ethical tensions. A whistleblower is
usually a single individual, subordinate to the accused, a well-informed
insider, deeply agitated, highly motivated, a participant turned judge,
and is perceived in a two-valued light of being either a traitor or hero.
Whistleblowing is increasing and is receiving encouragement and protection in various ways. Yet it remains a highly risky undertaking, likely
to bring much economic and psychological pain to whistleblowers and
their families and close associates. The contribution by J. Vernon Jensen
(Chapter 11) views whistleblowing as a communicative act within the
context of employee and employer rights and responsibilities. His exploration maps out and examines various characteristics of whistleblowing and whistleblowers. Jensen also sketches the current status of
whistleblowing, with particular attention to legal protection and other

social, market, and organizational mechanisms that encourage (and discourage) whistleblowing. Based on his analysis, Jensen concludes that society needs to find ways to protect the reliable whistleblower in order to preserve and foster individual integrity, responsible corporate values, and public well-being and safety.

If the 1980s are remembered for any major events, among them will certainly be the acts of those in high places that affronted the moral equanimity of members of our society. It was in that decade (specifically 1980–1982, and exposed in 1985) that E. F. Hutton & Company, a major American brokerage firm, engaged in enormous accounting gymnastics to defraud tax payers, the federal government, and its own clients of billions of dollars. Managers of the big New York brokerage house operated a massive check-writing scheme that fraudulently obtained money from many of the company's 400 banks without paying interest. More than $10 billion, and as much as $250 million on some days were involved (see, e.g., the *Wall Street Journal* stories by Andy Pasztor and his colleagues, May 3 and 5, 1985). Consider, further, the spring 1987 case of Ivan Boesky of the Drexel Burnham Lambert company. The investment executive sought and obtained insider information as his firm negotiated acquisitions for other, client, companies. Using this information just before it was made public, Boesky and his company would engage in insider trading, acquiring enormous quantities of the stocks of the target companies (i.e., the firms being acquired). Once the acquisition deals became public knowledge, triggering an increase in the price of the target company stocks, Boesky would sell his holdings at literally millions or billions of dollars in profits. It was also during that decade (particularly 1986–1988) that several top managers of even the religious and spiritual organizations (e.g., Jim Bakker, Tammy Bakker, Jimmy Swaggart, Oral Roberts) engaged in financial and sexual conducts that smacked of executive decadence and shocked the conscience of the nation, while tremoring society at large.

These and the numerous other widely reported excursions into the moral and ethical twilight of corruption and misconduct by business managers, public administrators, and finance bankers have resulted in an unparalleled decline in public confidence in the leadership of contemporary organizations. It is not surprising, therefore, that management education is undertaking a reappraisal of its part in the development of the moral character of students who have aspirations for management jobs. However, what is done in education today reflects the way that management evolved (Osigweh, 1985a).

Modern management and the preparation of tomorrow's business leaders through management education and professional training grew as the administrative state evolved in America. It became a distinguishing feature of American life spawning a "self-aware" field of knowledge and a class of executives. The identity of both this field and this class depended upon orthodoxy of thought that had three elements: markets, positive science, and myths. They governed the nature of practice, research, and theory in management.

Chapter 12 by William G. Scott revolves around the premise that management education is the captive of practice. This is to say that the needs of practice determine what is researched, theorized, and taught in management education. Scott holds, in conclusion, that this link must be broken for management education to exercise moral autonomy in the ethical development of students.

In short, much of the concern with the impact of employee rights and responsibilities problems focuses on what the employer can do to forestall or resolve those problems (see, e.g., the chapters by Westin, Waxman, and Kavanagh). Departing from that mold, Scott underscores an additional emphasis. Perhaps the beginning point for addressing these problems should be in the training schools or management education programs. Accordingly, Scott invites us to reevaluate the responsibilities of management educators, or the management professoriate, in fulfilling the rights of students or business leaders of tomorrow—which include sharpening their conscience and moral development through intellectual preparation. Scott therefore calls for the reformation of management training programs, based on a moral scheme that rises above prevailing management orthodoxy, while emphasizing freedom of choice and the expansion of learning alternatives and ethically fortifying management-related schemata.

One major theme of this book is that the legal perpective has severe limitations in dealing with rights and responsibilities problems and that the practical, if moral, perspectives are more promising. Part IV, the book's "Conclusion," begins with a contribution by Paul F. Salipante, Jr., and Bruce Fortado (Chapter 13), reexamining this premise while casting light on the question of whether employee rights strategies are desired or required in the contemporary industrial relations system. They share some newly collected actual cases on employee grievances from a wide range of organizations. The cases were derived from "workers" in the broad sense of the term—that is from managers and subordinates alike. Drawing upon a set of fifty grievance interviews, Salipante and Fortado analyze employees' views of their rights and the actions that individuals utilize when frustrated in attempts to resolve their grievances. Employees' expectations are summarized in a comprehensive list of eight rights that reflect moral and practical orientations transcending the legal perspective. How the grievances and similar problems affect line managers, plus practical implications for both employers and employees within a rights-responsibilities context are presented. The expansive view of employee rights that emerged from the interviews and the past history of managerial reaction to employment law illuminate the limitations of law in resolving employee/employer conflict. The authors also find that (1) a large gap exists between the treatment workers expect from their employers and popular conceptions of employee rights, and (2) an even greater gap exists between the treatment workers expect and what they actually receive from their employers. Data from the study help illustrate the nature, shape, and consequences of the resulting worker frustration and how they may impose unwanted costs on the modern organization. Salipante and Fortado conclude that the costs the aggrieved employees impose on their organizations create a practical incentive for organizations to address a far wider range of rights than can be defined in law.

Finally, in Chapter 14, Walter R. Nord develops an "interpretive/ critical political economic" perspective, which provides useful guidance for examining the conditions that affect the existence and exercise of employee rights (and the responsibilities associated with them). The interpretive component suggests that the exercise of rights at the micro (individual) level is heavily influenced by the social construction of reality. The critical component emphasizes the goal of individuals to exercise emancipatory self-control or conscious self-determination over outcomes that are important in their lives. The "political economic" component calls attention to aspects of the macro structure (institutional, public policy, market conditions—for example, laws, unemployment, alternative jobs, systemic assumptions, etc.), which affect and are affected by behavior and social construction at the individual (micro) level. From this perspective, a combination of social and psychological processes and concrete "real" conditions are seen as central to understanding and advancing employee rights. Thus, Nord concludes that although macrolevel variables centrally emphasized by many rights-responsibilities perspectives continue to be important, greater attention ought to be devoted to the fact that the existing treatments of employee rights need to explore the combined input of psychological, social, and political economic factors on the social construction of reality at the microlevel.

Comments by Paul F. Salipante, Jr., Patricia H. Werhane, and Frederick A. Zeller are gratefully acknowledged. I would like to express my special thanks to Krystal Curry and Sandra Parker for painstaking research assistance, and to my secretary, Aretha Harris, for typing and putting together the final manuscript.

PART I

INTRODUCTION

The Challenge of Employee Rights and Responsibilities in Organizations

CHIMEZIE A. B. OSIGWEH, YG.
AND MARCIA P. MICELI

Organizations have been experiencing several unprecedented occurrences in employer-employee relationships (Westin, Schweder, Baker, and Lehman, 1985). According to reports appearing almost daily in the media, the workplace is being transformed by conflicts over such issues as employee versus corporate free speech; employee privacy versus testing for drug use, truthtelling, and personality traits; employee rights to continued employment versus employers' rights to terminate the employment relationship "at will"; prevention of or remedying of unfair discrimination versus "reverse" discrimination; and a host of related issues. Several authors (e.g., Ewing, 1983) have suggested that increasingly, employees are challenging their organizations' practices, and this upward trend is expected to continue.

Issues pertaining to employee rights and responsibilities may at first appear disparate; for example, it may be difficult to see a connection between (1) the privacy and testing issue and (2) employee versus corporate free speech. However, they are in fact similar in that all involve a rethinking of traditional views of employer-employee relationships. Moreover, empirical studies clearly suggest that many problems associated with the issues have undesirable effects on productivity-related workplace processes such as occupational satisfaction, creativity, and credibility perceptions (Gorden and Infante, 1987). Thus, practitioners and academics can no longer avoid paying more careful attention to rights-related concerns and the organizational practices mandated by them.

Concerned practitioners and acdemicians are only beginning to discover and examine these issues and their implications for employees
and for management practice. This introductory chapter represents an
attempt to further this discovery and examination process. In this introductory chapter, we attempt to do three things: (1) define in very
general terms what is meant by employee rights and responsibilities; (2)
describe factors that may have influenced the transformation of traditional employer-employee relationships; and (3) provide a framework
for understanding the various manifestations of employee rights and
responsibilities. We begin with the definition.

DEFINING EMPLOYEE RIGHTS AND RESPONSIBILITIES

Our focus in the present chapter is on employee rights and responsibilities. By the term "employee rights" we employ a very broad definition in referring to the general injunction to "do no harm." Thus,
rights in the workplace may be justified or evaluated by reference to
some basic standards or moral principles. Hence, workplace rights can
be defined in terms of the basic injunction that an employer should do
no harm to workers (Osigweh, 1988b; Sashkin and Morris, 1987). Obviously, many definitional issues that are beyond the scope of this introduction can be raised; for example, at what point does an action that
has both helpful and harmful consequences for others violate the injunction to do no harm? Such issues are raised or suggested by other
contributors to this volume (e.g., Gordon and Coulson, Chapter 2, infra;
Perritt, Chapter 4, infra. See also Munchus, 1987).

Although attention conceivably could be focused on employee rights
exclusively, such treatment would be incomplete, because rights imply
responsibilities. Specifically, each set of rights has its own set of obligations, and is therefore tied to one or more particular set(s) of role
responsibilities (Osigweh, 1987a; Werhane, 1985, 1987). Thus, for example, a worker's right to protection from irrational employer job demands has the corresponding obligation that the worker carry out
legitimate instructions fully and in the best way possible. Thus, just as
workers have a right to be protected from harm, they have a responsibility to do no harm to others in the workplace.

This is equally true for both employers and employees (Werhane, 1987;
Osigweh, 1988a). Because workplace relationships have a reciprocal
character, this same employee right also underpins the employer's right
to the worker's best possible performance and complete attentiveness
to legitimate orders, while implying that the employer has the responsibility of ensuring that the relevant instructions are not irrational. Thus,
for example, management's rights to discipline and fire workers in settings where collectively bargained agreements exist has the correlative

responsibility of ensuring that the decision is just. It is the responsibility of the employer to adhere to the mutually established grievance procedure to ensure organizational justice.

Table 1.1 shows an illustrative listing of employee rights and corresponding responsibilities. As can be seen, employee rights are frequently linked to managerial responsibilities; employee responsibilities can be viewed as linked to managerial rights as well.

FACTORS AFFECTING THE TRANSFORMATION OF EMPLOYEE-EMPLOYER RELATIONSHIPS IN THE CONTEMPORARY WORKPLACE

We make an underlying assumption that the phenomena pertaining to employee rights and responsibilities are so closely related in important ways, that factors affecting rights and responsibilities of one type will also affect those of other types. This is an untested assumption that should be examined empirically. However, we think that it is reasonable to make the assumption at this time. To the extent that the same factors affect a set of rights and responsibilities, it is useful to identify these factors, because the identification of influences will help us understand why a fundamental change in workplace relations is occurring and why it is likely to continue.

Changing Characteristics of the Work Force

Professionalization and the Rise of Highly Paid, Highly Visible, and Very Powerful Workers

The increasing professionalization of the labor force is a well-documented phenomenon (Hall, 1986; Osigweh, 1985a, 1986). Individuals are obtaining higher levels of education, and a higher proportion of the work force is employed in jobs requiring higher levels of skills and responsibility than in the past. This trend is of particular interest in the examination of changing employer and employee relationships, because professionals may be more cognizant of, or more likely to assert, both rights and responsibilities (Graham, 1986). For example, Chimezie A. B. Osigweh's (1983) study of participation in problem-solving, using 458 members of five transnational organizations, has documented that knowledge inspires confidence to act. Similarly, Marcia P. Miceli and Janet P. Near (1988a) have shown that persons of higher educational and professional status are more likely than other persons to "blow the whistle" on perceived wrongdoing.

The propensity of professionals to be more aware of rights and responsibilities, and their propensity to exercise them, may stem from a

Table 1.1
Some Examples of Rights and Corresponding Responsibilities

Employee Right (Management Responsibility) Principle	Employee Responsibility (Management Right) Principle	Illustrative Employee (Employer) Activity
Employees have a right to, and managers have a responsibility to make, hiring and promotion (selection) decisions based on objective, job-related information	Employees have a responsibility to accept management's right to select whomever management pleases so long as the selection procedure is just and legal	Employees allow managerial documentation of valid performance and service records and participate in studies to improve recruitment and selection; management should train and monitor
Employees have a right to work in, and managers have a responsibility to provide, climates free from discrimination based on race, sex or other characteristics	Managers have a right to manage without consulting with employee representatives on a day-to-day basis so long as the decisions are consistent with legal and ethical standards	Employers should maintain a channel for employee voice, communicate rights, and review policies and procedures; employees should learn about rights and help others assert them responsibly
Employers have the responsibility to maintain safe working environments; employees have the right to walk off jobs under objectively dangerous conditions	Employers have the right to expect workers to remain on their jobs under safe and healthy conditions that meet legal and moral standards	Employers must design and enforce safe and healthy environments (e.g., through hiring of safety and health specialists, implementation and monitoring compliance with OSHA, training of managers and employees)
Employees have the right to protection from, and management has the responsibility to refrain from, intrusive employer practices	Employers have the right to perform (and employees have the responsibility to submit to) valid tests or make (respond to) inquiries that are necessary and job-related	Employers must not seek disclosure of private information or use polygraphs unless they are shown to be reliable and job-related

6

Table 1.1 (continued)

Employee Right (Management Responsibility) Principle	Employee Responsibility (Management Right) Principle	Illustrative Employee (Employer) Activity
Employees have the right to fair and good faith dealings in all practices	Management has a right to expect fair and good faith dealings with employees	Managers and employees must keep recruiting promises, follow employment the employee handbook guidelines, and communicate clearly and in timely fashion
Employees have the right to avoid being expected to participate in, or work in an organization where others engage in illegal, immoral, and unethical practices, and management has the responsibility to ensure that organizations and their members behave in ethical and legal ways	Managers have the right to make strategic and operating decisions without consulting employees or their representatives where such decisions take into account the effects of policies on others and meet the organization's moral and legal responsibilities	Employees should give opportunities to managers and other organization members to respond to complaints if the organization can be expected to take corrective action without retaliation
In settings where collectively bargained agreements exist, management must adhere to the grievance procedure to ensure organizational justice, through the right to due process	In settings where collectively bargained agreements exist, employees must behave, and management has a right to discipline and fire workers, in accordance with contractual provisions	Management should maintain grievance mechanisms, train employees and management about contractual provisions, use positive discipline; Employees should perform as expected and not file frivolous grievances or break rules
In non-union settings, employees have right to job security and management should ensure job security as long as performance and service record meets reasonable standards	In non-union settings, employers have right to to discipline and fire workers in good faith	Employer should maintain valid performance appraisal systems, consistently apply rules, train in policy application, maintain internal hearing forums; Employees should perform at levels expected and file no frivolous complaints

7

variety of factors. These factors include: (1) the skill and facility to examine, analyze, and critically reevaluate prevailing circumstances; (2) the confidence to press for change in the modern workplace; (3) increasing power ascribed to high-status positions. Also, professional status or interactions with other professionals may affect the assessment of responsibility (Graham, 1983) or the level of support from outside the organization (Miceli and Near, 1988a; Near and Miceli, 1987a). Professionals may have greater opportunity for alternative employment and hence they may be less dependent on their employers, who may react negatively to the questioning of employer practices (Near and Miceli, 1985). Thus, as the level of professionalization increases, individuals may be more likely to seek or even demand that their voices be heard by management, rather than to accept direction without question.

One other hypothesis that has attempted to link professionalization with increased awareness of workplace issues is that the socialization processes embodied in codes of ethics may impart a "service ethic" or "sense of social responsibility" (Perrucci, Anderson, Schendel, and Trachtman, 1980, p. 150). However, Derek Bok (1986) has pointed out that ethical dilemmas "are seldom treated systematically and directly in professional education" (Scott and Mitchell, 1986, p. 7). Thus, professionals may be no better prepared than other workers to identify or address ethical dilemmas and more empirical research is needed to examine this issue.

Many other employees, including those who might not meet academic definitions of "professionals," may be immensely powerful, in the sense that they are sources of ideas or decision-making hubs who must work closely with various levels of management, or by virtue of certain unique competencies that they bring to the organization. As one example, witness the case of Amy Guohland, who went to work for a large high-tech firm on the West Coast in August 1985 (Osigweh, 1987b). Guohland's ceramics and metallurgical engineering training and experience landed her an entry-level nonmanagerial position, a salary of $29,500, and excellent fringe benefits. Although her job involved working with a team of eight other materials engineers, her unique background rendered her a one-person ceramics department emphasizing product design. Although her position was several levels away from the lowest managerial rung on the organization's hierarchy, her decisions were vital and management depended on them. She could paralyze, devastate, cripple, or hold for ransom the company's ceramics operations because she alone possessed a ceramics background.

Guohland's case suggests that some organizations employ workers in specialty areas, and each specialty may be crucial to continued and profitable operations. The interdependency of workers means that when one fails or refuses to carry out responsibility, the productivity of others falls to zero (Thurow, 1975). Thus, as the levels of professionalization and specialization rise, the power held by these workers increases. This trend can be expected to put pressure on organizations to reform work-places and rethink what once might have been considered as sacred management prerogatives.

The Size of the Working Population

The size of the employed work force in the United States is greatly increasing. In 1978, 96 million people were employed during the fourth quarter (Bureau of Labor Statistics, as cited in Flaim and Fullerton, 1978). By 1983, this figure had grown to 106 million employees, including 70 million persons employed by 80,000 businesses with 100 or more em-ployees (Ewing, 1983). Recent data show that the civilian labor force was 117.2 million in 1986 (USDOL, 1986a, 1986b).

The implications of this growth for employee rights and responsibil-ities issues are obvious. As more and more persons enter the work force, the opportunity for conflicts between employers and employees in-creases (Schumacher, 1973).

Worker Mobility

Americans are more mobile than in the past; people are changing jobs and leaving organizations with greater frequency than previously. Ac-cording to the Department of Labor, as of January 1987, 69 percent of employees had been with their current employer for five or fewer years (Rosenberg, 1988). Newcomers to organizations often bring different perspectives reflecting their prior experiences in organizations with dif-ferent cultures. They are unlikely to accept a diminution of rights that they enjoyed at previous organizations. As cross-fertilization of ideas occurs, organizations may be more likely to confront attempts at change.

Worker Diversity and the Variegated Societal Culture

The work force in the United States has undergone a tremendous transformation in the past few decades in terms of its demographics. American workers are not only white, Anglo-Saxon, and Protestant men. This faulty characterization ignores the work force presence of people of diverse backgrounds, including various races (e.g., black), ethnic origins (e.g., Italian, Polish, Scandinavian), and religions (e.g., Catho-lics, Jews, Mormons, Moslems, atheists, and agnostics). Finally, there has been a dramatic increase in the labor force participation of women (Norwood, 1982). Women of all races now comprise more than 40 percent of the labor force and this percentage is increasing (Flippo, 1980). At the same time, white males continue to control the most powerful positions in many organizations (e.g., Darr, 1987), and the policies that exist understandably are based on their values, perceptions, and ideas about appropriate organizational behaviors.

The diversity of cultures and individual characteristics plays an important role in employee-employer relations, because this diversity may be associated with differences in values, perceptions, and responses of persons to organizational policies. To the extent that these values, perceptions, and responses call for a modification of employer thinking concerning rights and responsibilities, the opportunities for conflict and change will increase as the work force evolves.

Another important demographic change is the aging of the work force and the concentration of a large number of "baby boomers" in the middle-range jobs during the present decade (Fullerton, 1980; Gottschalk, 1981). As Ewing (1983) points out, "baby boomers" may feel compelled to challenge organizational authority in asserting their rights, because of their experiences in protesting the draft and their participation in (or influence by) the social upheaval of the 1970s, including the civil rights movement and increasing awareness of environmental issues. These movements were relatively successful in bringing about some social change, though observers may disagree about the extent of this success and the expeditiousness of its implementation. Success may reinforce and give confidence to persons who see change happen (Miceli and Near, 1985).

Changing Organizational Structures

Bureaucracy vs. Flexibility and the Protection of Employee Rights

One issue that has yet to be explored in depth empirically is whether bureaucracies, with their attendant formalized rules and rational bases for decision making, can more effectively ensure employee rights than can more flexible, open organizations. In recent years, organizations have shown increasing interest in participative decision making, quality circles, gainsharing, employee stock ownership, and similar workplace innovations. For example, Edward E. Lawler and S. A. Mohrman (1985) estimated that over 90 percent of the Fortune 500 companies now have quality circle programs, which they (and Rafaeli, 1985) say are groups of employees who seek to "identify, analyze, and solve various work-related problems" (Tang, Tollison, and Whiteside, 1987, p. 800).

One goal of such innovations is to provide greater flexibility in response to environmental pressures, such as increased competition, and in response to increased knowledge and skill of workers who would like to offer greater input and to assume greater control. Frequently, such changes are hailed as beneficial to workers, but there may be disadvantages of limiting bureaucracy.

Bureaucracy may serve to ensure that the principle of "doing no harm" while invoking the rational-legal authority framework within which the organization operates (Osigweh, 1988b; Sashkin and Morris, 1987) is upheld by requiring that rules be formulated, reduced to writing wherever possible, and applied consistently across similar situations (Weber, 1947). In more open structures, it is conceivable that no one will have thought of rules to be applied and that similar situations will be handled very differently. Differences may be interpreted as inequities. For example, in an effort to be "fair," a graduate admissions committee may allow applicants with incomplete application forms to submit the remaining needed materials after the published due date. But some applicants who did not know of this policy deviation will not attempt to apply because they did not believe they would be able to assemble complete files by the due date. It is understandable if these applicants would complain of unfairness upon learning that rules were "broken" for other applicants. Similarly, an employee who is denied access to resources such as long-distance telephone privileges, travel, copying, or secretarial support, ostensibly because "the organization cannot afford it," will complain justifiably of unfairness if she or he learns of other employees who obtained resources after "being in the right place at the right time." In a well-functioning bureaucracy, there is a rational basis for denying certain employees access to certain resources (e.g., if one's sales aren't sufficiently high, one cannot attend the annual sales meeting in Hawaii). Rules exist to protect the rights of similarly situated persons to similar organizational treatment.

It is not difficult to generate other instances in which the rights of employees may be better protected by bureaucracies than by flexible structures and systems. For example, the Uniform Guidelines on Employee Selection (EEOC, 1981) call for careful record keeping regarding availability of minorities and women, wider advertising and posting of job openings than might originally be contemplated, complex validation requirements, and other bureaucratic procedures designed to encourage the hiring of the best-qualified applicants without regard to race, sex, or other irrelevant characteristics. A more decentralized hiring process carried out by persons (1) untrained in the law or in selection techniques, and (2) not sufficiently sensitized to the fair treatment of all persons, may promote a positive sense of "ownership" in the hiring process, but may lead to unconscious abrogation of the rights of other individuals as well as a failure to carry out one's own managerial responsibilities.

Not surprisingly, research on procedural justice in organizations is now emerging (Greenberg, 1987). In contrast to distributive justice theories such as equity theory (Adams, 1965), which focus attention on relative *outcomes*, attention in the procedural justice literature is focused on how individuals come to view organizational *procedures* as fair and satisfying (Miceli and Near, 1988b). This research suggests that employees are more satisfied when rules are applied consistently; for example, employees believe that their performance should be evaluated in accordance with written performance appraisal standards (e.g., Greenberg, 1986; Miceli and Near, 1988b). Other procedural rules also imply that bureaucracy could be beneficial in ensuring organizational justice; for example, that decisions (e.g., about performance) should be based on accurate information (Leventhal, 1976).

However, empirical support also exists for the notion that flexibility and openness promote desirable organizational outcomes (e.g., Baucus, Near, and Miceli, 1985). Indeed, the procedural justice literature further suggests that greater employee participation will lead to perceptions of justice (Greenberg, 1987). Clearly, more empirical research is needed to determine whether the trend toward more flexible systems will continue, and if so, whether such systems can be managed in such ways as to preserve the benefits of well-run bureaucracies without sacrificing the benefits of flexibility. In any case, the increased interest in "open" organizational cultures will heighten awareness of issues involving employer-employee relations.

Managerial Orthodoxy

The influence of managerial orthodoxy (Scott, 1985)—and the low regard for the dignity of workers associated with it—provides another stimulus for the revolution in rights thinking in modern workplaces. According to William Scott (1985, p. 150) the "orthodoxy of managerialism" is a "value system that encourages the treatment of humans in ways that deprive them of their humanness."

Managerial orthodoxy can be understood in terms of two sets of distinct but interrelated elements (Osigweh, 1988a; Scott, 1985). The first is a worldview in which market considerations and their attendant quantitative and rational analyses are supreme. A market emphasis is justified because it fosters objective analysis and predictive rigor, while providing reliable yardsticks for allocating management's resources. The resulting value system underscores an orientation in which markets are the only reference points for management decisions, including those affecting human behavior at work. Second, managerial orthodoxy calls for the manipulation of the values of organization members in order to foster management's objectives. As described in Scott's contribution to this volume (Chapter 12), managerial orthodoxy relies on "myths, fables and fairy tales that management 'enacts' in order to secure control over individuals and groups within organizations," activities which he calls "not straightforward, not innocent and certainly not unhypocritical."

The pervasive magnitude of both elements of the orthodox value system has been well documented (Beam, 1986; Jenkins and Reizenstein, 1984; Nussbaum and Beam, 1986). One study of (1) personnel managers and chief executive officers of Fortune 500 firms, and (2) business school deans, alumni, and faculty, suggested that organizations and business training programs emphasize quantitative and market-driven considerations more than 75 percent of the time (Jenkins and Reizenstein, 1984). The more "humane," if less doctrinaire, areas of ethics, psychology, and human behavior receive considerably less attention. Yet it has been clearly shown that a basic component of all work activities and relations in organizations should be the moral and psychological injunction to "do no harm" (Sashkin and Morris, 1987, p. 114).

Another study suggested that managers tend to follow conventional utilitarian rules when making ethical decisions (Fritzsche and Becker, 1984). These researchers used a categorization of ethical reasoning in organizations (Cavanagh, Moberg, and Velasquez, 1981) to formulate vignettes depicting ethical dilemmas to which managers could respond. Managers tended to rely on a utilitarian orientation, in which acts or rules that lead to the greatest social benefit (immediately or over the long run) would be viewed as ethical. They tended not to rely on (1) a theory of rights, in which the decision maker is primarily concerned with respect for the rights of individuals, or (2) a theory of justice, in which the decision maker is guided primarily by concern for equity, fairness, and impartiality. Fritzsche and Becker (1984, p. 174) speculated that "such an orientation possibly could be explained by the strong role economics plays in managerial decision making."

In short, researchers, employees, and sometimes employers are taking a critical look at workplace rights thinking. Employees in particular may view with concern issues of orthodox management values while demanding that their rights not only be protected, but respected as well.

Corruption in Organizations

A factor related to managerial orthodoxy concerns corruption in organizations. By corruption we mean the incidence of questionable activities carried out by organizational members either to benefit the organization or to benefit themselves. Examples include employee theft, acceptance of bribes, "creative accounting," fraudulent marketing, or any other activities that are illegal, immoral, or illegitimate. Organizational corruption may occur because organizations and their managers perceive threats to their survival, coming from the business environment; research suggests that poor financial performance is frequently linked with organizational crime, that is, illegal activity to benefit the organization (Finney and Lesieur, 1982; Staw and Szwajkowski, 1975). Other employees may engage in wrongdoing for their own professional

benefit or because organizational reward systems exert pressure to behave unethically (Jansen and Von Glinow, 1985).

Although reliable data concerning the incidence of organizational
wrongdoing are not widely available, some surveys suggest that in the
federal government, between one-third and one-half of all employees
have observed activities they consider wrongful (USMSPB, 1981, 1984).
Likewise, a recent study revealed that about one-third of the research
scientists surveyed believed they were aware of at least one researcher
who engaged in questionable practices at their own or other institutions
(Tangney, 1987). Some observers maintain that corruption is on the
increase (Schutt, 1982); greater awareness of corruption also may now
occur because of increased media publicity and household access to the
media (e.g., through cable television, satellite disks). In either case, the
existence of organizational corruption seems relevant to the increased
concern with workplace justice. Employees may question whether they
have a responsibility to act to halt it and whether their rights to do so
will be protected. Greater levels of corruption in the organization may
suggest to individuals that corruption is an entrenched part of organizational climate that will consequently be difficult to change because of
organizational dependence on it (Miceli and Near, 1985, 1988a; Pfeffer
and Salancik, 1978). Thus, corruption may be self-perpetuating without
external regulation, and its interference with employee rights and responsibilities may lead to increased legal intervention to ensure that
rights and responsibilities are respected.

Changing Societal Institutions

The Moral Void of Business Education

Managers make decisions that affect the lives of others; thus, in many
ways managerial behavior involves the exercise of practical ethical judgment (Osigweh, 1988a; Scott and Mitchell, 1986). However, there is
evidence that students are receiving insufficient grounding in ethical
decision-making, and this void is coming under increasing scrutiny by
observers interested in employee rights and rsponsibilities.

Because students seeking business degrees and specialized vocational
training have a limited amount of time to spend in school, business
schools have been forced to make difficult choices about curricular of-
ferings. The common approach has been to emphasize the type of subject
matter that business school leaders believe is most valued by their constituencies, which may comprise business managers, public-sector administrators, the students themselves, or other parties. These
constituents frequently demand courses that appear to provide job-related skills. Often, the subject matter that is emphasized or required of

all students lends itself to quantitative analysis—for example, account-ing, finance, or economics. Other subjects, such as strategic planning, marketing, and management, are frequently taught in terms of the mar-ket and orthodox ideology (as discussed earlier).

Under such constraints, there may be little time devoted to a ques-tioning of the value orientation of business itself or to the values un-derlying the instruction designed to meet the needs of future business leaders. A critical omission from the curriculum in many business schools today therefore is coursework designed to examine ethical is-sues. This omission is critical because members of modern organizations frequently face difficult ethical dilemmas for which they may be unpre-pared. For example, what is the appropriate response when one learns of clear wrongdoing committed by one's organization or fellow workers against the shareholders or the public? If a new manufacturing inno-vation is highly profitable but somewhat risky to worker health and safety, how much risk should be tolerated, and at what cost? If there is little likelihood of a lawsuit by a member of a protected class, is it acceptable to promote a job candidate because higher management is more comfortable with that candidate than with the protected class mem-ber? Business educators could conceivably help prepare future organi-zation members by discussing these dilemmas and the implications of various resolution alternatives. Thus, business education should ideally seek to foster learning in the exercise of practical moral judgment. Fur-ther, as more and more scandals (e.g., involving insider trading or vi-olations of worker safety laws) are reported in the media, greater pressure may be brought to bear on educators to take some responsibility for and to rectify the problem.

Unfortunately, as noted earlier, attention to ethical issues is not often provided in business schools, in part because of the preference for train-ing viewed as more "productive." Another reason why ethical issues are not addressed may be that educators themselves lack the skills nec-essary to lead discussions involving ethics or to analyze complex ethical problems. They may be uncomfortable talking with students where they believe there are "no right answers." Professors may themselves be imbued with the utilitarian value system and may be unaware of alter-native ethical perspectives. Further, reward systems for professors rarely treat the ethical development of students as an important dimension of professorial performance. But such difficulties must be confronted if students are to be prepared to carry out their future responsibilities consistent with the trust that employees and the public place in them.

The implications of the moral void in today's business schools are clear, with respect to employee rights and responsibilities: to the extent that organizations engage in practices that at least some employees consider to be immoral, opportunities for conflict, reduced morale, and withdrawal will abound (Hirschman, 1970). Continuing failure on the part of business schools to address moral and ethical issues will result in the perpetuation of organizational behaviors that are insufficiently examined and potentially very costly in the long run (Scott and Mitchell, 1986).

The Favorable Legal Climate

There is evidence that lawmakers and courts are increasingly sympathetic to employee interests (Coulson, 1981; Ewing, 1983; Elliston, Keenan, Lockhart, and Van Schaick, 1985; Estreicher, 1982; Stieber and Murray, 1983; Westin, 1980; Youngblood and Tidwell, 1981). This trend has contributed to the heightened attention to rights and responsibilities. Some observers, in fact, feel that the pendulum has swung too far in the direction of the exercise of legal initiatives. In one New England organization, for example, lawsuits are such a frequent occurrence, that twenty-five have been filed by workers in three years. Although this is hardly funny, employees in this organization now joke about the "lawsuit of the week" (McMillen, 1987). Other observers, of course, disagree and call for more sweeping or pervasive legislation (e.g., Blades, 1967; Perritt, 1984; Stieber, 1986; Stieber and Murray, 1983; Summers, 1976, 1980).

The evidence that statutory protection has increased can be seen most vividly in four areas: (1) antidiscrimination laws; (2) occupational safety and health and workers' "right to know" legislation; (3) laws concerning privacy and polygraph testing; and (4) state and federal whistleblower protection laws (see Osigweh, 1987b). Courts are also carving out exceptions to the "employment-at-will" doctrine, which in earlier times permitted employers to terminate employees without cause (Steiber, 1984). The "erosion" of this doctrine is expected to continue (Perritt, Chapter 4, infra).

Rejection of Traditional Collective Bargaining

Workers are opting out of traditional collective bargaining arrangements while still pressuring for their rights, even though collective bargaining mechanisms and their grievance and arbitration frameworks provide perhaps the "best existing protection" against perceived unjust managerial practices (Osigweh, 1987b; Stieber, 1984). It has been estimated that the current union membership attrition rate is 3 percent per year (Freeman, 1985, p. 49. See also Feinstein, 1988, p. 1). Moreover, only about 14 percent of the nonunionized work force is being organized (Osigweh, 1987b). This lack of interest relative to earlier decades is probably attributable to many factors (Hoerr, Glaberson, Moskowitz, Cahan, Pollock, and Tasini, 1985). In one case, for example, workers in a multifacility organization in Missouri eventually rejected the efforts of a union attempting to organize them because they believed that their rights would be equally protected in the absence of a union (Osigweh, 1987a). As collective bargaining declines in prevalence, there will be a greater potential for conflict over rights and responsibilities that once were spelled out in contracts that also provided for a formal grievance process.

In summary, a variety of factors account for the increased attention focused on employee rights and reponsibilities today. Some of the factors challenge traditional views about appropriate employee-employer relations, while others are causing fundamental changes in the workers, their workplaces and their organizations. How do we attempt to examine the issues raised by the challenge of workplace rights and responsibilities?

EXAMINING EMPLOYEE RIGHTS AND RESPONSIBILITIES: A FRAMEWORK

Although the issues pertaining to employee rights and responsibilities are complex and interrelated, we suggest that these issues—as introduced in this chapter and detailed in several of the other chapters—can be categorized loosely as pertaining to (1) rights and responsibilities arising before membership in an organization (e.g., rights to obtain a job); (2) rights and responsibilities arising during employment (e.g., rights to certain conditions while working); and (3) rights to retain employment (e.g., rights to keep a job). These three considerations relate to one dimension—the level of conceptual focus of examining workplace rights and responsibilities (see Table 1.2).

A second dimension deals with the variety of approaches that can be used to focus on these issues. This dimension is not continuous but rather comprises a set of five categories. One approach is to examine these issues through philosophical strategies for ensuring rights and responsibilities. This may be the oldest tradition, as suggested by Jeremy Bentham (1948/1780) and exemplified by William G. Scott (1985). Discipline-specific works adopting this approach are quite abundant, especially among individuals who come from philosophy backgrounds (e.g., Donaldson, 1982; Goodpaster and Mathews, 1982; Werhane, 1985). A second approach examines the reliance on collective activity, such as the economic power of unions representing bargaining units of employees, as a means for bringing about greater recognition of employee rights (e.g., Osigweh, 1985b, 1985c).

A third approach focuses on legal strategies and is exemplified by works examining the various statutes, constitutional protections, and tort law relevant to employee rights. This is probably the most widespread approach (e.g., Blumrosen, 1978; Peck, 1979; Summers, 1976). A fourth and emerging approach emphasizes human resource management strategies, and focuses on motivation, communication, rewards, and other human resources and industrial-relations systems and their consequences. The contributions to Part III of this volume are primarily examples of works that fit this mold. Finally, a fifth and frequently neglected approach involves strategies that focus on managerial and professional education. Detailed justifications for increased attention to management education strategies can be found in Osigweh (1988b, 1988a) and Scott and Mitchell (1986).

Table 1.2 not only depicts the two dimensions of the study of employee rights and responsibilities, but also reflects a framework for examining the relevant issues. Chapters in the current volume tend to emphasize rights and responsibilities during employment, from the perspective of human resource strategies; however, as Table 1.2 implies, by no means can this be considered an exhaustive treatment of all potential combinations of strategies and levels. Table 1.2 lists the chapters in this volume (by author) according to the nature of the perspective taken and the issues examined. The exceptions are some of the introductory and concluding contributions, particularly Chapter 1 (Osigweh and Miceli), Chapter 13 (Salipante and Fortado), and Chapter 14 (Nord). As material designed to introduce and conclude this book, they jointly cut across each component of the framework and therefore are not listed in Table 1.2. In addition, Table 1.2 shows that this volume devotes a great deal of attention to strategies for approaching employee responsibilities and rights within a human resource context. Further, it calls attention to the need for strategies for managing employee responsibilities and rights based on management and professional education.

SUMMARY

This introductory chapter had three purposes. First, we attempted to define in very general terms what is meant by employee rights and responsibilities. Because each employee right has a corresponding responsibility, it is essential to discuss both rights and responsibilities within the same context. To illustrate, we provide a table listing some examples of employee rights and corresponding responsibilities.

A second purpose was to describe categories of factors that may have influenced the transformation of traditional employer-employee relationships. It is our view that there are a number of trends in the United States that are contributing to the increased attention on worker-management relationships, and that these trends can be loosely categorized. These categories, by no means exhaustive, include the changing characteristics of the work force, such as increased professionalization

Table 1.2
A Framework for Examining Employee Rights and Responsibilities

Level of Conceptual Focus on Employee Rights and Responsibilities

	R/R Before Employment	R/R During Employment	R/R to Continued Employment
Philosophical Strategies			
Collective Activity Strategies		Some mentions contained in Gordon & Coulson (Ch. 2)	
Legal Strategies	Perritt (Ch. 4) Baysinger & Youngblood (Ch. 5)	Perritt (Ch. 4)	Stieber (Ch. 3) Perritt (Ch. 4)
Human Resource Management Strategies		Gordon & Coulson (Ch. 2) Hutchison & Osigweh (Ch. 6) Humphreys et al. (Ch. 7) Westin (Ch. 8) Waxman (Ch. 9) Kavanagh (Ch. 10) Jensen (Ch. 11)	Gordon & Coulson (Ch. 2) Hutchison & Osigweh (Ch. 6)
Managerial and Professional Education Strategies	Scott (Ch. 12)		

(Left margin vertical label: Strategies for Defining and Assuring Employee Rights and Responsibilities)

levels, increased size of the working population, increased participation by minorities and women, and increased worker mobility. A second category concerned changing organizational structures, which raises questions concerning conflicts between bureaucratic rules, which may protect employee rights, and the increasing interest in "flexibility." The rise of "managerial orthodoxy" as a philosophy of management is also identified as raising structural issues, as does organizational corruption. A third category focused on changing societal institutions, including educational institutions that attempt to provide management education that may or may not address moral and ethical concerns. Another societal institution is its legal climate, which researchers suggest is increasingly sympathetic to employee interests, as noted earlier. Another societal institution is reflected in traditional collective bargaining arrangements; the weakening of unions' power to insure recognition of employee rights, which ironically may create greater interest in and conflict over employee rights.

A third purpose of this introductory chapter was to propose a framework for understanding the various manifestations of employee rights and responsibilities. Although our framework is preliminary and therefore rather crude, we believe that it may serve as a useful first step in suggesting two dimensions around which attention to employee rights can be focused. The first dimension represents the stage or level in the employee-employer relationship that gives rise to the employee rights and responsibilities issue (e.g., before employment, during employment, or termination versus continued employment). The second dimension represents categories of strategies for defining and assuring rights and responsibilities. We propose that these strategies can be categorized as involving philosophical strategies, collective activity strategies, legal strategies, human resource management strategies, and managerial and professional education strategies.

It is our hope that this chapter helps to set the stage for the other chapters in this volume. Further, we hope that it provides some context for future inquiry and research into the important arena of employee rights and responsibilities.

A Perspective on Workplace Justice for Organized and Unorganized Workers

MICHAEL E. GORDON
AND ROBERT COULSON

> Justice is only possible when to every man belongs the power to resist and claim redress for wrongs.
>
> *Robert S. Briffault*

Justice in the workplace is a subject of vital importance and, consequently, a matter in which there has been long-standing and widespread interest. Historically, concern for workplace justice was responsible in part for the creation of labor unions, the establishment of public policy that provides workers with equitable wages and safe working conditions, and the rise of political movements that sought to empower working people by reducing or eliminating capitalist control over the means of production. In view of the importance of the subject, it is not surprising to find scholarly treatises in a variety of academic disciplines that deal with workplace justice. Each academic perspective offers useful insights into the subject. Nonetheless, we will argue that the behavioral perspective requires special attention. Given that legal scholars and philosophers cannot agree on what fairness really is in any absolute sense, it is, perforce, imperative to study justice as it is perceived to be (Greenberg, 1988). By acknowledging the importance of subjective standards of workplace justice, research on the issue will remain incomplete lacking the behavioral study of workers.

In this chapter, behavioral theory and research on workplace justice are reviewed. After discussing the concept of workplace justice in terms derived from the study of social cognition, it will be argued that, at least implicitly, workplace justice has been a salient issue in behavioral science for about thirty years. This brief historical introduction will be followed by a more thorough description of conceptual foci that have evolved from the recent proliferation of research on reward and due process systems in administrative and organizational contexts. This research has identified a number of procedures that are consistently viewed as fairer than others and, consequently, are more likely to engender acceptance of outcomes.

Regardless of what researchers have discovered about constructing more equitable human resource programs that promote workplace justice, in actuality most disputes between individual workers and owners are resolved through patently unequal negotiations, with most of the bargaining power held by the latter. Given this power differential, questions have been raised about the ability of workers to *resist and claim redress for wrongs* without institutional support. Unions and negotiated grievance systems are, respectively, institutions and institutionalized mechanisms for providing due process. The chapter will conclude with a discussion of the effect that recent common-law precedents are having on the effectiveness of traditional employee institutions and due process mechanisms.

JUSTICE DEFINED

The most unmistakable characteristic of the voluminous writing on justice is the absence of agreed-upon definitions of the concept and procedures for due process. Ralph Newman's (1973) collection of papers on comparative law makes it evident that what is considered fair or just has changed continuously since the age of the Academy in Athens, and that within any particular era the meaning of justice frequently appears ambiguous. Hence, any attempt on our part to define the concept is unlikely to satisfy the requirements of all the various disciplines and institutions concerned with the issue of justice. We can, however, try to place the concept in the context of the social and industrial psychological literatures to be reviewed.

In common parlance, the term "just" is applied evaluatively to describe perceptions of social exchanges. Social exchanges are transactions between two interdependent parties, Self and Other. The list of such human transactions is endless, especially when one considers that role interdependence is the basis of all social organizations, including families, educational institutions, and societies at large, to name a few (Graen, 1976). One of the most familiar, and clearly most relevant, of such social exchanges is that between employee and employer. This exchange often is characterized as "just" if employees receive "a fair day's pay for a fair day's work."

Scientific study of social exchange has attempted to identify the motives, procedures, and rules that govern behavior in interdependent relationships where Self and Other(s) intend to trade valued resources with one another. According to Charles McClintock and Linda Keil (1982), "social exchange theories are concerned with the structural and functional nature of relationships that obtain between two or more actors who are outcome interdependent, and who reciprocally determine the delivery of various classes and amounts of resources to one another" (pp. 348, 349). In the employment context, it should be clear that the valued resources representing the bases for the transaction may be quite varied. Employees customarily consider their work experience, specialized skills, company loyalty, and level of effort to be commodities with which they can "negotiate." Employers, on the other hand, regard wages and benefits, and type of supervision to be resources that may be "traded."

Expectations about the particular social exchange between employees and employers involving these resources was entitled the "psychological contract" by Edgar Schein (1980). "The notion of a psychological contract implies that there is an unwritten set of expectations operating at all times between every member of an organization and the various managers and others in that organization" (p. 22). The psychological contract is implicit in the concept of organization roles. Associated with each formal role in the organization is a set of formal and informal behavioral expectations. Not only do these expectations pertain to the quality and quantity of work that should be performed for given amounts of financial compensation, but there are highly salient expectations concerning the rights, privileges, and obligations each party has with respect to the other. "Many of these expectations are implicit and involve the person's sense of dignity and worth" (p. 23).

Descriptions of workplace justice focus on the perceived fairness, or psychological acceptability (Folger and Greenberg, 1985), of these exchanges comprising the psychological contract. The psychological acceptability of social exchanges appears to be determined by the outcomes of the transaction and/or the procedures used to produce these outcomes. Because of the importance of subjective factors in shaping the psychological contract and assessing whether the actions of Other(s) have met the expectations of Self, it should not be surprising that employees and employers often find themselves at odds. Even though public negotiations ostensibly deal with more tangible matters such as pay, working hours, and job security, "some of the strongest feelings leading to labor unrest, strikes, and employee turnover have to do with violations of these aspects of the psychological contract" (Schein, 1980, p. 23).

The frailty, yet concomitant significance, of the psychological contract was described as follows: "The literature of industrial relations abounds with examples of broken contracts and crushed expectations on both sides of the exchange. Considerable time and resources have been spent by organization management and industrial relations researchers on attempts to discover why contracts are broken" (Hammer and Bacharach, 1977, p. 1).

With this background, we are prepared now to define a few relevant terms. *A social exchange will be perceived as just by Self if it has been conducted properly and has produced psychologically acceptable outcomes.* In other words, *justice* is defined in terms of the subjective states and experiences of Self, ignoring Other's perceptions of the transaction unless these are of some consequence in determining the psychological acceptability of the outcomes for Self. Such a view is consistent with a voluminous literature that emphasizes justice as a subjective state or quality. In this regard, it is important to acknowledge a conceptual distinction between what is expected and what is just. Joanne Martin (1986) demonstrated in a sample of blue-collar subjects that expectations and perceptions of justice did not coincide. However, visions of perfect economic justice did not depart radically from existing norms for industrial wages. This outcome is consistent with a great deal of research that has documented a fundamental conservatism in people's views of a perfectly just world. Martin accounts for such conservatism in terms of the cognitive limits of imagination. Specifically, she cites prospect theory as an explanation for a natural tendency to construct "perfectly just world views that focus on minor perturbations in current economic distributions, not too different from current realities" (p. 332). Also, an availability argument suggests that it is difficult to conceptualize matters that are not readily at hand. Taken together, these musings recommend that "visions of perfectly just worlds should not deviate strongly from what has been experienced and is expected to recur" (p. 332). The implication of this line of reasoning is that, short of a statement of absolute standards of justice, subjective standards operationalized in terms of expectations will offer a reasonable approximation of workplace justice.

Not all behavioral scientists are sanguine about subjectivist conceptualizations of justice. For example, according to social psychologist Edward Sampson (1983), the psychological study of justice has uncritically adopted pure psychology's empirical, individualistic, and subjectivistic research approach. As a result, "the work thereby has inadvertently functioned to legitimate the present configuration of society and, in deleting some of the important socioeconomic factors involved in issues of justice, has deflected our attention from effectively understanding and transforming conditions of justice" (p. 145).

Despite the reservations about subjective conceptualizations of justice, we will make no attempt to identify moral absolutes. Nonetheless, justice is more than a matter of arbitrary, personal taste. As we will see, certain normative principles regarding just procedures appear to be emerging from behavioral research. Further, at least in the context of the workplace, these principles seem capable of evoking similar perceptions of justice in a variety of situations involving the administration of human resource management programs which confer rewards on employees, settle disputes, and evaluate performance.

Justice in the workplace involves social exchanges between employees and employers. Such exchanges will be considered just if the procedures and outcomes are consistent with Self's expectations of the psychological contract. Our orientation in this chapter is to examine issues of workplace justice from the perspective of the worker. Consequently, we identify Self with the employee and Other with the employer.

BACKGROUND

Psychology and sociology are the academic disciplines in which the study of justice in organizations had its beginnings. In fact, the earliest investigations of justice-related behavior developed within the context of work organizations. The Hawthorne studies, for example, directed attention toward workers' concerns with issues of fairness as opposed to the physical characteristics of the work environment (Roethlisberger and Dickson, 1939). Early theoretical developments such as the principle of equity were based upon observations gathered in the series of investigations comprising the Hawthorne studies.

World War II military organizations were the setting for research that led to the concept of *relative deprivation* (Stouffer, Suchman, DeVinney, Star, and Williams, 1949; Stouffer, Lumsdaine, Lumsdaine, Williams, Smith, Janis, Star, and Cottrell, 1949). A variety of studies suggested that people judge the fairness of their present circumstances by comparing their outcomes with those of others in apparently similar situations. Stouffer and his colleagues described eleven cases in which soldiers who received higher actual outcomes from military service were less satisfied than others who were in objectively poorer positions. For example, despite more favorable socioeconomic conditions in the North, black soldiers stationed in northern bases were less satisfied with life in the army than blacks stationed in the South. This finding was explained in terms of black soldiers in the South feeling relatively well-off in relation to their civilian counterparts, whereas black soldiers in the North were feeling relatively less privileged vis-à-vis their Northern counterparts. These findings were interpreted as indicating that evaluations of justice were a consequence of social comparisons as opposed to absolute standards.

The socially comparative character of justice was elaborated in the work of George Homans (1961) and Stacy Adams (1965). Homans reported that Self has two significant expectations from social exchanges: first, Self will receive rewards that are proportional to costs; and, second, Self's net rewards will be proportional to investments. Self is expected to respond emotionally if actual outcomes are different from those expected, anger and guilt being the emotional states associated with receiving less than and more than anticipated outcomes, respectively.

Adams formalized these notions in his more carefully articulated theory of inequity in social exchange. Inequity was defined as lack of proportionality between Self's outcomes and investments relative to Other's outcomes and investments. In other words, if Self perceives that he or she receives less compensation (the outcome) than Other while performing comparable work (the investment), then inequity and, therefore, injustice is experienced. Adams described the manifestations of dissatisfaction and behavior intended to redress the imbalance in proportionalities of outcomes and investments. For example, in a series of provocative experiments Adams demonstrated that workers who felt unqualified for a job, and hence had low investments, tended to produce less if they were on piecework compensation. Lower production reduced their outcomes, making the latter more commensurate with their investments. By contrast, when unqualified workers were compensated on an hourly basis, they produced more as a way of bringing their investments into line with their outcomes.

The last important development of equity theory may be traced to the work of Elaine and William Walster (e.g., Walster, Berscheid, and Walster, 1973; Walster and Walster, 1975; Walster, Walster, and Berscheid, 1978) which increased the breadth and sophistication of this conceptual approach to justice. The range of phenomena to which equity theory may be applied was expanded outside of the workplace to a variety of situations involving friendship, altruism, exploitation, and other social motives. Also, the Walsters fashioned a broadly defined distinction among techniques used by Self to restore equity. Restoration of "actual equity" encompasses actual modifications of either Self's or Other's relative gains from the social exchange. On the other hand, restoration of "psychological equity" involves cognitive distortions of reality or "justifications" of imbalance in relative gains from a social exchange.

Underlying all these theories is a focus on the manner in which organizational resources are allocated and the reactions of Self to these allocations. The basic conern is with the perceived fairness of the *outcomes* or *consequences* of resource allocation decisions, or what Homans (1961) referred to as *distributive justice.* In terms of its application to the workplace, the basic premise of this stream of research is that the outcomes allocated to a worker or department should mirror the level of investments provided to the organization by the worker or department. For instance, when better-performing workers receive higher rewards (e.g., pay, promotional opportunities, etc.) than poorer-performing workers, these outcomes will be perceived as just. Should the better-performing worker receive rewards that are equal to or less than those of a poorer-performing worker, these outcomes will be perceived as unjust. As another example, collective bargaining agreements frequently specify two-tier wage systems as a form of union concession, thereby establishing a wage structure based exclusively on company tenure or date of hiring. Because workers with identical job titles and duties receive different pay outcomes for similar investments of effort, two-tier systems violate the conventional expectations of equal pay for equal work. Research has shown that the concepts of equity theory may be used to predict perceptions of the fairness of pay (Martin and Peterson, 1987). Not unexpectedly, low-tier workers perceived significantly lower pay equity than high-tier workers.

Although research on distributive justice, especially equity theory, once was a hotly debated topic among behavioral scientists, interest appears to be waning. According to Harry Reis (1986), ''It seems to me that equity theory proper is mostly of historical interest. It was never laid to rest by a final battle of empirical disconfirmation; instead, it seems to have slipped away quietly through benign (albeit affectionate) neglect'' (p. 187). It would be a mistake, however, to attribute this lessening of research activity to decreased concern among behavioral scientists in workplace justice. Instead, beginning in the 1970s, social psychologists began investigating another aspect of workplace justice, viz., procedural justice.

Procedural justice refers to the perceived fairness with which decisions are made to allocate organizational resources. It is the *processes* used to resolve disputes or the *how* of decisions rendered to allocate rewards that are considered in this stream of research. Organizational administrators have devoted less attention to the concept of procedural justice than distributive justice in managing personnel and human resources programs. Nevertheless, the implications of research on procedural justice may be implemented more easily to affect relations with workers than those for distributive justice. Even if unable to grant all those outcomes perceived to be equitable by its various constituents, the organization can at least handle these decisions in a manner that will be perceived as just, thereby salvaging some goodwill.

Research on procedural justice began as an interdisciplinary exercise involving social psychologist John Thibaut and law professor Laurens Walker (1975). The participation of Professor Walker should not be considered unusual given that legal scholars have taken as an article of faith the proposition that the procedures used to make judicial decisions will have a profound influence on the public's acceptance of them. Besides, it is customary to view issues of justice from a legal perspective (see Osigweh and Miceli, Chapter 1, supra). Thus, Thibaut and Walker's conceptual model of dispute resolution was developed in the context of comparative law, but its applicability has been discussed for analyzing the kinds of procedures used by managers to intervene in workplace conflicts (Sheppard, 1983). Procedures in this model are differentiated with respect to whether a third party or the disputants themselves control (1) the development and presentation of information that will constitute the basis for resolving the dispute (process control), and (2) the degree to which any one of the participants may determine unilaterally the outcome of the dispute (decision control). "Third-party control can take the form of process control, much as a football referee controls the flow of the game but has no direct influence as to the outcome, or decision control, the way a diving judge does not influence the dive in progress but simply decides on the dive's quality" (Sheppard, 1984, p. 150).

Thibaut and Walker used the concepts of process and decision control to describe a system of five "dispute intervention" procedures. The most familiar of these procedures are arbitration, in which the third party has decision, but not process control, and mediation, in which the third party has process, but not decision control. Two standards were suggested for assessing the effectiveness of these procedures, one objective in nature, the other psychological. *Actual effectiveness* pertains to the procedure's capacity to reveal the most evidence while maintaining the neutrality of the decision-making party. *Perceived fairness*, on the other hand, pertains to the degree to which the involved parties feel that the procedure is fair.

A second model of procedural justice was developed by Gerald Leventhal and his colleagues (1976, 1980). Whereas the orientation of Thibaut and Walker was toward process, Leventhal's approach was structural. Seven procedural elements were enunciated, each of which is used as a basis for judging the fairness of allocations. For example, one of these procedural elements is the availability of *appeals*, that is, a procedure for reconsidering an initially unsatisfactory allocation decision. The *selection of agents* is a second procedural element that pertains to the manner of choosing the individual who ultimately will decide the allocation issue.

Leventhal proposed six procedural rules that gave rise to fair allocation decisions. These are:

- Consistency rule—allocation procedures ought to be consistent from one person to the next and from one time to the next
- Bias suppression rule—self-interest should not be permitted to influence the allocation decision

- Accuracy rule—accurate information must be the basis for the allocation decision

- Correctability rule—mistaken allocation decisions should be correctable

- Representativeness rule—all relevant constituents must be represented

- Ethicality rule—allocation decisions must be consistent with prevailing ethical and moral standards

In the wake of these and other conceptual developments on justice has come a need to create a framework for the different theories. Such a framework might highlight similarities and dissimilarities among various theoretical perspectives and identify trends in research as well as gaps in current knowledge about workplace justice. Jerald Greenberg (1987) developed a taxonomy of theories that represents a useful attempt to integrate the different perspectives and to characterize the state of knowledge in the field. Two conceptually independent dimensions are the foundation for the taxonomy. The reactive-proactive dimension reflects the distinction between behavior that seeks to redress injustice and that which attempts to attain justice. Reactive theories focus on behavior designed to escape from or to avoid perceived unfair situations, whereas proactive theories focus on behaviors intended to promote justice. Distinctions between theories that focus on the ends achieved and the means used to acquire those ends are represented in the process-content dimension. Whereas process theories are concerned with how outcomes such as pay and recognition are determined in organizations, content aproaches deal with the fairness of the resulting outcome distributions.

The two dimensions taken in concert form a taxonomy consisting of four categories. According to this taxonomy, Adams' (1965) equity theory, with its focus on individuals' responses to unfair treatment, was classified as a reactive content theory. Thibaut and Walker's (1975) work was categorized as a reactive process theory given its preoccupation with how individuals respond to decision-making procedures that differ with respect to process and decision control. Greenberg (1987) goes a step further by using the taxonomy to identify representative research questions and prototypical dependent measures characteristic of each of the four types of justice theories.

In sum, the very existence of Greenberg's taxonomy is a significant indicator of the burgeoning theoretical developments in the domain of organizational and workplace justice. It is beyond the scope of this chapter to delve into additional conceptual perspectives and, therefore, other sources are recommended (e.g., Bierhoff, Cohen, and Greenberg, 1986; Greenberg and Cohen, 1982; Lerner and Lerner, 1981).

JUSTICE INHERENT IN DISPUTE RESOLUTION PROCESSES

Because interpersonal conflict is almost inevitable in organizations, methods must be developed to *avoid* or *settle* disputes about competing claims in as amicable and fair a manner as possible. A great deal of research has been devoted to the identification of process and outcome variables that affect the extent to which dispute-resolution procedures are perceived as just. Our brief review can touch upon only two such issues, one dealing with procedural justice, the other distributive justice.

The procedural justice inherent in two popular dispute resolution techniques, viz., arbitration and mediation, is a topic that has evoked considerable disagreement among researchers. The controversy centers on the importance of disputant control over process and outcome. On the basis of a series of simulation studies, Thibaut and Walker (1978) concluded that arbitration was a more satisfactory technique than mediation in terms of both actual effectiveness and perceived fairness. Arbitration was regarded as more advantageous, especially in situations of high conflict, because it provides disputants "control over the development and selection of information that will constitute the basis for resolving the dispute" (p. 546). By implication, mediation (a technique that was not researched very thoroughly by Thibaut and Walker) is the less preferred technique among disputants who consider it less effective and fair. Thibaut and Walker's work thus emphasized the importance of process control.

Several field studies have called into question these alleged advantages of arbitration (e.g., Brett, 1983; McEwen and Maiman, 1981). In her research in the bituminous coal industry, Jeanne Brett reported that grievants were less satisfied with arbitration than mediation of their grievances. The preferability of mediation was attributed to the decision control afforded the disputants. It also was argued that mediation had a salutary effect on a broader range of criteria including the time required to resolve a grievance and the costs incurred (Brett, 1986). The internal validity of these field studies has been questioned by Larry Heuer and Steven Penrod (1987) who point to the lack of random assignment of cases to dispute-resolution conditions and several sources of confounding of decision control with such variables as "the protractedness of the dispute, the savings in time and money that result from mediation, and the likelihood of outcomes that are more creative than simple compromise" (pp. 16, 17).

In order to eliminate these threats to internal validity, Heuer and Penrod compared arbitration and mediation under experimental conditions using college students as subjects. Contrary to the field research, the experiment found that decision control did not affect disputant satisfaction with dispute-resolution procedures or outcomes. However, *perceptions* of decision control were related to perceptions of procedural fairness. This leaves open the possibility that situational variables other than *actual* decision control in both the experiment and field studies influence these perceptions, which in turn influence procedural satisfaction.

The final word on this controversy obviously has not been written. The generalizability of the Heuer and Penrod results to uncontrived instances of dispute resolution has yet to be demonstrated. Evidence of external validity is an especially important requirement of experimental research in the domain of dispute resolution (Gordon, Schmitt, and Schneider, 1984). Also, experimentation on college students leaves in doubt the manner in which actual disputants, that is, nonstudents involved in a real conflict, would react to similar dispute-resolution conditions (see Gordon, Slade, and Schmitt, 1986). Finally, Robert Folger's (1986) review of research that compares the justice afforded by mediation and arbitration ought to be consulted for a more detailed analysis of the conceptual questions associated with this stream of research.

If one is willing to assume that equitable decisions about resource allocations may be considered as a way of resolving conflicting claims, and thereby obviating the need to implement other formal dispute-resolution procedures, it is appropriate to discuss the research of Morton Deutsch (1975) on distributive justice. Deutsch discussed the suitability of different criteria for resource distribution in terms of the goals of the social unit to which Self belonged. Rules for entitlement should be pertinent to the problems confronting organizations such that distribution of resources promotes organizational and, consequently, individual goal attainment. According to Deutsch, "the essential values of justice are those which foster effective social cooperation to promote individual well-being" (p. 143).

Based on the premise that social unit goals must be considered in establishing criteria for the allocation of rewards, Deutsch made several recommendations about distributive justice. First, if the primary goal of the social unit is economic productivity, then equity should be the basis for allocating resources. By making rewards contingent upon contributions to organizational productivity, people can maximize their outcomes by increasing their investments. Both they and the organization are likely to attain their goals using the equity criterion. Second, should enjoyable interpersonal relations be the goal of the social unit, equality is the best criterion of distributive justice. Envy or a sense of superiority among members of the social unit is likely to be aroused if relative productivity was the basis for allocating resources among members.

Finally, need is the dominant principle of distributive justice when the goal of the social unit is fostering personal development and personal welfare. Organizational resources such as food, shelter, or education may be distributed in the most beneficial manner for recipients and, in the long run, for the social unit as well. Although Deutsch (1986) has elaborated these ideas about context-specific preferences for distributive justice, they nonetheless demonstrate the important linkage between social unit and personal goals that must be considered in establishing a system of organizational justice to deal with ineluctable concerns and, possibly, overt disputes about resource allocation.

JUSTICE INHERENT IN OTHER ORGANIZATIONAL PROCESSES

Behavioral scientists have examined issues pertaining to workplace justice under a variety of guises. Concerns about procedural justice are implicit in the literature dealing with a number of organizational processes. Although the vocabulary is not utilized, procedural justice issues may be discerned in research on performance appraisal, feedback, group processes, and leadership. For example, Daniel Katz and Robert Kahn (1978) introduced the concepts of equity and rule enforcement as important aspects of leadership. Administrators were admonished to understand the system of organization rules and to be concerned with the effects of their application. Further, studies of leadership evaluation suggest that fairness, inferred from within-group reward distributions, is an important dimension on which the conduct of formal leaders is judged (Michener and Lawler, 1975).

A second research domain that has dealt with workplace justice is performance appraisal, although once again the research was not couched in terms of distributive and procedural justice. Frank Landy and his associates (Landy, Barnes, and Murphy, 1978; Landy, Barnes-Farrell, and Cleveland, 1980) reported that workers' perceptions of the fairness of performance appraisals were associated with a number of process variables including the frequency of evaluations, the raters' familiarity with the workers, and the opportunities presented to the workers to express their opinions. Interestingly, perceptions of fairness were unrelated to the favorability of the workers' performance rating, thereby discounting any suggestion that the outcomes of the appraisal affected perceptions of fairness.

Over the past few years, study of these same organization processes has been conducted from a perspective that specifically identifies fairness components and attempts to evaluate the effects of these components on a number of behavioral criteria. By contrast with earlier work, current writing has made explicit those elements inherent in organizational processes that affect perceptions of justice. Leadership is an organizational process that has been explicitly investigated from the standpoint of workplace justice. Tom Tyler (1986) reviewed a series of investigations of the role of distributive and procedural justice as inputs into leadership endorsement in political, legal, and industrial settings. Among his conclusions was that justice-based judgments have a major impact on leadership evaluations, thereby confirming the earlier speculative statements of Katz and Kahn. "Overall, the results reviewed suggest that, in formal settings, group members' leadership . . . evaluations are heavily justice based in character, with group members acting as naive moral philosophers, judging the actions of leaders against abstract criteria of fairness" (p. 309). Further, the studies point to procedural concerns as key factors in leadership endorsement. This line of research offers significant insights given that previous studies of leadership have focused on outcomes, that is, the benefits provided group members as a consequence of leader behavior (e.g., Hollander and Julian, 1970).

On a related matter, the applicability of Leventhal's rules to issues of workplace justice was examined by Blair Sheppard and Roy Lewicki (1987) who studied the bases for assessments of managerial fairness. Forty-four executives described incidents of fair and unfair treatment in seven domains of management responsibility: planning, staff development, delegating, motivating, coordinating, daily activities, and representing the organization to the public. Content analysis reduced the responses to sixteen rules guiding judgments about perceived managerial fairness. The results were consistent with earlier theoretical propositions about the determinants of perceived fairness. For example, Leventhal's six principles emerged from the analysis as did Thibaut and Walker's notion of process control. Nine new fairness principles were identified, however, that could not be subsumed readily under existing distributive and procedural justice frameworks. Six of the new principles, viz., accountability, communication, information, role description, meaningful assignment, and structural integrity, relate to activities which were not considered in traditional theorizing about fairness, but for which employees consider fairness to be relevant. One important finding of this exploratory study is the fact that the majority of these rules for evaluating managerial fairness did not fit either the distributive or procedural classification well. Obviously, more empirical work that relies upon statistical methods of categorization should follow up the research of Sheppard and Lewicki.

Finally, Robert Folger and Jerald Greenberg (1985) have led the discussion of the manner in which concerns about procedural justice manifest themselves in several areas of personnel practice. Performance evaluation, compensation, and participatory decision making were examined for evidence of process fairness and its impact on program effectiveness. This analysis revealed that programs that provide workers with a modicum of decision control were perceived to be fairer than those programs which did not involve workers in making choices that affect their conditions of work. In the realm of compensation, observations of worker satisfaction with cafeteria-style benefit programs were attributed in part to the availability of the choice mechanism. Similarly, the positive attitudinal effects of flextime programs were explained in terms of workers' involvement in the determination of working hours. This analysis also indicated that program components were preferred that afforded workers a chance to influence decision makers by providing information. The voice mechanism is a form of process control that enhanced outcome acceptance and perceptions of procedural justice, especially in programs designed to allocate rewards.

Folger and Greenberg reached several conclusions as a result of scrutinizing these human resource management programs. First, a fair-process effect appeared to typify reactions to these programs; that is, one may expect more enthusiastic acceptance of program outcomes if procedures are perceived as fair (rather than unfair). Employee suggestion systems, for example, must be administered in a manner that promotes confidence among workers that their suggestions will be evaluated in a fair manner, that is, suggestions will be evaluated by a representative group of decision-making agents according to the public set of standards. Second, certain structural features of the programs and psychological mechanisms engender perceptions of procedural justice. For instance, the voice mechanism offers workers a means for social influence on decisions. Even when unaffected by the workers' views, the decision-making process is considered fairer by workers afforded a voice. Finally, consistent with previous social psychological research in a variety of laboratory and field situations, more variance across a wide range of measures of global satisfaction was attributable to procedural concerns than to distributive concerns.

JUSTICE IN THE WORKPLACE

Despite the emergence of behavioral principles with the potential for promoting perceptions of justice in the workplace, transference of same to actual organizational contexts is problematical. Equity is not always achievable given two realities of organizational life: (1) the goals of various constituent groups in organizations are not necessarily the same and, therefore, what is perceived as fair is not necessarily the same; and (2) constituent groups differ in their ability to impose outcomes judged to be unfair on other groups. Institutional economists (e.g., Perlman, 1928), organization theorists (e.g., Cyert and March, 1963), and an increasing number of behavioral researchers (e.g., Gordon and Nurick, 1981) recognize that the goals of employees and owners are not entirely compatible, and that each party may use the power at its disposal to achieve its goals upon recognition that its immediate interests are at odds with those of the other party. Such attempts even may include subverting those mechanisms established to resolve disputes between employees and employers. In this section we will examine the effectiveness of dispute-resolution procedures for unorganized workers and those who are represented by a union.

Due Process for Unorganized Workers

Justice in the workplace for unorganized workers typically is a weak gruel made up of unequal parts of goodwill, the individual worker's contribution to the productivity of the enterprise, worker-protection legislation, and the common law of master-servant fashioned by the various state courts. As Jack Steiber points out in Chapter 3, infra, there are about 60 million such workers, many of whom encounter unfair treatment. Depending upon the particular employment situation, these issues are likely to be decided unilaterally within the hierarchy of the corporate employer. Even discharge cases are not subject to impartial review. If a disagreement can't be resolved informally, a nonunion employee must "lump it" or litigate. Often, the employee finds it impractical to retain a lawyer for such litigation, even if a competent attorney could be found who would take the case. The unorganized worker's only practical option may be to quit, then look for another job. Justice for the unorganized worker is often notable by its absence. David Ewing's (1977) seminal work on the civil liberties of American workers spoke directly, yet eloquently, about the plight of the employee at will.

For nearly two centuries Americans have enjoyed freedom of press, speech, and assembly, due process of law, privacy, freedom of conscience, and other important rights—in their homes, churches, political forums, and social and cultural life. But Americans have not enjoyed these civil liberties in most companies, government agencies, and other organizations where they work. Once a U.S. citizen steps through the plant or office door at 9 A.M., he or she is nearly rightless until 5 P.M., Monday through Friday (p. 3).

An increasing number of nonunion employers are implementing programs that offer their workers due process of complaints (Berenbeim, 1980). One of the first systematic investigations of such personnel policies was Fred Foulkes' (1980) study of twenty-six large nonunion companies. A variety of programs were reported such as open-door policies, appeal boards, or feedback mechanisms. Only two of the companies had formal grievance procedures with arbitration as a final step, and these procedures rarely were used. In many companies, the motivation to create these due process mechanisms was to obviate the perceived need for a union by voluntarily offering dispute resolution without the intrusion of organized labor. Indeed, many of the firms that have implemented grievance procedures do so as a cynical tactic to maintain their nonunion status (Freedman, 1985; "Antiunion Grievance Ploy," 1979).

Because a vast majority of the literature on workplace dispute resolution is confined to unionized employees in firms with contractually established grievance procedures, little empirical information exists on nonunion appeal systems. The most pregnant issue associated with nonunion dispute-resolution mechanisms has always been whether justice can be afforded to individuals without institutional backing. When employees are not supported by a union or by government regulation, questions remain about whether private systems of dispute resolution can redress grievances without reprisals against grievants—that is, whether they will be guaranteed "safe passage" (Foulkes, 1980). Even though John Aram and Paul Salipante's (1981) conceptual analysis of the parameters of organizational due process "offers conditional positive support for the possibility of private systems of conflict resolution" (p. 203), disquieting evidence of possible reprisals recently was brought to light.

David Lewin (1987) examined the appeal system files and personnel records over a four-year period from 1980 to 1983 for three large nonunion companies: a diversified financial services company, an aerospace firm, and a manufacturer of computing equipment. Each company maintained a multistep system that required appeals to be put in writing in order to progress through the system. The effects of a variety of demographic variables and work experience factors were studied in relation to appeal system usage, types of appeal issues filed, and levels of appeal settlement. Of greatest relevance to the present discussion was the creation of two matched groups, one consisting of employees who had used the appeal system, and one with similar background characteristics that had not used the appeal system. These groups were compared to examine the consequences of invoking the appeal procedure. The results indicated that appeal-filers and their supervisor-managers suffered significantly lower promotion rates and performance ratings, and significantly higher turnover rates in the postappeal period than comparable nonfilers and their supervisor-managers. Consistent with these findings were data collected in each of the companies on surveys designed to identify the reasons for nonuse of the appeal systems. Twenty-one percent of the nonsupervisory respondents reported "fear of management reprisal" as the primary deterrent to filing an appeal. Lewin concluded that "employees and their supervisors learn over time that formal appeals systems which are ostensibly established to resolve workplace disputes are more likely to result in punishments and sanctions than rewards and benefits for appeal filers" (p. 500). It appears that without institutional or regulatory backing as a safeguard against action taken by management as retribution against grievants, many unorganized workers will continue to silently grin and bear perceived violations of the psychological contract.

Due Process for Organized Workers

Contrast the circumstances described above with the situation of unionized workers. When differences arise about how a unionized worker is treated, the dispute can be grieved. If not settled, it may be arbitrated. According to the most recent figures, 100 percent of collective bargaining agreements in a sample of 400 contracts contained provisions that specified a grievance procedure. Of these, 99 percent relied on arbitration as the final step (Bureau of National Affairs, 1986; see also Osigweh, 1987b). The arbitrator will be an expert, impartial outsider who takes evidence on the issues and renders a binding decision based upon the language of the collective bargaining contract and the facts of the case. The union worker's rights under the collective contract are enforced under a specific procedure negotiated by the union. More important, the union is obliged to act as advocate for every worker in the bargaining unit, even those employees in open shops who are not dues-paying members.

The grievance system, considered to be the most significant American innovation in collective bargaining (Thomson and Murray, 1976), offers organized workers a number of benefits. Most important, the grievance system affords unionized workers a system of industrial jurisprudence, thereby protecting their rights to the employment condition mutually agreed upon by the union and management. Beyond the security provided by such institutionally supported legal protection, the grievance procedure assures a measure of economic security as well. Because the grievance procedure is an orderly mechanism by which the employer and union can determine whether or not the contract has, in effect, been violated, it is unnecessary to resolve such disputes by recourse to strikes or lockouts, both of which interrupt income flow. Workers, as well as industry in general, would be in a frightful state if the strike or the lockout were utilized to effect compliance with the contract in even a small percentage of the hundreds of thousands of grievances filed each year.

While the public tends to attribute the primary appeal of unions to their influence on wages and benefits, empirical evidence suggests that the role of organized labor in helping to provide workplace justice may be the most important determinant of how members feel about their unions. Unsatisfied economic needs are clearly an important indicator of unorganized workers' propensity to support unionization (e.g., Getman, Goldberg, and Herman, 1976; Gordon and Long, 1981; Schriesheim, 1978). Nevertheless, several studies have demonstrated that member satisfaction with the union was closely associated with perceptions of how well it was handling grievances. For example, in an investigation involving a small sample of union members, Charles Lawshe and Robert Guion (1951) reported a correlation of .53 between measures of attitudes toward the union and toward grievance handling. This suggests that the manner in which the union was judged to have dealt with grievances was an important factor in the tenor of its relations with the membership. As another example, Thomas Kochan (1979) analyzed data from a national probability sample of 1,515 full-time employees, approximately 400 of whom were union members. These results showed that union members gave highest priority among union activities to the handling of grievances.

The most comprehensive study of the relationship between member satisfaction with the union and grievance handling was reported by Michael Gordon (1987). Four union samples, varying in size from 138 to 1,578 respondents, were involved. Public- and private-sector unions were represented, as were both blue- and white-collar workers. Three measures were developed to evaluate the grievance systems in the unions. A scale of distributive justice examined the ends attainable as a consequence of invoking the grievance procedure to redress a perceived injustice (e.g., protection of job security, or the ability to advocate proper but unpopular positions). A second scale measured the procedural justice afforded by the grievance system (e.g., the probability of receiving a fair hearing, or the effect of personal friendship with union officials on the vigor of union representation). Last, the grievance system as a whole was evaluated. Development of these scales was necessitated because neither specific nor generic scales of procedural and distributive justice were available.

In each of the samples, the strongest correlates of satisfaction with the union were the three evaluative measures of grievance handling. Interestingly, these three measures were significantly better predictors of satisfaction with the union than satisfaction with management. This suggests that successes and failures in grievance handling reflect more strongly on how workers feel about the union than management. By contrast, three measures of job satisfaction, including one based on satisfaction with pay and fringe benefits, were the strongest correlates of satisfaction with management in each of the samples. Further, the three job satisfaction measures tended to be significantly better predictors of satisfaction with management than satisfaction with the union. Hence, the intrinsic and extrinsic rewards provided by the job are most likely to be associated with feelings about management. In sum, the workers represented by a union appear to evaluate it less in terms of the satisfaction provided by their jobs, and more in terms of the procedural and distributive justice afforded by the grievance procedure.

The data gathered by Gordon also offered the opportunity in the context of grievance administration to test the previously reported proposition that the overall evaluation of organizational processes is more closely associated with the procedural justice rather than the distributive justice provided by the process (Folger and Greenberg, 1985). In each of the four samples, scores on the procedural justice measure were more highly correlated with the overall evaluation of the grievance system than were scores on the distributive justice measure, and in three of the samples the difference between the magnitudes of these correlations were statistically significant. Hence, the procedures followed, rather than outcomes attained, have the greater influence on the overall evaluation of the grievance system. These results should not be interpreted as suggesting that the outcomes are unimportant. (Indeed, the salience of distributive justice was indicated by the fact that the correlations between it and the overall evaluation measure were significantly greater than zero in all four samples.) Nevertheless, it is how you play the game, and not whether you win or lose, that is the strongest correlate of the way people feel about grievance administration.

In view of the concerns expressed earlier about the potential for reprisals against employees who utilize appeal procedures in nonunion companies, it is surprising that so little research has been conducted in unionized facilities to determine the organizational outcomes that are perceived to be consequences of grievance-filing behavior. Only the work of Lewin and his associates (Ichniowski and Lewin, 1987) has begun to address this matter among organized workers. Individuals in four unionized companies who filed grievances in a baseline year were reported to have had a significantly higher probability of quitting by the end of the following year than did individuals who had not filed grievances. Further, subsequent voluntary turnover was always higher for workers whose grievances were ultimately decided in favor of the company than for those whose grievances were decided in the worker's favor. These results parallel Lewin's findings about the consequences experienced by appeal filers in nonunion companies.

As a general proposition, methodologically sound behavioral research on grievance systems is a scarce commodity (Gordon and Miller, 1984). In particular, none of the existing research has consulted grievants in order to determine the fairness of the system. Given the importance of

subjective factors in perceptions of workplace justice, research on grievances will be incomplete lacking the perceptions of the grievants themselves about the consequences of using the system.

The senior author recently completed a study designed to examine
whether specific characteristics of a grievance-filing incident are associated with attitudes about justice in the workplace (Gordon and Bowlby,
1988). This study investigated the relationship between grievance characteristics (e.g., the issue involved in the grievance, the step at which
the issue was resolved, and the nature of the settlement) and a variety
of organizational outcomes and perceptions of procedural and distributive justice. Among the outcome measures, respondents indicated the
impact of filing a grievance on relations with the union, relations with
management, and job satisfaction. The research was based on the reports
of 324 employees about a particular grievance they had filed that had
been processed through to settlement.

The clearest and most surprising finding of this research was that
none of the outcome or justice measures were affected by the level at
which the grievance was settled. In contast to economic analyses that
suggest obvious cost (Zalusky, 1976) and productivity (Ichniowski, 1986)
disadvantages of considering the same issue at several organizational
levels of both union and management, these behavioral data do not
reveal that settling a grievance at the lower steps of the system was any
more effective than settling the dispute at higher steps in terms of improving relations with the union or management, increasing job satisfaction, or raising confidence in the justice provided by the system. It
is probably true that, *ceteris paribus,* workers would prefer to have grievances settled quickly, thereby implying resolution of the matter informally or at the first step. However, the benefits derived from quick
resolution may be outweighed in certain situations by constraints that
limit the type of settlement that can be reached by stewards and first-
line supervisors. For example, it may be that the union and management
representatives who deal with a grievance at the first step do not have
the experience, authority, or time to fashion a truly integrative and
meaningful solution to the grievance.

The research also found that the issue involved in the grievance had
a bearing on the outcome measures. Settlement of grievances about
disciplinary matters and, to a lesser extent, work assignments were
associated with improved relations with the union, whereas resolution
of staffing grievances did not affect these relations. The grievance issue
also had an influence on relations with management. Because first-line
supervisors handle work assignments, it was not surprising to find that
grievances involving this matter harmed relations with the immediate
supervisor more than with higher-level management. On the other
hand, since staffing decisions tend to be made by higher-level manage-

ment, relations with these officials were found to be more adversely affected when an employee grieved about a promotion, layoff, or recall.

Finally, the measures of procedural and distributive justice were closely related to the nature of the settlement. Winners were satisfied with the fairness of the grievance process and its outcomes, while losers were far less sanguine. These findings support previous research that identified an "egocentric bias" for dispute resolution procedures that produce favorable outcomes (Greenberg, 1983).

In sum, these data suggest that organized workers may experience both pleasant as well as unpleasant consequences as a result of filing a grievance. Relations with the union or management may be either improved or adversely affected, depending upon the issue involved and the nature of the settlement. Given the exploratory character of this work, additional research is necessary before definitive conclusions can be reached.

CURRENT LEGAL EFFORTS TO EXPAND WORKER RIGHTS

Perceptions of workplace justice have changed over the last twenty years. Clearly, the expectations for due process among both organized and unorganized workers appear to have increased markedly. Perhaps because the expectations of organized workers about fair and effective union representation have not been realized, or because enterprising attorneys have helped to create unrealistically high expectations about the availability of procedural and distributive justice in the workplace, there has been a flood of litigation involving worker rights. Both unorganized and organized workers have been swept up by this litigious tide.

Assistance for Unorganized Workers

In recent years, state court decisions have strengthened the individual rights of unorganized workers, creating more demanding criteria for unjust dismissal, for dealing in good faith, and for emotional injury. For example, some courts are providing protection for unorganized workers when their discharges are based upon narrowly interpreted violations of statutory law (Youngblood and Bierman, 1985). These judicial developments augment justice in the workplace. Nonetheless, nonunion workers frequently are forced to endure inequitable treatment short of dismissal without being able to seek redress. Compared to other developed countries, government in the United States seems relatively disinterested in worker protection. For example, British workers who feel that they were unjustly fired may argue their cases in front of industrial tribunals. The three-person tribunals are inexpensive, render verdicts quickly, and are public. Their decisions have the force of law, although verdicts may be appealed to higher judicial bodies (Newman, 1986).

Unorganized employees in the American private sector are relegated to their own resources or to private lawsuits. Some observers believe that government should play a more active role in protecting nonunion workers. This is the thrust of "just cause" legislation proposed by Professors Jack Steiber (Chapter 3, infra) and Henry Perritt (Chapter 4, infra). In any case, the choice is largely political.

Legal Challenges to Union Exclusivity for Providing Due Process

The labor movement is being challenged increasingly by protective legislation and the availability of litigation. Until recently, labor unions were secure in their exclusive right to represent employees. A union, once elected, was the exclusive advocate. Members paid dues and agreed to be bound by majority decisions. That was the system, and when attorneys talked about labor law, it was in terms of organized labor. In the past two decades, however, a plethora of worker-protection statutes have changed the working environment, creating potential employer and union liabilities in many areas of employment.

Now, workers frequently sue employers and, if represented by a union, sometimes they sue their union, claiming discrimination, failure to represent (McKelvey, 1985), or some other breach of statutory or common law. Whereas workers used to be content with union representation during arbitration proceedings, today it is not unusual for the grievant to retain independent counsel. Labor unions and employers have been sensitized to the risk that they may have to face potential legal liabilities.

A struggle has evolved between unions, whose right to represent workers is guaranteed by the National Labor Relations Act (NLRA), and trial lawyers, retained to represent individual workers under a variety of emerging legal theories. The conflict involves labor unions, which seek to represent their members through Section 301 of the NLRA, and tort lawyers, who want to process the legal claims of individual workers in state and federal courts. This fundamental struggle can be viewed as an epic battle for controlling access to justice in the workplace. Two recent court cases highlight this conflict.

In *Garibaldi* v. *Lucky Food Stores, Inc.*, 726 F. 2d. 1367 (1984), the U.S. Court of Appeals for the Ninth Circuit held that a claim for wrongful termination, based on state public policy, was not preempted by Section

301 of the Labor Management Relations Act. Garibaldi was a member of the International Brotherhood of Teamsters. When he noticed that the milk in his milk truck was spoiled, Garibaldi called his employer, but was told to proceed with the delivery. Instead, he notified the local health department, which condemned the milk.

Garibaldi was discharged in October 1980, ten months after the incident. His union filed a grievance. An arbitrator decided that Garibaldi had been terminated for other reasons, not because of the earlier incident. If the arbitrator had found for the union, Garibaldi would have been reinstated, the traditional remedy in labor arbitration.

On October 2, 1981, Garibaldi sued Lucky Food Stores in the California state court, for bad faith, wrongful termination, intentional infliction of emotional distress, and violation of the public policy of California. Lucky Food Stores removed the case to federal court under Section 301. The federal district court dismissed the wrongful-termination count and remanded the "emotional distress" charge to the state court.

On February 27, 1984, the Circuit Court held that the wrongful-termination claim was not preempted by Section 301, balancing state and federal interests and pointing out that "inflexible application of the doctrine of preemption in industrial relations is to be avoided, especially where the State has a substantial interest in regulation of the conduct at issue and the State's interest is one that does not threaten undue interference with the federal regulatory scheme."

The court analyzed the law of California on "wrongful termination" and weighted the effect that its decision might have upon arbitration. The court pointed out that in *Alexander* v. *Gardner-Denver Co.*, 415 U.S. 36 (1974), the Supreme Court of the United States had held that an individual's statutory rights under Title VII of the Civil Rights Act were not preempted by arbitration. "We find the same considerations relevant here . . . the state law may protect interests separate from those protected by the NLRA provided the interests do not interfere with the collective bargaining process."

If workers sue under state law for compensation and punitive damages, they may be tempted to avoid arbitration, under which they can only be reinstated at work with back pay. If discharged employees can be handsomely rewarded by state courts, arbitration becomes a less attractive mechanism through which to seek redress. Should a union member have such a choice of remedies? This is an issue of concern for all employers and unions. The *Garibaldi* case was taken to the Supreme Court for further review.

In the meantime, another case arose in Wisconsin, *Allis-Chalmers Corp.* v. *Lueck*, 105 S.Ct. 1904 (1985). UAW member Roderick S. Lueck hurt his back while carrying a pig to a friend's house for a pig roast. He filed a claim under the collectively bargained disability plan, administered for the employer through Aetna Insurance Company. Aetna approved the claim, and Lueck began to receive disability benefits.

Sometime thereafter, Allis-Chalmers instructed Aetna to stop the payments, pending further physical examinations. After several days, the payments were continued. Ultimately, all of Lueck's disability claims were paid.

In January 1982, Lueck filed a lawsuit against Allis-Chalmers and Aetna in the Circuit Court of Milwaukee County, alleging that the defendants "intentionally, contemptuously and repeatedly failed" to make disability payments under the negotiated disability plan without a reasonable basis for withholding the payments. He claimed that they had failed to act in good faith and sought compensatory and punitive damages.

The trial court ruled in favor of the defendants. The Wisconsin Court of Appeals affirmed the judgment: Aetna owed no fiduciary duty to the plaintiff and federal law preempted the claim against Allis-Chalmers. The Supreme Court of Wisconsin reversed as to Allis-Chalmers on the basis that the suit did not arise under Section 301 and, therefore, was not subject to dismissal for failure to exhaust the arbitration procedures. The court reasoned that a Section 301 suit arose out of violation of a labor contract. Here, the claim was in tort. The court concluded that Aetna might be liable as an agent of the employer for the purpose of administering claims. It remanded the case to the trial court to determine whether Aetna exercised discretion in the processing of the disability claim.

The U.S. Supreme Court, on certiorari, decided that Section 301 preempted the state claim based upon bad faith. Justice William Blackmun gave several reasons for overturning the Wisconsin ruling. The employee's rights to prompt payment were not independent of the collectively bargained rights under the disability benefit plan. "It is a question of federal contract interpretation whether there was an obligation under this labor contract to provide the payments in a timely manner, and, if so, whether Allis-Chalmers' conduct breached that implied contract provision."

The plaintiff's right was derived from and, consequently, must be defined by the contract. Therefore, any attempt to assess liability must inevitably involve contract interpretation. The parties' agreement that such issues should be decided by arbitration is binding upon the individual employee. Congress provides that federal law governs the meaning of collective bargaining contracts. If state tort law attempts to give life to these terms in a different environment, it is preempted.

The Court also based its decision on the need to preserve the central role of arbitration in industrial self-government. *United Steelworkers* v. *Warrior & Gulf Navigation Company*, 363 U.S. 574 (1960). If the respondent had sued on a contract claim, he would be obligated to take it through the arbitration procedure established in the bargaining agreement before filing suit in court. "Perhaps the most harmful aspect of the Wisconsin decision is that it would allow essentially the same suit to be brought directly in state court without first exhausting the grievance procedures established in the bargaining agreement."

The Court emphasized that unless this kind of lawsuit was preempted, the parties' federal right to decide who is to resolve their disputes would be lost. In this case, the union and the employer had opted for arbitration.

Since nearly any alleged willful breach of contract can be reinstated as a tort claim for breach of a good-faith obligation under a contract, the arbitrator's role in every case could be bypassed easily if Section 301 is not understood to preempt such claims. Claims involving vacation or overtime pay, work assignment, unfair discharge—in short, the whole range of disputes traditionally resolved through arbitration—could be brought in the first instance in state court by a complaint in tort rather than contract. The rule that permitted an individual to sidestep available grievance procedures would cause arbitration to lose most of its effectiveness. A central tenet of federal labor contract law under Section 301 is that the arbitrator, not the court, has the responsibility to interpret the labor contract in the first instance.

When resolution of a state-law claim is substantially dependent upon analysis of the terms of an agreement made between the parties in a labor contract, that claim must either be treated as a Section 301 claim or dismissed as preempted by federal labor-contract law. This 8–0 decision by the Supreme Court seemed to dispose of the *Garibaldi* question. A claim for unjust discharge under state law would seem conclusively preempted if the plaintiff was covered by a contractual grievance procedure providing for binding arbitration. On May 13, 1985, the U.S. Supreme Court denied review of *Garibaldi* v. *Lucky Food Stores.*

Both these legal challenges resulted in decisions that left intact the primacy of the grievance system as a way of resolving disputes that pertain to worker rights guaranteed by the collective bargaining agreement. Nevertheless, it is not our expectation that lawyers will cease questioning the obligation of union members to rely on the grievance procedure to provide workplace justice. Therefore, it is intriguing to ponder the potential consequences of judicial verdicts that might support the intervention of attorneys in dispute resolution for unionized workers.

The spector raised by *Garibaldi* is that private litigation could replace organized labor in its capacity of advocate. Unions provide many services, but advocacy is primary. If unions lose their exclusive right to represent workers in dispute resolution, their mandate may be substantially reduced.

Although workers might believe that the availability of private law suits to redress grievances would expand their rights to due process, such a perception overlooks certain long-term consequences to the individual who might win a favorable verdict from such litigation. For example, tort lawyers can only sue for damages. If such a lawsuit reinstates a discharged worker, the plaintiff may be at the mercy of the employer. Compensation and punitive damages may not be appropriate remedies. Further, tort concepts that reward workers for suing their employer may have a poisonous effect upon the American workplace.

The actions of attorneys currently threaten other traditional and emerging institutions in American labor relations. In particular, the traditional role of arbitrators is under fire. In a speech to the Upstate Labor Advisory Council of the American Arbitration Association in Rochester, New York, in May 1985, Judge Harry T. Edwards of the Court of Appeals of the District of Columbia described the nature and extent of legal incursions into the process of arbitration.

In recent years, I have noticed what appears to be an increase in judicial activity affecting the arbitration process. There seem to be more suits seeking to challenge arbitration awards, and there are even cases in which the arbitrator is personally joined as a defendant in a lawsuit or in which a party sues to obtain the arbitrator's notes or tapes. There are several possible reasons for this increase in judicial activity. One that seems most clear to me is the general increase in activity in employment law. With the advent of legal actions for discrimination and unjust dismissal, and with the expansion of the duty of fair representation, more lawyers who are unschooled in collective bargaining have had occasion to represent employees. The natural instinct for many of those lawyers is to sue whenever a problem arises. Not surprisingly, the number of their suits have affected traditional practices in collective bargaining.

Finally, a new trend in labor relations may escalate the conflict between unions and trial lawyers. The AFL-CIO is trying to establish individual relationship with workers outside of traditional collective bargaining. A 1985 report by an AFL-CIO Committee on the Evolution of Work, entitled "The Changing Situation of Workers and Their Unions," suggests that unions should reach out to nonunion employees, offering to provide them with various personal services, including representation. The offer would be made on TV and radio. The union would seek to help such a worker protect individual rights, rather than collective rights. In such relationships, conflict between labor unions and trial lawyers would be even more direct.

As a result of this spate of litigation, unions, the institution of collective bargaining, and the process of contract administration are burdened severely. Rather than devoting their full attention to working on behalf of their members, union officials and their attorneys must concern themselves with defending against dissident claims. Even though unions have been relatively successful in protecting their interests—for example, unions win nine out of ten duty of fair representation cases (Tobias, 1985)—there are attendant costs and aggravations imposed upon the participants. And perhaps more debilitating to the union, it can no longer assure an employer that all employee grievances will be resolved through the contractual procedure.

CONCLUSION

In theory, the contrast between the rights of organized and unorganized workers would seem favorable to employees represented by a union. In actuality, worker job security depends upon more than contractual guarantees against unfair treatment by the company. A job with a profitable company can be more secure than tenure under a collective bargaining agreement in a declining industry where contractual rights are staunchly defended by the union through the grievance process. Words on paper can mean little when business is bad.

Nevertheless, justice in the workplace exists in the shadow of the law. As matters stand now, both statutory and common law provide greater assurance that the rights of unionized workers will be protected. The law recognizes and enforces collective bargaining. Unionized workers have common-law protection of procedural justice in duty of fair representation doctrine which helps to assure that union representatives will not negotiate their grievances in bad faith, arbitrarily, or perfunctorily. Section 9(a) of the Taft-Hartley Act affirms organized workers' right to present their own grievances, thereby instilling confidence in the fairness of the procedure whenever individuals feel that they can be more persuasive in arguing their cases than union representatives. The implications of Thibaut and Walker's (1975) research on control over the presentation of evidence as a determinant of perceptions of procedural justice should be obvious in this statutory guarantee.

Organized workers also have the opportunity to influence distributive justice as well. Despite the evidence that grievance filing is associated with some unpleasant consequences among organized workers, effective union representation can result in the restitution of entitlements and restoration of rights. All in all, the availability of procedural and distributive justice determines workers' evaluation of grievance systems and their satisfaction with their unions. Consequently, unions have an important stake in workplce justice. It also is significant that employers have something to gain from the existence of viable grievance systems.

One reason for the lower turnover rates among unionized workers is their access to a voice mechanism as an alternative to leaving the organization when dissatisfied with working conditions (Freeman and Medoff, 1984). Finally, union and management both are likely to benefit from favorable worker perceptions of their grievance systems since it may deter employees from turning to attorneys to satisfy needs for procedural and distributive justice.

What the future holds for the rights of unorganized workers is less certain. Workers generally win greater rights during expanding phases in the national economy. Now, our industrial establishment is hard pressed by foreign competition. Perhaps legislatures will be more cautious. The answers to such questions develop through experience, not through philosophy or logic. Politics and economic reality drive the legislative process.

PART II

LEGAL PERSPECTIVES

Legislation as the Best Protection Against Unjust Discharge

JACK STIEBER

Much has been made of the so-called erosion of the employment-at-will doctrine as a result of court decisions during the last two decades. If by "erosion" we mean that the idea that an employer may, as one court held over one hundred years ago, terminate an employee "for good cause, for no cause, or even for cause morally wrong" (*Payne* v. *Western & Atlantic R.R.*, 1884) is no longer literally true, the phrase has some validity. But it is a gross exaggeration to conclude, as many would have us believe, that employment-at-will (EAW) has been eroded to such an extent that the doctrine is all but dead in the United States and that employers are generally prohibited from discharging employees without just cause. The thrust of this chapter will be that court decisions have made only very narrow inroads into EAW and that legislation is both necessary and desirable to protect all employees against unjust discharge.

Almost without exception, court decisions start from the presumption that an employee hired for an indefinite period is terminable at will (Cathcart and Dichter, 1985). This presumption can be rebutted in a majority of states by a showing that the termination was in violation of public policy, in somewhat fewer states that it violated an implied contract between the employer and the employee, and in a handful of states that the termination was not made in good faith.

The exceptions to the EAW doctrine have been interpreted narrowly by most courts. Thus, the Texas Supreme Court ruled in 1985 that its recognition of a public-policy exception "covers only the discharge of an employee for the sole reason that the employee refused to perform an illegal act" (*Sabine Pilot Services, Inc.* v. *Hauck,* 1985). The case involved an employee's refusal to pump bilge water from the boat on which he worked in violation of a state law. Many courts have similarly limited their rulings to discharges in violation of a specific statute before finding a public-policy exception.

Oregon recognizes both the public-policy and implied-contract exceptions to EAW and would probably be considered among the more liberal states in its rulings on wrongful discharge cases. The Oregon Supreme Court has held that an employer may not discharge an employee for a "socially undesirable motive." The question then becomes what is a "socially undesirable motive." In 1986 the court ruled that an employee of twelve years duration could be fired for refusing to break off dating a female coworker. The court said: "Private employers who engage in the free enterprise system and risk their own capital can fire employees at any time and at will." The store manager's behavior was "rude, boorish, tyrannical, churlish and mean—and these are its best points," according to the court, but it was not "outrageous in the extreme" and was not "beyond the bounds of socially acceptable behavior" (*Patton* v. *J.C. Penney Co., Inc.,* 1986).

Interpreting the implied-contract exception in another case the Oregon Supreme Court ruled that even though an employee handbook said discharge could only be for just cause, the court inquiry was limited to whether the company had a good faith belief that the discharge was for just cause and not whether there was in fact just cause (*Simpson* v. *Western Graphics Corp.,* 1982). This places upon the discharged employee the extremely heavy burden of proving what was in the employer's mind rather than that the employee was not in fact guilty of the behavior that allegedly led to his termination.

These examples, which are by no means atypical, of the ways in which many courts interpret exceptions to EAW, indicate that one must go beyond the principles enunciated by the courts in their opinions in order to understand whether there has been a meaningful departure from the doctrine.

The most common basis for finding a public-policy exception involves cases in which an employer discharged an employee for filing a claim under the state's workers' compensation law. But, even in such cases, some states have held that EAW must prevail. The Mississippi Supreme Court explained its ruling as follows:

Our Workmen's Compensation Law does not contain a provision making it a crime for an employer to discharge an employee for filing a claim. If we create the remedy sought by plaintiff in this case, we would thereby engraft on the law an exception different from that expressed by the Legislature. This is not the function of the judicial department... (*Kelly* v. *Mississippi Valley Gas Co.*, 1981).

The reluctance of courts to act without legislative support is further illustrated in the decision of a federal court of appeals, even though federal courts have generally been much more expansive than state courts in finding exceptions to EAW. In 1981 the Fifth Circuit Court of Appeals reversed a trial court award of $400,000 to a plaintiff who had worked for a company in both Georgia and Texas and alleged that he had been discharged for giving damaging testimony against his employer in an antitrust suit. The court gave the following explanation:

the at will rule is itself grounded in important, although arguably outmoded considerations of public policy.... While the "public policy" exception may well be "wise and progressive social policy," recognition of our role as a federal court sitting in diversity precludes us from creating a "public policy" exception to the at will rule in the absence of any indication that the courts of Georgia and Texas might recognize such an exception (*Phillips* v. *Goodyear Tire and Rubber Co.*, 1981). [As noted above, the Texas Supreme Court subsequently recognized a public-policy exception in 1985.]

The Tennessee Court of Appeals was more forthright than some other state courts in giving its rationale for affirming a lower court decision granting summary judgment for the defendant in an implied contract case:

Tennessee has made enormous strides in recent years in its attraction of new industry of high quality designed to increase the average per capita income of its citizens and, thus, better the quality of their lives. The impact on the continuation of such influx of new businesses should be carefully considered before any substantial modification is made in the employment-at-will rule (*Whittaker* v. *Care-More Inc.* 1981).

The limited significance of court rulings in discharge cases is further evidenced by considering discharge in a broader perspective. Upwards of 60 million private-sector employees in the United States are subject to the EAW doctrine. About 2 million of them are discharged each year for noneconomic reasons without the right to a hearing by an impartial tribunal (Stieber, 1983). Only an infinitesimal proportion of these discharges could conceivably be considered as coming within the public-policy or implied-contract exceptions to EAW which have been recognized by state courts. This is apparent from thousands of published decisions of arbitrators appointed to decide discharge grievances under collective bargaining agreements.

These decisions indicate that the typical discharge is for such everyday occurrences as excessive absenteeism, fighting at work, insubordination, falsifying application forms or other employment records, negligence, theft, dishonesty, coming to work under the influence of alcohol or drugs, leaving work without permission, etc. (Elkouri and Elkouri, 1985). There is no reason to believe that reasons for discharging nonunionized workers are different from those in unionized establishments. Absent an implied contract to discharge only for cause, a nonunionized employer would not have to justify terminating an employee for any of these reasons. Yet, in more than half of the discharge cases going to arbitration under a collective bargaining agreement, arbitrators have found insufficient evidence to sustain the discharge and have reinstated the employee with full, partial, or no back pay depending on the circumstances in each case (Stieber, Block, and Corbitt, 1985). This suggests that even if only 1 out of 10 discharged EAW workers exercised a right of appeal to an impartial tribunal about half of them, or some 100,000, would be found to have been discharged without just cause.

Why should *discharge* be singled out for special treatment? After all, unionized employees generally have higher wages and better working conditions than nonunionized workers. What is so special about discharge? The answer is that in a modern industrialized society the difference between having a job and being unemployed is so fundamental that it cannot be compared to differences in wage rates and fringe benefits. It has become widely accepted that workers have a property right to their jobs which increases with length of service. Not only does a discharged worker lose a job and the income that goes with it. In addition, being fired for cause carries opprobious connotations which stigmatize an employee both as a worker and as a person. Prospective employers prefer to hire workers who have been laid off or have voluntarily quit their previous jobs rather than equally or even better-qualified individuals who have been discharged for cause (Stieber and Block, 1983). Consequently, discharged workers are likely to encounter considerable difficulty in finding new jobs and will probably have to accept less remunerative employment than they enjoyed on their previous jobs.

Various courses of action have been proposed to deal with wrongful discharge. Many believe that increased unionization is the answer. But this is an illusory solution. With unions losing more than half of all NLRB representation elections, many workers who join or want union representation remain unprotected against unjust discharge (U.S. Bureau of Labor Statistics, 1981). In addition, there are several million supervisory employees who are not covered by the National Labor Relations Act. Finally, and most important, the tide of unionization in the United States is receding rather than advancing, leaving little likelihood that this is a practical solution to the wrongful discharge problem.

A second approach is voluntary employer action to provide due process in the workplace. A small number of progressive employers have established grievance procedures including impartial arbitration for discharged employees. But this approach cannot begin to address the magnitude of the wrongful discharge problem (The Conference Board, 1980).

There are those who believe that the judiciary holds the best promise for doing away with the anachronistic employment-at-will doctrine. They point out that the courts, through creation of exceptions to the doctrine, have been moving in the right direction, and expect that eventually this movement will provide protection for all employees against unjust discharge. But there is no evidence that the courts are moving toward adoption of full-scale protection against unjust discharge (BNA Special Report, 1982). Indeed, some courts have begun to draw back from earlier decisions in wrongful discharge cases in favor of the view that it is up to the legislatures, not the courts, to explicitly address the employment-at-will issue (*Murphy* v. *American Home Products Corp.*, 1983).

My own view is that there will be fewer rather than more successful court suits over wrongful discharge in the future. Employers, concerned over highly publicized jury awards, have sought advice on how to avoid or, if necessary, to prevail in such suits, and lawyers and consultants have been quick to respond. Conferences and seminars on employment-at-will have proliferated to the point where they rival union-avoidance meetings. The advice rendered to employers ranges from introducing sound personnel policies and due process procedures for employee grievances to incorporating explicit language in employee handbooks stating that employment is at will, and having employees sign an agreement stating that they may be terminated at any time with or without cause.

The shortcomings of unionization, voluntary employer action, and reliance on the courts lead to consideration of legislative action to provide due process protection against wrongful discharge. Legislation has been proposed at both the federal and state levels (Stieber and Murray, 1983; Summers, 1976).

At the federal level, a bill was proposed in 1980 to amend Section 7 of the National Labor Relations Act to add the following language: "Employees shall have the further right to be secure in their employment from discharge or other discrimination except for just cause." Section 8(a) was to be amended by adding a new unfair labor practice: "To discharge or otherwise discriminate against an employee except for just cause" (Green et al., 1979). The bill did not come to a vote.

A federal statute would have the advantage over state legislation in that it would make irrelevant the argument that a state providing statutory protection against wrongful discharge would make it less attractive for industry. I think this is a phony argument because it magnifies a single factor far beyond its significance in plant location decisions. Nonetheless, it has been used effectively to discourage support for legislation against wrongful discharge.

Notwithstanding the advantages of federal over state legislation, it is not realistic to expect congressional action in the foreseeable future. We must, therefore, not rule out state legislation, despite the problems inherent in decentralized action.

Bills have been introduced in several state legislatures to provide protection against unjust discharge to employees (Perritt, 1984). In 1987 Montana became the first state to enact a law protecting at-will employees from unjust discharge. The Montana law prohibits employers from discharging employees without "good cause" as defined in the statute. Wrongfully discharged employees may be awarded compensatory and punitive damages (Montana, 1987).

Comprehensive bills to prohibit unjust discharge have been introduced in Michigan and California. The Michigan bill provided for notification to an employee of the reasons for discharge, mediation by the State Employment Relations Commission and, if mediation was unsuccessful, the right of appeal by the employee to final and binding arbitration. The arbitrator was to be selected jointly by the employer and the employee from a list provided by MERC, and his or her fee and expenses would be shared equally by the parties. The arbitrator's fee for study and decision writing was limited to twice the number of hearing days. The arbitrator could sustain the discharge, reinstate the employee with full, partial, or no back pay, or order a severance payment to be made to the employee. The arbitrator's award was to be reviewable by the circuit court only for the reason that the arbitrator exceeded his authority or did not have jurisdiction; the award was not supported by competent material and substantial evidence; or was secured by fraud, collusion, or other unlawful means.

An employer with a grievance procedure providing for impartial, final, and binding arbitration would be exempt from coverage. A discharged employee who filed a court action against his or her former employer was barred from seeking relief under the act. The act would apply to employers of ten or more employees. To be eligible to seek relief under the act an employee must have worked for an employer for at least fifteen hours per week for six months, and not be protected against unjust discharge by a collective bargaining agreement, civil service, or tenure. Managerial employees and others with a written employment contract of not less than two years would not be covered (Michigan, House of Representatives (1983), House Bill No. 5155).

The original California bill, introduced in February 1984, followed closely the majority recommendations of an ad hoc committee appointed by the State Bar of California (Ad Hoc Committee, 1984). It contained many provisions similar to those found in the Michigan bill. Major differences included a requirement that both the employee and the employer deposit $500 with the State Mediation and Conciliation Service to help pay for the costs of administering the act; defining employees as those employed for two or more years for an average of twenty hours per week; providing for attorney fees and costs to a prevailing plaintiff or to a prevailing defendant where the charge was made for vexatious reasons or for the sake of harassment (California Assembly Bill 3017, 1984).

In both Michigan and California, employers have opposed statutory protection against unjust discharge. Despite some extremely generous awards by juries to discharged employees, employers seem to prefer changing personnel procedures and policies to avoid or reduce their liability in wrongful discharge cases to extending protection against unjust discharge to employees generally, even though the remedies available under arbitration would be much more limited than those awarded through the judicial process.

Unions in California and Michigan have indicated that they would support unjust discharge protection legislation and in 1987 the AFL-CIO Executive Council adopted a resolution supporting both "federal and state measures that safeguard workers against discharges without cause" (AFL-CIO, 1987). But thus far, unions have not actively lobbied for or pressured legislators to support unjust discharge legislation.

The most vociferous opposition to legislation to substitute arbitration for litigation has come from the trial lawyers who represent plaintiffs and defendants in wrongful discharge suits. Removal of such suits from the courts to arbitration would deprive attorneys of generous fees, whether they represent plaintiffs on a contingency fee basis or defend employers against compensatory and punitive damage claims often running into six and seven figures. Obviously fees to be derived by representing relatively high-salaried employees who have been discharged far exceed possible income from suits involving hourly and low salaried workers.

In order to have a chance for passage, any bill must represent a compromise among the various interest groups. Such a compromise might well take the following form:

1. The employment-at-will doctrine would be abolished in favor of the general rule that employees may be discharged only for just cause.
2. Discharged workers who are interested primarily in being reinstated to their former jobs with compensation for economic loss that they have suffered would be given an opportunity, first to have a government conciliator try to resolve differences with their employers and, if conciliation fails, to appeal

to an impartial arbitrator. Arbitrators should be empowered to award monetary damages in cases of unjust discharge where reinstatement is not considered to be practicable.

3. Discharged employees who seek monetary damages and who are not interested in reinstatement would be permitted to sue their former employers in the courts. Employers should be protected against exorbitant jury verdicts by establishment of a cap on such awards. This is the approach that has been adopted by several states in medical malpractice suits to put a stop to sharply rising insurance premiums for physicians. Certainly the emotional distress suffered by discharged workers is not greater than the pain and suffering of victims of medical malpractice cases.

4. Recovery of attorney fees and costs should be permitted to prevailing plaintiffs or to defendants, when charges against them are found to be totally without merit and made primarily for purposes of harassment.

These guidelines go beyond the severe limitations of the public-policy or implied-contract exceptions. But they leave considerable room for negotiation with respect to such issues as employee eligibility, employer coverage, arbitrator selection, allocation of cost, remedies, and other compromises that are inherent in the legislative process.

NOTE

Mark D. Baines, former graduate assistant in the Michigan State University School of Labor & Industrial Relations, provided case citations for this chapter.

4

The Terrain of Wrongful Dismissal Legislation

HENRY H. PERRITT, JR.

INTRODUCTION

In 1976 University of Pennsylvania law professor Clyde Summers wrote a law review article saying that it was time for a statute to protect employees from wrongful dismissal (Summers, 1976). Ten years later many employers think a statute is a good idea to protect *employers* from wrongful dismissal suits.

The law has been reducing employer autonomy during the last half-century, and the trend is likely to continue. In the last decade, rapid development of common-law wrongful dismissal theories reduced the residue of the employment-at-will doctrine nearly to the vanishing point. Wrongful dismissal is merely the most recent step in a process of increased regulation that began with state and federal statutes obligating employers to pay minimum wages, to participate in collective bargaining, to refrain from sex, race, religious, age, and handicapped discrimination, to provide safe and healthful workplaces, and to meet certain requirements if they elect to establish employee benefit plans.

Wrongful dismissal differs from the other enumerated restrictions on employer autonomy in that it is a common-law, rather than a statutory, restriction.

Increasingly, legislatures are being asked to consider whether the law of dismissal should be codified. Legislative response to this request can begin to unify the law of employee dismissal, or it can fragment it further. Moreover, in framing their response, legislators will be asked to weigh conflicting societal interests with major implications for individual free-dom and economic efficiency. The important policy question for em-ployers, employee representatives, labor lawyers, and the legislatures is not whether employer dismissal authority should be restricted. Such restriction has been increasing for fifty years and it is unlikely to be reduced—although the wisdom of existing restrictions is likely to be debated. The important questions are how new restrictions should be integrated with old ones, and whether it is feasible to strike the balance between individual liberties and economic interests on the one hand, and the societal need for efficient enterprise on the other, in a way that adequately provides for both.

So far, the dialogue about legislation has been too narrowly focused. Most of the contemporary state proposals would prohibit dismissals of employees except for just cause. Such legislation, if enacted, would represent a revolution in American private-sector employment law. Most federal proposals protect employees against dismissal for a specific rea-son. At last count, federal law already prohibited dismissal for twenty specific reasons, with the prohibitions contained in as many separate statutes. For example, federal law prohibits dismissing employees be-cause they engage in concerted action, because they protest race, sex, or religious discrimination, because they complain about occupational safety and health violations, because they serve on federal juries, or because they report asbestos hazards.

The time is ripe for integrating and rationalizing employee dismissal law (see Perritt, 1984a, b, c, proposing single tribunal for adjudicating wrongful dismissal claims; Dotson, 1986, opposing creation of super-administrative agency to handle all employment disputes). The practi-cability of legislative reform always is determined by political reality. The purpose of this chapter is to broaden the policy dialogue about the range of legislative options available in the wrongful dismissal area.

An enormous literature has developed recently regarding wrongful dismissal common-law developments, and the extinction of the em-ployment-at-will rule (Perritt, 1987, pp. 21–23).

It is appropriate to summarize the three basic wrongful dismissal doc-trines that are reasonably well-defined in the case law, and discussed in the literature. About forty states have recognized one or more of three wrongful dismissal theories, sometimes referred to as exceptions to the employment-at-will rule.

The first is the Public-Policy Tort theory. It permits terminated em-ployees to recover damages resulting from their terminations when they can show that a termination jeopardized realization of a public policy reflected in a state or federal constitution, statute, administrative reg-ulation, or formal code of conduct for a profession. Early cases accepting this theory were *Nees* v. *Hocks* (1975), involving dismissal of an employee for performing jury service, and *Sheets* v. *Teddy's Frosted Foods, Inc.* (1980), involving dismissal of a quality-control inspector for protesting short-weighting of consumer products. The courts have required plaintiffs seeking recovery on a public-policy tort theory to show how their terminations jeopardize clear public policies, contained in statutes, administrative regulations, or state or federal constitutions.

The second is the Implied-in-Fact Contract theory, permitting a terminated employee to recover damages when he or she can prove breach of an implied-in-fact contract. Under this theory, employees are permitted to establish a contract right not to be terminated at will, based on informal employer promises of employment security, such as those made orally at the time of hire, or those contained in employee handbooks or personnel policies. The leading case recognizing this theory is *Toussaint* v. *Blue Cross and Blue Shield of Michigan* (1980), involving an employee who was dismissed in violation of commitments made in an employee handbook. Courts have been meticulous in requiring plaintiffs seeking recovery on implied-in-fact contract to plead and prove promise, detrimental reliance, and breach elements, although a tendency to relax the detrimental-reliance requirement for breach of implied-contract dismissal suits has surfaced (*Woolley* v. *Hoffman-LaRoche*, 1985).

The third is the Implied Covenant of Good Faith and Fair Dealing—a contract theory with tort aspects. It permits dismissed employees to recover damages for breach of an "implied covenant of good faith and fair dealing." It was one of the earliest exceptions to the employment-at-will rule, recognized in *Petermann* v. *Teamsters* (1959), involving an employee dismissed for refusing to commit perjury, and embraced in *Monge* v. *Beebe Rubber Co.* (1974), involving a woman dismissed for refusing to "date" her foreman, and *Fortune* v. *National Cash Register Co.* (1977), involving an employee dismissed to deprive him of sales commissions. The implied-covenant theory has declined in importance as courts have developed public-policy and implied-in-fact contract theories. The weaknesses of the implied-covenant theory are that it leaves too much to the jury (*Thompson* v. *St. Regis Paper Co.*, 1984), and that it potentially duplicates the public-policy tort concept (*Brockmeyer* v. *Dun & Bradstreet*, 1983). Nevertheless, few courts have repudiated the theory entirely because it may permit relief in apparently deserving cases that do not fit the evolving requirements for public-policy tort or implied-in-fact contract.

This chapter reviews the power and preferences of six salient interest groups, and suggests that the only type of wrongful dismissal legislation likely to receive appreciable political support in the near term is legislation enumerating reasons for which dismissal is *not* permitted. What is needed is a statute encompassing basically the grounds for which recovery is permitted under the Public-Policy Tort and Implied-in-Fact

Contract common-law theories, a limitation on damages recoverable, and attorney's fees for plaintiff's counsel. Significantly, this statute would encourage all legal claims related to a particular employment termination to be presented in a single proceeding. The issues explored in this chapter are developed more fully in Henry H. Perritt, Jr. (1984a), which contains draft federal and state statutes reflecting the considerations discussed in this chapter.

The Politics of Statutory Reform

The political alignment of six salient interest groups will determine the fate of any proposed wrongful discharge legislation. They are: employers, defense lawyers (the "defense bar"), trade unions, plaintiff lawyers (the "plaintiff bar"), nonunion employees, and academic lawyers.

Employers historically have opposed any legislative or judicial action that would restrict their employment practices or impose increased liability for adverse action against employees. Employers are well organized politically and influential in legislative assemblies. In the past, employers opposed legislation expanding legal protections against wrongful discharge. But employers also historically have favored legislation as an alternative to common-law liability when it seemed that legislation would permit greater predictability of outcome and limit the size of damage awards. The continued rapid growth in common-law liability for wrongful discharge could shift the preference of this key group toward legislation of an appropriate form.

The defense bar generally opposes legislative measures that would increase exposure to liability by defendants. This predisposition would militate against support of wrongful discharge legislation by this group. But for the same reasons that employer preferences may shift—the burden of increased common-law liability and the desire for predictability and order through statutory reform—the preferences of this group also may change in favor of comprehensive legislation.

Ironically, the following three groups who would benefit most from wrongful dismissal legislation are either too poorly organized to effect a change or are simply ambivalent toward such a change.

Trade unions historically have favored legislation granting new rights to employees. Furthermore, the trade union movement is well organized and influential with legislators. The labor movement, therefore, might be expected to favor, and its support could be effective in behalf of, wrongful discharge legislation. Yet, organized labor also knows that statutory expansion of employee rights may dilute the incentive for employees to organize. It is well recognized that one of the benefits that union organizers can offer to employees is protection against arbitrary dismissal. Accordingly, trade union groups have been ambivalent toward proposals for wrongful discharge statutes.

The plaintiff bar is ambivalent also. Plaintiff lawyers make their living by litigating, and by receiving portions of judgments or settlements large enough to compensate them for work done on cases in which the plaintiff receives nothing—a form of cross-subsidy. This segment of the bar has favored expansion of common-law wrongful dismissal doctrines, but that does not translate into support of legislation. Wrongful dismissal legislation would most likely include a cap on damages, thus limiting the opportunity for cross-subsidy of plaintiff litigation. But if legislation simplifies litigation or permits attorney fee awards, it could reduce the need for large potential damage awards to provide cross-subsidy. Also, if legislation broadens the substantive rights of dismissed employees, it could increase the probability of success for plaintiffs and their lawyers. Consequently plaintiff lawyers may oppose or favor legislation, depending on its effect on attorneys' fees, damages levels, and opportunity for recovery.

Undoubtedly, nonunion employees would benefit most from expanded protection against wrongful discharge. Such protection would enhance their economic security without imposing any identifiable costs directly on them. But this interest group is poorly organized and largely ignorant of the legal issues involved. Moreover, there is no "public-interest" group that regularly speaks for nonunion employees. Accordingly, the nonunion employee group will not be influential unless the subject of wrongful discharge gains prominence in election politics, so that the individual votes of members of this group are influenced by candidates' positions on the wrongful discharge issue. Wrongful discharge has not become such a prominent issue yet.

There really is only one group that seems strongly to support wrongful dismissal legislation of the type most frequently discussed: academic lawyers. Law professors generally have favored legislative initiatives expanding legal protection for individual employees. This predisposition has been manifest with respect to wrongful discharge law. Indeed, the common-law, wrongful discharge concepts may be attributed in part to the academic legal literature. Academic lawyers are influential because they provide technical assistance to legislators and because they link new proposals to well-accepted legal doctrines, and thus improve the perceived legitimacy of proposals for legislative change. At present, there is no indication that this group will lessen its support of comprehensive wrongful discharge legislation.

The foregoing interest-group analysis suggests that the balance of political power would shift in favor of wrongful discharge legislation only if employers and the defense bar react against expanded common-law liability for wrongful discharge, and if the plaintiff bar perceives that proposed legislation would enhance—or at least would not diminish—the economic feasibility of representing dismissed employees. If these groups decide that legislation is a desirable alternative to continued expansion of common-law liability, they may become proponents of legislative action.

Clearly, the group needs and desires are at variance and therefore compromises must be made. Enactment of wrongful dismissal legislation is unlikely unless it satisfies the essential needs of the major groups. Fortunately, the content of legislation meeting the essential desires of the key groups also appears desirable from a policy perspective.

Employers seek order and predictability. To meet these aspirations legislation attractive to employers would include:

1. Clear criteria to distinguish legitimate from prohibited dismissals
2. A procedure for eliminating frivolous claims
3. Protection against multiple claims
4. A cap on damages
5. Limited expansion of existing prohibitions (i.e., retention of the employment-at-will rule to the extent possible)
6. Deference to voluntarily adopted internal grievance mechanisms

The preferences of the defense bar parallel those of employers. Trade unions are likely to want:

1. Increased protection of employees
2. Protection of incentives to unionize
3. Fewer fair representation claims against unions

Nonunion employees need:

1. Low-cost claims procedure
2. Closest thing possible to just-cause protection
3. Protection of private off-duty conduct and freedom of speech
4. Maximum potential damages
5. Speedy claim resolution
6. The opportunity to present claims in as many forums as possible and with maximum opportunity for review

The plaintiff bar would like:

1. Potential for large damage awards
2. The opportunity to present claims in as many forums as possible
3. Statutory award of attorney's fees

Academic lawyers, for the most part, have supported legislation providing:

1. Just-cause protection
2. Arbitration of claims of wrongful dismissal

The Shortcomings of Prominent Legislative Models

Wrongful dismissal legislation can take two basic forms: It can forbid employment terminations except for cause, or it can forbid employment terminations for enumerated reasons. Most of the proposals for wrongful dismissal legislation are of the first form. Most existing employment dismissal statutes, such as Title VII of the Civil Rights Act of 1964, the Age Discrimination in Employment Act, the National Labor Relations Act, and the several federal "whistleblower" statutes are of the second form (Perritt, 1987, 1984a, pp. 79–92). As early as 1981, a committee of the Bar Association of the City of New York recognized that wrongful dismissal legislation can take a variety of forms, on a spectrum ranging from broad just-cause protection at one end to a simple codification of common-law protections at the other (Committee on Labor, 1981). Regrettably, this observation largely has been neglected in the wrongful dismissal legislative discussion since then.

Examples of just-cause legislation are plentiful. British labor law provides a comprehensive remedy for employees believing they have been subjected to "unfair dismissal." Federal law in Canada has provided comprehensive remedies for unjust dismissal since 1978, and three provinces provide at least limited protection. In 1976 Professor Clyde Summers proposed enactment of just-cause legislation at the state level in the United States, channeling the adjudication of cases arising under the statute into the arbitration process (Summers, 1976, pp. 521–22). A special committee of the State Bar of California endorsed, over employer dissent, a comprehensive legislative scheme establishing a just-cause standard for dismissal, arbitration, and reinstatement with back pay as the primary remedy. Other proposals have been similar. Colorado, Michigan, New Jersey, and Pennsylvania legislatures have considered, but have not enacted, just-cause legislation. The just-cause bills all are basically similar to Summers' proposal. The Philadelphia Bar Association has appointed a committee to evaluate the current version of the Pennsylvania bill. The author of this chapter is an advisor to that committee. The American Bar Association Labor and Employment Section is collecting information on legislative alternatives, and the commissioners on uniform state laws have undertaken to draft a model, state wrongful dismissal statute.

Five states have enacted statutes generally modifying the employment-at-will rule, though stopping far short of prohibiting dismissals except for just cause. Whistleblower statutes exist in California, Connecticut, Maine, Michigan, New Jersey, and New York. All of these statutes refer claims of violation to the regular common-law courts rather than to a new system of arbitration. In addition, South Dakota has had an employment-term statute for some time, establishing a presumption that employment is to continue for a period of time defined by the pay interval, and Missouri has a statute requiring employers to disclose the reasons for termination. Many more states, of course, have statutes addressing discrimination and collective bargaining (Perritt, 1987: Appendix A—table of state statutes).

The prevalence of just-cause/arbitration models tends to obscure the reality that other forms of wrongful dismissal legislation are feasible and may attract more political support.

The most significant development has been the enactment of a comprehensive wrongful dismissal statute by the Montana legislature. This statute, discussed below, generally follows the suggestions presented in this chapter.

CONTENT OF WRONGFUL DISMISSAL LEGISLATION

The choice between just-cause legislation and enumerated-prohibitions legislation should be made explicitly, revisiting the same policy question addressed by the courts that have modified the employment-at-will rule: To what extent must the reason relied upon by an employer for terminating an employee bear a rational relationship to the employer's business needs? This is a substantive question. In addition, the choice between arbitration and judicial enforcement raises a procedural question: Once acceptable reasons for dismissal have been prescribed, what machinery should be available to ascertain and evaluate the basis for dismissal in a manner likely to result in a reasonably accurate factual decision? For ease in exposition, the first aspect will be called "substantive fairness," and the second, "procedural fairness."

Before superimposing the political calculus, it is useful to develop, explicitly, the basic alternatives for substantive and procedural fairness.

Substantive Fairness

Choosing between a just-cause approach and an enumerated-prohibitions approach to wrongful dismissal involves a balancing process, in which the needs of an employer to have broad discretion to make dismissal decisions are weighed against the harm to the employee adversely affected by the decision. The use of a balancing process implies that one should be able to identify the interests being weighed. Commonly, the rights and needs thus drawn into the balance must be recognized as "legitimate" if the law is to take them into account. Defining the scope of "legitimate" rights and needs accomplishes the hardest part of the substantive fairness analysis.

The analytical process involved is embraced by the prima facie tort concept, recognized in Section 870 of the Restatement of Torts. The prima facie tort concept provides for the imposition of liability on one who intentionally, without justification, causes legal injury to another. The Restatement drafters contemplated that a court would engage in a balancing process, in which the legal injury to the plaintiff would be weighed against the legitimate needs of the defendant attempting to "justify" her action. In prima facie tort analysis, as in constitutional due process analysis, legitimacy enters into the equation on both plaintiff's and defendant's sides. If the plaintiff has been hurt in some way not recognized as legal injury, prima facie tort will afford him no damages and no injunction. Once the plaintiff proves legal injury (and causation, of course), if the defendant cannot offer legally recognized justification, her conduct will subject her to liability.

In prima facie tort analysis, the challenger of a decision cannot obtain scrutiny by legal institutions unless he can show impairment of an interest formally recognized by the law. The defender can be successful only if she shows that the decision was supported by interests formally recognized by the law.

Another example is constitutional substantive due process analysis. In substantive due process analysis, the needs of the state are weighed against the rights of the individual claiming denial of due process (*Beller v. Middendorf*, 1980; *Major v. Hampton*, 1976). The balancing process is not necessary unless the person claiming denial of due process can implicate rights recognized as appropriate for constitutional protection, either liberty (*Connick v. Meyers*, 1983) or property interests (*Cleveland Board of Education v. Loudermill*, 1985; *Perry v. Sindermann*, 1972; *Board of Regents v. Roth*, 1972). Once either of these rights is shown to be involved, the decision under scrutiny can be sustained only if a "legitimate" state interest in making the scrutinized decision can be shown. The analogy between the property or liberty interest in constitutional analysis and the individual right in substantive-fairness analysis is obvious. Similarly, the legitimate state interest is analogous to the institutional need in substantive-fairness analysis.

The history of employment law in the United States has been the history of adding legally recognized employee interests. Once a new category of interests is recognized, these interests are weighed against legitimate employer interests—either in a statutory formula or in individual cases. The courts and legislatures have expanded recognized employee interests in the following ways:

First, when the reason for the termination is based on a racial, religious, gender, or age characteristic, or when it is based on certain conduct, the legislature has said that the termination is at least prima facie illegal, and has afforded remedies to employees terminated for these reasons, unless the employer can offer overriding justification.

Second, when the reason for the termination arises from conduct within constitutional guarantees against governmental interference with free speech, association, privacy, and religion, the termination is prima facie illegal, under either a deprivation-of-liberty/due process or an equal-protection/fundamental-rights analysis. A governmental employer must offer legally adequate justification to escape liability.

Third, when the reason for the termination is conduct that is protected by "public policy," the discharge is a tort, unless the employer can offer justification.

Fourth, when the employing organization has promised that it will terminate only for certain reasons, or only after following certain procedures, the employee's expectations created thereby will be protected by enforcing the employer's promise in a common-law, breach-of-contract suit, or, if the employer is the government, in an action under the constitutional guarantee against governmental deprivation of property without due process.

Formulating a standard for substantive fairness in wrongful discharge legislation requires consideration of all the recognized interests enumerated above. A major weakness in most of the proposals found in the law review literature is that they address only one, or a few, of the types of substantive fairness (see Pierce, Mann, and Roberts, 1982–83; definition of "just cause" primarily by reference to "whistleblowing"). Reinforcing these employee interests are societal interests in favor of certain types of conduct by employees. These interests are recognized by the public-policy tort. They include interests in the jury system, in the workers' compensation system, and in safe products.

Arrayed against these interests are employer and societal interests favoring effective management of organizations. These interests require that employees not be shielded from the consequences of their poor performance or misconduct and that supervisors not be deterred from exercising their managerial responsibilities by the inconvenience of litigating employees' claims. An employer should be allowed to justify removing an employee in pursuit of these interests when such interests outweigh the adverse effect on legitimate employee interests. "Free enterprise," the preference for regulating economic relations by market forces instead of by law, is a societal value on the employer's side. The free-enterprise value militates against legal regulation of discharge decisions regardless of whether an employer can justify a particular discharge.

This is the way I explain the interest balancing to my first-year torts students:

An employment dismissal case can be represented by the scales of justice, on which various weights, representing interests, are placed. If the scales tilt toward the employer, the employer wins; if the scales tilt toward the employee, the employee wins. The scales of justice in a dismissal case start out with a "weight" on the employer's side of the scales—the employment-at-will rule—opposing a "weight" always on the employee's side of the scales—the employee's interest in job security. If no further weights are placed on the scales, our society has decided that the employment-at-will rule is "heavier" than the employee's economic interest, and the employer wins. But other weights may go on the employee's side in a particular case: nondiscrimination rights granted by statute, "public policy," or implied employer promises of job security. Similarly, specific justification for dismissal is another weight that goes on the employer's side.

In balancing the competing interests involved in workplace governance, the workable substantive-fairness standard should draw upon the experience of the common-law courts and the expressions of the legislature.

Possible substantive-fairness standards range from the simple to the more complex. The simpler proposals unfortunately tilt the balance of interests against the employer and present problems of administration. Such an imbalance detracts from the likelihood that employers would support wrongful discharge legislation that encompasses a simple substantive-fairness standard.

1. *Prohibiting Dismissals Without Just Cause.* A simple substantive-fairness standard would be a requirement of "cause" for dismissal in all cases. This corresponds to the "maximalist" approach discussed in the New York City bar report (Committee on Labor, 1981). This is the approach taken or suggested by most of the unfair dismissal schemes adopted in other countries and proposed for adoption at the state level in the United States. Such a substantive standard burdens the employer to articulate the interests justifying the dismissal. Imposing such a standard would have the effect of making private employment like public employment, in that employees would enjoy something resembling civil-service tenure.

2. *Prohibiting Bad Faith Dismissals.* Another simple possibility is a requirement that employer dismissal actions be accomplished in "good faith." This corresponds to the "intermediate" approach discussed by the New York City bar report (Committee on Labor, 1981, p. 190). This presumably is a less burdensome standard for employers than a "for cause" requirement; the employer's action would be allowed to stand based on the subjective motivation for the employer's decision, rather than on application of an external substantive standard.

A "good faith" standard, however, gives broad discretion to the reviewer of employer decisions, resulting in considerable unpredictability, and possible bias against the employer.

3. *Disadvantages of Broad, Simple Prohibitions.* A weakness with any simple substantive-fairness standard articulated in general terms such as "cause" or "good faith" is that it authorizes individual decision makers outside the workplace to make basic value tradeoffs that perhaps should be made by the employer.

Adopting a broad general substantive-fairness standard almost certainly would result in less predictability in employment relations and reduced acceptance of the system. A just-cause standard would represent a revolutionary change in private-sector employment relations. Even if this were desired by the poorly organized nonunion employee group, and by the plaintiff bar, it would materially restrict employer flexibility in enterprise management. Such an initiative is not feasible politically, because of the strong employer opposition that would be aroused, and because of a public perception that civil-service employees who are protected against discharge without cause enjoy too much job security. The broad English protection against unfair dismissal emerged from a complete overhaul of English labor law in 1971. The unfair dismissal program was a proemployee piece; most of the rest of the legislation was perceived as proemployer.

4. *Prohibiting Discharges for Specified Reasons.* In addition to the disadvantages of the broad, simple prohibitions, there are clear advantages to a substantive-fairness standard that builds on existing, specific statutory and common-law restrictions on employment terminations by enumerating the reasons for which dismissal is *not* permitted. This approach to substantive fairness would incorporate into one wrongful discharge doctrine the various standards contained in the Constitution, in federal statutes, and articulated in common-law cases. While this would result in a more complex set of rules, it would be consistent with an attempt to rationalize, rather than to revolutionize, the law of wrongful discharge. This approach is similar in many respects to the "minimalist" approach discussed by the New York City bar committee (Committee on Labor, 1981, p. 191). The order and predictability stemming from this consolidation could reduce employer opposition.

The first step in developing such a standard is to identify those types of employee interests that are entitled to legal protection under existing law. Each of these interests should be incorporated in the new substantive-fairness standard.

The interests of employees to be free from discrimination based on race, religion, gender, age, handicap, and sexual orientation should be recognized. These interests presently are protected by statute and it is unlikely that any credible opposition to include them in a comprehensive wrongful discharge doctrine could be mounted. Interests of employees to be free from discrimination based on specified conduct also are recognized to some extent by statutory law, and also should be protected in conjunction with protections afforded presently under public-policy tort concepts. Conceptually, it is hard to distinguish from the conduct-based protection afforded by the public-policy tort doctrines.

The expectations of employees, generally protected under common-law contract principles, in having employers live up to promises made to them also should be recognized. Recognition of these contract principles does not greatly involve external reviewers of termination decisions in striking difficult balances among competing interests; the organization itself struck the balance when it made the promise of employment tenure. If the employer wishes to change the way the balance is struck, it can forbear to make the promise.

Inclusion of these protections in a new substantive-fairness standard would not tilt the balance of interests appreciably against employers. On the contrary, codification would reduce uncertainty and permit reponsible employers to design better employee policies and thus from a political standpoint would attract employer support.

Incorporation of two other, overlapping categories of existing common-law protection presents more difficult questions of balance. These categories relate to off-duty conduct, and to rights protected by the Constitution against governmental interference as "liberty" interests.

Including termination for off-duty conduct in an enumerated-prohibitions statute has two virtues: It would not jeopardize legitimate employer interests, though it undeniably diminishes employer power, and it would protect certain interests recognized by the Constitution without eviscerating the state-action barrier to full constitutional scrutiny of private employer decisions. Off-duty conduct protection, widely afforded by labor arbitrators, shields employee interests in privacy and personal freedom from employer coercion unrelated to employer economic interests. Unless the employer can sustain the burden of demonstrating a nexus with its business needs, it should not be able to escape liability for terminating employees on account of political views expressed outside the workplace, marital status, or sexual orientation. Affording protection to off-duty conduct is not the same thing as imposing a just-cause requirement. Adding off-duty conduct to the enumerated reasons for which dismissal is not permitted leaves the burden of proof on the employee to demonstrate that she was fired for off-duty conduct. A just-cause protection burdens the employer to articulate the reason for the dismissal and to demonstrate that the reason amounted to just cause.

These substantive-fairness rules might be expressed in a statute like this:

A discharge of an employee shall be wrongful if one or more of the following was a determining factor in the discharge:

1. The employee's age, sex, race, religion, national origin, handicap, or sexual orientation

2. The employee's exercise of rights of political expression, religious activities, association or privacy guaranteed under the United States Constitution against governmental interference

3. The employee's performance of an act or refusal to perform an act, the performance or refusal being a furtherance of public policy, as expressed in statute, administrative regulation, or formal statements of professional ethics applicable to the employee

4. Off-duty conduct of the employee bearing no reasonable relationship to the employee's job performance

A discharge of an employee shall be wrongful if the discharge occurred in violation of an employer's express or implied promise that the employer would dismiss the employee only for certain reasons or only after following certain procedures.

None of the suggested enumerated rights would be absolute; employers would be able to escape liability for infringing the rights when they can show legitimate business reasons for doing so. Such justification occurs in applying substantive due process scrutiny to public employer decision, and when an employer is allowed to justify class-based discrimination on BFOQ or business-necessity grounds recognized in the discrimination statutes. A BFOQ is a "bona fide occupational qualification" defense to a prima facie case of sex, religious, or age discrimination, recognized by Section 703(e) of Title VII, 42 U.S.C. Section 20003e–2(e) (1984), and by Section 623(f) of the Age Discrimination in Employment Act, 29 U.S.C. Section 623(f) (1984). This is not a revolutionary proposal; virtually all of these grounds for dismissal would give rise to statutory or common-law liability under present law. The political motivation for this approach to substantive fairness is the need to attract support from employers and the defense bar; the needs of the plaintiff bar are addressed primarily through the selections made regarding procedural fairness.

Procedural Fairness

Whether a wrongful dismissal statute should send claims to arbitration, to an administrative agency, or directly to the regular courts raises procedural-fairness questions. The issue of procedural fairness in private employment termination decisions primarily involves striking a balance between deferring to decisions made by the employer through the organization's own procedures and retrying the termination decision in an external forum.

Procedural fairness is a relative rather than an absolute concept. At minimum, it requires some external check on the decision procedures utilized by employers, as a counterweight to natural employer interests potentially antagonistic to employee interests. Procedural fairness can be ensured by a review of procedures used by the employer or it can involve a *de novo* decision by an external tribunal. Determining the appropriate level of procedural fairness, like determining the appropriate approach to substantive fairness, requires a balancing of values. Acceptance of this proposition is reflected in the balancing approach to procedural due process adopted by the Supreme Court in *Mathews* v. *Eldridge* (1976).

Selection of Forum

A new statute could direct wrongful discharge disputes to any one of three forums: the regular courts, an existing or new administrative agency, or alternative dispute resolution tribunals, such as arbitration. As noted earlier, most of the proposed wrongful dismissal statutes involve an arbitration forum. Most of the statutes actually enacted involve a judicial forum.

The serious burden on regular courts by the existing volume of civil litigation militates against sending additional wrongful dismissal claims directly to court (Perritt, 1984). A search for civil-litigation alternatives enjoys wide support within the legal community and elsewhere. Legislative action perceived as increasing burdens on the courts would contravene the movement to reduce the burden. Wrongful discharge legislation designed to attract maximum support should avoid this and should, if feasible, be perceived as reducing the existing burden.

Similar reasons militate against sending wrongful dismissal claims to administrative forums, the approach traditionally elected in twentieth-century labor legislation. Administrative regulation has been subjected to increasing criticism since 1970, and "regulatory reform" has been high on the list of priorities of the last two presidents of the United States. Wrongful discharge legislation should be designed so as not to contravene this political movement, although there might be some merit in integrating wrongful dismissal into the unemployment compensation system.

The arbitration alternative is attractive because it avoids these problems with judicial and administrative alternatives. In addition, arbitration already is in wide use to protect against wrongful discharge in the union and government sectors of the economy and has proven to be generally successful in protecting the legitimate rights of both employers and employees. Also, presumably the economic barriers to arbitral resolution are lower for the dismissed employee than the barriers to judicial litigation. A California study has estimated that plaintiff legal fees for wrongful dismissal cases that go to trial average $7,500 to $8,000 per case (Ad Hoc Committee, 1984). A typical labor arbitration case probably costs about $1,000. It is not surprising that many of the concrete proposals for wrongful discharge legislation, and the methods actually adopted in Britain and Canada, utilize some form of arbitration.

Arbitration has a number of disadvantages, however. The civil courts already exist, and referring claims under a new wrongful dismissal statute to the courts has the virtue of avoiding the establishment of a new institution. Moreover, the constitutions of all but one state afford the right to a jury trial for common-law claims. Serious constitutional issues may be raised by a statute that apparently leaves intact common-law tort and contract claims for wrongful dismissal and purports to require that they be heard in a nonjudicial forum. The constitutional problem might be avoided if a new statute expressly extinguishes the common-law claims and substitutes a new statutory claim. This approach is followed in the Montana statute.

Also, statutory arbitration suffers from disadvantages not present with collectively bargained arbitration. Individual claimants, unlike unions, are largely ignorant as to the qualifications and biases of potential arbitrators. Of course, it is possible that the plaintiff bar would develop knowledge about potential arbitrators commensurate with that exercised by unions on behalf of grievants.

Ironically, arbitration deprives employers of more decision-making authority than common-law litigation in the regular courts. If common-law judges review dismissals, the appellate process can correct major excursions from rules of decision that reflect competing societal values accurately. Even then the price is high in terms of the time required, and the resulting uncertainty, before basic standards of conduct stabilize. If arbitrators make the tradeoffs, the resulting transfer of authority over employment decisions is potentially greater because most labor arbitration decisions are insulated from meaningful judicial review on the merits of individual cases. This may not be a problem in the collective bargaining contest, where union and management negotiators can change or make more definitive the basic document that arbitrators are interpreting. But in the statutory wrongful discharge setting, the discretion of an arbitrator to give his own interpretation to a statutory term such as "cause" or "good faith" is troublesome. This is because it is difficult to provide a convenient means of controlling the arbitrator's exercise of discretion in specific cases without vitiating the advantages of arbitration.

Regardless of the forum selected, it could exercise more or less deference in reviewing employer decisions, ranging from a strictly appellate role to authority to decide the termination question *de novo*.

1. Deference to Employer Procedures. Voluntarism decentralizes decision-making, thereby reducing the load on central political institutions. It permits experimentation, provides opportunities for employers and employees directly to participate in making decisions that affect them, and usually results in procedures and substantive norms that are tailored to the needs and priorities of a particular enterprise and its employees. A wrongful dismissal statute that promotes voluntarism is more likely to be favored by the employers because it allows them to design dispute-resolution procedures that accommodate the needs of a particular workplace.

Voluntarism can be promoted by ensuring that substantial deference is paid by legal institutions to procedures adopted by employers for deciding discharge controversies voluntarily.

Two polar alternatives can be identified. The first alternative, least intrusive into employer prerogatives, but also the least protective of fairness, would be to permit employers to make discharge decisions, immune from any external review, so long as they follow *some* formal process that embodies the rudiments of procedural fairness (e.g., notice, an unbiased decision maker, and an opportunity for the employee to tell his side of the story to that decision maker). This is similar to the minimum due process required for student suspensions in *Goss* v. *Lopez* (1975) (notice of charges, explanation of evidence against student, and an opportunity to present student's side of story). In Judge Friendly's list of ingredients of procedural due process, this would include only the first three rights: (1) an unbiased tribunal, (2) notice, and (3) an opportunity to present reasons why the proposed actions should not be taken ("Some Kind of Hearing, 1975"). The other alternative would be more intrusive, but also would enhance substantially the protection afforded to employees. It would involve a trial *de novo* of the fairness of the discharge decision by a jury in a regular court of law, following the usual rules of evidence.

An intermediate approach to procedural fairness can be borrowed from administrative law. Under this approach the employer would be allowed to adopt procedures meeting generic requirements of procedural fairness. Employer decisions reached under such procedures would be accepted unless they were arbitrary and capricious, or made in "bad faith."

Such an approach should be built into proposed legislation. If an employer affords no procedures protective of employee rights, then an external tribunal should decide the merits of a wrongful discharge claim. However, if the employer does have formal procedures within which the grounds for discharge are adjudicated, then the external tribunal should confine itself to an appellate role, ensuring that those procedures are followed. Decisions reached by the employer in compliance with those procedures should be final and binding, unless there is a substantive-fairness problem. Substantive issues need not be reached until it is determined that employer procedures were followed.

Such an approach will provide incentives for employers to continue to adopt their own disciplinary procedures and may reduce employer resistance to new wrongful dismissal legislation. Any other approach would create a disincentive for the continuation or adoption of such procedures because the employer always would face the threat of relitigation of questions already decided in its own internal procedures. Precedent for a deferential approach to procedural fairness includes arbitral review of discharges in the railroad industry and court review of public-employee discharges under the civil-service laws.

Despite the desirability of deferring to certain employer decisions, however, a number of difficulties arise. One obvious difficulty is deciding what standards the employer-established procedure must meet in order to be entitled to deferral. Whether procedural fairness existed in the employer's forum cannot be determined by an external decision maker without scrutinizing what the employer did, and what the employee was allowed to say in his defense. It is difficult for an external decision maker to ensure procedural fairness without having a record of the employer's proceedings or else retrying the case on the merits. But requiring employers to make transcripts or otherwise to create a "record" formalizes employer procedures, creating economic and other disincentives for adoption of such procedures.

A deferential procedural-fairness standard can confront this problem in two steps. First, it can confine the statutory tribunal to the question of whether the employer procedures were fair before proceeding to address the substantive-fairness question. In this first stage, evidence could be offered as to procedures actually followed by the employer. In the hypothetical case offered, the statutory tribunal could hear testimony and decide whether the employee was given a meaningful opportunity to present her version of the facts to the president of the employing enterprise. Second, if the employee alleges that the reason given by the employer was pretextual, the statutory tribunal can proceed to hear evidence on the merits. This compromise is far from perfect, but it represents a reasonable attempt to defer to employer procedures without rendering the opportunity for external review entirely illusory.

At the very least, a new statute should ensure the finality of final and binding arbitration agreed to in individual cases or in a class of cases. In those states adopting the Union Arbitration Act, or similar statutes, little more will be necessary than a savings clause preserving the effect of such statutes. In other states, specific language should be included.

The Montana statute requires employees to exhaust any available employer procedures before suing for wrongful dismissal, but does not address what effect the decision reached in such procedures would have in subsequent litigation (Montana statute, Section 6[2]).

2. *Treatment of Collectively Bargained Arbitration.* Employees with a right to be discharged only for cause and to litigate the fairness of terminations within collectively bargained procedures should not gain the right to relitigate such claims in a new external forum. Exclusions of statutory coverage for employees covered by collective agreements should be provided. This approach which appears in the British statute and in the Pennsylvania and Michigan bills has been suggested by Professor Summers.

There are signs, however, that some unions are willing to support wrongful dismissal legislation only if the legislation gives the union an opportunity to submit a dismissal claim either to collectively bargained arbitration or to submit it under a new statutory procedure. The rationale for this position is that submitting an individual employee to a forum not controlled by the union probably would lessen the number of subsequent fair-representation claims against the union.

One of the difficulties with this proposal is that union control over the arbitration process reduces individual employee discretion to press her claim as far as possible, since the standard of review of collectively bargained decisions is so deferential that it makes reviews highly impracticable.

3. *Preclusion, Exhaustion, and Election of Remedies.* One major shortcoming of present employment law is that employers are subjected to multiple litigation in various forums over adverse employment actions. If a particular employee enjoys statutory protection, she may be able to arbitrate a grievance over her discharge, file a charge with the NLRB, file a complaint with the EEOC alleging sex, race, or age discrimination, and file a suit alleging wrongful discharge. In *Olguin* v. *Inspiration Consolidated Copper Co.* (1984), the employee filed a state public-policy tort action for wrongful dismissal after having administrative claims dismissed under the Mine Safety and Health Act and the National Labor Relations Act. He also filed a grievance under the collective agreement, which the union refused to take to arbitration. Also, it is not unusual for the legitimacy of an employee's termination to be litigated before an unemployment compensation tribunal as well as in a claim of wrongful dismissal.

All these separate claims may go to a hearing. Enactment of comprehensive protection against wrongful discharge obviates the need for these separate procedures and also creates the opportunity to build political support in the employer community for wrongful discharge legislation by simplifying the machinery for deciding disputes.

Any wrongful discharge statute should force all legal claims related to a discharge into a single proceeding, and should preclude relitigation of the discharge in any other forum. Of course this objective is difficult to meet entirely through state legislation. Federal preemption would guarantee employees access to federal forums despite establishment of new state remedies.

State legislation could be framed, however, so as to preclude access to the state forum by an employee electing to pursue federal forums. In this situation, the employee would still have access to multiple forums, but it is unlikely that an employee would choose to litigate several narrow federal causes of action to the exclusion of the broad state causes of action for implied-in-fact contract and public-policy tort. Thus, protection against multiple claims is established indirectly by abolishing the two causes of action at common law, including them in a comprehensive state statute and disallowing actions under this statute where the federal forum is utilized. The Montana statute avoids the constitutional problems in two, mutually reinforcing ways. It extinguishes common-law claims for dismissals covered by the statute (Montana statute, Section 8). It also makes arbitration optional, while imposing the economic burden of attorney's fees on a party who refuses arbitration and loses (Montana statute, Section 9[4]).

If the employee presents a claim to the new state tribunal, loses, and then proceeds to a federal forum, the federal forum might apply judgment- or issue-preclusion principles, though preclusion would be uncertain.

A number of problems arise in connection with defining the appropriate relationship between new wrongful dismissal tribunals and administrative agencies already established to hear issues related to a wrongful dismissal claim. The problem is evident currently when an employee brings a common-law, public-policy tort claim premised on employer violation of health or safety regulations. Health or safety regulations commonly are enforced by administrative agencies. If the agency decides that a health or safety violation did not occur, the question then arises what effect should this have on the wrongful dismissal case. One can argue that, since the agency did not decide the retaliatory dismissal question, the administrative decision should have no effect. Conversely, one can argue that the public-policy basis for the wrongful dismissal claim evaporates when the responsible agency has found that there was nothing wrong with the employer's conduct. The soundest view is that the issue is not whether the employee was *correct* in her complaints; rather the issue should be whether the employee's right to complain *in good faith* without fear of retaliation promotes public policy. Accordingly, a finding of a serious violation by the responsible administrative agency would be persuasive evidence that the employee's concern was in good faith. A finding of no violation might support an argument that the employee's complaint was frivolous.

When the responsible agency has not yet addressed the employer's compliance with law, exhaustion-of-remedies principles should preclude decision on the wrongful dismissal claim prior to the agency having an opportunity to interpret its own statute or regulation.

4. *Burdens of Proof.* Under a just-cause statute, the practical burden of proof (at least the burden of producing evidence) rests with the employer to show that the reason for dismissing an employee was justified. Under a "bad faith" statute, the burden would rest with the employee to make the initial showing that the employer dismissed him in bad faith.

Under an enumerated-prohibitions statute, the employee would be burdened with establishing that one of the enumerated reasons motivated the termination. The employer then can defend successfully by offering legitimate business reasons for the discharge. The ultimate burden of persuasion should rest with the employee. This order of proof comports well with what presently is required under federal statutes.

5. *Judicial Review.* If the new wrongful dismissal tribunal is not judicial in character, a wrongful dismissal statute must address the appropriate standard of judicial review. The term "arbitration" leads most labor lawyers to assume a very deferential standard of review, similar to that applied under Section 301 of the National Labor Relations Act. But, the plaintiff bar, unorganized employees, and employers may be unwilling to trust a new form of arbitration to this extent.

Practicable alternatives are hard to formulate, however. Affording *de novo* judicial trial after arbitration negates much of the benefit from including a nonjudicial tribunal in the statute. On the other hand, the experience of court-annexed arbitration programs, which are reviewable *de novo*, suggests that perhaps the availability of a nonbinding decision, combined with threshold costs for access to the judicial forum, may result in a large proportion of cases stopping at the arbitral step.

If one takes an intermediate approach, and wishes to have an arbitrary and capricious standard of review, or a substantial evidence in the records standard of review, one then must force the initial tribunal to create a record, or at least to write opinions. Many of the benefits of arbitration result from requiring neither records nor opinions.

6. *Remedies.* Deciding upon the remedies to be afforded under a comprehensive wrongful dismissal doctrine presents three difficult questions: (1) whether reinstatement should be allowed; (2) whether "front pay"—pay for lost earnings in the future, as opposed to back pay— should be allowed; and (3) whether statutory attorney's fees should be granted.

Reinstatement is almost universally available in labor arbitration and under existing statutes protecting individual employees, such as Title VII and the ADEA.

If reinstatement is permitted, there is less reason to provide for front pay. This represents a compromise between the common-law contract rule, which permits "expectation damages" when a breach of contract has been shown, and the tort and statutory rules, which generally would permit only back pay.

On the other hand, if remedies are circumscribed too much, strong opposition can be expected from the plaintiff bar. Statutory attorney's fees would benefit the plaintiff bar. A reasonable compromise might be to cap damages, as desired by employers, permitting front pay in cases where reinstatement is not desired or appropriate, but not permitting punitive damages or compensation for mental distress, and providing an award of attorney's fees to successful claimants.

Estimate of Case Volume

A relatively unsophisticated analysis of arbitration cases and caseload under existing federal statutes suggests that the number of cases filed annually under the proposed statutes could range from 30,000 to 103,000 (Perritt, 1987, pp. 539–42).

The Montana Statute

The most significant development at the state level has been the enactment by the Montana legislature of the Wrongful Discharge From Employment Act. This statute follows many of the suggestions expressed in this chapter.

The Montana statute authorizes damages actions for dismissals that violate public policy (Section 4[1]), are not for good cause after employees complete probationary periods (Section 4 [2]), or which violate express written employer personnel policies (Section 4[3]). Compensatory damages for lost wages and benefits for up to four years are available, but not any other form of damages unless the employee can establish actual fraud or actual malice by the employer (Section 5). The statute expressly preempts common-law tort and implied-contract claims (Section 8), and excludes employment terminations subject to state and federal whistle-blower and discrimination statutes (Section 7[1]), or covered by collective bargaining agreements (Section 7[2]). Arbitration of claims arising under the statute is optional, but attorney's fee awards are provided for against the party declining to arbitrate (Section 9). The Montana statute is a peculiar combination of just-cause and enumerated-reasons legislation. It is not entirely clear why the specific provisions relating to public-policy dismissals or dismissals contravening employer personnel policies are included, given the board prohibition against dismissals without just cause, unless the narrower prohibitions are intended to protect only probationary employees.

CONCLUSION

   This chapter has reviewed the basic substantive and procedural alternatives for wrongful dismissal legislation, and supports the conclusion that the best approach is one similar to that recommended by Perritt (1984a) and adopted by the Montana legislature: prohibiting dismissals for enumerated reasons, and providing procedures that defer to established employer and collectively bargained mechanisms and that replace unnecessarily fragmented administrative and judicial proceedings. The substantive protections incorporated in such an enumerated-prohibitions statute should codify existing employee interests reflected in scores of federal and state statutes and in the three common-law wrongful dismissal theories.

5

Trends in Title VII Discrimination Legal Theories: The Future of Disparate Treatment and Disparate Impact

REBECCA A. (BAYSINGER) THACKER
AND STUART A. YOUNGBLOOD

In today's rights-conscious society, few employers have employment policies that operate to discriminate illegally against entire groups of minorities. Yet there continues to be a call for legislative and judicial remedies to correct perceived inequities between employer rights and employees' rights (see, e.g., Stieber, Chapter 3, supra and Perritt, Chapter 4, supra). In particular, there is some sentiment to have the courts use the disparate-impact theory as the vehicle for fighting illegal discrimination at upper levels of the organization (see, e.g., Bartholet, 1982).

The purpose of this chapter is to investigate the recent use and application of disparate impact and disparate treatment, the two legal theories used to analyze Title VII discrimination cases. The chapter will also investigate the challenge that disparate impact is the appropriate legal remedy for righting perceived inequities caused by illegal discrimination and, as such, should be the vehicle for analyzing minority claims of discrimination at upper levels of the organization. The chapter will proceed with a five-year review of Title VII cases, and then address the disparate-impact challenge.

DISPARATE TREATMENT AND DISPARATE IMPACT: EXPLANATION AND ILLUSTRATION

Disparate-treatment theory is the mechanism used to define illegal discrimination against an individual, although it can also be used to prove illegal discrimination against a group of individuals. Disparate impact defines discrimination against a group of individuals based on the composition of the employer's work force, or the employer's rejection rates. The key distinction between the two theories is that with disparate-treatment analysis, the employee must prove that the employer *intended* to discriminate. With disparate-impact analysis, intent is irrelevant.

The need for disparate-impact analysis is not as great today as it was immediately following passage of the Civil Rights Act of 1964. At that time, many organizations had policies or employment practices that blatantly discriminated against minority groups. For example, some organizations had separate lines of progression for blacks and whites that resulted in the exclusion of blacks from the organization's highest levels and most attractive jobs. This is systematic discrimination against an entire category of individuals, and is the type of discrimination addressed by disparate impact.

However, most obvious forms of discrimination have disappeared; thus, the objective of future discrimination suits should be to make *individuals* prove that they are victims of discrimination. For example, the Supreme Court decision in *Firefighters Local 1784* v. *Stotts* (1984) stated explicitly that Title VII does not permit preferential treatment to non-victims of discrimination. In *Wygant* v. *Jackson Board of Education* (1986), the Supreme Court rejected an affirmative-action plan allowing black schoolteachers in Jackson, Michigan, to retain their jobs while more senior white teachers were laid off. The value of remedies that penalize the majority population while giving preferential treatment to nonvictims of discrimination was scrutinized closely in both these cases. In particular, the statistical evidence so frequently found in disparate-impact analysis was called into question.

The argument against the disparate-treatment philosophy is that use of the disparate-treatment theory does not allow for fulfillment of the social goal of getting more minorities into upper-level positions of the organization (see, e.g., Bartholet, 1982). The argument continues to state that disparate-impact theory is the appropriate vehicle for achievement of this goal; thus, disparate-impact analysis should be applied to upper-level Title VII discrimination cases.

The choice of whether to use disparate-impact or disparate-treatment theories is complex, and deserves further examination before making a normative recommendation that disparate impact should be applied to upper-level discrimination cases. For example, the employment practice or employer behavior that led to the filing of the discrimination suit will usually determine the legal theory used to analyze the case. Moreover, the type of evidence required to prove employer guilt will differ, depending upon whether the disparate-impact theory or the disparate-treatment theory is utilized. Two recent Supreme Court decisions, *Local*

28 of the Sheet Metal Workers' International Association v. *Equal Employment Opportunity Commission* (1986) and *Local Number 93, International Association of Firefighters, AFL-CIO* v. *City of Cleveland* (1986), illustrate the kinds of employer behavior that are applicable to disparate-impact analysis and disparate-treatment analysis. In both cases, a combination of intentional discrimination, which implies disparate-treatment analysis, and more benign (in the sense that the discriminatory outcome was not intended) discriminatory behavior, which implies disparate-impact analysis, was evident.

In *Sheet Metal Workers*, the Union (Local 28) was sued for failure to include blacks in the union and in the apprenticeship program. Evidence presented in court indicated that no blacks had ever been admitted to the union. In addition, the union was accused of engaging in nepotism when admitting individuals into the apprenticeship program. Individuals were sponsored by a union member, and this practice constituted "an impenetrable barrier for nonwhite applicants" (*Local 28*, p. 109).

The situation was exacerbated by the union's refusal to abide by the New York State Supreme Court's "cease and desist" order. The union had also refused to comply with a plan by the New York City government to require city contractors to hire one minority for every four journeymen union members.

The behaviors that proved troublesome for the union in *Sheet Metal Workers* were as follows: use of criteria (an entrance examination and high school diploma requirement) that had an adverse impact on minorities and were not related to job performance; creation of a fund subsidized by the union to set up training sessions for members' friends and relatives taking the apprenticeship examination; restriction of membership size to keep out nonwhites (the union had refused to administer yearly journeymen's examinations despite increased need for their services, relying instead on pensioners and temporary workers to meet demand); admitting to membership only whites when the union organized nonunion sheet metal shops; and, finally, accepting only white transfers from other locals.

The behavior of the union in *Sheet Metal Workers* appears to be a combination of purposeful, intentional discriminatory behavior and benign, albeit discriminatory, behavior. Relying on current members to supply new members had been the union's practice in the past, and the practice provided an adequate supply of satisfactory members. The fund for training purposes was an outgrowth of the practice of relying on the network set up by union members. These two practices, although discriminatory in outcome, may not have been followed with the *intent* of keeping minorities out of the union.

By the same token, the entrance examination and the high school education requirement were probably not used to intentionally exclude minorities. The examination and high school degree requirement are facially neutral, yet in practice they serve to exclude a disproportionate number of minority applicants. The situation is compounded when the employer cannot show the job-relatedness of the selection criteria. Indeed, many employers are unaware of the validity of their selection criteria. Hence, these employment practices are more appropriately categorized as disparate-impact practices.

The remainder of the behaviors exhibited by the union in *Sheet Metal Workers* appear to be motivated by an intention to keep minorities out of the union; that is, intentional discrimination. Certainly, refusing to admit nonwhites from newly organized shops and accepting only white transfers from other locals is a clear indication of restricted policy by the union with intent to discriminate against minorities. These behaviors are more appropriately categorized as disparate-treatment behaviors.

In the *Firefighters* case, the promotion examination for firefighters used by the city of Cleveland was found to be discriminatory. In addition, the court determined that the city contrived to keep minorities at the bottom of the promotion list by manipulating retirement dates and relying on a system of seniority points to determine promotion status. Finally, the city had refused to administer a promotional examination after 1975, resulting in limited minority advancement.

Employer behavior in *Firefighters* is also a combination of intentional and benign discrimination. Again, use of an examination for promotion purposes that results in discriminatory outcomes is not necessarily an indictment of the city's employment practices, and can more appropriately be termed disparate-impact behavior. However, manipulating retirement dates, reliance on the seniority points system, and refusal to administer the promotional examination appear to be purposeful, intentional discriminatory behaviors. The latter behaviors are disparate-treatment behaviors.

Under the standards of Title VII, both kinds of employer behavior described in these two cases are potentially illegal. An employer who relies on past practices to make employment decisions can be in violation of Title VII, if the practice results in adverse impact for a minority group, and if the employer cannot prove that use of the employment practice is related to the job. Purposeful, intentional discrimination on the basis of a physical attribute is clearly proscribed by Title VII.

REVIEW OF RECENT TITLE VII LITIGATION: METHOD AND RESULTS

To assess the use and frequency of application of the disparate-treatment theory and the disparate-impact theory in the lower courts,

Table 5.1
Outcomes of Content Analysis of Eighty-One Discrimination Cases*

LEGAL THEORY

		DISPARATE IMPACT		DISPARATE TREATMENT		DISPARATE IMPACT & DISPARATE TREATMENT	
		Employer Wins	Employee Wins	Employer Wins	Employee Wins	Employer Wins	Employee Wins
HIERARCHY	Upper Level Positions		1	35	3	1	1
	Lower Level Positions	3	4	10	16	7	5

- - - - - - - - - - - - - - - - -

*A total of 86 claims were analyzed. The number of total claims reported exceeds 81, as some cases had multiple claims. Each claim was counted once.

a review of recent Title VII discrimination cases was conducted. Eighty-one Title VII discrimination cases filed between 1980–1985 were reviewed (see Appendix 5.1). The cases were selected using the West Law data base. Use of this data base involves a computer search that is initiated with the use of several key words and phrases. For this search, phrases such as "disparate treatment" and "disparate impact" were used to identify Title VII cases. Cases were content analyzed for judicial reasoning concerning the use of either the disparate-treatment or disparate-impact theory, as well as for outcome. In addition, cases were categorized by type of job, either upper level or lower level. The upper/lower-level distinction was based upon the job's position in the organization's hierarchy. For example, an assembly-line worker is a lower-level job, but a superintendent of schools is an upper-level job.

Table 5.1 depicts the number of cases by type of position that were decided using each of the legal theories. In Table 5.1, a few of the lower-level cases have multiple claims and each claim is counted once. In the multiple claims cases, the employee alleged discrimination regarding more than one employment practice. For example, the employee may have alleged discrimination because of the employer's performance-evaluation process as well as the promotion practice. Multiple claims may have also resulted from the use of both disparate impact and disparate treatment to analyze the same claim. Eighty-six claims are included in total. Table 5.1 is further broken down by outcome; that is, whether the employer or the employee won the case.

Seventy-four percent of the total claims analyzed were disparate-treatment claims; 9.3 percent were disparate-impact claims; and 16.3 percent involved both disparate-treatment and disparate-impact analysis. Ninety-three percent of the upper-level positions claims were disparate-treatment claims; 57.8 percent of the lower-level cases were disparate-treatment claims. Almost 5 percent (4.9 percent) of the upper-level claims involved both disparate impact and disparate treatment; 26.7 percent of the lower-level claims involved both disparate-impact and disparate-treatment analysis.

Moreover, employees in lower-level positions using a disparate-treatment theory of discrimination won 62 percent of the time while upper-level plaintiffs using a disparate-treatment theory won only 8 percent of the time. In summary, disparate-treatment theory appears to be the dominant theory used in discrimination cases and appears to be significantly more successful for plaintiffs in lower-level positions.

No attempt has been made to interpret these results in terms of statistical significance. As the cases were not selected randomly, these results may not be representative of all the Title VII claims that came to court during the 1980–1985 period. Nonetheless, the results are interesting and suggest some patterns that warrant further research.

DISCUSSION

Based on preliminary results, the courts have apparently begun to rely less on disparate-impact analysis in Title VII litigation, and are beginning to rely more upon disparate treatment. The important question is why disparate treatment has become the dominant theory. As suggested earlier, blatant and obvious forms of discrimination, as well as employment practices that yield noticeable imbalances in work-force composition have, in general, disappeared. The focus is on *individual* cases of discrimination.

For the disparate-impact theory to be applied, the employee must prove that the challenged employment practice affected the composition of the employer's work force, or was responsible for disparate rejection rates. Under this requirement, fewer and fewer claims of disparate impact actually succeed past the first stage of disparate-impact analysis, which requires the employee to prove a *prima facie* case of discrimination against the employer.

Another issue concerns the technicalities of the two theories. The theories require different kinds of evidence and shift the burden of proof to the employer or employee for different reasons. Thus, they are not easily interchangeable.

For example, many of the cases in Table 5.1 involved promotion decisions. It would seem that disparate-treatment theory is more suited to claims involving promotion or transfer decisions, rather than hiring decisions. Upper-level promotion and transfer decisions (particularly for companies with a promotion-from-within policy) generally involve a smaller pool of candidates; thus, the employee will not be able to mount a challenge against the composition of the work force based upon the particular promotion or transfer policy.

A challenge to the composition of the work force or the organization's selection/rejection rates is the cornerstone of disparate-impact analysis. Yet, often the number of candidates considered as the relevant internal labor pool is simply too small to claim systematic discrimination in most upper-level promotion and transfer decisions; hence the need for disparate-treatment analysis. Athough the two recent Supreme Court cases cited earlier, *Firefighters* and *Sheet Metal Workers*, provide clear examples of disparate impact against an entire group of people in selection and promotion, only lower-level jobs were involved. If many upper-level discrimination claims involve promotion or transfer decisions, then they are more likely to be analyzed with the disparate-treatment theory, as the "fit" with the requirements of disparate-impact analysis is not a good one.

Another reason that the two theories are not interchangeable is that disparate-treatment theory requires proof of employer *intent* to discriminate. Proof of discriminatory motive is irrelevant to a disparate-impact analysis, as the composition of the work force or the organization's rejection rates may be the result of benign and facially neutral, albeit discriminatory, employment practices. To suggest that minorities are excluded from upper-level positions simply because of their (supposedly undesirable) minority status is to suggest that employers *intend* this result, or design their promotion and transfer policies with this goal in mind. If an employee is going to succeed in a discrimination suit that claims that the employer *intentionally* discriminated, then disparate-treatment analysis is the only legal recourse available. Hence, disparate impact is technically inappropriate for addressing a claim that minorities are *intentionally* barred from upper-level positions.

Beyond the question of the technicalities of disparate-impact and disparate-treatment analysis, the root causes of discrimination itself must be examined in order to suggest appropriate remedies. Discrimination is a complex phenomenon and takes many forms. The roots of discrimination are in the socialization patterns of both men and women (Sears and Whitney, 1973; Thompson, 1967; Terborg, 1977; Ahrons, 1976). For example, the home environment and the role that the mother takes in the family have proven to be important contributing factors toward female offsprings' career decisions (Almquist and Angrist, 1971; Waite and Berryman, 1985). The result is that those women who have career-oriented women for mothers are more likely to take on nontraditional roles when they enter the work force than are those women who had mothers adopting traditional female roles (e.g., stay at home with the children).

In addition, socialization influences the amount and kind of training and education individuals choose for themselves. In other words, if women and blacks, for example, accept the traditional roles in life they have been socialized to accept, they will be less likely to prepare themselves for careers that lead to the upper levels of the organization. That is, they will be less likely to invest in post–high school education, or they will receive the type of college degree best suited to their accepted traditional role (e.g., nurse or schoolteacher), or they will be less likely to accumulate work experience that is relevant to nontraditional roles. The theory of human capital accumulation (Mincer and Polachek, 1974) focuses on the voluntary choices of individuals rather than the effects of discriminatory employment decisions as explanations for the lack of minorities in upper-level positions of the organization (Blau, 1984).

Another result of socialization is sex-role stereotyping. Sex-role stereotyping rests on the premise that the stereotypical man and woman will consistently exhibit characteristics or qualities that are inherently male or female. Organizations treat men and women according to socialized expectations (Powell, 1980). As a result, employers may not consciously treat individuals differently on the basis of a physical characteristic, but may react unconsciously to their socialized expectations about appropriate roles and behaviors for females or blacks or other minorities.

While socialization's effects may result in various forms of discrimination, its origins are not well understood. Disparate treatment does not address the subtle influence of socialization as a form of discrimination because disparate treatment requires proof of discriminatory motive. The effects of socialization are so subtle that most people are not aware of their influence. Furthermore, employees will have difficulty proving that their employers had discriminatory motives because of a lifetime of socialization.

Moreover, to apply the disparate-impact theory, the employee would have to challenge a specific employment practice that resulted in discriminatory outcomes for the specified minority group. Once again, it would be difficult to challenge socialization as a specific employment practice because socialization began at a very early age and had its effects long before individuals entered organizations and began to make employment decisions.

Thus, the effects of socialization and an individual's voluntary human capital accumulation choices are not the result of intentional employer discrimination. Rather, the lack of minorities at upper organizational levels is at least partially the result of influences on the individual that began long before the individual entered the organization. Socialization and voluntary choice are not the types of influences Title VII legal theories were designed to correct, as Title VII theories are limited in scope, as well as application.

SUGGESTIONS FOR FUTURE RESEARCH

Future research should take a more scientific approach to analyzing Title VII discrimination cases. That is, random selection of cases would provide more support for generalizing the consequences associated with judicial application of the disparate-treatment and disparate-impact legal theories. Such an analysis could also analyze the stage of proof at which a case succeeds or fails under both theories. For example, under disparate-impact analysis, the employee is first required to prove the adverse impact of the challenged employment practice. If the employee succeeds, the employer is then required to defend the employment practice through a defense of job-relatedness, business necessity, use of a bona fide occupational qualification, or a bona fide seniority system. If the employer defends the employment practice to the court's satisfaction, the employee has the option of suggesting an alternate employment practice that achieves the same employer goal but with less discriminatory impact. Failing to do this, the employer is allowed to continue with the challenged employment practice.

Much valuable information could be gained from an investigation of the points at which the employee's claim fails or succeeds. Much could be learned about judicial interpretation of the public policy from such an analysis, and perhaps trends for future Title VII litigation could be identified. Certainly, judicial tolerance (or intolerance) for the kinds of evidence presented in disparate-impact analysis (i.e., statistical evidence) could be determined, along with the extent to which this tolerance has increased or decreased over the years.

Research of this kind might also be able to identify patterns in application of the two theories. For example, disparate impact may be the more effective theory for employees who claim discrimination at the point of entry into the organization, while disparate treatment may be the more effective theory for the employee who alleges discrimination in intrafirm mobility decisions, for example, promotions or transfers. Such evidence would be useful for organizations designing selection, promotion, and transfer policies.

Finally, public-policy research would be meaningful if a logical, rather than a normative, approach is taken. For example, Henry H. Perritt's analysis of wrongful dismissal legislation in Chapter 4 is to be commended for including perspectives of four affected constituent groups before making recommendations about the viability of wrongful dismissal legislation. Such an analysis facilitates understanding and, hopefully, improves public policy.

CONCLUSION

First, judicial experience with Title VII claims is at odds with those who claim that the disparate-impact theory can be applied to all upper-level discrimination cases. Of the few cases pursued under the disparate-impact theory in this review, 88 percent involved *lower-level* positions. Moreover, the majority of the Table 5.1 *upper-level* cases were decided using disparate-treatment analysis. Because the disparate-impact theory relies on large numbers to assess the consequence of facially neutral employment practices, while disparate treatment looks at employer intent, these two theories are not interchangeable. Each theory has specific requirements, and it would appear that, in general, disparate treatment theory is the best "fit" with upper-level discrimination cases that typically involve promotion or transfer decisions.

However, the courts have not accepted *entirely* the philosophy that disparate-impact analysis has outlived its usefulness. The Supreme Court found discrimination against entire groups of minorities in its two recent findings, *Sheet Metal Workers* and *Firefighters*. Nevertheless, in time courts may begin to rely more on disparate-treatment analysis, emphasizing statistical evidence less, in favor of an emphasis on specific incidents of an employer's discriminatory behavior.

Second, Title VII legal theories are limited in scope and application. Hence, they are ineffective in redressing socially based inequities that have as their root causes other factors besides illegal discrimination. Illegal discrimination is only one part of a complex problem that manifests itself in few minorities at upper levels of the organization. However, when illegal discrimination, as defined by both disparate-treatment and disparate-impact theory, is the cause of the problem, then both legal theories are available for analysis of the problem.

Discriminatory behavior rooted in either lifetime socialization or the voluntary choice of individuals cannot be effectively addressed by either disparate-treatment theory or disparate-impact theory remedies. An individual (or a group of individuals) challenging such institutionalized barriers via the disparate-treatment or disparate-impact theory route will have difficulty proving illegal discrimination on the basis of adverse impact; these barriers are too subtle to be defined within the confines of the two available legal theories.

Advocates of legislated remedies for perceived employee rights' problems (see Stieber, Chapter 3, supra) might be mindful of the results of this study. The imposition of controls sometimes does not have the intended effect because the underlying causes for the perceived inequity are not well understood.

Finally, because the two Title VII legal theories are limited in scope and application, they are incapable of redressing social inequities that are the product of years of socialization. In effect, disparate impact attempts to redress discriminatory or prejudicial treatment of an entire group of minorities by allowing one or several employees to file a claim on behalf of that minority group. While only several employees may have been directly affected, the theory rests on the assumption that an entire category of minorities could have been adversely affected.

For those individuals who are victims of illegal discrimination, a legal remedy in the form of the disparate-treatment theory is available. However, disparate impact is not the appropriate remedy for moving minorities into the organization's upper levels. Implicit in this statement is the notion that there are other, more subtle causes for the lack of minorities in high-level organizational positions. Two of those possible causes are socialization and voluntary choices. Thus, the legal remedies, at least in their present form, may be inadequate for dealing with the multifaceted problem of discrimination. Not only are the two legal theories technically incapable of providing the mechanism for increasing the number of minorities in upper-level positions, but a thorough understanding of the causes of discrimination might reveal that what appears to be illegal discrimination is, in fact, a consequence of individual choice and socialization.

Appendix 5.1
The Legal Cases Studied

Spearmon v. Southwestern Bell, 506 F. Supp. 761 (1980)

Farrakhan v. Sears, Roebuck, & Co., 511 F. Supp. 893 (1980)

Smith v. Univ. of North Carolina, 632 F.2d 316 (1980)

Sklenar v. Central Board of Education of the School District of the City of Detroit, 497 F. Supp. 1154 (1980)

Murphy v. Middletown Enlarged City School District, 525 F. Supp. 678 (1981)

Womack Shell Chemical Co., 514 F. Supp. 1062 (1981)

Valentino v. U.S. Postal Service, 511 F. Supp. 917 (1981)

Texas Dept. of Community Affairs v. Burdine, 101 S.Ct. 1089 (1981)

Bauer v. Bailar, 647 F.2d 1037 (1981)

Page v. Bolger, 647 F.2d 227 (1981)

Coe v. Yellow Freight System Inc., 646 F.2d 444 (1981)

Harris v. Group Health Assn. Inc., 662 F.2d 869 (1981)

Dickerson v. Metropolitan Dade County, 659 F.2d 574 (1981)

St. Peter v. Secretary of the Army, 659 F.2d 1133 (1981)

Williams v. Colorado Springs, Colorado School District, 641 F.2d 835 (1981)

Stinson v. Tennessee Dept. of Mental Health and Mental Education, 553 F. Supp. 454 (1982)

Pouncy v. Prudential Ins. Co. of America, 668 F.2d 795 (1982)

Burrus v. United Telephone Co. of Kansas, Inc., 683 F.2d 339 (1982)

Milton v. Weinberger, 696 F.2d 94 (1982)

Knight v. Nassau County, 649 F.2d 461 (1982)

Stones v. Los Angeles Community College Dist., 572 F. Supp. 1072 (1983)

Peters v. Lieuallen, 568 F. Supp. 261 (1983)

Burrows v. Chemed Corp., 567 F. Supp. 978 (1983)

Mohammed v. Callaway, 698 F. Supp. 978 (1983)

Foster v. MCI Telecommunications Corp., 555 F. Supp. 330 (1983)

Grano v. Dept. of Development of City of Columbus, 699 F.2d 336 (1983)

Mason v. Continental Illinois Natl. Bank, 704 F.2d 361 (1983)

Bell v. Bolger, 708 F.2d 1312 (1983)

Lewis v. St. Louis University, 573 F. Supp. 300 (1983)

Verniero v. Air Force Academy School District, 705 F.2d 338 (1893)

Nord v. United States Steel Corp., 758 F.2d 1462 (1985)

Holsey v. Armour & Co., 743 F.2d 199 (1984)

Gilchrist v. Bolger, 733 F.2d 1551 (1984)

Walker v. Jefferson Co. Home, 726 F.2d 1554 (1984)

Lewis v. Univ. of Pittsburgh, 725 F.2d 910 (1983)

Whatley v. Skaggs Companies, Inc., 707 F.2d 1129 (1983)

Cuthbertson v. Biggers Bros. Inc., 702 F.2d 454 (1983)

Hebert v. Monsanto Co., 682 F.2d 1111 (1982)

Royal v. Missouri Highway & Transportation Comm., 655 F.2d 159 (1981)

Crawford v. Western Electric Co., Inc., 614 F.2d 1300 (1980)

Carroll v. Sears, Roebuck & Co., 708 F.2d 183 (1983)

Carpenter v. Stephen F. Austin Univ., 06 F.2d 608 (1983)

Rowe v. Cleveland Pneumatic Co., Numerical Control, 690 F.2d 88 (1982)

EEOC v. Korn Industries Inc., 662 F.2d 256 (1981)

Nanty v. Barrows Co., 660 F.2d 1327 (1983)

Movement for Opportunity, Etc. v. General Motors, 622 F.2d 1235 (1980)

Fisher v. Procter & Gamble Mfg. Co., 613 F.2d 527 (1980)

Conner v. Fort Gordon Bus Co., 761 F.2d 1495 (1985)

Bibbs v. Block, 749 F.2d 508 (1984)

Walls v. Mississippi St. Dept. of Public Welfare, 730 F.2d 306 (1984)

Page v. U.S. Industries Inc., 726 F.2d 1038 (1984)

Hill v. K-Mart Corp., 699 F.2d 776 (1983)

Eastland v. Tennessee Valley Authority, 704 F.2d 613 (1983)

Eubanks v. Pickens-Bond Const. Co., 635 F.2d 1341 (1980)

Stastny v. Southern Bell Telephone & Telegraph Co., 628 F.2d 267 (1980)

Ramirez v. Hoffeinz, 619 F.2d 442 (1980)

Falcon v. General Telephone Co. of the Southwest, 626 F.2d 369 (1980)

Griggs v. Duke Power Co., 402 S.Ct. 424 (1971)

Atonio v. Wards Cove Packing Co., 38 FEP Caess 1170 (1985)

Rowe v. General Motors, 457 F.2d 348 (1972)

Chisholm v. U.S. Postal Service, 665 F.2d 482 (1981)

Nieves v. Metropolitan Dade Co., 598 F.2d 995 (1984)

Colon-Sanchez v. Marsh, 733 F.2d 78 (1984)

Craik v. Minnesota State University Board, 731 F.2d 465 (1984)

Parker v. Board of School Commissioner of the City of Indianapolis, 729 F.2d 524 (1984)

Robinson v. Polaroid Corp., 732 F.2d 1010 (1984)

Rossini v. Ogilvy & Mather, Inc., 597 F. Supp. 1120 (1984)

Hawkins v. Bounds, 752 F.2d 500 (1985)

Jayasinghe v. Bethlehem Steel Corp., 760 F.2d 132 (1985)

Smith v. St. of Georgia, 749 F.2d 683 (1985)

Lewis v. N.L.R.B., 750 F.2d 1266 (1985)

Catlett v. Missouri Highway & Tansportation Comm., 589 F. Supp. 929 (1983)

Paxton v. Union Natl. Bank, 688 F.2d 552 (1982)

Lilly v. Harris-Teeter Supermarket, 545 F. Supp. 686 (1982)

Wilmore v. City of Wilmington, 533 F. Supp. 844 (1982)

Ellison v. Best Foods, 598 F. Supp. 159 (1984)

Reynolds v. Sheet Metal Workers Local 102, 498 F. Supp. 952 (1908)

McKenzie v. Sawyer, 684 F.2d 62 (1982)

Jackson v. Seaboard Coast Line Railroad Co., 678 F.2d 992 (1982)

Thompson v. Sawyer, 678 F.2d 257 (1982)

Johnson v. General Tire & Rubber Co., 652 F.2d 574 (1981)

PART III

HUMAN RESOURCES AND MANAGEMENT EDUCATION PERSPECTIVES

Positive Discipline: A Nonpunitive Approach to Managing Human Resources

WILLIAM R. HUTCHISON
AND CHIMEZIE A. B. OSIGWEH, YG.

In the introduction to a popular book in 1985, Tom Peters argued that "a revolution is on, and managers in every field are rethinking the tried and, as it turns out, not so true, management principles that have often served their institutions poorly" (see also Osigweh, 1987b, 1988a). In this chapter, we will argue that the traditional industrial discipline system ignores the great majority of organization members who do their jobs well and, for the few who do not, emphasizes punishment instead of individual responsibility and recommitment to the organization's goals. Further, we will argue that this traditional punitive system is one of the most significant "tried and not so true" management principles that today serves institutions poorly. We shall accomplish these while describing a model of discipline that has been implemented at Union Carbide Corporation where the first author serves as director of corporate employee relations, and where the traditional approach to dealing with disciplinary problems has been abandoned and is being replaced with an entirely different model known as *positive discipline*.

Positive discipline is a performance management system that retains the benefit of progressively serious contacts with an employee when performance or behavior problems arise, but eliminates quickness to use punishment as a means of getting the individual to decide to change and abide by company standards. It also provides a complete administrative system that helps assure fairness and consistency in dealing with individuals. Furthermore, and most important to Union Carbide, the system places great emphasis on the recognition and reinforcement of the good performance delivered by the great majority of the company's employees.

TRADITIONAL "PROGRESSIVE DISCIPLINE"—A
BANKRUPT SYSTEM

The traditional discipline system, still in use in a great majority of America's organizations, provides for increasingly serious punishments to be inflicted on members of the organization who fail to attend regularly, perform properly, or behave acceptably. An oral warning is followed by a written warning if performance does not improve; the final step prior to termination is typically an unpaid, multiday suspension.

This system of discipline was perhaps appropriate when it was originally developed in the 1930s in response to union demands that disciplinary action and discharge be taken only for "just cause" (see Osigweh, 1987b, pp. 13–14). Today, however, the system seems counterproductive to building an organization committed to common goals and dedicated to excellence. Consider the characteristics and effects of this traditional punitive approach to problem solving:

The Objective Is Punishment. Faced with the commission of an offense against the organization, management marshalls the facts, scrutinizes the evidence, and determines the punishment that fits the crime. What practitioners would call organizational "misdemeanors," such as casual absenteeism and tardiness, result in a "chewing out" or "Dutch Uncle" discussion. More serious transgressions—including workplace "felonies" such as violations of a serious safety rule, chronically substandard work performance, or horseplay; and industrial "capital crimes," such as sabotage, thievery, or gross insubordination, are met with warnings or suspensions.

It Applies to Few. At Union Carbide, as at most organizations, only a tiny minority of employees were ever involved with the formal traditional discipline system. It is our belief that that a system for encouraging true self-discipline should apply to every member of the organization.

It Focuses on the Past. Traditional systems of discipline focus entirely on the past. The employee who has broken one of the organization's rules or who has otherwise transgressed receives a written warning or some other disciplinary action in response. In effect, a "crime" has been committed and the penalty has been assessed. The individual may well feel, "I done the deed; I paid the price; and now everything's back to normal." If so, little or no commitment for future good performance may be received, suggesting that little or none is implicit in the traditional system.

It Encourages Adversarial Relationships. In the traditional industrial discipline system, the employee stands as "the accused" against whom the supervisor "builds a case." The outcome of their discussions, particularly when a union is involved, may well be the development of an "us vs. them" climate inside the organization where supervisors and workers view each other as the enemy.

It Treats the Employee as a Child. The traditional progressive discipline system incorporates the assumption that the errant employee is a child who must be punished for misbehavior, not an adult with a problem to solve. By concentrating on punishment, this view of the employee as an irresponsible adolescent too often becomes a self-fulfilling prophecy.

It Offers Nothing Affirmative. The traditional discipline system is concerned only with wrongdoing. There is rarely a provision in the system that requires managers to recognize good performance. In effect, the system ignores the good, work-related behavior of the majority of organization members and concentrates primarily on punishing those few who fail to meet company or location expectations.

It Is Resisted by Managers. Few managers want to be seen as "disciplinarians." Managers are frequently reluctant to take very apropriate disciplinary action because they are unsure of the exact procedures to follow. Further, they fear that their decisions may be reversed "upstairs," and are also concerned about the negative impact that taking a disciplinary action can have on their relationship with the individual involved. In addition, managers tend to be slow in acting when employee behavior indicates the need for a discussion about performance, because of the negative view held by many managers and supervisors about the traditional discipline process. As the employee's behavior begins to deviate from the norm, managers frequently delay taking appropriate action, waiting until that behavorial deviation becomes serious. William Fulmer (1986) has documented that when this occurs, managers become confronted with additionally more problematic questions such as, How do you say you're fired?

When supervisors wait until the final stages of performance degradation, the likelihood of their actions being reversed by third parties increases since the necessary prework of coaching, counseling, and documenting has frequently not been done. Positive discipline tends to make the face-to-face encounter with the employee a more positive one, thus encouraging the supervisor to act at an earlier stage in the disciplinary process.

UNION CARBIDE AND POSITIVE DISCIPLINE

More than eleven years ago, an analysis of performance difficulties among domestic Union Carbide employees numbering about 48,000 indicated that traditional systems of discipline were not having a successful effect on modifying employee behavior. Additionally, the nature of Union Carbide's business and the change in the character of the company's work force were producing evolutionary pressures toward an environment where employee commitment and excellence of job performance were becoming significant new requirements. It seemed that the traditional system was becoming increasingly counterproductive to the changing aims and goals of the organization.

If the quality of supervisory action and judgment ultimately determines the effectiveness of any human relations policy, the traditional system's lack of effectiveness indicated the need for a more contemporary approach that would enhance the relationship between supervisor and subordinate. The basic adult-to-adult precepts of positive discipline suggested a model that could serve as a catalyst to enhance the relationship between the two and thus contribute to the goals of the organization in a more positive manner. At the same time, the misapplication of traditional discipline policies and procedures was viewed, within Union Carbide, as causing the erosion of effective employee-supervisor interface and contributing to adversarial labor relations in those facilities where employees were represented by a collective bargaining agent. To change this, Union Carbide embarked on a systematic strategy of selectively installing positive discipline, not just as a new discipline system, but as part of an overall cultural modification that would complement both the business and the evolving human relations environment of the company in the 1980s and beyond.

Union Carbide began implementing positive discipline on a pilot basis in a small nonunionized manufacturing facility in Brownsville, Texas, in 1977. The rationale for starting small was to gain understanding and comfort with the program. After adapting the approach to fit the local culture, the corporation concluded that the success of the program was sufficient to install positive discipline as part of a new plant start-up. In this case, positive discipline was used to create a culture rather than the more difficult task of modifying an existing one. Since 1981, when the first new plant was started up using positive discipline as one of its operating practices, all new Union Carbide facilities have employed the system of discipline. Finally, in 1984 the company devised a corporate strategy to encourage all of its facilities to make the transition. Performance Systems Corporation, a Dallas consulting firm, has worked with Union Carbide to implement its positive discipline approach.

THE STRUCTURE OF POSITIVE DISCIPLINE

Positive discipline, as a management system, seeks to prevent problems through formal and informal managerial practices and the recognition of good performance. When problems do arise, it attempts to address them early through coaching and counseling. If informal coaching discussions fail to bring about the required changes, positive discipline provides for three formal levels of disciplinary action—an oral reminder, a written reminder, and a decision-making leave.

These three formal levels of discipline concentrate not on punishing the individual for committing some offense against the company, but on building commitment and individual responsibility. We suggest that the employee commitment fostered by positive discipline flows from, among other things, the participatory nature of the approach—a component whose dynamics have been well described by Marshall Sashkin (1984, 1986) and Chimezie A. B. Osigweh, Yg. (1983, 1985a). The approach reinforces the belief that each individual employee possesses personal dignity and high self-worth. It recognizes that each member of the organization has the right to know exactly what is expected, as well as the right to be advised promptly and professionally when those expectations have not been met. Thus, the approach assumes that the individual has a right to know where he or she stands—to know what the manager's specific concerns are and the seriousness of the situation. Further implied is the assumption that each employee has the right to correct problems that arise in the workplace and be allowed the time required to return to fully acceptable performance. All of these rights are reflected in each formal level of the approach.

The Oral Reminder

The *oral reminder* is a formal conversation between a supervisor and a subordinate about a performance or behavior problem. The oral reminder is most frequently used when informal discussions about a problem have failed to produce change, or when a single incident is of sufficient seriousness that a formal level of discipline is the appropriate response.

In conducting an oral reminder discussion, the supervisor, rather than threatening more serious disciplinary action if the problem is not resolved, formally reminds the employee of two things:

• First, the performance standard or behavioral expectation that the organization has of its members
• Second, the employee's individual responsibility for meeting that standard

The supervisor explores the causes and possible solutions, and concentrates on gaining the employee's agreement to change and return to fully acceptable performance. The supervisor communicates the specific change that is expected and expresses confidence that the individual will indeed solve the problem as a result of this discussion.

The supervisor documents this conversation with a handwritten memo for his or her own working file. A copy is usually not placed in the employee's permanent personnel record unless required by a collective bargaining agreement. In this way, the supervisor can provide a strong incentive for improvement by advising the employee that even though this is the first formal level of the discipline procedure, no record will appear in the permanent file unless the problem arises again. Should the problem continue and the individual move to the next formal level of discipline, the second-step documentation will reflect that the oral reminder discussion did occur as well as the facts surrounding that transaction.

The Written Reminder

If the problem continues following an oral reminder (or should a problem of sufficient seriousness arise that formal written notice to the employee is considered appropriate), the employee is given a *written reminder*. The supervisor talks to the individual again, seriously, but without threats. He or she reviews the good business reasons why the problem must be solved and again gains the employee's agreement to perform properly in the future. At the end of the meeting, the supervisor advises the employee that he or she will write a memo documenting the conversation and that a copy will be placed in the employee's personnel file.

To foster the understanding and acceptance of this procedure by managers, Union Carbide's supervisor training stresses that the purpose of a disciplinary discussion is to gain the employee's agreement to change. This agreement is important for two reasons. First, the individual is more likely to improve performance if he or she agrees to do so, as opposed to having compliance be mandated by the supervisor. Second, and more important, if the problem continues and another disciplinary transaction is required, the subsequent discussion will focus not only on the continuation of the original problem but also on the employee's failure to honor his or her agreement—a much more serious concern.

At Union Carbide locations where positive discipline has been implemented, few problems move beyond the point of a written reminder. The company's experience suggests that almost without exception employees so trusted with such a procedure choose to perform or behave as mature and responsible adults. While variations from corporate expectations will inevitably occur, those variations are predominantly resolved in Union Carbide through honest discussions that focus on both the employee's resonsibility to meet reasonable organizational standards and his or her ability to do so. It would seem, then, that by dealing with individual responsibility, supervisors encourage responsible behavior in return.

It does happen, however, that some problems continue following a written reminder. In addition, some problems of great seriousness do occasionally arise that require the individual to decide about his or ability to continue to work for an organization. This is the point at which Union Carbide moves to the level of the decision-making leave.

Decision-Making Leave

Instead of suspending an individual for several days without pay, giving him a "final warning," or placing her on probation (strategies that Union Carbide, like so many other organizations, had emphasized in the past), positive discipline's final level is a one-day paid disciplinary suspension. The employee is told that he or she is not to come to work on the following day. This is called the *decision-making leave.* The individual is to remain at home making a final decision: Whether to solve the immediate problem and make a "total performance commitment" to fully acceptable performance in every area of the job; or to quit and find more satisfying work elsewhere.

When the employee returns on the following day, he or she does not immediately begin work. Instead, the worker meets with the supervisor to advise of the decision he or she has made. If the worker decides not to resign, the supervisor again expresses confidence that the employee will be able to live up to his or her commitment to change, correct the situation, and maintain fully acceptable performance in all areas of the job. Further, the supervisor and the worker jointly identify the precise change(s) to be expected in the worker's behavior. In addition, the supervisor advises the employee, in the form of a reminder, that if another problem requiring disciplinary action arises in the future, the logical consequence is termination. This statement is repeated in the formal documentation of the step, a copy of which is placed in the employee's personnel file. An employee's failure to correct his or her misconduct following the leave results in termination. Because the emphasis is on joint identification of desirable changes, and on employee/employer commitment to and responsibility for achieving the changes, worker dismissal is not viewed as a disciplinary step when it does occur; rather, it is viewed as a failure of the behavior modification system within the context of positive discipline.

A PAID DISCIPLINARY SUSPENSION?

The provision for paying the employee for the decision-making leave day is certainly a novel aspect of the system. While managers frequently express some initial misgivings about paying an employee during the period of disciplinary suspension, upon close examination of the approach they come to realize that the decision-making leave provides many benefits unavailable with other "final-step" strategies. Indeed, using a suspension from work (whether paid or unpaid, one day or several days) as a final disciplinary step has several advantages over other approaches. A disciplinary suspension demonstrates the seriousness of the situation, while allowing a "cooling-off" period for both worker and management. It provides a dramatic gesture that fully brings home the seriousness of the situation. Most important perhaps—at least from a corporate view—the use of suspensions has been fully accepted by arbitrators and other third parties as sufficient notice to the employee that the job is at risk.

While a disciplinary suspension is effective as a final step, withholding the employee's pay during the period of suspension rarely provides any benefits to the organization. Consider the possibility of the following occurrences:

- When workers return from an unpaid suspension, the anger, resentment, or apathy provoked by the suspension may result in subtle sabotage, reduced output, and other forms of costly anti-organizational behavior
- Paying the employee may reduce the tendency of the individual to "save face" by striking back at the company
- Paying for the decision-making leave day also avoids the employee's becoming a victimized martyr in the eyes of peers, thus reducing peer support for any "get even" behavior

There is, of course, the concern with employee abuse, such as intentional misbehavior in order to gain a "free day off." Such concerns have proved to be unfounded at Union Carbide. Employees at the company treat the leave seriously and do make a real decision about changing their behavior and maintaining employment. One possible explanation is that the employees themselves are actively involved and participate in the various levels of the system of discipline, thus making its acceptance likely. If so, their tendency toward making a commitment to improvement by deciding, more often than not, in favor of changing their behavior and maintaining employment can be further explained by the fact that each worker is given the prerogative to personally decide whether to resign or stay on and improve. The worker fully recognizes that the decision to stay on and improve carries with it something of a "self-selected" termination sanction, if he or she does not deliver on this final (commitment-to-improve) promise. In addition, fears of resentment by good workers have not been encountered at the company. Employees see the decision-making leave as a very serious and appropriate step. Indeed, what good workers do seem to resent at Union Carbide is management's failure to confront a poor performer, since they typically bear the brunt of the additional work generated by their less-committed colleague.

While the cost of paying for the day the employee is absent is very visible and easy to calculate, it typically is the only cost associated with the use of the system. Thus, one would expect that the traditional unpaid suspensions frequently generate much higher actual costs in production disruption, overtime coverage, increased grievances, and reduced output by the returning worker following suspension.

Generally speaking, an unpaid disciplinary suspension is rarely considered appropriate for professional and managerial employees. However, a decision-making leave has been used with similar success with exempt and nonexempt as well as hourly employees at Union Carbide. This leads us to conclude that it is a mature and nonpunitive way of gaining recommitment to organization standards and acceptable performance from the professional and managerial as well as the nonmanagerial and nonprofessional cadres.

One more element of this approach needs to be mentioned. By attempting to convince and encourage individual workers toward improvement-oriented change, the approach underscores the sincerity of management's good faith toward its employees. Thus, the installation of positive discipline can reduce the chances of a termination decision being reversed by a third party, or the decision being challenged by an employee through a wrongful discharge suit, by helping demonstrate the employer's good faith dealing, should an employee be ultimately terminated.

A SOFTER APPROACH?

A first glance at positive discipline suggests that it is a "softer" system than traditional punitive disciplinary practices. In some ways, the system may understandably be perceived as "softer." It assumes that the employee is an adult with a problem to solve and not a child in need of punishment. It places as much emphasis on recognition of good performance as it does on confronting poor performance. And as a final disciplinary step it allows people to take a day off at Union Carbide's expense to contemplate their future. It does these while inviting and maintaining the employees' active participation in the entire process of problem-solving and decision-making.

The question, however, is whether mature treatment, fair dealing, and an emphasis on individual responsibility is indicative of softness. We think not.

While the traditional approach to discipline is certainly quick to be punitive, we would be hard pressed to describe it as "tough," since it demands nothing of the employee except that he or she accept the punishment and, in the case of an unpaid suspension, serve out the time. When the individual returns from the traditional disciplinary suspension, the worker simply picks up from where he or she left off. The individual is not explicitly required or encouraged to make any commitment for the future even though, admittedly, it is implicit in the traditional approach that the worker is expected to improve his or her situation or else face termination. Thus, the traditional approach proceeds from the premise that (1) although workers may be likened to children who need not bear personal responsibility for decisions affecting their future, (2) they nevertheless possess the "divine wisdom" to know and pursue organizational expectations that have not been clearly communicated to them, and to which they have not personally made a commitment, and (3) an individual who does not possess this divine wisdom should be summarily discharged. With positive discipline, the employee is not only fully informed through effective communication techniques such as dialogue, or even "directivity" (see Osigweh, 1983) and other participative strategies, he or she must take personal responsibility for future performance and behavior. Employees discover that, in spite of the pay, they are confronted with a far tougher personal and company response to their failure to meet standards.

Traditional unpaid suspensions are actually "softer" in another way. When an employee returns from the standard three-day disciplinary layoff, he or she is typically told that another disciplinary incident will result in termination. However, the fact is that in many instances another disciplinary incident rarely brings about the threatened termination. Instead, management responds with another, perhaps longer, suspension. This process may continue through several suspensions, each time accompanied by the recurring idle threat of "termination next time." And when the company finally does terminate, the chances of the employee being returned to work by an arbitrator are greater since the company has inadvertently established a pattern of inconsistent as well as successively longer suspensions. The arbitrator is likely to decide that the logical next step after a three-day and a five-day and a ten-day suspension is not termination but a twenty-day suspension. In addition, an employer's lax enforcement of work rules and policies, such as those pertaining to suspensions, may force an arbitrator to reinstate a discharged employee under the just-cause provision of labor agreement. That positive discipline provides for one and only one disciplinary suspension also reduces the possibility that an arbitrator hearing a discharge case will decide that the period of time between the employee's termination and the hearing of the grievance is a sufficient "disciplinary suspension" and return the individual to work without back pay.

The continuing saga of suspension after suspension is avoided by positive discipline. This is because upon a suspended worker's return to work, and his or her announcement of a decision to stay and improve, the employee is reminded that another problem requiring disciplinary action will result in his or her termination. If another disciplinary problem arises, he or she is ultimately discharged. In short, an ultimate problem with traditional punitive approaches is that they identify a problem employee, punish him or her, and leave the individual a punished problem employee. Positive discipline requires the problem employee to make a choice: to become either a committed employee or an ex-employee; this requirement is also clearly known to the worker.

EMPLOYER AND EMPLOYEE RIGHTS AND RESPONSIBILITIES

As already noted, workers have some rights (e.g., the right to explicit knowledge of what is expected of them), and management has responsibilities that are corresponding to these rights (e.g., the duty to convey clearly what it expects of each employee). Just as this is the case, organizations have their own legitimate and reasonable rights, while employees have responsibilities that are concurrent with the rights. For example, organizations have the right to expect employees to be on time; to attend regularly; to put in a full day's work; to respond positively to direction; to be mentally and physically prepared for work; to learn the job at hand and the jobs to come; to adapt to change; to get along well with customers, supervisors, and coworkers; to follow the rules; and to meet the technical and ethical standards of the organization. On the other hand, the employee not only has the right to a paycheck, but also the obligation to fit in and fulfill the responsibilities underpinned by the employer rights.

Positive discipline suggests that most people do fit in, and that most perform at a fully acceptable level. When they do not, however, the difference between what is expected and what is delivered must be confronted. Should the need for such confrontation arise, the rights of the employee must also be respected. These include, among others (see, e.g., Osigweh, 1987b, 1988a; Salipante and Fortado, Chapter 13, infra; Kavanagh, Chapter 10, infra), the right to prompt and specific notice of the need for change; an opportunity to improve; fair and consistent treatment; maintenance of one's dignity and self-esteem; clear and reasonable rules and requirements; the opportunity to mount a defense and to appeal to a neutral party.

Thus, an effective process for assuring a well-disciplined organization preserves and reinforces the rights of both parties. According to James Redeker (1988), formerly chairman of the Labor Law and Employee Relations Department of the Philadelphia law firm, Saul, Ewing, Remick and Saul, and currently a member of the Wolf, Block, Schorr and Solis-

Cohen Law Corporation in the same city: "Central to most workplace problems is the failure of employer and employee to satisfy the expectations of each other. Employers often fail to inform employees adequately concerning what is expected of them. This goes far beyond simple job descriptions and most frequently involves poorly designed codes of conduct. Absenteeism rules, for instance, are often so confusing that employees have little knowledge of what the criteria for acceptable behavior are. In addition, most systems allow so much abuse that supervisors cannot verbalize or apply the employer's standards."

THE IMPLEMENTATION OF POSITIVE DISCIPLINE AT UNION CARBIDE

In general, the implementation of positive discipline involves more than a training program. It deals with efforts to resolve some specific organizational issues. It focuses on particular questions such as: How will the organization maintain discipline among its members? Who will decide who stays and who goes? How will that decision be made? Accordingly, positive discipline involves the belief that worker discipline is an arena in which an organization ultimately displays its most deeply held beliefs and values about people, professionalism, and productivity.

At Union Carbide, to assure that the rights of all parties and stakeholders are preserved, and that responsibilities are placed with those most capable of meeting them, positive discipline is not simply implemented by executive fiat. For example, the role of the corporate director of employee relations is to encourage and assist each of Union Carbide's facilities toward positive discipline, not to mandate or direct. While the implementation process is similar at every Union Carbide facility that has adopted positive discipline, the end product always varies from one location to another. The guiding principle seems to be in the knowledge that people are likely to support what they help create. Accordingly, the implementation process is designed to assure inputs from everyone involved in the system.

The process of implementation at any Union Carbide facility begins with an *executive overview*, which is a presentation about positive discipline to the facility's senior management group. This group explores the results that the approach has achieved at other Union Carbide locations, resolves any arising questions or concerns about the approach, and makes the decision to implement. All concerns about the approach must be raised prior to a decision to implement, since the ultimate success of the system will depend on top-management understanding and support.

Senior management's final decision to begin the implementation of positive discipline involves appointing an *implementation team*. This group, typically twelve to twenty individuals, is appointed to serve as a task force and is charged with the responsibility of managing the transition from the facility's current practices to positive discipline. The team represents a cross-section of plant management and includes managers and supervisors from all different locations and levels within the facility.

This implementation team is usually subdivided into three working subgroups, each with its own area of responsibility:

1. *Policies, Practices, and Procedures.* This subgroup is responsible for developing the actual policies that will be recommended to top management for adoption. The subgroup is charged with answering such questions as: What are the appropriate roles of personnel and top management? To which categories of employees will the system specifically apply? How will the severity of different problems and offenses be determined? How will unrelated offenses by the same individual be handled? What specific authority and responsibility will first-line supervisors have at each step of the system?

   While the work of this group is aided by the previous decisions in each area made by previous implementation teams from other Union Carbide locations, ultimately each facility must decide for itself how performance will be managed.

2. *Measures, Monitoring, and Management.* This subgroup concentrates on developing program measures and ways to maintain the system after the official implementation date. In addition to tracking the number of disciplinary incidents, the reasons and results, other measures concentrate on areas such as productivity improvements, attendance, safety records, and improvements in commitment and morale as measured by employee attitude surveys.

3. *Understanding, Support, and Acceptance.* This subgroup is responsible for assuring appropriate and timely communication of the new system throughout the organization. Members of this subgroup prepare articles for in-house newsletters. They create slides or videotape programs to introduce the system to all employees, and prepare agenda and question-and-answer guidelines for supervisors to use in employee meetings. They are also charged with the responsibility of recommending appropriate action for those employees currently on an active step of discipline under the existing system at the time of transition to the new one.

The work of the implementation team typically involves a series of meetings as an entire group and within subgroups, over a four-month period. Working closely with the external consultant, the team and its various subgroups prepare all of their recommendations. These are typically adopted by senior management prior to the beginning of any management training in the workings of the approach.

TRAINING MANAGERS IN POSITIVE DISCIPLINE

Before the actual implementation, all managers attend a two-day training program at Union Carbide. This is based on the realization that dealing with disciplinary problems is one of the most difficult and stressful, yet essential, parts of any supervisor's job. It is particularly difficult for the great majority of first-line supervisors who were previously members of the work group they must now supervise. The object of the training, therefore, is to assure complete familiarity with the new policies and practices, while building the managers' skills and self-confidence in dealing with performance problems. The training also must deal with the natural tendencies of managers to respond to performance problems in a punitive way. Many managers are reluctant and have never before been encouraged to abandon their traditional parent-child approach to the supervision of subordinates.

During the course of training, the managers' traditional perceptions of discipline are challenged and hopefully changed. Initially, most managers perceive a disciplinary discussion as a painful and distasteful duty that they are required to perform. Most have never been previously told the objective of the disciplinary discussion, which in positive discipline is to gain the employee's agreement to correct the situation. Similarly, most have never learned techniques for assigning responsibility for appropriate behavior to the individual. Furthermore, many have no clear models for documenting their discussions specifically, factually, and defensibly.

In the management training sessions at Union Carbide, the participants are advised of the implementation team's recommendations about policies and practices. These policies, although adopted, are not formally approved by senior management until the completion of all management training. This enables managers attending the training to have the opportunity to review the proposals and provide suggestions before final executive approval.

EMPLOYEE COMMUNICATION

Following the management training sessions and before the official date on which each trained individual can actually begin to implement what he or she has learned about positive discipline, the changes in the facility's policies and practices are communicated to all employees. Meetings are held with all employees to review the key elements and operation of the new system of discipline, the reasons for the change, and the philosophy behind the program. Individual meetings are held with each employee who is currently on an active discipline step under the old system and to advise him or her of the status of that previous action following the implementation of the new system.

These employee meetings provide several additional subtle but significant benefits. For example, there are employees who will never be directly impacted by the formal levels of positive discipline. The approach impacts this group through its stress on the importance of "positive contacts," in the form of regular and formal recognition of good performance. Moreover, positive discipline communicates to employees management's subtle commitment that any workers who encounter a performance problem will be dealt with as adults in a participative and problem-solving rather than punitive manner. In addition, the approach underscores, to the good worker, the assurance that any coworkers who do not perform acceptably will be confronted with the need to change.

MAINTAINING THE NEW SYSTEM

Following the official date after which implementation is authorized, the program is maintained through measuring the results, feeding information back to supervisors and senior managers at regular intervals, and reinforcing supervisory coaching skills. In addition, the discipline system is integrated with all other human resource systems (performance appraisal, Employee Assistance Programs, attendance control, etc.) to assure consistency among them.

THE RESULTS

We believe that Union Carbide's history with positive discipline has been very beneficial to the company. The system has now been installed in some fifteen manufacturing facilities in the United States and Canada, and currently covers over 10 percent of the corporation's 48,000 domestic work force. Additional implementations are being planned for a 2,800-person chemicals and plastics research and development center, as well as for one of the corporation's newest business groups. The program has been used in both union and nonunion facilities with equal success. The application of the concept to both blue- and white-collar workers and local management's ability to customize the program to its needs and culture have added tremendously to employee receptivity and favorable management response.

Data generated from ongoing employee attitude surveys conducted before and after implementation of the approach show a significant upturn in several key categories. For example, survey results indicate a positive shift in employee perceptions of the quality of their relationship with their immediate or near-immediate supervisor or manager. Other areas that have displayed positive changes include general morale, quality of communications, and increased synergy between organizational and individual goals. In nearly every case of the attitude surveys and other "soft" data collected, the company's employees expressed the view that the system represents a more realistic approach to modifying the organization's culture. In one employee's words, positive discipline has put "company actions in a superior status to company words." Indeed, the approach has almost attained the status of being considered a "benefit plan" in the perception of employees at Union Carbide—to the extent that reverting to the traditional approach would create a serious negative impact with attendant increases in absenteeism, grievances, and employee complaints.

Another major result emerges in the willingness of supervisors and managers to react early to performance slippage, rather than delay until the employee's performance problems have become so serious that correction is probably not attainable. While not universal, the general feeling among Union Carbide's management is that the adult-to-adult mode of personal dealings improves supervisory job performance, output, and cooperation. Furthermore, positive discipline provides for ongoing training of supervisors and managers. It offers refresher training and incidental learning essential for program maintenance.

In more measurable terms, studies in five facilities have shown an average decline in absenteeism of 5.5 percent with a range from 2 percent to nearly 8 percent. This suggests that cost-savings from reduced absenteeism alone could justify the installation of positive discipline. Nevertheless, other measurable advantages exist such as reduced levels of employee complaints and grievances. For example, in one unionized facility at Union Carbide Corporation, thirty-six disciplinary grievances had been processed in a twelve-month period prior to positive discipline. Following implementation of the approach, however, the number of grievances sharply dropped to eight. Based on executive estimates (from some corporate managers at Union Carbide), an employee complaint through all steps of the grievance procedure short of arbitration costs approximately $400 at the facility. Using this figure, a savings in excess of $11,000 per year in grievance reduction can be estimated for the facility.

INDIVIDUAL RESPONSIBILITY AND SELF-DISCIPLINE: SOME CONCLUDING REMARKS

The traditional industrial discipline system ignores the great majority of people who are performing well and requires management to sit in judgment of the individual who is not. By assessing a penalty for unacceptable performance or behavior, management subtly assumes responsibility for that behavior. The supervisor is forced into the uncomfortable role of constable and judge, catching "bad guys" and punishing the guilty.

Implementing positive discipline requires managers to abandon some long held notions about discipline and punishment. They must realize that the decision to perform well or poorly, to follow the rules or ignore them, to commit to excellence or merely to comply with minimum standards is always and exclusively the individual's.

At Union Carbide, management recognizes that it is always the individual who makes his or her own decision about commitment to the company and the quality of job performance. By implementing positive discipline, Union Carbide is abandoning the traditional approach of "doing discipline" to poor performers and ignoring the great majority of employees who perform well. Instead, the company is approaching discipline as a human resource system for building a truly committed and self-disciplined, self-responsible work force.

7

Positive Discipline from the Worker's Perspective

RICHARD W. HUMPHREYS, FREDERICK A. ZELLER, AND SARAH S. ETHERTON

Because of the need for appropriate behavioral regularity, formal organizations generally make use of systems to encourage some kinds of behavior and discourage others. Disciplinary systems are one such effort to ensure compliance with organizational rules.

Presumably, the most effective disciplinary system is one that maximizes organizational goal attainment over time. However, a review of the studies of the theory and practices of discipline suggests that the knowledge needed to support such an outcome has not yet been produced. For example, while it is easy enough to relate punishment to changes in an individual's behavior in the short run, it is far more difficult to demonstrate that punishment of an individual will cause short- and long-run changes—intended or unintended—in the behavior of others who in some way are witness to that punishment.

Research has shed some light on such questions, most often relying on observation rather than on the attitudes and opinions of those who have received discipline. The research reported here primarily examines two systems of discipline (progressive and positive) suggested or described in Chapter 6 by William Hutchison and Chimezie A. B. Osigweh, Yg. The study was conducted among sixteen union members in two separate plant locations, one using positive discipline and the other considering a change from progressive to positive discipline.

To understand the worker's perspective, it is necessary to have some background in the development of the employment-at-will doctrine as it has been interpreted by the courts, modified by social-policy legislation and limited by contractual agreement. It also is important to keep in mind the commonly held practitioner view of discipline as power- or authority-based, in contrast to "discipline without punishment" which emphasizes counseling as its tool and reform as its goal.

This chapter is organized into six sections, beginning with a review of the development of the employment-at-will doctrine. Administration of discipline as part of the contractual relationship is taken up next. The third section describes the organizational behavior perception of positive discipline. The fourth section reviews the concept and practice of positive discipline. In the fifth section, empirical research is reported that details worker experience in a firm that uses positive discipline, and a second that employs a progressive discipline system. In the last section, some comment on the use of positive discipline is offered.

BACKGROUND

Common-law doctrine dating to the nineteenth century enunciated the principle of employment-at-will (Baer, 1972). Under this doctrine, employers had the right to administer corporal punishment without recourse to the courts and to subject workers to public humiliation because workers were viewed as inferior beings while employers were superior beings (Stessin, 1960). The more extreme manifestations mercifully fell early into disfavor, but when the public continued to question the employer's presumed rights, the National Association of Manufacturers in 1903 "codified" the employer's right to discipline and discharge employees (Stessin, 1960).

A somewhat mellower view of the work force emerged in the 1920s when the scientific management movement, inspired by Frederick W. Taylor, advocated the view that workers were not indolent by nature, but rather were capable of yeoman service if properly trained and fairly treated (Stessin, 1960). However profound and diffused this change of heart may have been, it did not alter reality enough to avert growing sympathy among workers for collective bargaining. As a matter of fact, one author has suggested that "the promiscuous use of dismissal is one of the primary factors in the twentieth-century dissolution of employer-employee loyalties and the substitution therefor of employee self-protection through collective bargaining" (Phelps, 1959).

In 1960 the Supreme Court reaffirmed the employment-at-will doctrine when it held that in the absence of a collective bargaining agreement and "except as limited by published law" employers are free to execute management functions at their discretion (*United Steelworkers of America* v. *Warrior and Gulf Navigation Co.*, 46 LRRM 2416). The reference to published law serves as a reminder that the scope of the employment-at-will doctrine has been substantially modified by state and federal minimum standards, labor-management relations developments, and antidiscrimination legislation.

Workers' compensation legislation has deprived employers of their right to assert common-law defenses against employee claims for recompense for work-related injury. Unemployment compensation internalizes the cost of seasonal and/or cyclic reductions in force. Old Age, Survivors, Disability and Health Insurance (Social Security) require employers to contribute to income maintenance programs for retired and disabled workers and health care for the elderly. The Fair Labor Standards Act requires employers to pay employees time-and-one-half their normal hourly rate for work in excess of forty hours a week. Occupational health and safety legislation requires employers to provide a safe place to work and defines what constitutes safe working conditions. Benefits legislation requires those employers who offer retirement and welfare benefits to conform to certain reporting, funding, fiduciary, and administrative standards. The National Labor Relations Act of 1935 and the Labor-Management Relations Act of 1947 confirm and reconfirm public policy with respect to encouraging the practice of collective bargaining. The Equal Pay Act of 1963, Title VII of the Civil Rights Act of 1964, and the Age Discrimination in Employment Act of 1967 limit employment actions with respect to affected classes of employees.

However, neither restrictions imposed by legislative fiat nor judicial redefinition of the doctrine in recent years has stripped the employment-at-will doctrine of its power as is pointed out by Jack Stieber in Chapter 3 (supra). This reshaping of common law means that employers now are required to be more precise about their employment practices and policies—particularly those that are in writing—and to avoid statements that explicitly or implicitly suggest continuity of employment. Having satisfied this requirement, employers remain free to discipline and discharge workers with or without cause except as limited by a collective bargaining agreement and applicable law. (For an evaluation of the prospects for statutory modification of the employment-at-will doctrine see Henry H. Perritt, Jr., Chapter 4, supra.)

THE JURIDICAL VIEW

Union negotiators, as surrogates for the workers they represent, have seldom if ever questioned the need for discipline. They have, however, sought contract language that restricts management's right to discipline and discharge. Any of three major philosophies of discipline may be encountered (Phelps, 1959). Most readily recognized is the authoritarian philosophy, which is often identified with the armed forces where, particularly in time of war, the needs of the organization are considered to be paramount to individual needs. At the opposite end of the continuum, the anarchic view could be described as the antithesis of discipline. This philosophy holds the rights of the individual superior to the rights of the organization; coercion is absent and cooperation is paramount. However, the anarchic view does not eliminate discipline but merely transfers responsibility for discipline from the organization to the individual. The third relies on rights of due process, recognizing the need for organizational discipline but asserting respect for the rights of individuals and provision for assuring those rights.

This moderate view has prompted and propelled union negotiators as they have addressed the subject of discipline and discharge at the bargaining table and during the life of the working agreement. As early as 1936, more than 80 percent of working agreements contained provisions spelling out the steps that must be taken by labor and management in disciplinary cases (Stessin, 1960). The bargaining goals unions ordinarily embrace do not include negotiating with respect to the makeup or composition of the list of offenses that constitute grounds for discipline and discharge. The dominant, although by no means universal, pattern is for unions to assume that employers are responsible for preparing and posting worksite rules and regulations and that unions are responsible for guarding against unjust administration of those rules.

This pattern continues despite the 1958 U.S. Supreme Court decision (*NLRB* v. *Borg-Warner Corp.*, 42 LRRM 2034) that established the concept of mandatory, voluntary, and illegal bargaining subjects, placing discipline and discharge in the "mandatory" category. When asked, employers are required to engage in good-faith bargaining regarding discipline and discharge, and bargaining may proceed to impasse if agreement cannot be reached (Baer, 1972). Most unions are reluctant to participate in the formulation of rules of conduct and to incorporate those rules in the collective bargaining agreement. This attitude appears to arise from concurrence with management's assertion that it has the unilateral right to formulate the rules required for safe and efficient conduct of business and some union reluctance to "endorse" those rules. The length and grimness of disciplinary offenses (Tables 7.1 and 7.2) are self-explanatory reasons for the union's reluctance to incorporate rules in the agreement.

If unions are reluctant to address the employer's rules of conduct directly at the bargaining table, how do they deal with discipline and discharge? The answer is consistent with the focus on due process. Unions seek to restrict the employer's power to discipline and discharge, under the employment-at-will doctrine, by acknowledging the employer's right to direct the work force but limiting the right to discipline and discharge workers except for "cause" or "just cause," or subject to the provisions of the agreement. This language is often found in the management rights clause, where its presence transforms that clause from

Table 7.1
Forms of Conduct for which Severe Discipline Is Generally Concluded

Intoxication	Defective work
Insubordination	Restricting production
Violation of no smoking rules	Falsifying work records
Deliberate destruction of company property	Stealing
Sleeping on the job	Gambling
Absenteeism without permission	Use of drugs
Dishonesty	Immoral conduct
Repeated tardiness	Improper language
Dangerous "horseplay"	Disclosure of confidental data
Failure to observe safety rules	Political activity in the plant
Incompetence	Distributing literature or spreading rumors
Negligence on the job	
Disobedience	Failure to report communicable diseases
Disorderly conduct	Failure to use safety devices
Giving or taking bribes as an inducement to obtaining a job	Carrying weapons
Failure to meet work standards	Throwing objects outside windows
Infraction of health and safety rules	Violation of Sanitation rules
Subversive active	Reading books or magazines not required in the line of duty
Quitting early	Failure to immediately report accidents or personal injuries
Loitering	
Selling goods in plant	Falsifying or refusing to give testimony when accidents are being investigated
Leaving job, department or plant	
Receiving outside visitors or phone calls	

Source: Stessin, Lawrence (1960). _Employee discipline_. Washington, D.C.: Bureau of National Affairs, Inc., pp. 25-26

Table 7.2
More Usual Grounds for Industrial Discipline

Absenteeism	Moonlighting
Tardiness	Unsatisfactory performance
Loafing	Refusal to accept job assignment
Absence from work	Refusal to work overtime
Leaving post	Negligence
Sleeping on the job	Damage to or loss of machine or materials
Assault and fighting among employees	Prohibited strike
Horseplay	Misconduct during a strike
Insubordination	Refusal to cross picket line
Racial Slur	Union activities
Threat or assault of management representative	Slowdown
Abusive language to supervision	Possession or use of intoxicants
Profane or abusive language	Possession or use of drugs
Falsifying employment application	Obscene or immoral conduct
Falsifying company records	Gambling
Disloyalty to government	Attachment or garnishment of wages
Theft	Abusing customers
Dishonesty	Abusing students, patients or inmates
Disloyalty to employer	Sexual harassment

Source: Elkouri, Frank, & Elkouri, Edna A. (1985). How arbitration works. 4th
         Edition. Washington, D.C.: Bureau of National Affairs, Inc., pp.
         691-707.

a unilateral declaration of the employer's right to manage the enterprise into one that strips the employer of historic common-law authority.

In addition to imposing a contractual limitation on common-law doctrine, unions also have sought a number of procedural provisions such as advance notice of intent to discharge, the assurance of representation before disciplinary action is taken, expeditious processing of discipline and discharge cases, and language indicating what is to happen in the event a disciplinary action is not upheld.

Management's right to promulgate rules required to maintain order and efficiency is often acknowledged either in the management functions clause or in the opening language of the agreement, but its absence does not impair management authority. Under the residual rights doctrine, arbitrators uniformly uphold management's right to establish reasonable rules (Baer, 1972). On the other hand, where the term "cause" or "just cause" does not appear in the contract, arbitrators regularly hold that there is an implied "just cause" restriction on management's right to discipline employees (Baer, 1972).

THE ORGANIZATIONAL BEHAVIOR VIEW

Practitioners have focused on a power- or authority-based approach to discipline that largely ignores the behavioral implications of traditional discipline systems. It might be assumed that students of human resources management, industrial relations, and organizational behavior were concurrently engaged in collecting data that would indicate whether the traditional system is effective or ineffective. In actuality, there is a dearth of information on employee discipline which "has left a gaping void in the . . . literature linking . . . theory to [practice]" and "what the body of literature on employee discipline consists of is conventional management wisdom!" (Belohav, 1985). Indeed, at least one observer has remarked that "it is remarkable how little is written or said about the topic of punishment in organizational settings." The explanation may lie in the fact that "punishment is a rather controversial topic" (Business Publications, 1978).

The data available do not support clear conclusions about the effects of punishment on job performance: "[W]e are largely lacking in our knowledge about organizational discipline and punishment" and the "research that does exist has produced somewhat confusing results" (Arvey and Jones, 1985). Personnel literature tends to omit or neglect coverage of industrial discipline (Phelps, 1959), and writers in the fields of human resources and industrial relations tend to "consider discipline as something unavoidable in managing deviant employees" (Beyer and Trice, 1984).

The preceding comments illustrate the difficulties encountered when reviewing the organizational behavior literature on discipline. Not only is there very little guidance to be derived from empirical data, but what few data there are reflects information gathered from managerial sources. We were unable to identify any empirical data in the organizational behavior literature derived from worker sources. This characteristic of the data finds expression in the functions of discipline in an organizational setting as visualized by Richard Arvey and Allen Jones (1985). They suggest that the functions are:

1. To serve as a direct behavior control mechanism

2. To provide cues to employees regarding what is acceptable behavior

3. To establish and maintain a boundary system

4. To maintain in-group and out-group relations with supervisors

5. To create an illusion of strict behavior control

It is clear that these functions reflect an exclusively management-oriented view of the role of discipline.

In spite of this management orientation, the organizational behavior literature offers little or no encouragement to employers bent upon the continued implementation of a traditional discipline system. Studies that have investigated the use of punitive systems in combination with a reward system (e.g., a reward for good attendance and punishment for poor attendance) suggest that these systems are generally effective, although the number of such studies is limited (Arvey and Jones, 1985).

And, while Janice M. Beyer and Harrison Trice found no studies on the effects of milder forms of formal discipline, their own study (Beyer and Trice, 1984, pp. 760–61) tended to support the opinions found in human resources and industrial relations literature: If discipline must be meted out, "mild discipline is most effective" and the more severe forms—written warnings and suspensions—are counterproductive. A partial explanation of the nature of guidance, and its scarcity, may lie in the fact that "organizational researchers generally tend to pay much more attention to positive sanctions as ways to encourage conformity . . . than to negative sanctions as ways to discourage deviance" (Beyer and Trice, 1984). Therefore, in spite of the fact that very few empirical studies question punishment as a means of dealing with errant behavior, there is a widespread belief that punishment is counterproductive or of little value. It is suggested that punishment may not extinguish the undesirable behavior and, perhaps worse yet, may have undesirable side effects.

Empirical data or no empirical data, the literature does provide guidelines for effective discipline. Managers intent upon implementing the most prevalent form of discipline (i.e., progressive discipline), with emphasis on increasingly severe penalties for repeated infractions, will find that several of the guidelines are inconsistent with common practice. Table 7.3 presents these guidelines.

Table 7.3
Conditions under which Punishment Can Be Effective

1. Punishment is more effective when it immediately follows the offending behavior

2. Punishment is more effective when it is
   "intense and quick"

3. Punishment should focus on the offending
   act rather than the offender

4. Punishment should be administered in a
   consistent manner

5. Punishment should have instructional value

6. Punishment if more effective when it is
   administered by persons who are the
   source of rewards

7. Punishment should not be followed by non-
   contingent rewards

Adapted from: Organ, D.W., & Bateman, Thomas
(1986). Organizational behavior: An applied
psychological approach, 3rd edition. Plano, Texas:
Business Publications, Inc., 326-328.

POSITIVE DISCIPLINE

The most common disciplinary system (*Employee Discipline and Discharge*, 1985) is a product of the due process orientation of practitioners on both sides. Under progressive discipline, repeated infractions of the rules are subject to increasingly severe disciplinary measures. While practices may vary, the most common measures include oral warnings, written warnings, suspension without pay, and discharge.

Critics argue that this system tends to emphasize punishment rather than reform (see Hutchison and Osigweh, Chapter 6, supra). They contend that the focus of a disciplinary system should be on counseling rather than on punishment. The founder of this school of thought, John Huberman, formulated an alternative called "discipline without punishment" (Campbell, Fleming, and Grote, 1985). Although Huberman's proposal was made more than twenty years ago, he found few converts. According to proponents, several factors limited interest in this new approach. One of the major reasons for reluctance to adopt a new style of discipline was simply that firms were satisfied with the traditional approach. Two decades ago very few firms were concerned about developing a corporate culture; now interest is growing, and discipline is seen as a part of that culture. Then, too, Huberman did not suggest an implementation strategy that would enable a firm to move from one system to another.

It is also true that twenty years ago the work force was dominated by a generation committed to traditional values, including self-discipline. Today the work force includes a large number of workers who are products of an era that spurned discipline for permissiveness. In addition, a large number of wrongful termination suits has caused corporations to give discipline a higher priority on the agenda.

The basics of discipline without punishment, or positive discipline as it has come to be known, are as follows (Campbell, Fleming, and Grote, 1985):

First Step. The supervisor meets privately with the offending employee and tries to convince the employee of a personal responsibility to meet "reasonable standards of performance and behavior." The employee is advised that no record of the problem will appear in the employee's file unless the problem arises again.

Second Step. The supervisor and employee again meet privately to discuss the employee's failure to abide by the original agreement and again invites the employee to solve the problem. This discussion is followed by a written reminder, a copy of which is placed on file. In both the first and second steps, emphasis is placed on the reasonableness of the rule and the employee's responsibility for complying with it.

Third Step. If the deviant behavior persists, management places the employee on a one-day, paid "decision-making leave." On returning to work, the employee meets with the supervisor to report the decision. If the employee chooses to reform, a formal memorandum documenting the step is prepared and entered into the employee's file with both written and verbal notation that failure to abide by the agreement is grounds for termination.

Supporters of positive discipline maintain that the paid suspension clearly demonstrates the seriousness of the problem, that the paid leave reduces the errant employee's need to save face, that "good" workers do not resent the paid suspension, and that unpaid suspensions generate hidden costs. In unionized environments, grievance arbitration takes on a new dimension because the appropriateness of the penalty is no longer an issue. Further, the paid suspension is evidence of the company's desire to convince the errant employee to change, and arbitrators accept it as sufficient notice to employees that their job is at risk.

Since some unacceptable behaviors are more serious than others, employers are encouraged to classify disciplinary problems as "minor," "serious," and "major," and to initiate the positive discipline procedure at a step commensurate with the severity of the offense (Grote, 1979). In the case of major violations, the system might be bypassed altogether. That is to say, the first and only step may be discharge.

EMPIRICAL ANALYSIS

While research would be most useful if it could relate the costs and benefits of disciplinary arrangements directly to specific problem behaviors, this would require complex research and data that would be very expensive to obtain. Without abandoning this as a desirable longer-term strategy, we accepted two opportunities to interview workers about their experiences under divergent disciplinary systems. Attitudinal, perceptual, and evaluation data on the design and administration of discipline systems were obtained from two small samples of workers' representatives who were elected or appointed officials. Thus, to the extent that elected union officials are representative of their constituents, these samples are representative of the workers in both plants.

The two samples were located in two different firms in the same industry, one plant using a positive discipline system that replaced a progressive system, and the other installation having no other history than a progressive system. The general goal of this research was to determine workers' views of the strengths and weaknesses of discipline systems. A more specific goal was to test the hypothesis that worker-supplied data would show the positive system superior to the progressive system.

Positive Discipline

Closed-end Questions. Each person in an eight-member study group working under a positive discipline system completed a written questionnaire, which was preceded by a written (see Appendix 7.1 [a]) and an oral explanation of the characteristics of progressive and positive discipline (see Appendix 7.1, a and b), before taking part in a two-hour group interview. For the most part, the questionnaire consisted of statements reflecting the alleged advantages of positive over progressive discipline, and the workers were asked to indicate whether they agreed with each of those statements. The questions used in the interview session were designed to elicit less-structured responses to matters such as:

1. What workers like best and least about positive discipline
2. Perceived problems with positive discipline
3. Whether any kind of a discipline system is needed
4. Perception of an ideal discipline system

The workers included in the study group ranged from thirty to forty-eight years of age, with ten to twenty years of experience with the employer. All had from twelve to fourteen years of formal schooling. They included employees from all production departments of this industrial plant, where they worked as operatives and maintenance personnel. All members of the group held either elective or appointive office in the local union. The incumbent union president and the immediate past president of the local were members of the study group. The change in disciplinary policy was made about two years before the study, so all eight had extended experience with the previous progressive system as well as significnt experience with the current positive system.

The questionnaires contained thirty-one items. Twenty-seven of the items represented advantages claimed for positive discipline over the traditional and more prevalent alternative, progressive discipline. Participants had an opportunity to indicate whether they agreed or disagreed with each item or whether they had no opinion. The completed questionnaires were collected before the group discussion occurred.

The magnitude of the group's disagreement with positive discipline's supposed advantages is illustrated by the fact that out of the 216 responses possible for Items 1 through 27, only 44 (20.4 percent) were recorded in the "agree" column. Negative responses were far more common: 156 responses (72.2 percent) were in the "disagree" column. A high rate of "don't know" responses might have cast a shadow on the weight of the findings, but with only 16 responses in that column it is reasonable to conclude that the participants understood the issues involved and had clear convictions about those issues.

The weight of the findings also might be suspect if the participants had revealed antipathy toward discipline. However, the survey results are rather conclusive. Asked to register an opinion about the need for a discipline system, none of the eight participants questioned the need for a discipline system: four said a system was needed to "some extent," three said it was needed to a "great extent," and one said it was needed to a "very great extent." And seven of the eight believed that it was possible for an employee discipline system to contribute to the mutual interests of management and employees to at least "some extent." However, their replies were quite different when asked, "To what extent, in your opinion, does the employee discipline system used by your employer (i.e., the positive system) actually contribute to the mutual interests of management and employees?" Five replied "little extent" and three checked "no extent."

Table 7.4 represents the portion of the questionnaire based on advantages claimed for positive discipline over other disciplinary arrangements. On only five items did four or more of the workers believe that positive discipline was superior. And of these five items, three reflect a belief that positive discipline more effectively strengthens the position of management relative to employees (Items 4, 10, and 26). There is little, if any, evidence in the data of workers' belief that the present disciplinary system (i.e., positive discipline) contributes in areas that affect the plant's economic performance, such as increased work productivity (Item 7) or the development of a more collaborative management/employee climate (Item 11).

Yet, while the study group's experience led the members to disagree emphatically with the advantages of positive discipline claimed in the literature, seven of the participants (see Item 25) agreed that the system has "important potential advantages." The explanation for this seeming contradiction can be found in the belief that positive discipline is not immune to corruption in the hands of negatively motivated administrators.

Open-end Questions. Responses to the question "What do your members like best (if anything) about the positive discipline program?" could not be isolated from responses to the next two questions. "What do your members like least about the positive discipline program?" and "Are there any problems with the positive discipline program?" are different facets of the same issue.

Replies of nearly all of the study group to these three questions indicated that its members perceived adoption of positive discipline as being motivated by a desire to build a stronger case for continuing management's past policies, not by a fundamental change in policy, posture, or style with respect to discipline. For example, interviewees maintained that the positive discipline program made it more likely that management would win arbitration cases and that the system is used to "negatively motivate" and "intimidate" employees. One participant suggested that management used positive discipline as a motivating program and then quickly added, "motivation through threat." Everyone agreed with the observation of one participant that "the company is using positive discipline to support old-style management practices."

Other responses to program problems, advantages, and disadvantages included a number of uniformly negative and/or hostile comments. One significant problem is that, as positive discipline has been admin-

Table 7.4
Possible Advantages of Positive Discipline Compared to Other Disciplinary Arrangements

Possible Advantages	Number under		
	Agree	Disagree	Don't Know
1. Reduce employee turnover	0	8	0
2. Reduce employee absenteeism	3	3	2
3. Reduce the disciplinary actions	0	8	0
4. Make it harder for workers with infractions to say they didn't know the rules	4	2	2
5. Contribute to good workplace morale	0	8	0
6. Reduce the incidence of grievances	1	7	0
7. Reduce the use of sick leave	3	2	3
8. Contribute to increased work productivity	0	7	1
9. Contribute to consistent administration of company policy	1	7	0
10. Stronger supervisory self-confidence in confronting problem workers	4	3	1
11. Develop more collaborative management/employee morale	0	8	0
12. Paid decision-making leaves more likely to reduce the involved individual's need to "save face" through later expressions of anger and resentment	0	6	2
13. Involved employees are more likely to assume greater responsibility for future performance and behavior	1	6	1
14. More likely to be preferred by good workers (i.e., those who avoid rule infractions)	0	7	1
15. Provide equitable employee treatment	1	7	0
16. Make it less likely to result in need to punish employees	1	7	0
17. Produce timely identification of employees' behavioral problems	3	5	0
18. Produce appropriate treatment of employees' behavioral problems	0	6	2
19. Produce adequate treatment of employees' behavioral problems	0	7	1
20. More likely to produce management/employee agreement about the definition of behavioral problems	1	7	0
21. More likely to result in punishing cases of management's behavioral problems	3	5	0
22. Produce discipline without punishment	0	8	0
23. Different from progressive punishment	4	3	1
24. Employees prefer positive discipline	1	7	0
25. Does have important potential advantages	7	1	0
26. Tells employees that they, not management, are responsible for their job performance	5	3	0
27. "I prefer the positive discipline system"	1	7	0

istered, workers do not know what punishment is associated with what offense. The consequence is that workers do not know what kind of discipline to expect when an infraction occurs. Other comments pointed to a perceived lack of "evenhandedness" in the program's administration. According to one participant, the company is using positive discipline as a vehicle for employing pressure tactics and for "going after" and "riding" workers. The consensus was that the positive discipline program fails to provide any incentive to improve performance.

Answers to "Is it necessary to have a discipline program?" were affirmative, consistent with responses to Item 29 of the closed-end questionnaire. Pressed for an explanation of their response, group members expressed views that support the belief that a disciplinary program is required for two reasons: (1) maintaining and assuring adequate productivity, and (2) regulating the conduct of those workers who are unwilling or unable to assume their share of the responsibility for achieving that goal. The spontaneity with which group participants responded to this question was impressive. It suggests that while the group strongly disapproves of management's administration of *the* discipline program there is, at the same time, strong support for *a* discipline program.

The fifth and final directed question asked the study group to describe the elements of an ideal discipline system. This question included an elaborative statement that invited the respondents to consider role responsibilities. Some stresses were evident at this juncture. The accepted view was that an ideal system should be characterized by a high degree of certainty and predictability. Participants favor a system that makes the rules of conduct clear and evident to all concerned and specifies the penalty associated with infractions. On the other hand, there was also insistence that an ideal system must make provision for mitigating circumstances. This tension was resolved by the group in the form of the suggestion that the system provide for both classification of infractions *and* consideration of circumstances. In general, the data produced by question five appeared to be quite consistent with the criteria found in Table 7.3, entitled "Conditions under which Punishment Can Be Effective."

Defining role responsibilities also caused some discomfort among group members. They recognized that although it is the union's responsibility to negotiate a working agreement reflecting favorable wages, hours, and working conditions, the union also must administer that agreement. Thus, while group members were comfortable when asked to identify the elements of an ideal discipline system, it was much more difficult to reconcile role responsibilities. After some wavering, the group concluded that the union should not share responsibility for administering discipline; the union's role in the discipline system should be to concentrate on fair and impartial implementation of the system through representation of aggrieved workers.

A number of other comments by participants are worth noting. One such comment might have come straight from a textbook on organizational behavior: "You can't force or make a person produce. You have to give an incentive to produce." This observation, quickly embraced by all study group members, summed up a frequently expressed feeling that, from the workers' perspective, positive discipline has been and is being administered as "negative discipline." Words and phrases such as "pressure tactics," "scared to death" of making a mistake, "stress," "uncertainty," "demoralized," and "unfair" dotted the discussion. From the perspective of this study group, there was no discipline problem under the progressive system before it was replaced by positive discipline. Now there is a problem and the problem is the positive discipline system itself. There was agreement with the contention that "the net effect of the program is the existence of an addition of stress to the environment."

A number of specific complaints about the positive discipline system were reported by most or all of the study group members. They represent criteria applicable to evaluation of any discipline system.

1. Employees do not like the positive discipline system because it is not being administered uniformly or equitably.
2. Some of the infractions are hard to interpret. Management appears to determine the seriousness of the punishment on a basis having nothing to do with the seriousness of the offense.
3. The standards for determining whether a worker should be subject to the positive discipline program appear to change from month to month.
4. Positive discipline is more complicated than progressive discipline. More layers of management, each progressively farther removed from the point of origin, are now involved.
5. Workers do not always know when they have been put in the program. Once they know they are in, they can be harassed and intimidated.
6. The paid day off subjects workers to a new, insidious form of pressure from family and friends (i.e., Since the company is being so "nice," what's the problem?).

Conclusion. All indications were that the study group strongly believed that a discipline system was necessary for a productive organization and that the concept of positive discipline was more promising than the concept of progressive discipline. Yet, in their opinion, most of the benefits claimed for positive discipline were not being attained in their plant because of its flawed application. Indeed, based on data supplied by the group, one would suspect that a comparison of production records before and after the discipline system change, *ceteris paribus*, would reveal some productivity decline. At the same time, before-and-after records of arbitration awards might also reveal a higher proportion of company victories and/or fewer cases reaching the arbitration stage. While such data are not available at this time, and while the study group was small, this research has at least underscored the possibility of complex effects from discipline systems' operations and changes in them. More intensive research in this area might reveal that the choice of a discipline system has profound implications for productivity and organizational competitiveness.

Progressive Discipline

In general, the study of a plant using positive discipline led to the conclusion that while workers believe the concept of positive discipline holds promise, the potential benefits were not being realized because of the system's faulty application. In order to contrast their experience against a worksite using progressive discipline, arrangements were made to interview a comparable group: eight elected union officials in another plant in the same industry, working under a progressive discipline system. Workers' attitudes represented by this group were expected to be less contaminated by the possible effects of a change from one discipline system to another, and thereby to provide a "cleaner" set of information about whether certain benefits can be produced by positive, progressive, or any other discipline system.

The methodology used with this second group was similar to that applied to the first: Each person in the second study group completed a written questionnaire and then was included in a group interview which lasted two hours. The content of thirty-one written questions was altered to be appropriate for the discipline system in effect. Similar to the discussion questions used with the "positive" group, the second group was asked to define:

1. What workers like best and least about progressive discipline
2. Perceived problems with progressive discipline
3. Whether any kind of a discipline system is needed
4. Their perception of an ideal discipline system
5. Following a description of the positive discipline system, whether their members would prefer the progressive or positive system
6. Their perception of the relationship between "good" managers and "good" discipline systems

The workers in this study group ranged from twenty-nine to sixty years of age (with six over forty years of age), and had from four to forty years of experience with their employer (four had thirty-five years or more while four had less than ten years). All had between twelve and fourteen years of formal schooling. The group included representatives from all of the plant's production departments, and participants worked at semiskilled jobs in the plant.

Closed-end Questions. The questionnaire used with this group contained three questions dealing with the need for a discipline system, its potential and realized benefits. All eight said a discipline system was needed at least to some extent and that the system had the potential "to contribute to the mutual interests of management and employees." In this respect the two groups were similar. However, 50 percent of the progressive group reported that the discipline system used by their employer contributed to the mutual interest of management and labor to at least some extent; in contrast, none of those in the positive group rated their discipline system so highly.

Twenty-three items in the questionnaire were drawn from the advantages claimed for positive discipline. The eight participants were asked whether their progressive system produced those advantages. Of the 184 responses possible, 47 were recorded in the "yes" column, 115 as "no," 14 in the "don't know" column, and 8 responses not recorded. In other words, only 26 percent of this group's answers were "yes"; however, an even smaller proportion, about 20 percent, of those in the positive discipline group replied "yes."

The eight workers in this second plant also were asked if they could visualize any other system that could produce the twenty-three benefits listed. In this case, 109 responses were recorded as "yes," 6 were marked "no," 40 were "don't know," 29 were blank. Thus, both workers under a positive discipline system and those under a progressive system were able to see the potential of greater benefits from properly administered disciplinary systems. Only their perspectives were different: Workers in the first study group were optimistic about their system administered in a certain way, while those in the progressive system visualized benefits of an alternative system. Discussion during the structured interviews shows that this group also is critical of their discipline system primarily for the way it is administered, rather than because of dissatisfaction with its concept.

Open-end Questions. The discussion produced additional evidence that a discipline system was needed. Reasons for this included "because some people are always going to be goof-offs" and "it's human nature to look for the limits on behavior." There was general agreement that, in principle, the discipline system was sound, although considerable dissatisfaction with the way it was administered also surfaced.

One of the principal criticisms was that the system is applied inconsistently. One claim of inconsistency rests on the assertion that some

Table 7.5
Possible Benefits from Present Discipline System (i.e., Progressive) versus Any Other Discipline System

Possible Advantages	Our System				Another System			
	Yes	No	Don't Know	No Response	Yes	No	Don't Know	No Response
1. Minimize employee turnover	4	4			3	1	3	1
2. Minimize employee absenteeism	3	4	1		5	1	1	1
3. Minimize disciplinary actions	2	6			6		1	1
4. Insure workers know company rules	4	4			7			1
5. Contribute to good workplace morale	1	6	1		4		3	1
6. Minimize incidence of grievances	1	7			4	1	2	1
7. Minimize the use of sick leave	1	6	1		2	1	4	1
8. Contributes toward a good level of work productivity	2	6			6		1	1
9. Contributes to consistent administration of company policy		6		2	5	1	1	1
10. Contribute to strong supervisory self-confidence in confronting problem workers	1	5	2		3	1	3	1
11. Contribute to collaborative management/employee climate	1	6		1	6			2
12. Minimize a disciplined employee's need to "save face"								
13. Encourages disciplined employees to assume greater responsibility for future performance and behavior	4	3	1		7		1	
14. Is supported by good workers (i.e., those who avoid rule infractions)	3	5			4		3	1
15. Provides equitable treatment of employees	2	6			6	1	1	1
16. Minimizes need to punish employees	1	4	2	1	2		4	2
17. Produces timely identification of employees' behavioral problems	1	6	1		4		3	1
18. Produces appropriate treatment of employees' behavioral problems	1	6	1		4		3	1
19. Produces adequate treatment of employees' behavioral problesms	1	5	1	1	4		2	2
20. Produces management/employee agreement about the definition of behavioral problems	3	5			7			1
21. Produces punishment in cases of management behavioral problems	2	4	1	1	2		4	2
22. Produces discipline without punishment	1	6		1	6			2
23. Tells employees tnat they, not management, are responsible for tneir job performance	6	1	1		7			1

workers are never disciplined regardless of their behavior, although the discipline system is used to harass others without good reason. Workers also claimed that a single discipline system was official plantwide policy when, in fact, it appeared that each department had its own system, enforcing different standards and policies depending on the views and goals of the various supervisors at particular points in time. One participant spoke for the group when he stated that the confusion resulting from these kinds of inconsistencies means that "in some cases we don't know what the rules are until we break them and get punished." Another added, "The big trouble is that everybody is writing discipline policies."

Much of the inconsistency was attributed to supervisors' lack of training in administering the discipline system. But at the same time, they also recognize that part of the problem probably was unavoidable because of the human tendency for supervisors to like some workers but not others, thereby resulting in different behavioral expectations and standards.

Another of the principal criticisms of the existing discipline system was that it is used harshly with regard to work-related mistakes. In other words, work-related errors of judgment and momentary skill inadequacies because of unexpected problems brought on harsh punishment regardless of the worker's relationship with the supervisor. It was claimed that this "leaves workers scared to death and error prone" and "impairs productivity, especially among longtime good workers, who may be punished more severely than others for the same thing."

After discussion of the current discipline system's weaknesses, the group was asked to describe the characteristics of an alternative discipline system that might produce more satisfactory results. As an introduction to this aspect of the inquiry, the investigators described positive discipline as a possible alternative.

The group's reactions to positive discipline as an alternative might best be characterized as uninspired. Several maintained that there was little conceptual difference between positive discipline and the progressive system that was in effect in their plant, except for the paid day off. They did speculate that under positive discipline employees might "choose" to quit, thereby virtually eliminating discipline and discharge arbitration. This, of course, is among the anticipated results from the installation of positive discipline.

Conclusion. The group coalesced around the conclusion that the problem is not with the nature of a discipline system expressed abstractly; the problem centers on the attitudes and behaviors of the managers and supervisors who administer the system. When asked what sort of managerial and supervisory behavior might be acceptable, the characteristics cited most often were consistency, uniformity, clarity, and predictability.

Further understanding of expectations for management's contribution to an effective discipline system emerged in discussion of the characteristics of an ideal system of discipline. In that context, the characteristics that enjoyed the most uniform support were:

1. Focus on the identification of real problems, calling them to the attention of those involved and counseling the appropriate parties regarding correction
2. Provide for impartial reviews
3. Treat managers and workers alike with regard to rules infractions, rather than operate on the fictitious assumption that managers are never wrong
4. Help workers solve their problems
5. Recognize the possibility that some rules infractions may be provoked and provide for a remedy short of punishment

In the group's opinion, a good manager would be open and frank, would involve the workers in development of the rules, or would at least make sure the workers knew what the rules were, and would be a good problem-solver.

DISCUSSION

Considering the data obtained from both of the small study groups, it is hard to avoid the conclusion that employees believe that the type of discipline system is less important than how it is used. If there is a qualitative difference between progressive and positive discipline, according to the study participants, it is not recognizable.

Carefully designed systems that are predicated on the use of positive motivation may produce negative results if their principles are not honestly implemented or if employees perceive a lack of conviction. Conversely, "rough and ready" progressive systems may be as acceptable as positive discipline if they are administered in a fair and impartial manner. Data collected from the first group of workers indicate that positive discipline may be the cause of more problems, including productivity loss, than the progressive system it replaced. Nor is positive discipline necessarily more rewarding or motivating, since workers under progressive discipline seemed more able to identify benefits derived from their discipline system than were the workers covered by the positive system.

Administration of discipline systems was criticized by both groups, who believed that much more effective discipline administration was possible under either progressive or positive discipline. Beyond dissatisfaction with application, however, is the possibility that current disciplinary practice in both plans may be the source of important productivity losses, particularly when the discipline system is used in an attempt to "correct" unfortunate judgments and skill lapses in work performance.

The proponents of positive discipline do not advocate systemic change. Instead, they advocate a reformed approach to administering discipline within the context of traditional, hierarchical administrative structures. Thus the change that occurs in employer-employee relationships may be so subtle that it is unrecognizable. In at least some measure, that is what the data suggest. The group operating under a positive discipline system did not believe it was superior to the progressive discipline system that it replaced. On the contrary, they believed morale had deteriorated. And the group operating under a progressive discipline system saw little difference between the two.

Positive discipline proponents obviously believe that a conversion from "cursing" to counseling—from authority to alliance, as it were—in the administration of discipline will bring about a profound change in the quality of employer-employee relationships. But one source suggests that being called into the boss's office for counseling regarding errant behavior may prompt an aversive reaction just as surely as being "called on the carpet" (Business Publications, 1978). This same source has suggested that "discipline without punishment" may turn out to be "punishment without discipline" (Business Publications, 1978). And, here again, our data bear this out: The group operating under positive discipline agreed that "the net effect of the program is the existence of an addition of stress in the environment."

This reaction to positive discipline may be attributed entirely to administrative shortcomings rather than program deficiencies and to flawed execution rather than to inadequate design. On the other hand, there may be merit to the view that the changes that accompany conversion from progressive to positive discipline are virtually imperceptible. The organizational chart remains unaltered and working conditions, in the absence of independent action, will remain unchanged. There may even be a risk that the employer's motives will be questioned and the changes that do occur may be perceived as merely cosmetic.

There is no power-sharing involved, as is the case with labor-management participation programs, and there is no reward for conforming to company rules and regulations, that is, no positively reinforcing reward. For instance, some firms have eliminated tardiness as a disciplinary problem by instituting flexible hours. Others have minimized absenteeism as a disciplinary problem by making vacation and holiday pay contingent upon the degree of absenteeism. And others have resolved lagging productivity problems by turning to profit-sharing, employee stock ownership plans, and group incentive programs.

These are changes in employer-employee relations that are substantive as well as procedural. They tend to encourage the self-discipline that is sought by proponents of positive discipline, not by elevating the discipline system to a new level of visibility, but by relegating the system to a minor and even irrelevant role in the industrial milieu.

In any event, we have become convinced by our limited research that companies' employee discipline systems may be the source of serious inefficiencies in resource use and, in the absence of other research to confirm or deny this possibility, that this problem merits the attention of both researchers and practitioners in the field of organizational behavior.

Appendix 7.1(a)
In Capsule: Positive Discipline

BACKGROUND

The most common form of disciplinary system—known as progressive discipline—operates on the basis that repeated infractions of the rules are subject to increasingly severe disciplinary measures. While practices may vary, the most common measures include oral warnings, written warnings, suspension without pay, and discharge. In contrast, an alternative to standard practice, called "positive" discipline, is said to emphasize "correcting the problem rather than punishing the offender." Under this system, the first step involves a private discussion during which the supervisor counsels the worker regarding the importance of maintaining certain standards of conduct. Since this is an oral reminder, no permanent record is made, although the supervisor may place an informal note in the file. If the rules infraction continues, the supervisor arranges a second meeting. At the end of this meeting a written memorandum summarizing the conversation is placed on file. This step is followed by a paid, "decision-making" leave during which the worker is invited to make a final decision about whether he/she can conform to the employer's rules and regulations. If the worker returns with the indication that he/she can "live by the rules" the supervisor and the worker meet once again. The supervisor reminds the worker that if the problem behavior recurs the worker will be subject to discharge. This meeting is documented with a memorandum that includes a description of the specific change in behavior that is expected and confirmation of the claim that recurrence of the offending behavior will result in discharge.

The Questionnaire

Q. 1. Have you had experience working with any discipline system other than positive discipline?

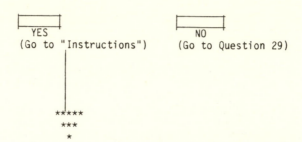

    YES   NO
(Go to "Instructions")   (Go to Question 29)

```
        *****
         ***
          *
```

"Instructions" - Comparing positive discipline with other disciplinary arrangements you have worked under, please indicate whether you agree or disagree with the following statements: (check only one box by each statement beginning with Q. 2. and continuing through Q. 28).

	Agree	Disagree	Don't Know
Q. 2. "Positive discipline is more likely to reduce employee turnover".	☐	☐	☐
Q. 3. "Positive discipline is more likely to reduce employee absenteeism".	☐	☐	☐
Q. 4. "Positive discipline is more likely to reduce disciplinary actions".	☐	☐	☐

	Agree	Disagree	Don't Know
Q. 5. "Positive discipline makes it harder for workers with infractions to say they didn't know the rules".	☐	☐	☐
Q. 6. "Positive discipline is more likely to contribute to good workplace morale".	☐	☐	☐
Q. 7. "Positive discipline is more likely to reduce the incidence of grievance".	☐	☐	☐
Q. 8. "Positive discipline is more likely to reduce the use of sick leave".	☐	☐	☐
Q. 9. "Positive discipline is more likely to contribute toward increased work productivity".	☐	☐	☐
Q.10. "Positive discipline is more likely to contribute to consistent administration of company policy".	☐	☐	☐
Q.11. "Positive discipline is more likely to result in stronger supervisory self-confidence in confronting problem workers".	☐	☐	☐
Q.12. "Positive discipline is more likely to contribute to the development of more collaborative management/employee climate".	☐	☐	☐

	Agree	Disagree	Don't Know

Q.13. "Positive discipline paid decision-making leave is more likely to reduce the involved individual's need to 'save face' through later expression of anger and resentment".

Q.14. "Positive discipline is more likely to result in the involved employee's assumption of greater responsibility for future performance and behavior".

Q.15. "The positive discipline system is more likely to be preferred than progressive discipline by good workers (that is those who avoid rule infractions)".

Q.16. "Positive discipline is more likely to provide equitable employee treatment".

Q.17. "Positive discipline is less likely to result in the need to punish employees".

Q.18. "Positive discipline is more likely to produce timely identification of employees' behavioral problems".

Q.19. "Positive discipline is more likely to produce appropriate treatment of employees' behavioral problems".

	Agree	Disagree	Don't Know
Q.20. "Positive discipline is more likely to produce adequate treatment of employees' behavioral problems".	☐	☐	☐
Q.21. "Positive discipline is more likely to produce management/employee agreement about the definition of behavioral problems".	☐	☐	☐
Q.22. "Positive discipline is more likely to result in punishing cases of management's behavioral problems".	☐	☐	☐
Q.23. "It is fair to say that positive discipline produces discipline without punishment".	☐	☐	☐
Q.24. "Positive discipline is considerably different from progressive punishment".			
Q.25. "Most workers who have experienced both positive and progressive discipline prefer the positive discipline system".	☐	☐	☐
Q.26. "The positive discipline system seems to have important potential advantages but in my experience management doesn't handle it very well".	☐	☐	☐
Q.27. "Positive discipline is more likely to tell the employee that they, not management, are responsible for their job performance".	☐	☐	☐

143

	Agree	Disagree	Don't Know

Q.28. "I prefer the positive discipline system". (Go on to Q. 29, through the end of the questionnaire).

| ☐ | ☐ | ☐ |

Q.29. To what extent, in your opinion, is an employee discipline system actually needed? (Check one box)

☐ Very great extent

☐ Great extent

☐ Some extent

☐ Little extent

☐ No extent

☐ Don't know

Q.30. To what extent, in your opinion, is it possible for an employee discipline system able to contribute to the mutual interests of management and employees? (Check one only)

☐ Very great extent

☐ Great extent

☐ Some extent

☐ Little extent

☐ No extent

☐ Don't know

Q.31. To what extent, in your opinion, does the employee discipline system used by your employer actually contribute to the mutual interests of management and employees? (Check one only)

    ☐   Very great extent

    ☐   Great extent

    ☐   Some extent

    ☐   Little extent

    ☐   No extent

    ☐   Don't know

Q.32. What is your age? ☐

Q.33. Are you an elected union leader? ☐ YES   ☐ NO

Q.34. What is your job title? _____

Q.35. How many years have you worked for your present employer? ☐

Q.36. How many years of formal schooling have you completed? ☐

The Questionnaire

Below is a list of benefits which are said to result from the use of a good discipline system. Indicate, for each of them, whether these results are produced by the discipline system you are covered by and whether they could, in your opinion, be produced better by any other type of discipline system you can visualize. (Check two boxes on each line)

	Results from					
	Our System			Another System		
	Yes	No	Don't Know	Yes	No	Don't Know
Q.1. Minimize employee turnover						
Q.2. Minimize employee absenteeism						
Q.3. Minimize disciplinary actions						
Q.4. Insure workers know company rules						
Q.5. Contribute to good workplace morale						
Q.6. Minimize the incidence of grievances						
Q.7. Minimize the use of sick leave						
Q.8. Contributes toward a good level of work productivity						
Q.9. Contributes toward consistent administration of company policy						
Q.10. Contribute to strong supervisory self confidence in confronting problem workers						
Q.11. Contribute to a collaborative management/employee climate						

	Results from					
	Our System			Another System		
	Yes	No	Don't Know	Yes	No	Don't Know
Q.12. Minimizes a disciplined employee's need to 'save face' through expression of anger and resentment						
Q.13. Encourages disciplined employees to assume greater responsibility for their future performance and behavior						
Q.14. Is supported by good workers (that is, those who avoid rule infractions)						
Q.15 Provides equitable treatment of employees						
Q.16. Minimizes the need to punish employees						
Q.17. Produces timely identification of employees' behavioral problems						
Q.18. Produces appropriate treatment of employees' behavioral problems						
Q.19. Produces adequate treatment of employees' behavioral problems						
Q.20. Produces management/employee agreement about the definition of behavioral problems						
Q.21. Produces punishment in cases of management's behavioral problems						
Q.22. Produces discipline without punishment						

147

Results from					
Our System			Another System		
Yes	No	Don't Know	Yes	No	Don't Know

Q.23. Tells employees that they, not management, are responsible for their job performance

Q.24. To what extent, in your opinion is an employee discipline system actually needed? (Check one box)

☐ Very great extent

☐ Great extent

☐ Some extent

☐ Little extent

☐ No extent

☐ Don't Know

Q.25. To what extent, in your opinion, is it possible for an employee discipline system to contribute to the mutual interests of management and employees? (Check one only)

☐ Very great extent

☐ Great extent

☐ Some extent

☐ Little extent

☐ No extent

☐ Don't know

Q.26. To what extent, in your opinion, does the employee discipline system used by your employer actually contribute to the mutual interests of management and employees? (Check one only)

    [   ]   Very great extent

    [   ]   Great extent

    [   ]   Some extent

    [   ]   Little extent

    [   ]   No extent

    [   ]   Don't know

Q.27. What is your age?   [   ]

Q.28. Are you an elected union leader?   [   ]   [   ]
                                          YES   NO

Q.29. What is your job title?   _____ .

Q.30. How many years have you worked for your present employer?   [   ]

Q.31. How many years of formal schooling have you completed?   [   ]

8

Internal Mechanisms for Resolving Employee Complaints in Nonunion Organizations

ALAN F. WESTIN

THE NEW ENVIRONMENT OF AMERICAN EMPLOYMENT LAW AND EMPLOYEE RELATIONS

American employment law and the conduct of employee relations in private, nonunion companies are in the midst of a profound transition. Our society is moving toward a new ethical, organizational, and legal framework of employee rights and responsibilities in the private sector, in what I have called the era of "socially mediated employment administration" (Westin, 1988).

Other contributions to this volume (particularly Osigweh and Miceli, Chapter 1; Gordon and Coulson, Chapter 2; Hutchison and Osigweh, Chapter 6; Humphreys, Zeller, and Etherton, Chapter 7; and Waxman, Chapter 9) explore the various social forces, changing employee expectations, new business and management operating environments, and shifts in statutory and judicial law that are involved in this emerging development. And since I have written at length about these forces elsewhere (Westin, 1979; Westin and Salisbury, 1980; Westin, 1981; Westin, 1983; Westin and Feliu, 1988; and Westin, 1988), there is no need to repeat these descriptions and analyses here, as background for my treatment of new complaint and appeal systems in nonunion employment.

However, one aspect of the shift from the era of employer prerogative (1890–1950) to the new era of socially mediated employment administration (1980–present) deserves mention. In the era of employer prerogative, three conditions guaranteed by law and sustained in dominant public opinion characterized the conduct of nonunion personnel administration: *invisibility, informality, and finality.*

1. Invisibility—decisions concerning hiring, administration, discipline, and termination were carried out as "back room" or "kitchen" work, known only to management and not subjected to the glare (and democratic influences) of public disclosure.
2. Informality—personnel decisions did not have to be documented extensively, or even at all in most instances. They did not have to be based on objective criteria formulated and communicated in advance to the employee, and did not have to be exposed to internal challenge by the affected employee in formal procedures.
3. Finality—under the prevailing employment-at-will doctrine, outside authorities—judges, juries, arbitrators, mediators, etc.—could not review the merits of the nonunion employer's personnel actions and compel changes in those actions.

These "good old days" (from the employer's perspective) are no more. The distinctive aspect of the new era of socially mediated employment administration is that nonunion employers must now conduct most of their personnel administration through visible standards, rules, and processes. They must document what is done and provide internal complaint procedures for many key employee relations activities. And many personnel actions are now subject to review, modification, reversal, or sanctions against the employer by "outside" bodies such as Equal Employment Opportunity (EEO) and human rights agencies, occupational health and safety agencies, and the civil courts, if those bodies are complained to by the employee and the reviewing authority finds violations of various employee-protection statutes or judicial doctrines.

With the loss of invisibility, informality, and finality, many nonunion employers have realized that they need to develop a very different kind of rule structure and personnel process than they had in the employer-prerogative era. Not to develop such a new system is to risk major costs and disruptions in today's employee-protection environment—heavy EEO-charge and civil litigation levels; sizeable awards to employees in such proceedings; bad publicity in the mass media; loss of prestige with customers and potential new employees; lowering of commitment and productivity by the existing work force; and even loss of face with peer companies and corporate customers that have themselves adopted a "progressive" approach to employee relations.

The challenge to nonunion firms over the past ten to fifteen years, therefore, has been to create a new personnel administration process that can successfully incorporate objective, merit-based rules and meaningful fair-procedure mechanisms into what remains a nontenured, subjectively judgmental, and competitively assailed social activity—organizational work in a capitalist system.

How well have American nonunion corporations been doing in making that transition, and in developing internal procedures that satisfy the legitimate interests of both employees and employers?

TEN YEARS OF EMPIRICAL RESEARCH INTO NEW COMPLAINT SYSTEMS

My studies of how the American corporate community was addressing this issue began in the mid–1970s, and grew out of earlier studies of employee rights issues in corporate life during the 1950s and 1960s. The data I collected have come from a wide range of sources: national conferences on individual rights in the corporation that I organized in 1978, 1979, 1981, 1982, and 1984; collection of company materials and interviews with management officials in more than 150 firms; surveys of over 200 companies; accounts volunteered to me by over 100 employees from different companies who alleged punitive treatment for engaging in whistleblowing activities; extensive contact with civil rights, minority-protection, and civil liberties groups at national and local levels that are active in defense of employee rights; and in-depth field work with employees, supervisors, middle managers, and executives with almost two dozen companies.

This work of a decade has produced one book on resolving employment disputes through formalized complaint systems (Westin and Feliu, 1988) and will also produce a book-length case study in 1990 of Federal Express Corporation's Guaranteed Fair Treatment Procedure.

In this chapter, I want to present one important product of this decade of research: a list and discussion of the requirements for effective adjudicative systems for resolving employee complaints, based on the common characteristics of the excellent company programs studied, as well as the failures generated in company programs when these requirements are not met. Some of these accounts are adapted from Westin and Feliu (1988).

REQUIREMENTS FOR EFFECTIVE ADJUDICATIVE PROGRAMS

The companies I have studied run the gamut from large to small; across industries such as financial services, transportation, insurance, manufacturing, utilities, computers and telecommunications, food service, and others; from old established firms of many decades to new-arrival firms less than a decade old; and with work forces of many different types and mixes of workers and managers. Despite this diversity, I believe there is a set of key factors that if successfully incorporated into adjudicative systems in the current era of socially mediated employment administration will produce high levels of success. Disregard or rejection of these factors will sharply imperil any company program, no matter how well-meaning or heavily promoted that system may be.

While these requirements could be divided and categorized in a variety of ways, to produce a consolidated list of four to five or even a further elaborated list in the twenty-five to thirty range, I think the following fifteen factors express usefully the vital elements involved.

A Complaint and Appeal System that Fits the Company

Whether done primarily by the CEO, the human resources department, or a task force drawn from various staff and line functions in the organization, the type and style of program chosen by leading companies reflect the special qualities and environment of the organization. The background and outlook of the employees (high-tech professionals, entertainment industry prima donnas, very diverse production and clerical work force, etc.); the formalized or informal atmosphere of operating units; the degree of decentralization or centralization of decisions; the reputation of and employee trust in the personnel department—all of these factors are considered in structuring the program and deciding which responsibilities to assign to various management and employee elements. A good program builds on the basic management style and corporate culture, or is used to help managements that are consciously changing their management style from traditional and authoritarian modes to more participative approaches.

A Positive View of Dispute-Resolution Machinery

In some large companies, top management sees employee complaints as a "bad" sign, and the creation of formal dispute-resolution systems as only "encouraging" discontent and protest. Top managements in good companies do not share that view. They see the presence of employee complaints as an inevitable part of managing large work forces for complex business tasks, and they consider it to be intelligent personnel relations to create formal mechanisms to solicit, process, and resolve such complaints. *Not* to have such a system, these managements believe, is to leave employee concerns to fester, leading to negative developments such as poor work attitudes, low commitment, absenteeism, possible substance abuse and emotional crises, susceptibility to unionization among unorganized employees, and (in EEO- or OSHA-type situations) unnecessarily high levels of complaints to regulatory agencies and the courts. In short, these managements see a formal dispute-resolution system as functionally valuable for sound organizational administration.

Top Management Commitment and Presence

Whether still under the direction of the original founder (as at Federal Express), in the third generation (as at IBM in the 1960s), or in firms that never had a "founding family," companies with effective fair-procedure systems recognize that a visible, committed role by the CEO is imperative. Given the frequent tension between employee fair treatment and hard-driving managers and executives "getting things done," it will always take the prestige of the CEO—or a top executive enjoying the CEO's full confidence—and occasional intervention by that executive, to protect the system from favoritism or the "management-team instinct." Also, only the CEO or other top executive can ensure that the visible and invisible reward system that spurs managers on is geared to recognize allegiance to the fair-procedure system, and to punish abuse of it by managers.

Merit-oriented Personnel Policies

No fair-prodedure system can be equitable and just in its decisions if it is called on to administer a subjectively cast, inequitable set of employment and personnel policies. Unless a company acknowledges the "rationality" standards of current employment law and commits itself to objective standards of excellence, professional performance evaluation, fair promotion policies, strong EEO and affirmative action programs, and similar "merit-based" approaches, it does not have the policy base from which to do justice in daily operations. Such policies have to be seen as right for a company in good economic times or bad ones, whether expanding or contracting the work force, and for old-tech or new-tech environments.

A Formal Justice System without Legalism

In good companies, employees are told that they are valued stakeholders in the total enterprise. They are expected to be wholly committed workers, joining in a common, concerted drive to make the company succeed. They are also told they are entitled to various positive rights, including equal employment opportunity and fair hearings for grievances. Under this concept of "rights," procedures are *informal* enough to foster use of the system, and to help draw out both the "employee's story" and the psychological feelings that are behind the sense of grievance. But they are also formal enough to give all participants in the process the sense that *justice*, not "cooling out" or "manipulation," is the commitment of the program. Each company must walk its own line between formalized procedures and a numbing legalism.

Communicating the Program's Availability to Employees

Good companies pay serious attention to communicating the availability of their complaint procedures to employees, recognizing that wide publicity and frequent reinforcement of the system's presence are essential to its use, and to influencing the behavior of supervisors and managers who might be tempted to act arbitrarily and unfairly if they felt use of the system by employees would not take place. This communication takes place in new employee handbooks and orientation programs, bulletin board announcements, articles in company newspapers, video programs shown throughout the company, and many other publicity techniques. In addition, employees are asked in internal surveys, among other things whether they know about the program, have used it, and if they have confidence in its fairness. If the results show low levels of awareness or support, many of these companies step up their communication efforts in response, or see whether elements of unfairness have, in fact, developed and need to be corrected. If so, they do that, quickly.

Providing Expert Resources to Employees

In nonunion companies, the resources of management and the individual employee are not equal. Since outside counsel or group representation are usually not brought in to assist an employee invoking the fair-procedure system, a committed professional staff unit or individual must be designated to take employee assistance as a moral and practical responsibility. This role must be institutionalized and protected by the organization. (This is especially needed when such advice seems to help the employee's presentation "too well" against those in management who made the contested decision.) Counselors skilled in dispute-resolution techniques must help employees to sort out the facts, identify what they feel their grievance is, specify what relief or action they are seeking, understand the other party's perspective and needs, and formulate a strategy for using the company's fair-procedure system effectively.

Installing a "Keeper of the Flame"

In good systems, there is usually one person who embodies and defends the integrity and pervasiveness of the fair-procedure system. This will usually be someone who knows the company intimately from long working experience there; understands the pressures and challenges of operations in that enterprise; knows the informal lines of influence and personality interactions of the senior management group; and has full access to and enjoys the confidence of the CEO. Such a "keeper of the flame" must have the personality to win the respect of employees and managers alike as a person dedicated to *fairness* as an achievable ideal in a real-world setting. He or she must also be perceived as someone who will pursue and protect the fundamental requiremens of that process no matter who is involved in a complaint.

Protecting Employees against Reprisals

Employees who challenge the decisions of their supervisors and other managers run the risk of having reprisals taken against them for their actions. Since the employment relationship involves continuous evaluation of the employee for pay, assignment, promotion, and other discretionary decisions, employees are highly vulnerable when they continue to be judged by superiors against whom they have complained. Recognizing this fact, and in the absence of any union to safeguard an employee from such reprisal, good managements explicitly promise employees that reprisals will not be permitted against any employee using the system. Some good firms have their staffs track the progress of employees who have used the complaint system, to see whether that promise is being fulfilled. In addition, publicity about antireprisal guarantees and their enforcement is widely disseminated among these companies.

Building Support among Line Managers

The way that line managers and executives relate to fair-procedure systems represents an important element in their success or failure. Good companies pay special attention to fostering the goodwill of these managers. They develop management communications and training materials that stress top management's commitment to this approach, stress the objectivity that will govern the hearings and appeals in the system, and communicate clearly the expectation that line managers will help to make the system work effectively. As noted earlier, compliance with such policies is not made "optional"; it is built into the reward system of every supervisor and manager.

Accepting the Duty to Change Policies and Remove Poor Managers

A common theme in good programs is a desire to discover and correct possible illegality or unfairness, and to correct such conditions quickly and completely. The remedial action taken must not only be appropriate under the facts of an individual case, but must be in line with company policy without losing the trust of employees. At the same time, where management policies have been revealed in a specific case to be faulty in formulation, or to have outlived their value, or to be creating problems of application, good companies correct the situation for this employee— *and change the policies.* They also deal directly with managers whose conduct is shown in a fair-procedure hearing to be lacking the sensitivity and fairness that the company expects of good managers. Either additional training is provided or that manager is transferred from a management role to a production, professional, or nonmanagerial staff position. In clear and extreme cases, unfair managers are terminated.

Publicizing the System's Operations and Outcomes

Since the credibility of a company-managed system cannot be taken for granted, many good companies report periodically to their employees about the system's use and outcomes. Such communications generally describe how many employees had used the system in a given period, the makeup of the user group, the kinds of issues being raised, and the outcomes of the process—including how many decisions accepted the employee's side, how many the management position, and those that were "mixed" results. Such publicity is also directed at supervisors and managers, to make the system's operations visible to them as well.

Honest and Probing Employee Surveys

While some companies either do not do specific periodic opinion surveys of their employees or else use surveys that are highly generalized "mood" measurements, many good companies ask detailed enough questions of all employees to learn how satisfied their employees are with the complaint and appeal systems. These survey results are used to spot pockets of discontent by such variables as work location, type of employee, and operating unit, and enable the personnel experts and senior management to dig deeper into the problem and to take corrective measures. Such surveys are also used to test particular features of the fair-procedure system, and to help decide how to keep the mechanisms "well-tuned."

Employee Representation in the System

Whether it is a "peer review" system or variations of employee role that we found at a dozen other companies, building employee representation into the hearing or appeal stage of the system is seen by many managements today as an essential credibility-building technique. In part, this arises from growing employee expectations that such is the fair way for a "management-run" system (without a union present) to protect employee interests. Partly it is a "professional" judgment that employee participation helps achieve better results over the long course, by building employee experiences and attitudes into the decision-making process. Also, employee participation usually makes rulings unfavorable to the complainant more acceptable, and earns more general employee trust in the system than one entirely presided over by management members.

Recognition that the Fair-Procedure System Is "Forever"

Companies that understand why managing in these times requires a good fair-procedure system—that management must "do justice well" inside or have it done for them by outside agencies and the courts—are committed to having a fair-procedure system permanently. The forms and procedures may change, modified to reflect new issues and organizational operations. But just as no nation could imagine abolishing its courts, so no effective company managing for excellence today can imagine eliminating its fair-procedure system, or allowing it to wither into ineffectiveness. In short, these systems are seen as necessities, not luxuries.

THE FUTURE OF EFFECTIVE ADJUDICATIVE SYSTEMS

Are these fifteen requirements "realistic" for most companies? My estimate is that there are probably no more than fifty to one hundred organizations that have installed fair-procedure systems that meet these fifteen critical requirements. Before the glaze of pessimism settles over the eyes of readers of this chapter, let me make two essential points about this situation.

First, the fifty to one-hundred organizations that have installed fair-procedure systems profited measurably and visibly from using their systems; by doing so, they have also avoided most of the negative consequences of employee discontent facing peer organizations, and employers generally. These systems can be found in leading organizations in various industries, of varying sizes and ages, and with varying styles of management, and they are working well. As scholars, the media, and industry associations publicize the successes of these firms, hundreds of "second-wave" managements and eventually thousands of "band wagon" firms will give serious consideration to installing new fair-procedure systems, and recognizing what it takes for them to succeed (Westin and Feliu, 1988).

Second, the deepening of social mediation of employment administration will press many other organizations to consider developing and installing such systems. At no time since the rise of the assembly-line system in American industry have there been so many changes under way in the content of work, the relationships of supervision, the structures and processes of organizations, and the recognition that new management philosophies and styles are needed to guide businesses and nonprofit organizations through this passage to more effective organizational performance.

There would have been little basis for optimism about large scale adoption of fair-procedure systems in nonunion firms in the 1950s, or even the 1970s. There is now a considerable basis for believing that such a trend—nurtured by the promise of internal benefits and the minimizing of external exposures—is an idea whose time has come.

9

Reactive and Proactive Resolution of Employee Responsibilities and Rights Staff Issues via the Ombudsman Concept

MERLE WAXMAN

The introduction of the ombudsman concept to organizations generally, as a vehicle for defining and insuring employee rights and responsibilities, has yet to gain wide acceptance. While there is a long history to the idea of the ombudsman, the development of the concept in universities is a recent one (Mundinger, 1967; Eddy, 1968). Even more recent is the application of the ombudsman concept to teaching hospitals and medical schools. This chapter provides a description of the ombudsman concept, in both theoretical and practical terms, as implemented at a large academic medical center, Stanford University Medical Center. While the term "ombudsperson" is preferable, we use the term "ombudsman" in this article because of the historical importance of this term.

In the context of the present volume, a medical center can be viewed as a relatively well-defined community in which there is a complex network of employer-employee relationships. A medical center presents a model system, in which the applicability of the ombudsman concept, in terms of conflict resolution and problem-solving, and in terms of defining and preserving employee rights and responsibilities, can be examined and refined.

The need for ombudsmen within academic institutions has been well outlined (Rowe, 1984). However, an academic medical center exhibits a high degree of complexity not present elsewhere in a university, and the confluence within a medical center of numerous professional groups poses the potential for a number of interactive issues (Waxman et al., 1986a, 1986b). Moreover, given the increasing complexity of health care, education, and research, as well as the growth of the institutions in which these missions are carried out, there is presently an increased potential for conflict and controversy within the modern medical center. Within this context, the ombudsman at Stanford University Medical Center has functioned as a facilitator not only in terms of problem-solving and conflict resolution, but also as a vehicle for the identification of generic issues as well as specific ones, and for the anticipatory discussion of newly recognized or emerging problems.

As has been pointed out by Rowe (1984), the ombudsman, by definition, does not function in isolation. In an institution as complex as a university, redundancy of problem-solving mechanisms is highly desirable, with a variety of routes to problem resolution, both formal and informal, being available to all constituencies. The ombudsman, appropriate dean's office, union representative, human resources representative, etc., are all accessible to a potential grievant. By providing a spectrum of potential sources of help in problem-solving, this redundancy helps to "humanize" a system that might otherwise be seen as bureaucratic. The multiplicity of problem-solving mechanisms provides a "safety net" and helps to meet the special needs of any potential grievant, in terms of finding a resource person whose gender, age, ethnic origin, etc., make him/her a comfortable and accessible source of help. This redundancy also provides, for a potential grievant, a sense that there are multiple options.

ORIGIN OF THE MEDICAL OMBUDSMAN'S OFFICE IN THE UNIVERSITY OMBUDSMAN'S OFFICE

The medical center ombudsman's office arose as an outgrowth of the university ombudsman's office, which serves the entire university. In 1970 Stanford University established the Office of the University Ombudsman. The goals of the office were outlined in its initial charge: "The Ombudsman's task is to protect the interests and rights of members of the Stanford community from injustices or abuses of discretion, from gross inefficiency, from unnecessary delay and complication in administration of university rules and regulations, and from inconsistency, unfairness, unresponsiveness, and prejudice in the individual's experience with university activities. The Ombudsman exists to receive, examine, and channel the complaints and grievances of members of the Stanford community, and to secure expeditious and impartial redress."

In establishing the Office of the Ombudsman, it was felt that the university ombudsman should be a member of the academic community who was widely perceived as having high ethical as well as academic stature. Well-honed administrative and interpersonal skills were also considered of primary importance. After a careful search and selection process, a psychiatrist was chosen as the first university ombudsman. Professors of humanities or natural or social sciences, clergymen, or in one case, an individual with experience in labor relations have been appointed as ombudsmen at other universities.

A wide range of problems have been presented to the ombudsman's office. Approximately 5,725 cases were dealt with by its fifteenth year of operation. Problems presented to the office range widely, extending from students' concerns about courses, grades, and instructors, to staff concerns about evaluations and promotions as well as harassment, to women's concerns about sexual harassment or gender-related discrimination, and to faculty concerns about inequities (or perceived inequities) in terms of salary, promotion, and teaching loads.

Despite the success of the university ombudsman's office in carrying out its mission, even early in its development a need was felt for a specific office dedicated to the needs of the medical center. This need reflected, in part, the geographic and physical sequestration of the Medical School at one end of the campus. However, it also reflected the unique culture of the medical community and the specialized types of issues that arise in a medical center.

CHARACTERISTICS OF A MEDICAL CENTER

A medical center possesses a number of unique characteristics (Waxman, 1986) that provide special potential for conflict:

1. It has *multiple interrelated missions*. These include patient care, research, and teaching. The institution also has to interface effectively with a variety of lay and patient advocacy groups, the community, government agencies, and other parts of the academic community.

2. The institution is characterized by considerable breadth and *represents many disciplines*. As viewed in academic terms there are nineteen departments including seven basic science departments such as cell biology, genetics, biochemistry, and pharmacology; and twelve clinical departments such as medicine, surgery, psychiatry, and pediatrics.

   Looked at in another way, the breadth of the institution involves a bringing together of multiple disciplines. Thus, for example, the operating room may include a senior surgeon supervising an assistant surgeon, a resident, an intern, and a medical student or two. But there is also an anesthesiologist, and there is a nursing staff headed by a chief nurse and involving its own hierarchy. There may also be a variety of technicians who are part of other organizational hierarchies. All of these individuals (and the hierarchies that they represent) have to interact in a productive and smooth manner.

   The situation in the research laboratory is somewhat isomorphic. Here one may have a hierarchy of faculty-scientists (professor, associate professor, assistant professor, research associate, postdoctoral fellow) but there is also

Figure 9.1
Interactive Relationships within the Academic Community

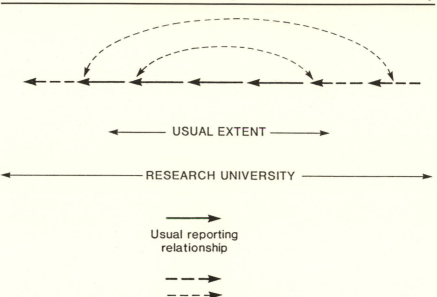

technical staff (possibly including both unionized and exempt staff), and there
are graduate and medical students.

3. A medical center embodies a variety of *hierarchical ladders,* each one with a
   tiered or pyramidal structure. But here the *extent of the hierarchy,* that is, its
   length along the vertical axis, *is greater than in many other organizations* (Figure
   9.1). Thus, at the upper end the hierarchy can extend to internationally noted
   Nobel Prize laureates. At the lower end it can include beginning undergrad-
   uates.

   Figure 9.1 shows the interactive relationships within the academic community. Traditional reporting relationships are shown as solid lines, whereas
   academic interactions are shown as broken lines. Note the expanded vertical
   extent of the academic hierarchy and that academic interactions often bypass
   the traditional reporting structure.

   If we look at the flow of communication and the potential for conflict within
   this structure, it becomes clear that the reporting system is often not explicit.
   Moreover, it does not necessarily adhere to the hierarchical structure. Thus,
   for example, a beginning undergraduate student, while junior to a graduate
   student, postdoctoral fellow, or assistant professor, may interact directly with
   his/her professor. Within this structure, open dialogue and debate are encouraged. Freedom of thought, and freedom of expression, are prized. Yet
   these may challenge the tiered structure.

The important point is that, within this structure, disagreement is encouraged, and conflict is not constrained to necessarily occur between neighboring levels along the vertical axis. For example, a student may bypass the entire structure because he or she has concerns about his/her professor, or conversely a professor may bypass the entire hierarchy and voice concerns about a beginning student. In each case, there is the potential for conflict between opposite ends of a very far-reaching spectrum.

4. At each level there is a high degree of *success orientation*. Especially as funding for research has become difficult to obtain, the question of *credit*, or *priority in terms of credit*, for various contributions has become increasingly complex. Within the academic domain, this can translate into conflict concerning authorship.

5. The *size* of the organization leads to the possibility of *duplication, or perceived duplication*, between various constituents. This becomes especially important as various constituencies are exposed to an increasingly competitive milieu in terms of government and public funding, and health-care-related dollars.

6. Medical education is an inherently *stressful* process. During their training, medical students and house officers are subjected to a variety of stresses and strains, ranging from psychological, to socioeconomic, to marital, to physical ones (see Mumford, 1980; Donnelly, 1983). Depression, for example, is a common complaint in house officers (Valko and Clayton, 1975; Small, 1981); sleep deprivation and the potential for drug and alcohol abuse may interject further stress (Friedman, 1971; Borsay and Leff, 1977). Many house officers experience a sense of isolation. Moreover, the role of "caregiver" provides little opportunity for the house officer or medical student to express his/her weaknesses and fears.

The stress of working in a medical setting can be especially difficult for women doctors (Potter, 1983), who face a spectrum of complex conflicts as well as the possibility of gender-related discrimination. Rinke (1981) has noted that women experience an increased sense of isolation during medical training. This may arise in part from a sense of exclusion from a peer group that consists primarily of males, and from the traditional male gender-oriented picture of the physician.

The above characteristics provide a fruitful substrate for the development of conflict. Moreover, conflict is often complex and can extend to issues or relationships for which there is no clear precedent. Moreover, given the sheer number of participants in the Stanford Medical Center community (4,711) and the fact that the Medical Center, like many others, had evolved its own interpersonal as well as administrative intrastructure, there was a widespread perception of the need for an in-house focus of problem-solving and conflict resolution. Thus, by 1980 it was felt that a separate ombudsman's office should be established within the Medical Center and an ombudsman was appointed at Stanford University Medical Center.

It was decided at that time that the characteristics necessary for an

effective Medical Center ombudsman's office should include: (1) inde-
pendence from the existing departmental and administrative structure
of the Medical Center; (2) knowledge of the administrative structure, as
well as policies and procedures of the Medical Center; (3) working knowledge of, and experience in, handling these policies and procedures and
also in terms of handling less well-defined situations for which no firm
policies exist, and/or situations where policies were not effectively implemented; (4) access to information (the ombudsman must be able to
request an audience with any member of the community and must have
access, when necessary, to records and files); (5) full authority to investigate (note here, however, that the ombudsman has no power to
compel); (6) confidentiality; (7) in addition, the office serves as an important source of information and referral. Figure 9.2 shows one model
for the relationship of the ombudsman to the academic hierarchy. Note
that the ombudsman does not have formal power to compel actions at
any level. As a result of the organizational structure, the ombudsman
can act as a facilitator of interactions between individuals at different
levels within various hierarchies.

The jurisdiction of the ombudsman includes students, house staff,
postdoctoral fellows, faculty, and staff at the Medical Center (patients
were, by design, not included in this group since they have a number
of other advocacy mechanisms at the Medical Center). Over the first
four years of its operation, the importance and value of the office have
become well established. Three hundred thirty-seven cases were seen
by the office during this period.

THE OMBUDSMAN'S OFFICE

The medical ombudsman's office itself has remained small in terms
of staff, and in terms of its need for fiscal and administrative support.
The ombudsman (appointed on a 25 percent effort basis) and his/her
assistant (50 percent effort) are supported by a small clerical staff. Despite
the part-time nature of their appointments, the ombudsmen, in fact,
serve in an "open-line capacity" with activities distributed throughout
the week. Both of these individuals are also accessible to their constituents throughout the week; it is interesting, in this context, that a number of individuals have chosen to communicate with the ombudsmen
outside of normal working hours. This may reflect a sense of urgency
or the need for confidentiality in some cases, or psychological issues in
others.

While the ombudsman operates in a manner that is functionally separate from the traditional reporting ladder of the Medical Center, he/
she interacts closely with other parts of the community. Since the medical
ombudsman's office has been established, the ombudsman and his as-

Figure 9.2
The Relationship of the Ombudsman to the Academic Hierarchy

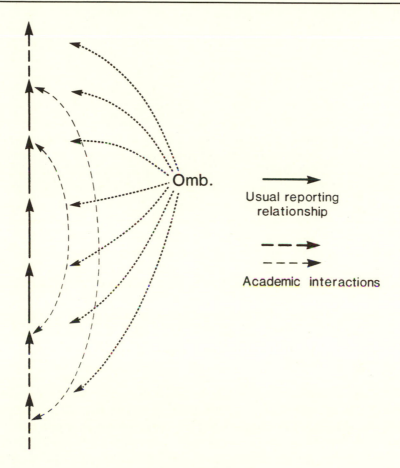

Omb.

Usual reporting
relationship

Academic interactions

sistant have participated, as members or in an *ex officio* capacity, in a number of Medical Center committees and working groups. These include a Committee on Well-Being of Medical Students and a Committee on House Staff Well-Being. They also attend periodic meetings held by the Medical Center's chief of staff with the chief residents representing various clinical services within the center. They meet periodically with members of the Human Resources Group. In addition, the office has participated in the development of workshops on stress management which have been made available to individuals throughout the Medical Center.

ISSUES

In its four years of operation, the Stanford Medical Center Ombudsman's Office has dealt with a broad range of problems and issues. At one end of the spectrum, the office has functioned simply as a referral source or a source of information. For example, a new member of the Medical Center community might visit the office for advice concerning housing, child care, etc. In subserving this function, the office does not attempt to duplicate the resources provided by other university or Medical Center administrative entities, but rather supplants them. In one case, for example, the ombudsman's office referred several student groups to appropriate Medical Center offices so that they could request support for curricular and extracurricular activities, and advised them of the most appropriate strategies to employ in obtaining support; this not only helped the student groups in obtaining much-needed support, but also channeled their request to the most appropriate Medical Center office, thus "streamlining" the request and obviating the need for it to be processed, and responded to, in inappropriate offices.

In other cases the office has participated in the resolution of conflictual issues. These have usually centered around interactions of a "vertical" type (for example, between a house office and attending physician, or a technician and supervisor, or a student and instructor). As is evident from Figure 9.1, these vertical interactions can extend over a large range. In some instances, however, conflict has arisen from "horizontal" interactions (for example, interactions between student and student, or resident and resident).

The degree of conflict encountered by the office has shown a wide range. In some cases the issues are seemingly minor and easily resolvable ones ("_____, who works at the laboratory bench next to mine, is a messy worker. This interferes with my work. What should I do?"). In other cases the issues are more complex, such as the following example.

A common scenario arises when an employee contacts the ombudsman complaining that he/she is about to be terminated for a seemingly inappropriate reason. In such a case, one of the ombudsman's first steps is to carefully study the situation. While a variety of themes have been encountered, the following theme is a common one: Despite the perception of inadequacies for some time by a supervisor, an employee has been receiving satisfactory evaluations; these evaluations do not reflect these inadequacies. When the system is perturbed (e.g., when the department is reorganized, or a new line manager assigned, or funding becomes restricted), the perceived inadequacies are expressed as justifying a termination. In this case, the ombudsman has several options. These include reviewing the case, and pointing out to the supervisor that prior evaluations did not focus on the employee's deficiencies; in such a case, counseling of the employee and a remedial program, including a realistic time frame for improvement, might be suggested. In some cases, this has resulted in marked improvement in employee performance, and thus benefited both the supervisor and employee. It may also be helpful to look for extraprofessional sources of poor performance (i.e., ones arising from domestic, economic, etc., sources), and offer help in dealing with them. We have encountered a number of instances in which inadequate performance evaluations did not reflect poor performance, but rather resulted from a mismatch in the supervisor's expectations as compared to those of the employee; in some cases, the ombudsman's office was able to arrange joint conferences between supervisor and employee that resulted in a better understanding of the position and its requirements, and ultimately to a superior performance. In other cases, the employee cannot meet the requirements of the position, but has other useful skills; in these instances, the ombudsman and/or Human Resources group can try to match these skills to the needs of another position. Even in cases where termination is unavoidable, the ombudsman can attempt to ensure that it is carried out in a way that preserves the dignity and rights of the employee. Moreover, in these cases, the ombudsman can function to help the supervisor learn how to critically, honestly, and constructively evaluate employees, and when necessary, to take disciplinary action in a constructive manner.

CONFLICT AS A SYMPTOM: INSTITUTIONAL DISEQUILIBRIUM

While, as outlined above, problems brought to the ombudsman in many cases reflect conflict between *individuals*, in other cases problems arise as a symptom of *institutional disequilibrium*. Thus, we have come to recognize that the individual grievance often represents the tip of an iceberg. This is illustrated by the following example: The ombudsman was approached by a resident with complaints about what he perceived to be inequities in the night-call schedule; he was particularly concerned about the impact of night call on his family life. Further discussion revealed that in this resident's department, there had been a number of simultaneous scheduling problems arising from illnesses, etc., which could not have been anticipated. This had precipitated a situation in which there were not enough house officers to provide night call without a considerable increase in the workload of the remaining residents. In exploring the issue further, it became clear that other departments had experienced similar problems. As a result of this, discussions were begun at the Medical Center level to examine the issue of night-call coverage during unanticipated resident absences.

The profile that emerged, for many departments, was one of tightly and efficiently organized clinical services with all residents (especially those at junior levels) being assigned heavy schedules. A significant problem for residents in all departments arose from the unanticipated absences of other residents resulting from illness, maternity leave, death in the family, etc. When the schedule was perturbed by the unexpected absence of even one resident, the remaining residents were called upon to increase their workload and adjust their schedules, often with little warning. This type of situation had become particularly acute when several residents were simultaneously absent in one department. The problem was further complicated by the feeling on the part of some residents that they could not be absent, even in case of serious illness or family problems requiring their attention, because of the added workload this would place on the remaining residents. This problem did not pertain to any single department, but was a more general one. Thus, *what had appeared as a complaint from a single individual reflected, in fact, an institutional problem that was affecting many workers.* In this case, the problem was resolved following joint discussions with the chief of staff and the dean of the Medical School, who arranged, together with the clinical departments, to allocate funds for alternative coverage in case of unanticipated resident absence. Thus, the problem was referred upward, within the appropriate hierarchy, for examination and solution. This has been termed "upward feedback" (Rowe, 1984), and it serves to involve the institution itself, when appropriate, in problem-solving.

Finally, some issues have involved an examination of principles of due process. In this context, the ombudsman's office has played a major role, not only in ensuring that due process procedures are properly employed, but also in the development of due process procedures. One illustrative case involved allegations of possible unethical behavior by a trainee. Examination of the issue by the ombudsman demonstrated that, while there had been poor communication between the trainee and instructor, there was little basis for the serious charge of unethical behavior. As an outgrowth of examining this case, however, it became clear that due process procedures had not been established for handling this type of situation. As in the prior example, a problem involving one individual reflected a more generalized issue, in this case reflecting the absence of a set of applicable policies. After studying the situation the ombudsman's office recommended that the Medical School adopt the due process protections. As a result, a set of explicit guidelines was developed. Again, the situation required "upward feedback."

MODES OF CONFLICT RESOLUTION

We have found, in developing the ombudsman's office, that it is important to maintain a flexible and open approach to conflict resolution.

In view of this, it is important to emphasize that, as seen from the vantage point of the ombudsman, there are no absolute or inflexible rules concerning conflict resolution. In fact, the success of the ombudsman approach depends on resourcefulness and on the ability to find, or to create, *ad hoc* solutions to new and complex problems. Nevertheless, a number of themes have emerged with respect to the implementation of the ombudsman concept at the Medical Center:

Confidentiality. It is clearly understood that the activities of the ombudsman's office are confidential. This protects the rights of both the grievant and the alleged offender. As part of this confidentiality, the policy is not to contact any of the secondary parties involved in a given issue unless the person seeking help agrees to this.

Institutional Informality. It is clearly understood that actions of the office result in recommendations and not informal actions. We have found that the informal nature of conflict resolution encourages an open approach to problems in which all of the involved parties are willing to examine a broad spectrum of potential solutions to a given problem. It also permits the ombudsman to "try out," in an experimental manner, various potential solutions, which might be viewed as threatening if suggested by a more formal administrative officer. The informal nature of the relationship with the ombudsman also fosters a degree of candor that might not otherwise be possible. Thus, for example, the ombudsman can tell a student "you were in fact wrong," in a manner that is less threatening, and hopefully more constructive, than when the same message is given by a formal administrative office.

Positive as Well as Negative Feedback. As viewed from the vantage point of the ombudsman, the trajectories of both grievants and supervisors can be improved by both positive and negative feedback. Thus, for example, in dealing with a supervisor who has handled X's job evaluation poorly, it can be useful to say "you handled Y's evaluation very well last year," in addition to pointing out the difficulties in X's evaluation. We have found that the use of both modes of feedback make it much easier to enter into a dialogue with managers and helps them to improve their supervisory styles.

Objectivity. In order for the ombudsman's office to achieve its mandate, it must be recognized as *objective and neutral*. Thus, while the office is available to and in fact serves a number of constituencies, it is clearly understood that the ombudsman's role is that of obtaining fair and equitable solutions, and not of automatically defending any particular party. In some cases, if it is appropriate, the ombudsman will function as the advocate for a student or staff member, but this role is explicitly defined. In cases where neutrality is inconsistent with functioning as a grievant's advocate, this can be openly and explicitly discussed. The grievant, when aware of the inconsistency of these two roles, can then request that the obmudsman assume one particular function. In fact, the role of the ombudsman does not have to be invariant, but can change according to the setting. Thus, the ombudsman may function as an advisor in confidential meetings with a grievant, but may be requested to act as an advocate, or as a neutral, in formal proceedings.

In this respect, our experience has shown that if a grievant can be made aware of the various points of view surrounding a conflictual issue, he/she will often discuss and resolve it informally without formal grievance actions. It has also become clear that neutrality per se can be a very important resource; thus, for example, in the case of alleged sexual harassment, the presence of a neutral individual can serve to protect the rights of all individuals involved.

Access. The ombudsman has, by virtue of the organizational structure of the ombudsman's office, access to university and Medical Center offices at a variety of levels (Figure 9.2). Thus, the ombudsman can function as a facilitator of upward, downward, and lateral communication at many levels. Moreover, the ombudsman can provide mediation that is not confined to any single level or organizational ladder. We have found that this flexibility has been rapidly discerned by, and utilized by, our constituencies. This flexibility reinforces, for the entire community, the idea that individuals in need of help have at their disposal a spectrum of problem-solving strategies and mechanisms, that is, that they have multiple options.

PROACTIVE PROBLEM-SOLVING

It has become increasing clear, over the past several years, that the medical ombudsman fills several needs. One role involves *reacting* to existing problems and conflicts. Another, more global, role is an *anticipatory* or *proactive* one. Here, the ombudsman's office is in a unqiue position to monitor the pulse of the medical center community. As noted above, specific complaints often turn out to be symptomatic of more general issues. In this regard, the ombudsman is in a position to identify centerwide problems or trends, and to anticipate issues and their solutions. We find that an increasing proportion of the ombudsman's efforts are directed toward generic issues, and to identifying potential problems and discussing them in a prospective manner.

This anticipatory function does not move forward in a case-by-case manner, but it is nevertheless partly consumer-driven. In view of this, we have found that it is very valuable to involve students, house staff, employees, etc., in proactive activities.

CONCLUSION

As outlined above, the development of the ombudsman concept is extremely helpful both to the individuals working within the institution and to the institution itself. It has become clear that the ombudsman represents an organizational development mechanism that can significantly promote effectiveness. In many cases, this increased effectiveness far outweighs the cost of developing an ombudsman's office. The ombudsman has the opportunity to function in a pivotal way both in a case-by-case manner and in a more general way.

10

How'm I Doin'? I Have a Need and a Right to Know

_____ MICHAEL J. KAVANAGH

INTRODUCTION AND BACKGROUND

When New York City mayor Ed Koch was running for reelection, the central theme of this campaign was contained in the question "How'm I doin'?" The reference was to his record during the previous term in the office of mayor. What he was seeking was an evaluation of his performance as mayor of one of the world's largest cities. Naturally, he felt he had done well in his previous term and expected this record of performance would lead to reelection. However, the phrase he chose, "How'm I doin'?" addresses an important function of performance appraisal in organizations and emphasizes the rights of employees in the process. Fortunately, most employees are not considering running for mayor of New York City. However, they, like Mayor Koch, want feedback on their performance—they want to know "how they are doing."

This general need to know how well one is doing, to receive feedback on job performance, is fundamental to understanding the rights employees have in the performance appraisal process. Of course, these rights are not contained in the employment contract, and only infrequently contained in union contracts; however, they are assumed by employees in the "psychological contract" (Schein, 1965), thus forming powerful underlying determinants of behavior in organizational settings.

Since the results of the performance evaluation process indicate the productivity level of the organization and the individual, they are central and crucial to the operation of the organization. These results serve as the basis for actions at the individual employee level such as promotions and pay raises, and at the organizational level as an indication of the overall productive capacity of the work force. As Richard S. Barrett (1966) noted, "Management has no choice as to whether it will have a program of performance evaluation. It has a program . . . and the results of the evaluations are continuously used . . . employees are transferred, promoted, demoted and fired on the basis of the opinions of management" (p. 1). As Kavanagh (1982) further notes, the performance appraisal program is the capstone of the personnel function, serving through the evaluation of the effectiveness of individual employees to evaluate the effectiveness of the personnel system that put them there. Given these considerations, it is not surprising that the functioning of the performance appraisal program, and, in particular, the nature of the performance feedback given, is of critical importance to both management and employees.

Support in the scientific literature for this need for feedback on job performance can be found in several places. Leon A. Festinger (1954), in a conceptual article concerned with attitude formation and conformity behavior, postulated a powerful need to evaluate one's opinions, beliefs, and abilities. As a corollary, he also argued that people want feedback to determine that their attitudes and opinions are correct, and that they possess good abilities. This basic need to validate one's attitudes, opinions, and abilities leads the person to seek information in terms of feedback. In the case of attitudes and opinions, Festinger uses these search activities to explain group norms, attitude formation, and conformity behavior. In terms of abilities, he argues for a unidirectional drive upward, which means the search for validating information continues longer. A primary place the person can receive such validating information on personal abilities is the workplace.

Another basis for the strong need for performance feedback can be found in the theoretical works of Jerome S. Bruner (1958, 1961). He argues that people need to structure their environment in order to make sense of it, and thus he postulated the existence of competence and mastery motives. It is through structuring their environment that people feel competent or that they have mastered it. In this process, people "discover" not only their environment but their place in it. Central to this discovery process is feedback about the use of one's skills and abilities on meaningful tasks, exactly the purpose job performance measurement and feedback is supposed to accomplish.

It is important to recognize that the power of the needs discussed in the previous paragraph can also lead to problems for employees in the form of *performance evaluation apprehension.* Most employees and supervisors find the annual performance review, whether it is tied to salary increases or not, a potentially explosive situation. As David L. DeVries and Morgan M. McCall (1976) cogently observed, at annual performance review time managers frequently ask the question "Is it tax time again?"

This natural performance evaluation apprehension is the other edge of the "double-edged sword" of the needs postulated by Festinger and Bruner. Employees have a powerful need to know how they are doing so that they can feel competent in their environment and validate the use of their skills and abilities on the job, but they are equally apprehensive about receiving any bad news in a performance evaluation review. Understanding these competing drives helps explain the rights employees have in the performance appraisal process.

Further background for understanding employees' rights in the performance appraisal process can be found in a variety of writings in the management literature that propose workplace changes in line with what is called "self-regulation" values (Kavanagh, 1982). The underlying assumption is that employees should have more charge in changing and regulating their environment in attempting to optimize a match between their capabilities and the job requirements. This is consistent with the transactional view of satisfaction (Jahoda, 1961), who postulated that a "best fit" of individual to environment has positive effects, whereas a "lack of fit" has negative effects. This argument also forms the basis for various theories of human performance motivation (Maslow, 1943, 1965; Herzberg, Mausner, and Syderman, 1959; Herzberg, 1966), which advocate that employees seek growth and fulfillment of their potential in their jobs.

In a similar vein, most organizational change programs included within the rubric of Quality of Work Life (QWL) involve an improvement in the quantity and quality of feedback about job performance. Most of these changes in the workplace result in the employees having more control over the feedback they receive about their job performance. For example, the implementation of a behavioral modification plan at Emery Air Freight (Hamner, 1975) required that employees keep records of their own performance for comparison against standards or goals. The use of autonomous work groups in the Volvo experiment ("Job redesign," 1973) improved the quality of feedback so that the workers could see a finished car rather than a single piece. A key element in most job enrichment programs (Lawler, 1969) is that employees exercise more control over elements of their jobs, one of which is the amount and quality of feedback about job performance. Greater involvement and control over the organizational results used to evaluate individual job performance is key to Management By Objectives (MBO) and other goal-setting programs. These examples illustrate the point that there is an underlying value in these programs called self-regulation of individual performance, achieved primarily through improvements in the quantity and quality of feedback.

Finally, to understand more fully the rights employees have in the performance appraisal process, one has to consider various applied research literature and legal decisions regarding performance appraisal practices. This applied research literature includes work on employee acceptability of performance appraisal programs in companies (DeBiasi and Kavanagh, 1984; Kavanagh, Hedge, Ree, Earles, and DeBiasi, 1985; Landy, Barnes-Farrell, and Cleveland, 1980; Landy, Barnes, and Murphy, 1978), implementation and evaluation of total performance appraisal programs (Beer, Ruh, Dawson, McCaa, and Kavanagh, 1978; Kavanagh, Hedge, and DeBiasi, 1983), the work on performance feedback (Ilgen, Fisher, and Taylor, 1979; Tannenbaum and Kavanagh, 1984; Taylor and Walther, 1981), and rater accuracy and rater training work (Borman, 1978; Latham, Wexley, and Pursell, 1975; Pulakos, 1984). In addition to this applied research concerned with practical issues in improving performance appraisal programs, knowledge of recent litigation on performance appraisal practices (Cascio and Bernardin, 1981) is necessary to understand more fully employees' rights in the performance appraisal process.

All of these factors considered together, from the theoretical arguments of Festinger and Bruner to the empirical research cited above, indicate that most performance appraisal programs within organizations need to be redesigned as what Alan F. Westin calls "innovative systems" (see Chapter 8, supra). As we examine the rights of employees in the performance appraisal process, many of the implications in terms of redesign of performance appraisal programs are consistent with the features of fair-process systems proposed by Westin. Westin's five elements of a fair-process system are reflected in the list of employee rights in Table 10.1.

EMPLOYEE RIGHTS IN PERFORMANCE APPRAISAL

Based on a consideration of both the conceptual and practical literature on human performance and the performance appraisal process, the rights employees have in performance appraisal were identified and are listed in Table 10.1. In considering these rights, keep in mind that they imply that employees have responsibilities in terms of their work performance and its evaluation. A general responsibility is best captured by the phrase "a fair day's work for a fair's day pay." Employees are expected to perform, on a daily basis, the job for which they were hired. Also, consideration of the employee rights in Table 10.1 implies some of the rights and responsibilities of management. Finally, the discussion of the employee rights in Table 10.1 will be done within the context of performance ratings from supervisors since this type of performance appraisal is used in over 90 percent of companies (Lochner and Teel, 1977). However, the employee rights apply to other types of performance measures, such as productivity indices, and can be easily generalized.

Table 10.1
Employee Rights in Performance Appraisal

1. Accuracy of evaluations

2. Individual fairness of evaluations

3. Understanding of relationship to rewards

4. Basis for judgment in performance standards

5. Privacy with need-to-know only access

6. Right of appeal within performance appraisal

7. Warnings and performance planning

8. Career planning for promotion

9. Performance feedback type and organizational results

10. Performance feedback frequency on event basis

11. Discriminate fairly among employees

12. Supervisor competent to complete evaluation

13. System used fairly throughout organization

14. Performance appraisal system is understandable

The first right of employees in performance appraisal is that it be accurate; that is, the evaluation of the employee's job performance is based on the duties and standards described in the job description. This means that important, relevant factors are not omitted nor is the evaluation based on nonjob factors. Accuracy in the ratings of job performance means the rater knows the relevant behaviors and accomplishments of an employee that indicate the employee's level of performance on the duties and standards as defined by the job description. The implication for management is that raters must be sufficiently trained to make the difficult judgments necessary to evaluate employee job performance accurately. The accuracy and fairness of performance appraisals are consistently the most important characteristics that determine employee acceptability of performance evaluations (Kavanagh et al., 1985).

In addition to accuracy, employees must feel they are treated fairly as individuals in the performance appraisal process, the second right in Table 10.1. This means that they were not inhibited or blocked in some way from performing at their maximum level due to machine, location, or other environmental factors. Or, if there were some factors that had a negative influence on their performance, these were taken into account when the evaluation of their performance was done. This fairness also implies an equity judgment in relation to how other employees are evaluated, particularly those in the same or similar jobs working for the same supervisor. Adams' (1965) theory of inequity applies directly to this situation in performance appraisal. Since one element in his theory is the person's output when comparing the equity ratio with others, the fairness of the performance appraisal process is critical to this determination. Considerable research on Adams' theory has indicated that there are serious negative effects on both the organization and the individual when inequity exists.

Third, employees have a right to understand the relationship between their job performance and organizational rewards, for example, merit increases and promotions, in the organization. This does not argue that specific rewards be closely related to performance levels, but only that employees need to know the relationship. In many organizations, management ties merit increases and bonuses closely to individual performance, while in other organizations, performance is one of several factors included in these rewards. Whatever the plan, management has a responsibility to communicate this relationship to employees. This communication should not only occur organization-wide, but also at the individual supervisor-employee level.

The relationship of individual performance to rewards has been perhaps the most difficult and confusing aspect of the performance appraisal process. This is due to the confusion between performance evaluations based on interpersonal versus intrapersonal differences. In most performance reviews, managers typically urge their employees to maintain and/or improve their performance, depending on the current performance level of the employee. This improvement is usually concerned with intrapersonal factors, that is, the current strengths and weaknesses of the employee, a determination not based on a comparison with other employees. When employees improve in terms of their previous performance, naturally they expect to be rewarded. However, organizational rewards are based on comparisons between employees—interpersonal differences. Failure to distinguish between these types of personal performance differences has been the undoing of many MBO and goal-setting programs that are based on improvements in intrapersonal factors. In MBO or any type of performance improvement plan for employees, the implications for organizational rewards of fulfilling the specific performance goals or levels must be clearly explained to employees.

Employees have a right to know the basis for the evaluation of their performance as indicated in the fourth item in Table 10.1. It is insufficient to simply provide them with a copy of their job description, although this is a good start. Specific performance standards must be established based on the job description, and these standards must be communicated to employees. Obviously, to meet these performance appraisal requirements, an accurate and up-to-date job description must exist.

It is the responsibility of both management and employees to be certain job descriptions are timely and accurate. It is management's responsibility to review and revise all job descriptions on at least an annual basis, and otherwise on an as-needed basis. If significant changes occur in a job, for example as the result of new technology, the job description needs revision. However, accurate job descriptions are not enough. Supervisors then need training in the difficult task of developing performance standards for jobs, and communicating these standards to the employees. Usually, the Personnel Department can aid in the first task of developing the performance standards based on an accurate job description. However, the final step of communicating the standards to the employees remains with the supervisor. Failure to follow these steps has led to negative outcomes against organizations in litigation involving performance appraisal programs (Cascio and Bernardin, 1981).

As seen in Item 5, employees expect their performance appraisals to be kept private, and not released without their approval. Considering the powerful needs being met or frustrated by the performance appraisal process, it is apparent that privacy of appraisal results can easily be an explosive issue. However, management has a right to access performance evaluation results on a need-to-know basis, since these results provide an indication of the efficiency of both the firm and its personnel practices. Management also has a right to share performance results as averages, with individual results thus not identifiable. However, performance evaluation results cannot be shared with other employers in reference checks unless the employee has agreed in writing.

Employees should have the right to appeal (Item 6) when they disagree with a performance appraisal. Although this is frequently part of union contracts via grievance procedures, nonunion organizations also need to have an appeal mechanism. The litigation on performance appraisal (Cascio and Bernardin, 1981) indicates that the absence of an appeal mechanism will have negative implications for the case presented by management. The existence of a grievance program can fulfill this requirement, but having a separate appeal system embedded within the performance appraisal program is considerably better. The performance appraisal form used to record the results of the performance evaluation should have space for the employee to indicate disagreement and a wish to appeal the results. One advantage is that this starts the appeal process at the supervisor-employee level. If not resolvable, the reviewing authority can attempt resolution informally. This is preferable to the more

formal and typically time-consuming process involved in a formal grievance program. This is similar to the ombudsman concept discussed by
Merle Waxman in Chapter 9, supra.

The employee rights numbered 7 through 10 in Table 10.1 are related
in that they are concerned with the supervisor-employee counseling
relationship over time in the performance appraisal process. These rights
are consistent with the notion of an ombudsman discussed by Waxman
in chapter 9, supra. Further, the characteristics of a positive discipline
approach, advocated by William R. Hutchison and Chimezie A. B. Osigweh, Yg., in chapter 6, supra, would form the basis of a performance
appraisal program that incorporated rights 7 through 10 in its design.

Considering rights 7 through 10, if supervisors have adequately communicated performance standards based on job duties, employees
should still have a right to warnings, as opposed to immediate termination, for substandard performance, particularly in the case of first-
time violations. After the organization has invested in the recruitment,
hiring, and training of individual employees, there should be a strong
effort to retain employees through effective employee-supervisor counseling on job performance. Employees have a right to expect warnings
for substandard performance, but also a responsibility to attempt to
respond and correct the performance deficiency. Management has the
right to expect employees to respond to counseling on performance
deficiencies, and the responsibility to train supervisors to counsel employees effectively. This entire process of dealing with substandard performance should be tied to the development of a performance
improvement plan to correct the deficiencies. Employees have the right,
and management the responsibility, to have reasonable performance
improvement plans that have specific actions to be taken by both employees and management, target dates, and specific information on how
the performance improvements are to be evaluated. These performance
improvement plans can be the basis of a contract whereby both management and the employee are aware of the consequences of both satisfying and failing to meet the defined performance levels.

By extension to longer time periods of employee performance within
an organization, employees should have the right to have career and
performance planning done at least at each annual review. Career planning in terms of specific skill, experience, and educational requirements
for advancement within the organization should be done during the
annual performance review and planning session. Most important, this
planning must be done in terms of a reasonable timetable so that both
the supervisor and employee understand that the advancement aspirations of the employee are in harmony with personal and organizational
realities. There must be room in the organization for advancement when
planned, and the employee must recognize personal obstacles in fulfilling needed skills within this time frame.

The type and frequency of feedback about job performance that employees receive are closely related to performance and career planning. Employees have a right to know when they will receive feedback on their job performance. Supervisors have a responsibility to provide feedback when appropriate, usually on a performance event basis, not necessarily on a "daily" basis as has been advocated in the management literature. This compulsive "daily" feedback can easily become meaningless for the employee; thus, providing feedback based on specific performance behaviors or accomplishments is a better approach. As part of performance and career planning, employees also have a right to know what type of performance feedback they will receive; that is, what behavior or accomplishments will be used to evaluate their level of job performance. These indicators of performance levels need to be defined as objectively and quantifiably as possible. However, there should be a clear recognition that some indicators of performance must remain qualitative and judgmental. This distinction should be made during the performance and career planning process so that misunderstandings do not arise later. Finally, employees have a right to receive clear and frequent performance feedback, but they also have a responsibility to respond to it in terms of changes in performance when appropriate.

Employees have a right to expect the performance measurements used will discriminate fairly (Item 11); that is, good performers will be correctly identified and differentiated from poor performers. This is closely related to the equity notions discussed in terms of the fairness of performance appraisals, but goes beyond it. It means the performance appraisal system, and particularly the form used to record performance results, must be designed to allow supervisors to adequately differentiate between good and poor performers. The ability of the supervisors to use the specific form to differentiate between good and poor performers is a major factor influencing employee acceptance of the performance appraisal system.

Clearly related to the right of discriminability is the employees' right to expect that their supervisor will be competent in completing the performance ratings (Item 12). Employees have a right to expect that their supervisor is competent to judge their job performance. This means that management has the responsibility to provide adequate training for new supervisors on how to rate employee performance using the performance appraisal system within the organization. In the case of changes and revisions in the system, management has the responsibility to inform and retrain supervisors in its use. Finally, management has a responsibility to monitor how well supervisors are using the performance appraisal system, and to provide corrective, refresher training as needed.

The employees have a right to expect that the total performance appraisal system in their organization is fair (Item 13). If they and their supervisor "play by the rules" in evaluating and reporting job performance, they expect other supervisors and employees to follow these same rules. The expectation is that all supervisors are attempting to be accurate and fair in their evaluations, not falsely elevating some employees to obtain more rewards for employees in their unit over other units in the organization. The classic problem of lack of comparability between raters is concerned with this system fairness issue. Management has a responsibility to monitor supervisors' ratings to detect "unfairness" in the form of consistently elevated ratings from individual supervisors. These high ratings, compared to those of other supervisors, need to be investigated to determine if they are true, or if a supervisor is using the system unfairly.

Finally, and perhaps most important, employees (and supervisors) have a right to be able to understand the performance appraisal system, particularly the form on which the performance evaluation is recorded. The performance appraisal form is the major point of contact and communication between management and the employee in regard to individual job performance, and thus must be clear and understandable. If employees do not understand the performance appraisal process, they have a responsibility to inquire. Often, the best-designed and communicated performance appraisal program is not understood by some employees. Management and individual supervisors have no way of knowing this unless employees inform them. As should be obvious, the best way to have an understandable performance appraisal system is to ensure the system meets the other rights listed in Table 10.1.

IMPLICATIONS FOR MANAGEMENT

A careful consideration of the literature on human motivation and the evaluation of individual job performance appraisal led to the list of employee rights in Table 10.1. Management, by designing and implementing performance appraisal programs that recognize these rights, can anticipate improved productivity and morale from employees. This can be accomplished by including specific design considerations in the development or revision of performance appraisal systems. Obviously, these design features should incorporate the characteristics discussed in relation to employees' rights, particularly with those identified in litigation involving performance appraisal.

Without going into lengthy detail, the following design features should be part of performance appraisal systems: (1) employees' involvement in parts of the design process to be certain they can express their expected rights; (2) development of performance standards based on job descriptions that are used to determine performance levels; (3) supervisory training on how to complete the ratings accurately and fairly, communicate performance standards to employees, provide performance feedback, and effectively counsel for individual performance improvement and for career planning; (4) an appeal procedure within the performance appraisal system; (5) the relationship between the performance evaluation results and organizational rewards should be clearly established and communicated to employees; (6) procedures to maintain the privacy of individual performance appraisals should be established; (7) where necessary, the quality of performance feedback should be improved through job design changes; (8) the performance ratings made by supervisors should be monitored to be certain they are completing the appraisal form correctly and using the system fairly; and (9) communicate with the employees, both organization-wide and at the individual supervisor level, about the performance appraisal system and any revisions to improve understanding. Integrating these design features into the operating procedures will help ensure that management can meet the needs and rights of employees, have a more productive work force, and avoid litigation on its performance appraisal system.

The Communicative Act of Whistleblowing

J. VERNON JENSEN

The employees' need and right to know their quality of performance as perceived by their employers or supervisors, as the previous chapter has discussed, serve as an important backdrop to an analysis of whistleblowing. In many instances, a fair system of appraisal and feedback, and a general openness and trust between employees and their employers or supervisors, would reduce greatly the need for whistleblowing.

In the last century whistleblowing has been increasing steadily (Westin, 1981), as a number of individual cases have been reported in newspapers, articles, books, and on radio and television. An engineer may reveal to the public that faulty brakes are being permitted on an automobile at his plant, a member of a senator's staff may publicize wrongdoings of her employer, an accountant may accuse her superiors of serious mismanagement of funds, or an athlete may publicly accuse his teammates of using drugs. Whistleblowing is all around us. The January 1986 space shuttle *Challenger* disaster was a devastating instance where there was a lack of warning given by some knowledgeable engineers, and a clear managerial ignoring or downplaying of warnings given by other engineers, who came to suffer various punishments for their outspokenness (Magnuson, 1988; Stewart, 1987; Jaksa, Pritchard, and Kramer, 1988).

Most discussions of whistleblowing have been in the context of episodes in business, industry, government, or the courts, rather than as communication phenomena. Articles by Lea P. Stewart (1980) and

Charles W. Redding (1985) are among the very few analyses from a communication perspective. My objectives in this chapter are to arrive at a fuller understanding of whistleblowing as a communicative act and a clearer view of the characteristics of a whistleblower. Finally, I shall briefly sketch the current status of whistleblowing in the courts and in the marketplace.

WHISTLEBLOWING AS A COMMUNICATIVE ACT

Whistleblowing is a communicative act that is (1) intentional, (2) responsive, (3) accusatory, (4) public, (5) in varying media, (6) refutational, (7) over a long period of time, (8) seeking support for claims, (9) straining a contractual arrangement, and (10) grappling with a host of ethical questions.

First, whistleblowing is an intentional communicative act. There is nothing accidental about it. The letter to the editor just did not happen to appear. The photocopied documents were intentionally secured and presented to the public. The communicator has usually given much thought and much time to the act. While there may be degrees of intentionality and some parts of the message may have unintentionally become known, intentionality is at the core of the process.

Second, whistleblowing is a responsive act. Whistleblowers are responding to a condition they feel is badly in need of correction. If nothing were wrong, they say, they would not be blowing the whistle. A referee does not blow the whistle until some foul has been committed; he responds to a rule infraction. Whistleblowing occurs because "other mechanisms of institutional control are failing" (Peters and Branch, 1972, p. 295). It becomes apparent to the whistleblower that corrections are not forthcoming from the group, therefore, a response is necessary.

Third, whistleblowing presents an accusatory message. It is an example of the genre of *kategoria*, accusation. The group, or a portion thereof, is accused of a specific wrongdoing, such as deception, secrecy, coercion, corruption, graft, mismanagement, bribery, unfairness, negligence, discrimination, harassment, or irresponsibility. The accused might be a single person, a small group of people, or the whole organization. The whistleblower, like a referee, identifies the violator, calls for public recognition of the malpractice, and urges punishment of some form to be meted out. The public is not merely being informed of something, they are being informed of a specific, significant willful wrongdoing. Whistleblowing is thus different from "leaking" information. Both are transmitting information from inside an organization to the outside, but the former is transmitting accusatory information (Bok, 1982). Whistleblowing is also different from a confession, which is a first-person accusation: "*I* did something wrong." Whistleblowing is a third-person accusation: "*They* did something wrong." It is, for example, a former attorney for the A. H. Robins Company accusing his firm of "lying and destroying documents" (Oberdorfer, 1984) in the Dalkon Shield law case; or it is two airmen accusing the air force of paying $426 for a hammer, $1,118 for a plastic stool-leg cap, and $7,600 for a ten-cup coffee maker (Goodman, 1984).

Fourth, whistleblowing is a public act. The whistleblower goes public. Some people define whistleblowing as including accusations made inside an organization (Werhane, 1985, p. 114), but it is more common to limit the definition to accusations sent outside the group. Since those inside the group would not listen, the rhetor delivers the message outside. Whistleblowers tell outsiders about the inappropriate things that go on inside a particular group. No group exists in a vacuum. A steel factory is in some city, an infantry squad is part of larger units, and a college sorority is part of a specific campus as well as a national organization. No group exists in and of itself. By definition, there is an "outside," and it is to this audience that whistleblowers present their messages.

Fifth, in so doing they use varying mediums. It might be a letter to the editor in a newspaper, through a reporter who subsequently writes an article in a newspaper or magazine or appears on television, in a public speech, or by informing a public official, a candidate for public office, or law enforcement officers. It may also be an eventual autobiographical exposé (Eveland, 1980; Wright, 1987).

Sixth, whistleblowing is refutational. The initial accusation is almost certainly to be followed, and quickly, by denials and counteraccusations, by demands for evidence and sources of evidence, by charges of self-serving motivation, by all kinds of developments that will call for refutation and counterrefutation. Indeed, the whistleblower's initial charges may even include considerable refutation of anticipated points to be brought up by the opposition. Whistleblowers know that charges will have to be substantiated in a lengthy refutational context. As Charles Peters and Taylor Branch (1972, p. 273) have expressed it, "You can count on the act [whistleblowing] being countered quickly by people threatened, who will raise all kinds of considerations that would put its propriety in question—whether the person had a right to do that sort of thing, whether it would lead to anarchy, whether it was the work of an unbalanced person, and so on." The conflict may well end up in court so that the refutational activity will operate under those procedures.

Seventh, such charges and countercharges are likely to continue for a long period of time, usually for years. Indeed, some court cases stemming from whistleblowing have gone on for a number of years. Thus, "long-range commitment is perhaps the first requirement of successful whistle-blowing" (Peters and Branch, 1972, p. 76). The person does not make merely a single accusation and then expect that to be the end of it.

Eighth, the objective of whistleblowers is to enlist support from some larger outside audience. The correction of the wrongdoing cannot be accomplished by the whistleblowers themselves, and corrections by the group were not forthcoming, so now they blow "the whistle of desperation" (Westin, 1981, p. 2), seeking outside allies who will help. Whistleblowers seek to inform, arouse, and actuate an outside audience, one that is probably initially uninformed and apathetic. The message has to be clear, credible, and compelling. Sometimes the whistleblower will have a specific audience in mind, such as bringing substandard nursing home conditions to the attention of certain medical authorities and relevant city officials. The goal is presented as benefiting the public and defeating or neutralizing those profiting from the status quo. Sometimes the objective may be larger and beyond the specific wrong. For example, when Daniel Ellsberg made public the Pentagon Papers, his objective was to go beyond merely exposing specific government deceit, for he really wanted to gain allies to his cause of altering U.S. policies regarding Vietnam. Whistleblowers assert that the larger outside audience will somehow suffer from the continuation of the malpractice. The public has to be convinced that its tax money *is* being squandered in huge defense contract overruns, that the atomic power plant in its vicinity *has* dangerous safety weaknesses, or that a particular automobile with an undependable braking mechanism *is* indeed a threat to safety. If the public cannot be convinced that somehow they would be exposed to possible injury, there is little likelihood that they would be concerned enough to act, or even to listen. The danger might be an immediate one of wasting millions of tax dollars, or an impending one of potential disaster due to probable leakage of dangerous gases from a chemical plant. It goes without saying that if the threat is in the too distant future, the audience's concern will be minimal.

Ninth, it becomes readily apparent that the act of whistleblowing strains contractual agreements, written or understood. In an organization, an employee agrees to give talent, effort, cooperativeness, and loyalty to the organization. But loyalty, freely and thoughtfully given, is different from blind, coercive subservience. On the other side of the contract, the company agrees to give the employee wages, facilities to use skills, decent working conditions, and miscellaneous other financial and social securities. In some cases, confidentiality is part of the contractual understanding. Industries have many trade secrets in order to protect themselves from their competitors. A government agency, such as the CIA, may require an explicit pledge to secrecy, as would many fraternities/sororities, lodges, religious cults, or underground gangs.

Families have an implicit understanding that members keep some aspects of their behavior secret from the outside world.

Finally, whistleblowing generates a host of ethical questions (Jensen, 1987). In addition to struggling with what is right regarding contractual commitments, whistleblowers grapple with their moral obligations to their profession, to their family and friends, to the general public, and to their own personal integrity. Past experience has amply demonstrated that repercussions, economic and pyschological, can be devastating for the whistleblowers and their families, but also that great satisfaction can come from doing what they thought was right and needed to be done.

CHARACTERISTICS OF THE WHISTLEBLOWER

To these rhetorical facets of the whistleblowing act we need to add the characteristics of a whistleblower in order to secure a full view of the communicative "happening" of whistleblowing. A whistleblower is (1) usually a single individual, (2) subordinate to the accused, (3) well informed, (4) an insider, (5) agitated, (6) highly motivated, (7) participant turned judge, and (8) perceived to be a traitor/hero.

First, a whistleblower is usually one person, though occasionally two or more may be involved. Generally, it is one person who has made an intensely personal decision to engage in the communicative act of blowing the whistle on his/her group. Often the whistleblower has to be a single person so that others do not prematurely reveal his/her plans, or so that others (colleagues, friends, etc.) do not get unfairly suspected or accused of being part of the effort. As an individual, the whistleblower takes on what can be a lonely task. It is one against a whole group, one against many. The group has enormous resources on which to draw— a large treasury, a fleet of lawyers and aides, a huge supportive clientele, and the power to dismiss or punish. The whistleblower has only his/her information, talent, and credibility. In this underdog role, the whistleblower has an enormous uphill struggle. The public serves as a potential power balancer if it rallies behind the whistleblower.

Second, part of the power differential is due not only to the numbers involved, but also to the whistleblower usually being subordinate to those he/she is accusing. After all, one does not need to go outside the group to accuse someone lower in the hierarchial structure of the group, for that usually can be accomplished within the organization itself. When parents need to reprimand their children, they can do so within the family structure, but how can a child "reprimand" an abusive parent without going "outside" the family? A supervisor in a factory punishes subordinates within the organization's framework. The whistleblower, then, is not only outnumbered but is in a subordinate relationship. The task to overcome this power differential is indeed great. It has been generalized that "the average whistle-blower comes from the middle levels of the bureaucracy—high enough to have an over-all picture of some pillage against the public interest . . . and yet low enough not to have truly close ties with those responsible for policy" (Peters and Branch, 1972, p. 285).

Third, the whistleblower is an "inside" person, one who is or was a regular member of a group who speaks about it from the point of view— the place of view—of one who has actually experienced the inner workings. The whistleblower has firsthand specific knowledge that outsiders cannot possibly have. A member of a college sorority or fraternity, for example, has experienced it from the inside, whereas other students have seen it literally only from the outside. Any member of a family unit is an "insider" to that circle, and knows about it in a way the next-door neighbor or anyone else "outside" cannot possible know. The whistleblower has usually been a member of the group for a considerable length of time, has accumulated a sizable amount of key information, has developed a close relationship with at least some members, and in general has become immersed in the culture of the group. This is quite different, for example, from an investigative reporter who tries to get "inside" an organization long enough to secure enough information for an exposé. It also means that someone like Ralph Nader, for instance, "is not a whistle-blower—having always been an outside muckraker— but he is often considered one [a whistleblower]" (Peter and Branch, 1972, p. 277). A whistleblower, then, is a legitimate "insider."

Fourth, whistleblowers are well-informed people. If they were not, they would have little significance and their message would largely go unnoticed. They possess something others do not possess—valuable inside information, which makes them potential, powerful communicators. A strategically placed engineer may have technical knowledge about the dangerous aspects of some machinery that others do not possess, or a member of a military unit knows the details of the inhuman behavior of that group, which outsiders have no knowledge of. Obviously a long-tenured, highly respected group member will have more credibility than a shunned chronic complainer, but the dimension of expertness gives even the latter's ethos a powerful quality. Being "well-informed" of course goes beyond just having a sizable amount of information—it means meeting the qualitative tests of accuracy, completeness, relevance, objectivity, and currency, together with proper analysis of the data.

Fifth, not only do whistleblowers possess facts, but they have interpreted those facts to constitute a "problem." Facts in and of themselves are not necessarily "problems," for humans have to conclude that those facts violate some value. Only then does a "problem" exist. For example, the fact of segregating different races is no "problem" in the eyes of white leaders in South Africa, whereas the blacks and people in most areas of the world perceive that "fact" of segregation to be a very serious "problem." On a more mundane level, two professors may agree on the fact that fifty-five students are in a given classroom. Professor A calls it a "problem" of overcrowded conditions, whereas Professor B sees it as a dramatically filled room. It comes down to whether there is a feeling that some value has been violated. Whistleblowers feel that one or more values have been violated, and their peace of mind, their conscience, is disturbed. They have become morally agitated, and their frustration is compounded by the feeling that the organization has not made sufficient efforts to correct the situation. Whistleblowing is "prompted by an event or condition that the whistleblower views as in some way morally objectionable and that would probably otherwise go unnoticed" (Werhane, 1985, p. 114). Many cases show that the whistleblowers "slowly and in disbelief, came to realize that nothing was going to be done to correct the wrongdoing that they had identified and had brought to management's attention" (Westin, 1981, p. 132). Whistleblowers are morally and intellectually convinced that there are "actions or conditions within a firm that are either illegal or harmful to the public or to consumers of the firm's product" (De George, 1985, p. 15).

Sixth, whistleblowers are motivated, at least from their viewpoint, by laudatory ideals, by an altrustic concern for the public. They challenge the assumption that what is good for the organization is good for the public. They are dissenters in the public interest, as the subtitle of the Peters and Branch (1972) book on whistleblowers labels them. Whistleblowers perceive themselves to be servants of "truth," "efficiency," "economy," "fairness," "justice," "safety," "human dignity," "freedom of expression," "courage," and other similar lofty values. Frequently, from the point of view of the group, or at least its threatened hierarchy, whistleblowers are perceived to be motivated by personal vendettas, disgruntlement, desire for revenge, hunger for notoriety, or a chronic venting of complaints. It is of course difficult to know when motives are chiefly self-serving and when they are altruistic. As in most social phenomena, one can probably assume that high and not-so-high motivations are part of a mix prompting the whistleblowing act. But we would still have to come back to the point that in the eyes of the whistleblowers, and of a large segment of their publics, the act is generated by commendable motives.

Seventh, whistleblowers by their very act assume the role of a judge. Can a prosecuting attorney also be the judge? Can a participant also be a referee? It is like a tennis player who constantly complains to the line umpire, thus creating an anomaly of wanting to be both player (participant) and line umpire (nonparticipating evaluator). One cannot be both. Either one plays or one evaluates. Thus, whistleblowers are looked upon by many as being presumptuous, or arrogantly wanting to be referees when they are only participants. It is this anomaly that makes the metaphor of "whistleblower" an apt one.

Finally, it should be clear by now that whistleblowers come to be viewed by their group as traitors and by many of the public as heroes, and the ensuing rhetoric is cast in this two-valued framework. The etymology of a "traitor" is one who has betrayed a trust or has "handed over" something. Whistleblowers have indeed handed over inside information and have betrayed a trust. Engineers who accuse their company of producing unsafe products are likely to be looked upon as traitors by their organization. Whistleblowers are usually accused of violating a sense of interdependence and mutual obligations within hierarchical arrangements that are so necessary to maintain a healthy organization (Drucker, 1981). They are accused of violating the implicit if not explicit "rule" of not damaging the harmony, the well-being, the reputation of the group. In the view of their critics, whistleblowers have not heeded the ancient Confucian warning against "those who mistake insubordination for courage . . . [and] . . . those who mistake talebearing for honesty" (Waley, 1938, p. 216). They are being disloyal to their "team," and the team is likely to inflict punishment of an infinite variety, such as demotion, unfavorable reassignment, loss of job, harassment, or ostracism (Jensen, 1987; Near and Miceli, 1987b; Magnuson, 1988; Kleinfield, 1986).

But on the other hand, whistleblowers often become heroes to the public, who are genuinely grateful to them for exposing the inefficiency in a governmental agency, the obsessive priority of scheduling over safety in a corporation, or the insensitive care in a nursing home. Obviously there are no guarantees that whistleblowers will be applauded for their efforts, and it is best for them not to expect it. Because they are willing to expose themselves to the public, to cross-examination and inevitable criticism, and possible severe punishment, whistleblowers are indeed often commended by many outsiders. Political émigrés are looked upon as traitors by the government leaders in the countries from which they fled; to other countries those émigrés may be persecuted defenders of high values and civilized principles. Whistleblowers exposing merely surface problems, such as waste and fraud, may well be honored as heroes, but whistleblowers exposing deeper faults in the "system" may face great hostility (Kosterlitz and Norrgard, 1984).

CURRENT STATUS OF WHISTLEBLOWING—
REFLECTIONS FROM THE COURTS AND THE
MARKETPLACE

What protection does a whistleblower have in the courts and in the marketplace? Public employees since 1968 have been explicitly protected in their exercise of free speech. In that year the Supreme Court ruled on the *Pickering* v. *Board of Education* case, which involved a schoolteacher who was fired for "writing letters to local newspapers regarding a proposed tax increase in which he strongly criticized his superiors" (Sanders, 1981, p. 398). The court ruling stipulated that "public employees have constitutional free speech rights. Although these rights are not as expansive as those enjoyed in society at large, the Court has felt that free speech is not only important for the individual but important in making organizations accountable to the taxpaying public" (Sanders, 1981, p. 398).

Since public employees have access to important information, the Court felt that such individuals improve the quality of the public debate by so participating, and that society suffers if such employees are afraid to speak out. A few years ago, a person was dismissed from the air force for testifying to Congress that a particular military transport plane would likely run $2 billion over estimates. He sued, eventually won his case in 1982, and was granted a promotion and legal fees ("Whistleblower wins," 1982). It appears that "the courts have held that government as an employer must follow basic constitutional rules that limit government power in the interests of individual rights. This means that government agencies cannot infringe upon an employee's right to freedom of expression on or off the job unless such conduct disrupts the workplace or interferes with supervisory authority" (Westin, 1981, p. 5).

Whistleblowers in the private sector, however, have less protection. Wayne Sanders has surveyed the applicability of constitutional rights to employees in private industry, and indicates that the main way to apply constitutional rights to private employees is to demonstrate that the firm's action amounts to state action, that is, show that "the State and the private organization [are] connected in such a way that the action of the private organization can be treated as that of the State itself" (Sanders, 1981, p. 401). However, after tracing cases since 1968, Sanders pessimistically concluded that "freedom of speech will probably not be protected in private organizations as a result of state action. The private employee seeking free speech should look not to the Constitution, but to the legislature" (p. 410). Patricia Werhane (1985) expressed the hope of many when she wrote that "employees should not be dismissed or demoted for responsibly exercising these rights [whistleblowing] on the job any more than they should be punished for doing so in society at large" (p. 114), and that "it is morally imperative that clear-cut and open policies for free expression and the protection of legitimate whistleblowers be in the workplace" (p. 119).

Some federal and state actions in recent years have come to the aid of whistleblowers. The federal Toxic Substances Control Act of 1977 "requires companies to instruct employees that any person *must* report information about a chemical they take to present a substantial risk of injury to health or to the environment" (Bok, 1982, p. 228). In 1984 a federal regulation forbade supervisors to force employees to take psychiatric tests for supposed fitness to work (Baldwin, 1985), which had sometimes been a not-so-subtle punishment for whistleblowers. In 1985 the Merit Systems Protection Board for the first time ordered the Pentagon to fire or demote and fine three officials who had improperly retaliated against a whistleblower ("Pentagon told," 1985). Michigan in 1981 "became the first state to enact a Whistleblowers Protection Act covering corporate employees. It allows courts to grant back pay, reinstatement in the job, and costs of litigation to employees who can demonstrate improper treatment" (Bok, 1982, p. 227). Martin H. Malin (1983) commented on how it worked. In 1985 Wisconsin passed a whistleblowers law which provided "that a state employee can report waste and mismanagement in state government without fear of retaliation" (Ritzenthaler, 1986, p. 4).

In 1980 and 1983 significant surveys were made by the U.S. Merit Systems Protection Board (MSPB) to determine how well the Civil Service Reform Act (CSRA) passed by Congress in 1978 was being adhered to. That act specified, among other things, that "employees should be protected against reprisal for the lawful disclosure of information which the employees reasonably believe evidences (a) a violation of any law, rule, or regulation, or (b) mismanagement, a gross waste of funds, an abuse of authority, or a substantial and specific danger to public health or safety" (U.S. Merit Systems Protection Board, 1984, frontispiece).

The major difference found in the 1983 survey was that whereas approximately 45 percent in 1980 "claimed to have observed one or more instances of recent illegal or wasteful activity" (U.S. Merit Systems Protection Board, 1984, p. 5), in 1983 the percentage was only 25 percent. In both 1980 and 1983 the same large percentage (70 percent in 1980 and 69 percent in 1983) did not report what they observed, mainly because they felt nothing would be done to correct it. Fear of reprisal was the second most important reason, with a notable increase from 20 percent in 1980 to 37 percent in 1983 claiming it as a factor. Actual reprisal was reportedly experienced by 20 percent in 1980 and 23 percent in 1983; the main punishment was perceived to be a poor performance appraisal, and the second was a denial of promotion. The 1983 report concluded that "the apparent odds in favor of experiencing some type of negative consequences if one reports an illegal or wasteful activity are high enough to discourage many employees from taking the chance" (U.S. Merit Systems Protection Board, 1984, p. 43). The report recommended, among other things, that each federal agency should maintain an organizational climate that manifested:

1. the active and periodic solicitation of employee viewpoints and knowledge regarding fraud, waste, and abuse;

2. the fair evaluation of employee-supplied information with timely feedback to the involved employees on the results of that evaluation;

3. consideration, during reviews of each manager's or supervisor's performance, of the actions they have taken to implement agency policy in this regard;

4. consideration, during reviews of each employee's performance, of the degree to which they have become constructively involved in identifying and resolving problems related to fraud, waste, and abuse;

5. positive and widely publicized recognition of employee contributions to the reduction of illegal or wasteful activities (U.S. Merit Systems Protection Board, 1984, p. 9).

Other supportive mechanisms for whistleblowers also exist. For instance, the Pentagon has a "hotline" number that employees can call to report waste and inefficiency. Support groups have been organized, such as the Clearinghouse for Professional Responsibility (Nader's innovation), the Government Accountability Project and The Project on Military Procurement in Washington, D.C., and The Educational Fund for Individual Rights, Inc., in New York City. Also, support mechanisms are located within professional organizations. For example, in 1975 the Committee on Scientific Freedom and Responsibility of the American Association for the Advancement of Science issued a report urging scientists and engineers to blow the whistle if their work was being used in a way harmful to the public. The appearance of ombudsmen (see Waxman, Chapter 9, supra) and grievance boards and procedures (see Hutchison and Osigweh, Chapter 6; Humphreys et al., Chapter 7; and Westin, Chapter 8, supra) in many corporations is helpful, but of course they have their limitations.

CONCLUSION

The communicative act of whistleblowing is not a simple phenomenon. It has multiple strands and involves balancing multiple values. A few years ago Blumberg (1971, p. 318) concluded:

The real question is to establish civilized perimeters of permissible conduct that will not silence employees from expressing themselves on the public implications of their employers' activities in the social and environmental arena and at the same time will not introduce elements of breach of confidentiality and impairment of loyalty that will materially impair the functioning of the corporation itself. A balancing of interest, not a blind reiteration of traditional doctrines, is required.

More recently Malin (1983) came to a similar conclusion. Linda Ferguson (1987) recently phrased the dilemma: "What is the trade off of employees' interests in safety and conscience vs. employers' interest in running a business?" (p. 103). Werhane (1985) expressed well the agonizing decision-making involved: "Whistle blowers often have to make moral choices between ideals that are of conflicting but equal weight" (p. 115).

It is clear that whistleblowing is increasing and is receiving encouragement and protection in various ways. "Protecting the whistleblower," Nancy Hauserman (1986b) has recently claimed, "is one way of reasserting individual morality in the corporate structure" (p. 9). But not everyone shares that view, and whistleblowing remains a highly risky undertaking.

In summary, to understand and evaluate better the role of whistleblowing in our society, it is important to see more clearly its rhetorical components. The communicative act of whistleblowing is intentional, responsive, accusatory, public, uses varying media, is refutational, lingers over a long period of time, seeks support for one's claims, strains a contractual arrangement, and struggles with many ethical tensions. A whistleblower is usually a single individual, subordinate to the accused, a well-informed insider, deeply agitated, highly motivated, a participant turned judge, and is perceived in a two-valued light of being either a traitor or hero.

Those who would be managers of human resources need to be enlightened about, and sensitive to, these rhetorical dimensions of whistleblowing. They need to appreciate the delicate balancing acts involved, to be open to the concerns expressed, and to handle them at an early stage. Not to do so is not to "manage." The fabric of the corporate culture and the larger society may well become seriously frayed, efficiency impaired, safety jeopardized, and individual lives filled with great agony.

The Responsibilities of the Management Professoriate in the Administrative State

WILLIAM G. SCOTT

The administrative state is a twentieth-century governance artifact. Its various incarnations, which in the second and third decades of this century ranged from Italian fascism to American New Dealism, were systems of national resource mobilization and coordination induced by the autarkic requirements of national power, the demands for mass consumption and production in mass societies, the advancement of technology, the growing complexity of organization, and rapid population growth. For these reasons and others, such as the social, political, economic, and ideological crises of those times, corporatism emerged as the realpolitik of administrative statecraft. It provided a rational form of centralized resource management, based on a social order in which national policy goals were decided and implemented by a management elite cooperating at the highest levels of government, business, and labor.

A highly articulated management practice and scholarship evolved along with the development of the administrative state. The two most important aspects of this evolution were the appearance of a "self-aware" elite in the public and private sectors, and the refinement of a single-set value orthodoxy that informed this elite uniformly across these organizational sectors.

Dwight Waldo (1980) documented the rise of self-awareness in both public and private administration. He held that it pertained to administration as an objective activity—"a mutation in human culture" (p. 10)—which could be studied, taught, improved, and communicated.

But there was also a subjective aspect to self-awareness, in the sense that administrators realized that they were a class apart from other classes with a calling and a legitimacy peculiar to their status and expertise.

Hand in hand with a self-aware administration came a value orthodoxy that began, according to Waldo (1980), with Henry Towne's 1886 speech to the American Society of Mechanical Engineers and Woodrow Wilson's famous 1887 essay on public administration. Towne and Wilson established the value framework for administration in an elementary form: Towne for the private sector, Wilson for the public sector. However, it is critical to note that the central elements of these frameworks were the same. Both authors valued a rational administration informed by science and economics. These values are still central to the orthodoxy of modern administration.

With rudimentary administrative values and a dawning managerial self-awareness in place by the turn of the century, all that practice and theory needed was an appropriate environment in which to flower. This environment appeared in the 1930s for the reasons mentioned above. The American response to these environmental imperatives was an Americanized version of the administrative state, and management is still acting out the consequences of this major revolution.

Management education was particularly influenced by this revolution, and it has measured and mirrored this social transformation in three ways. First, management theory spawned an "heroic" utopian literature with lionized gurus, such as Chester I. Barnard (1938), Herbert Simon (1947), Peter Drucker (1954), and Thomas Peters and Robert Waterman (1982). Their work reinforced orthodox values and heightened managerial self-awareness. Second, professional academic graduate programs in public and business administration arose partly to socialize students in the culture of the administrative state (Scott and Mitchell, 1986). And third, a dedicated professoriate in administration, itself inculcated by the orthodoxy of administrative statecraft, transmitted its values and culture to successive generations of students.

America had not advanced too far into the decade of the 1980s when evidence of corruption in management practice and paradoxes in management scholarship hinted that the field was in ruins. Seymour Lipset and William Schneider (1983) reported a serious erosion in the public's perception of managerial leadership legitimacy. William Scott and Terence Mitchell (1986) argued that "enacted" management cultures were grossly manipulative and tended to trivialize human participation in organizations. Loren Baritz (1960) charged that behavioral scientists sold out to practicing management, compromising the integrity of their research.

Given the current interest in "ethics," which has been variously underscored in this book by Osigweh and Miceli (Chapter 1), Gordon and Coulson (Chapter 2), Hutchison and Osigweh (Chapter 6), Kavanagh (Chapter 10), Jensen (Chapter 11), and Salipante and Fortado (Chapter 13), it is clear that both sides of the field—scholarship and practice—are not oblivious to the possibility of a fundamental moral decay in management. Indeed, this and some of the underlying concerns have been precisely documented by exploratory analysis in Chapter 1, and by field data in Chapter 13. In light of these concerns, it has not escaped the attention of scholars and administrators in education that schools of management bear some responsibility for the present state of affairs. More specifically, the management professoriate has obligations to promote the moral health of the field. It is not meeting them because of a curious paradox that has evolved in the field among practice, theory, and research. The next section of this chapter examines this contention. The last section proposes a moral stance for the professoriate which must be taken as a preliminary before any specific reforms in management education are undertaken.

THE SEEMING PARADOX IN MANAGEMENT THOUGHT

The paradox springs from the orthodox triad of management thought (Figure 12.1). On the one hand, management objectifies instrumental puzzles through the rigorous application of the methods of positive science. The results of this research are published in journals such as the *Academy of Management Journal*. On the other hand, management deobjectifies many other subjects that are beyond the reach of hard-core empiricism. Such work, usually written about on the level of frameworks and model-building, finds its way into journals of a broader orientation such as the *Academy of Management Review*. One obvious example are the studies that fall under the rubric of organizational culture, about which the *Review* has carried at least nine articles since mid–1983. Therefore, not to put too fine a point on the contention, it is generally the case that the domain of the *Journal* is the empirical objectification of instrumental management *problems* whereas the domain of the *Review* is the deobjectification of the substantive *values* of organizational life.

So that there is no misunderstanding about my position on these aspects of management scholarship, let me make it clear that there are many legitimate instrumental problems to be solved by positive science in behavioral research. This work is usually straightforward, unhypocritical, and often refreshing in its innocence.

However, there are substantive values of individual and organizational behavior that are as real as the research problems scientists try to solve. But our field seems to have drifted into the untenable position of holding that those things that transcend the limits of our empirical meth-

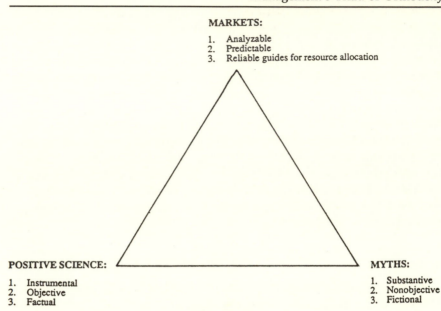

Figure 12.1
Management's Triad of Orthodoxy

MARKETS:

1. Analyzable
2. Predictable
3. Reliable guides for resource allocation

POSITIVE SCIENCE:

1. Instrumental
2. Objective
3. Factual

MYTHS:

1. Substantive
2. Nonobjective
3. Fictional

odology are somehow less than actual matters of fact. They are often referred to as myths, fables, and fairy tales that management "enacts" in order to secure control over individuals and groups within organizations. This aspect of management is not straightforward, not innocent, and certainly not unhypocritical.

But, substantive values are not always fairy tales, phenomenological constructions, or enacted realities as some current management writers want us to believe. Many are concrete "N-of-one" events that have explicit moral content. To illustrate this point consider Sidney Biddle Barrows' 1986 autobiography *Mayflower Madam*, one of the more recent examples of contemporary managerial barbarism.

This book is *not* vulgar or erotic. It is more on the order of sterile and amoral, although these words do not quite fit it either. Rather, Hannah Arendt's 1965 description of Adolph Eichmann more accurately expresses my sense of *Mayflower Madam*: It is Banal!! Not that commercialized sex and genocide are morally indifferent. Rather it is that banality stems from contrived, artifactual management processes such as those that were used to rationalize a sex business or an efficient procedure for mass murder. What horrified Arendt about Eichmann was the utterly prosaic nature of a man who solved process problems without regard to the substantive value ends served by the process. People such as Eichmann and Barrows define their personal identities in terms of processes. Therefore, if the processes are banal then the self of its managers is banal. Or as A.G. Ramos (1981) put it, "Only a defective self can find in contrived systems the adequate milieu for [personal] actualization" (p. 87).

Returning to the paradox, the professoriate in the management field works within the rings of two concentric circles: an inner circle, concerned with the empirical objectification of instrumental management problems, and an outer circle of those deobjectified substantive values of management that elude empiricism. This is a strange vision for a field of scholarship that makes pretenses about analytical rigor and scientific method. Its weirdness is only surpassed by the academics who take it seriously. This paradox, however, is not real because there is another circle that encompasses the other two. It represents the power of management practice presumably driven by markets which reconciles that which would otherwise be the irreconcilable worlds of management facts and management fictions (Figure 12.2). Thoughtful practitioners have known this since the early 1920s. However, it took Chester I. Barnard (1938) and Herbert Simon (1947) to compose a system of management theory that merged managers and academics into a partnership that models and guides current scholarship and teaching.

As Barnard and Simon visualized it, centralized management control of broad organizational purposes justified manipulating employee work motives and social realities in order to achieve the consolidation of top management power. If this included the shaping of people's moral values and the organization's culture without regard for truth, then so be it.

In constructing his analytical framework Barnard (1938) borrowed directly from Vilfredo Pareto (1935) or indirectly from others who used Pareto to shape their ideas. Since Pareto's theoretical and philosophical views were influential in the development of administrative statecraft (he was much admired in Italy during the 1920s), it is important to have a sense of the structure of his ideas.

Pareto chose five analytical categories for his interpretation of social dynamics:

1. The social system

2. Residues and derivations

3. Language (logical and emotive)

Figure 12.2
The Inner and Outer Circles of Management Thought

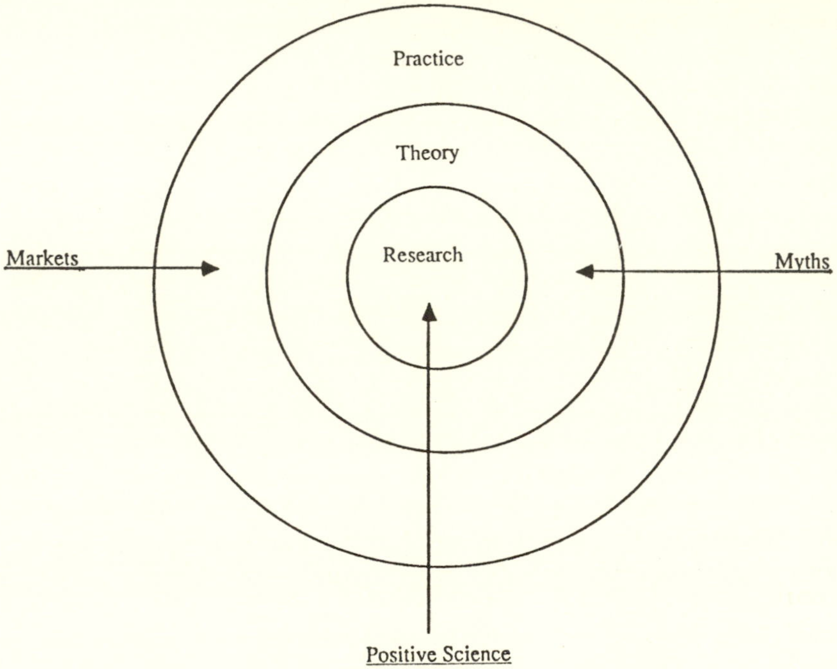

4. Equilibruim (balance within the social system)

5. The circulation of the elite

Pareto's dynamics worked this way. A society is an aggregation of interrelated and interdependent parts systemically connected and balanced in a state of dynamic equilibrium. The function of the elite is to maintain that equilibrium. One way they did this was through the control of behavior by manipulating residues and derivations, that is, nonlogical and logical values, motives, and attitudes. Language is the symbolic expression of the aspects of human behavior. Since most behavior is nonlogical, a product of emotive sentiments, the elite must invent myth systems and fictions that appeal to this side of human nature. These can elicit obedience from the masses more effectively than an appeal to logic.

The concept of myth, therefore, is the third indispensable element of the orthodox management triad because it permits management to contrive certain realities that are otherwise excluded by markets and positive science. The framers of modern management thought wholly accepted this point of view. This group, located at Harvard University during the 1920s and 1930s, included such notables as Elton Mayo, Fritz Roethlisberger and William Dickson, Lawrence Henderson, George Homans, Talcott Parsons, W. Lloyd Warner, R.K. Merton, and Thomas N. Whitehead. Their influence on Barnard (1938), his own reading of Pareto (1935), and his social and political milieu cannot be underestimated in the formation of his ideas about management's part in the modern administrative state. If there is any truth to the statement that Pareto was the "Karl Marx of the bourgeoisie" (Henderson, 1935, p. 45) then Barnard most certainly was Pareto's Lenin.

Barnard (1938) referred frequently to the Paretian categories, especially the social system, equilibrium, logical and nonlogical behavior, and language. Barnard does not mention the circulation of the elite because he thought the elite *had* circulated. That is, America's old aristocracy of industrialists, merchants, bankers, landowners, and the scions of inherited wealth had sunk into the obscurity of Pareto's historical graveyard, and their places were taken by a new elite of professional managers rising from the ranks of the petite bourgeoisie, farmers, urban industrial workers, and technicians.

The chief problem for this new elite to solve was the effective administration of the enterprises they controlled. Thus, Barnard's sole objective was to create a framework that legitimized this elite's authority, thereby securing the obedience of their followers. Simon (1947), in his book *Administrative Behavior* took this framework one step further and proposed an agenda of empirical research based upon positive science that would improve the verifiability of administrative facts about human behavior in organizations.

The significance of Barnard's (1938) and Simon's (1947) work did not rest in the specifics of their approach to administration for which they are most often cited. Instead, it rested in their views about the social order and how that order is maintained. Here Barnard and Simon were unequivocal: Organizations must have a management elite whose authority is unchallengeable because they have convinced others of the myth that they have the technical, social, and cooperative skills to do a job that no one else can do. Such myth-making is the practice of "cognitive politics" which Ramos (1981) defined as "a conscious or unconscious use of distorted language, the intent of which is to induce people to interpret reality in terms that reward . . . the agents of such distortion"(p. 76).

Barnard (1938) was aware of the significant problem raised by his commitment to this type of authority. How is democratic political freedom preserved and effective, centralized, elitist organizations nurtured at the same time?

He solved this problem through his consent theory of authority which is the ultimate statement of cognitive politics. This theory has bamboozled management scholarship for years. For example, H.E. McCurdy (1977) wrote in his public administration textbook, "With a stroke of the pen, Barnard did for organizations what John Locke has done for constitutions: he set the sources of their power in the people who made them up" (p. 44). While utterly wrongheaded about Barnard's intentions, McCurdy's accolades are typical in the administrative literature. The received wisdom is that Barnard introduced democratic management by his consent theory. However, there is not a shred of democracy in this concept. Rather, he argued that management ought to *engineer* consent by manipulating the motives of individuals and by influencing the norms of informal organizations to create the illusion of a democratic experience while at the same time enhancing the reality of centralized control by a management elite. So just as it is expedient for politicians to encourage people to believe that they exercise democratic control over their government, it is also expedient for managers to encourage subordinates to think they have some control over their work lives, regardless of the facts of the situation.

Few formulations in management theory are more elegant than this or more contemporary in their application, as Peters and Waterman demonstrated (1982) by documenting Barnard's and Simon's views on value manipulation. So Barnard and Simon, as the helmsmen of the management paradigm, set the course that our field has been on for fifty years. But what has this to do with our inner and outer circles?

We seldom acknowledge that the outer ring of managerial power drives academic management and reduces its professoriate to being servants of this power. Loren Baritz (1960) wrote, "The position . . . social scientists have taken regarding the ethics and politics of power obtrudes as a red thread in the otherwise pallid canvas on which they have labored. . . . Almost all industrial social scientists have either backed away from the political and ethical implications of their work or have faced these considerations from the point of view of management" (pp. 198–99). Following the same theme, twenty-five years later, Ellen Goodman (1986) pointed out in her column that, "with all the fascination on how to manage, there is little taught about what to manage." Returning to one of our earlier themes, the banality of management processes removes from managerial decision-making any vestige of concern about the moral value of the product or service. Sex as a commodity can be as effectively merchandised as hotel space. Similarly, mass murder and meat-packing are problems to be solved by queuing theory. Consequently, those disposed toward spinning out this logic have available to them a huge body of rationalized techniques to draw upon in order to be more effective in their enterprises.

THE RESPONSIBILITIES OF THE PROFESSORIATE

It is not enough for management academics to labor self-righteously in the orthodoxy of Simon's (1947) circle of empiricism or Barnard's (1938) circle of theoretical frameworks. Because surely as they do, they will become captives of the power of practice. And just as surely as the bonds of this captivity tighten, so will the unwitting complicity grow between the professoriate and this power's barbarisms. Therefore, we of the professoriate have a special obligation to occupy a territory that is at the center of the fray but at the same time above it—in short, a moral high ground.

To illustrate, consider first these quotations. Baritz (1960) wrote: "A major characteristic of twentieth-century manipulation has been that it blinds the victim to the fact of manipulation" (p. 210). Over twenty years later Alasdair MacIntyre (1981) observed that our age has become so morally dismembered that "any genuine distinction between manipulative and nonmanipulative social relations" has been obliterated (p. 22). The assessment made by MacIntyre the philosopher is the logical corollary of the assessment made by Baritz the historian.

The common theme in these quotations is manipulation. And we have already pointed out that its encouragement, as part of the overall management project, can be traced from Barnard (1938) to Simon (1947). Regardless of whether we express manipulation now in our literature as inculcation of morals, injection of values, symbolic management, management of culture, or the construction of phenomenological archetypes, it all reduces to one thing—managerial control. Such control is achieved by limiting people's choices and by narrowing their perception of alternative values, all of which is highly functional from the standpoint of practice since it produces obedient subordinates.

While managerial control of the sort just described is a questionable practice in a free society, it is entirely unacceptable as a point of view in universities. The ancient and honorable traditions of universities emphasized certain student rights that professors had the obligation to fulfill: their freedom of choice, expansion of their alternatives, their moral development, sharpening of their conscience, and their intellectual preparation to discern right from wrong. In this respect, the modern university has a dual function that is brought into perspective by the nature of a professional school, such as a school of business. Being part of the fray, it has an obligation to prepare students to solve instrumental management problems. At the same time, it has a traditional substantive obligation to rise above the fray, which in this instance means enhancing the moral development of its students as citizens of the larger society in which they will live. Why should the professoriate in management schools be exempted from the responsibilities entailed by this tradition?

They should not be exempted, but the problem is how to proceed. There are specific actions which Scott and Mitchell (1986) have recommended for the reform of management programs. They included the consideration of ethical and moral issues in all core management courses; the development of designated ethics courses integrated into management programs; the sponsorship of independent forums for moral discourse; the extension of such forums into the programs of professional associations such as the Academy of Management (the Council on Employee Responsibilities and Rights, chartered formally in 1985, has started to provide independent forums as well as an associational framework); and the establishment of an institute for study of management values and ethics jointly supported by the American Society for Public Administration, the Academy of Management, and the American Assembly of Collegiate Schools of Business. These proposals cannot be discussed in detail here. Instead, we propose a *Zeitgeist* for a professoriate occupying a moral high ground.

The essence of this *Zeitgeist* is a professorial spirit that is dedicated to the formation of an intellectual moral order in professional enclaves which are devoted to noetic reason and social action. This order moves among the managerial barbarians, but it is intellectually and morally detached from them. This order has a moral tradition; it is a moral community; and most important, its goal is the enhancement of citizen excellence.

Such enclave-thinking is alien to American culture. Indeed, its main contemporary exponents are French, English, and Brazilian: Barnard-Henri Levi (1979), Alasdair MacIntrye (1981), and A.G. Ramos (1981). Furthermore, in Poland today, Solidarity lives, not as an organization, but as a cultural enclave, under whose aegis is held meetings around the country that discuss everything from journalism, to poetry, to political philosophy. However, Europeans have had experience dealing with barbarians for thousands of years. Their strategy, in fact the only strategy possible when faced by the overwhelming power of barbarism, is to gather and preserve in enclaves what is good, and hope that when the dark age passes the good will be given to future generations.

Our age recommends just such a path of action to the management professoriate. Pertinent to the instrumental interests of our field we must be, but not at the cost of surrendering the high moral ground that is our privileged legacy from history.

PART IV
CONCLUSION

13

Employee Rights: Required versus Desired

PAUL F. SALIPANTE, JR.,
AND BRUCE FORTADO

Analysis of employee grievances suggests that a sizable gap exists between the treatment that employees expect from their employers and prevalent conceptions of employee rights. An even greater gap exists between employees' desires and the treatment that they actually receive. The accumulation of frustration that results from this gap has important repercussions for organizations and for the ability of employee rights law to regulate employment conflict. Frustration leads subordinates to resort to both overt and covert actions in order to create situations they feel are more equitable. The views employees have of their rights and the actions they utilize in attempts to resolve conflict are analyzed here based upon a set of fifty grievance interviews conducted by the authors and their students. These interviews revealed that a much wider range of employee actions takes place, over much longer periods of time, than has previously been emphasized.

CONCEPTIONS OF EMPLOYEE RIGHTS

The legal perspective on employee rights describes the court-enforceable obligations that management is required to provide due to legislation, union contracts, and voluntarily assumed personnel manual provisions. A second perspective on rights argues from moral grounds for the establishment of a much broader set of rights than does the legal view. Even this moral perspective falls short of what employees actually expect, suggesting that a third view of rights deserves consideration—

one emphasizing employee expectations and their practical implications for organizations.

Legal Conceptions of Employee Rights

Increments in legal rights have come primarily in bursts during critical historical periods. Many of the current legal rights were a product of the social climate of the Great Depression. From the depths of despair, workers were given protection in the areas of union representation, safety and health, child labor, social security, and unemployment and workers' compensation (Goldberg, Ahern, Haber, and Oswald, 1977). In the 1960s and 1970s legal rights were expanded in the areas of discrimination, safety and health, and pensions. The overall thrust of the legislation was to provide safe employment, a buffering from the loss of employment, and equitable treatment for certain protected classes.

Most recently, there has been an erosion of the employer's ability to hire and fire at will (Bierman and Youngblood, 1984). However, as Jack Steiber points out in Chapter 3, supra, the vast majority of workers in the United States have no substantial protection from unjust dismissal. With an estimated 150,000 workers per year being discharged without cause, and dismissal rates for nonunion employees being twice that of unionized employees, the doctrine of employment-at-will remains largely intact (Stieber, 1985). The courts in the progressive states have reached a plateau with the current legislation (St. Antoine, 1985), so further progress in legal rights will depend on the passage of new laws. New legislation will probably come slowly since, as Henry H. Perritt's discussion in Chapter 4, supra, makes clear, there are disagreements among the major groups that have a stake in wrongful dismissal legislation.

The Moral Perspective

The moral viewpoint contends that the legal perspective is too simplistic, because laws themselves may not be just. The remedy espoused by this perspective is the application of moral standards, based on each person's inherent value as a human being. These standards include the following: (1) the right to equal consideration, (2) the right to security and subsistence, (3) the right to life and the right not to be tortured, (4) the right to freedom, and (5) the right to private ownership (Werhane, 1985).

From this basic set of moral rights, other legitimate rights can be inferred. For example, controversies over privacy, autonomy, and free choice and actions are derivations of the generic category of freedom. Arguments over privacy extend beyond employee records and financial information to topics such as the ethics of lie detector tests. Timely and accurate disclosure by organizations of a broad range of information, beyond what the law requires, is needed so that employees can make prudent decisions and maintain control over their lives. Rumors, threats, innuendos, and coercive acts are clearly contrary to these dictums. Overall, the degree of respect given by the organization to individuals' moral rights will determine their dignity and quality of life in the work setting. If an organization expects its employees to give their full effort and loyalty, it must reciprocate by fulfilling these moral obligations (Gordon and Infante, 1987; Osigweh, 1988a; Selznick, 1969; Aram and Salipante, 1981).

The Practical Perspective

Even the moral perspective falls short of employees' expectations, so a third viewpoint warrants consideration. The practical perspective holds that (1) employees will act on their own expectations of the rights due them, and that (2) employers will adjust their behavior when they perceive it to be in their interest to do so.

In recent years little research has been devoted to the organizational consequences of day-to-day employee frustrations and employees' attempts to modify the situation in their favor. Early grievance studies did investigate these issues. Stanley B. Mathewson (1969) found that in the 1920s employee grievances sometimes resulted in output restriction. Later research found that work groups' expectations and power were dependent upon the amount of discretion that they exercised over their work, the replaceability of their output, communication channels among workers, the homogeneity of worker interests, and work group status (Sayles, 1958). More recent studies have found that grievance activity and outcomes also depend on factors external to the work group, including the organization's environment and its attitudinal climate (Peach and Livernash, 1974; Thomson and Murray, 1976).

Increasing the length and specificity of the union contract, the labor relations analog of the legislative approach, was found to be ineffective in reducing grievance activity; it merely gave unhappy workers more ammunition (McKersie and Shropshire, 1962). Employees want more than *post hoc* adjudication of their complaints. They also desire forewarning and inclusion in the decision-making process (Kuhn, 1961). In some instances the specific issue at stake is of less consequence than whether a rapport exists that allows the rules to be bent. Kuhn has demonstrated that, although the process of working through a grievance can be a disruptive one, if it is properly understood and managed, it can result in more motivated and democratic work groups.

The legal, moral, and practical views of employee rights may be considered as three concentric circles, with the rights expected by employees (the practical perspective) being a superset subsuming the other two conceptions. By examining large numbers of employee grievances from a variety of settings, we intend to move beyond the existing literature by more generally describing employees' expectations and their reactions when these expectations are not fulfilled.

RIGHTS DESIRED BY EMPLOYEES

A set of rights that employees desire could be surmised from the preceding literature review. Alternatively, a set of expected rights could be extracted from interviews with grievants. This study integrated these two approaches by outlining a theoretical list of rights that was amended by information contained in fifty grievance interviews. From this research process eight categories of desired employee rights were identified:

1. The right to *job stability*. This concerns transfers, demotions, layoffs, plant closings, discharges, severance pay, and unemployment compensation.

2. The right to *equitable treatment* concerning rewards and sanctions received and effort demanded. Among other issues falling into this area are discrimination, status, use of seniority versus merit, blocking of growth opportunities, and failure to praise.

3. The right to *accurate and timely information* and *meaningful responses* to questions. An important issue here is whether the organization is responsive to its employees' informational needs.

4. The right to *autonomy and privacy*, including issues of responsibility and trust, control over socializing and breaks, and the freedom to perform one's own job without undue meddling from superiors.

5. The right to *reciprocal commitment,* covering the loyalty shown to loyal employees, a manager's representation of subordinates' interests, and the effort that superiors put into their jobs compared with that demanded of subordinates.

6. The right to *rebalance inequities* without fear of retribution or being labeled an incompetent or troublemaker. Rebalancing may occur through either bilateral actions directly involving the other party or unilateral, often covert actions on the part of the grievant.

7. The right to be involved in *decision-making* that affects the employee's situation, local work group issues in particular.

8. The right to *technical and managerial support* useful to completing one's task with pride, such as being backed up by a superior when impediments are created by others.

As can be noted from the discussion earlier in this chapter, rights (1) and (2) stem primarily from the spirit of the legal perspective, (3) through

(5) from that of the moral perspective, and (6) and (7) from the practical perspective. Right (8) became evident from the grievance cases themselves, although in retrospect it is consistent with literature on employee motivation (see Dalton, 1971) and industrial democracy.

We do not claim that this list is exhaustive, and further research may well lead to modification or additions. Nevertheless, this general but concise list of rights does well when compared to rights proposed for specific applications. For example, each of the fourteen rights that Michael J. Kavanagh derives in Chapter 10, supra, for performance appraisals can be subsumed within the above categories.

Cases of Desired Rights

Two of our grievance cases are particularly illustrative of the rights categorized above. The first case involves a one-hundred-employee, nonunion subsidiary of a large corporation. A highly paid group of degreed professionals was supported in this subsidiary by less well-paid, hourly clerical workers. A conflict arose from the corporation's decision to transfer the operation from the Midwest to the Southwest. Formal notification came in the form of a terse memo, announcing that the move would occur in six months, and a press release stating that the relocation would be in the best interests of the corporation.

Although rumors of the move had been circulating for a year and half, the employees were angry. Among the many questions that they wanted answered were whether they would be transferred to the new location and, if not, whether there would be severence pay (Right 1). The employees found it difficult to obtain prompt, credible responses to their questions (Right 3), in no small part due to the president's having just left for an extended vacation! Many of the employees had earlier relocated from another geographical area to the Midwest location. When they discovered that only the ten people in the highest positions would make the move, those with long years of service were bitter about the one-sided commitment (Right 5). Anger was expressed over the unequal treatment they received compared to that accorded the highly educated employees retained by the firm (Right 2). Despite the deep feelings of discontent, the company emerged unscathed, except for some epithets in graffiti on the walls.

The second case, involving a unionized manufacturing operation, provides an important contrast to the first in terms of the cost of its outcomes to the organization. Management suspected theft and found a discrepancy between the tally of mechanized counters on the production line and the actual stock of finished goods. Through unobtrusive observation, Employee Z was found to be moving units made by a worker on an earlier shift to his machine, then manipulating his counter forward to overstate the amount of his work. After Z was caught with specially marked units, he was discharged (Right 1). The union conceded his guilt, but felt that the penalty of discharge was too severe (Right 2). Nine months later the case was taken to arbitration.

While this case was being pursued, Z's work group took action. Production was slowed and machines broke down with uncommon frequency. Unscheduled breaks and an excessive number of sick days were taken. A walkout was repeatedly threatened. Although the employees did not directly state the connection, it was clear that they wanted Z reinstated (Right 6). If management would not cooperate, then the workers would make sure that management would feel as miserable as did the work group.

What was it that the workers resented? They expressed the greatest indignation at having been spied upon, this invasion of privacy (Right 4) being seen as a dangerous precedent. If employees were observed long enough and closely enough, would not some fault be found with their work? Furthermore, management had not listened to their wishes concerning the discharged coworker. The workers had a right to be involved in making such decisions (Right 7), and now management would pay the price for having ignored them. Eventually, an arbitrator reinstated Z with no back pay. In the arbitration hearing, the union had emphasized Z's nearly twenty years of service (Right 5) and the trivial, $50 amount of the violation (Right 2). Management had failed to make their point and had absorbed considerable costs in the process. In addition, the discontent and militancy that were galvanized in the work group were certain to be continuing problems.

These two examples display aspects of the desired employee rights outlined earlier. Also note that a right primary to one party may be secondary to another. While the most important concern of employees in the second case was the right to privacy, the arbitrator focused on the reciprocal commitment created by long service. Each party in these situations had a somewhat different focus on the relevant rights, failing to come to a congruent viewpoint (Bouwen and Salipante, 1986).

METHODOLOGY

The methodology employed in this study was designed to explore employees' own perceptions of their complaints and rights. Two problems presented themselves. First, how could grievants be encouraged to disclose opinions and covert actions that often challenged their superior or organization? Second, how could employees be permitted to respond in their own terms and concepts rather than the researchers'? Traditional surveys of cross sections of employees do not handle these two problems well. An alternative approach is the analysis of formal, written grievances, but the written complaint is often a restriction and distortion of the grievant's full views (Kuhn, 1961).

Given that the sources of employee frustrations are relatively unexplored, and that the outcomes which result from employee discontent are frequently covert, a multiple case study based on personal interviews was the most appropriate design, allowing for description of cause-effect relationships and the generation of concepts (Yin, 1984). To counter respondents' reluctance to disclose, the interviews were conducted by people trusted by the interviewees. The interviewers, most of whom were full-time employees enrolled in part-time graduate business programs, interviewed personal friends and acquaintances. Given the importance of interviewee trust and the reluctance of a range of organizations to allow research into the potentially volatile topic of employee complaints, this data-collection strategy was the only practical path to pursue (Whyte, 1987). The existing relationship between interviewer and interviewee allowed the grievants to "open up" and tell their story.

Interviewees were asked to describe a personal complaint involving a superior or an organizational procedure, providing the relevant history and their opinions on its treatment by management. The dialogue followed an interview guide of general topic areas (Lofland and Lofland, 1984), allowing a joint construction of the framework for eliciting and interpreting responses. This approach represents one of several relatively unexplored techniques that can be used to empower respondents by giving them more control over the process through which their words are given meaning (Mishler, 1986). Interviewers then wrote the interviews in the form of cases, allowing them to emphasize those points most salient to the respondents.

Note that no claim need be made that a respondent's perceptions were "accurate" in the sense of being shared by others. The study's focus is solely on the aggrieved's feelings and the actions that ensued. Further, the study's purposes of identifying a variety of perceptions and behavioral responses are best served by a heterogeneous sample rather than a sample from a single organization. The breadth of the sample is important, but not the degree to which it is representative of the general work population, since the intent is to engage in analytic generalization rather than statistical generalization (Yin, 1984). Interviews covered employees from a broad range of service and industrial operations. Nearly 80 percent of the cases dealt with nonunion sites, approximately the unorganized percentage of the work force at large. Interviewers reported that better than one in every two people whom they approached for interviews had a complaint to relate. This suggests that many employees have complaints and that the sample was not composed primarily of chronic complainers.

Initially, five of the fifty grievance cases were read by one of the authors of this chapter and each incidence of a perceived employee right was coded. A further five cases were coded by both authors, showing good congruence in the codings; points of disagreement were discussed, a few of the initially developed categories were collapsed, and the definitions of the final coding categories clarified. No expressions of rights were found in the remaining forty cases that could not be easily subsumed into the eight categories listed previously.

The codings for each case reflected the grievant's perception of rights denied; rights granted were not coded. For example, a secretary who complained bitterly of receiving only two days' notice of a transfer to another unit was coded as Right 3 being "strongly felt as denied." The codes utilized were "right not mentioned as denied," "weakly felt as denied," "moderately felt," and "strongly felt." The one exception to the "rights denied" nature of the codings was for the right to rebalance inequities, which was coded according to whether the grievant actually attempted some form of rebalancing. The coding procedure was similar to the methods used by William J. Dickson and Fritz J. Roethlisberger (1966, p. 67) in analyzing counseling interviews; the length of comments, the repetition of topics, and the depth of emotion all played a role in discerning the severity of concerns.

THE EXPANSIVE EXPECTATIONS OF EMPLOYEES

Most interviewees believed that many rights were denied them, as indicated by the row totals in Table 13.1 summing to a number several times larger than 100 percent. Excluding Right 6 since it was not coded as a right denied, the mean number of unmet rights per respondent was 3.5. In fact, every case portrayed multiple problem areas, with 20 percent containing two transgressions coded as moderately or strongly felt, 44 percent containing three rights, and 34 percent containing four or more. Complexity was the rule rather than the exception in our cases.

The most striking aspect of the figures in Table 13.1 is that each right was noted in at least a moderate percentage of the cases. Even the right to involvement in decision-making, a right on which the U.S. labor movement has traditionally deferred to management, was moderate or strong in almost one-fifth of the cases. Clearly, employees have an expansive view of their rights.

In the table, the most frequently cited unmet right (84 percent) was a legally inspired right (equitable treatment), while the right with the next highest incidence (74 percent) was the morally inspired right of timely information and responsiveness. Labeling these categories as legally or morally derived masks the fact that many of the employee expectations falling within those categories greatly exceeded what writ-

Table 13.1
Incidence of Denied Employee Rights

Right	Moderate or Strong	Weak	Total
1. Continued employment	14 (28%)	5 (10%)	38%
2. Equitable treatment	40 (80%)	2 (4%)	84%
3. Timely information and responses	34 (68%)	3 (6%)	74%
4. Autonomy and Privacy	13 (26%)	3 (6%)	32%
5. Reciprocal commitment	19 (38%)	5 (10%)	48%
6. Rebalance inequities	20 (40%)	10 (20%)	60%
7. Involvement in decisions	9 (18%)	5 (10%)	23%
8. Technical and managerial support	13 (26%)	11 (22%)	48%

ers in the field of employee rights have claimed as legitimate employee rights. For example, employees' views that they should be free from observation by management, even when one of their number was guilty of theft, go far beyond the claim that others have made to an employee right of privacy. Greasing rungs on a ladder to the catwalk would not be viewed as a legitimate action under virtually any previous conception of rights, yet some employees feel that in response to spying such actions are justified. Unreasonable or not, employees' expansive claims drive behavior that can be costly to their organizations.

THE GROWTH AND EXPRESSION OF CONFLICT

Organizations run a risk when they minimize the importance of a grievance. Our first example above, involving a divisional relocation, did not draw a costly response from employees. Quite the opposite occurred in our second case of an employee discharge. Despite management's actions being less threatening in scope and more clearly linked to efficiency than in the first case, the grievant's coworkers acted in a manner that proved exceedingly costly to the organization. Often, it is not the substance of a grievance that determines employee action; rather, it is how management responds to the complaint.

Each individual absorbs some distasteful conditions at work, so grievances generally appear only after an individual's tolerance threshold has been surpassed (Bouwen and Salipante, 1986). Since some organizations suppress grievances, based on the false assumption that a low level of grievances is a sign of success (Rowe and Baker, 1985), grievances that could easily be addressed by management often are not. They remain latent and accumulate so that the eventual confrontation becomes more intense and destructive (Walton, 1969). A self-reinforcing process can start for the organization's managers, in which painful experiences with massive problems motivate further suppression, in a vain attempt to avoid unpleasant experiences. From the subordinate's side, the individual feels a force to redress a deviation from an acceptable state (Adams, 1963) and is driven to reblance the situation. If there is no continuing exacerbation of the problem, an attenuation process probably occurs over time. However, if related incidents occur, months or even years later, accumulation mounts and the latent conflict can burst forth in full force. When accumulation finally results in a confrontation, the stated conflict seldom resembles its original form or root causes, making it difficult for management to accurately diagnose the problem.

We term the process by which conflict changes form "metamorphosis." Four basic types of metamorphosis have been identified from analysis of grievance cases:

1. *restatement* of an issue, to make it appear more legitimate or to increase the grievant's leverage;
2. *pressure tactics* to influence a decision, as discussed in the discharge example above;
3. acts of *retribution;* and
4. *compensatory acts* on the grievant's part, including *denigration* of superiors and various *defiant acts* such as invasion of a superior's privacy, sham performance or other forms of *effort reduction*, and *theft*.

Examples of Metamorphosis

Several types of metamorphosis have been noted in previous research. Restatement of grievances has been found to occur when it is necessary in order to bring the grievance before a particular forum, such as a civil rights agency (Salipante and Aram, 1984), or to address issues that are formally out of bounds or were previously settled in an unsatisfactory manner (Kuhn, 1980). Pressure tactics by unions have received the most attention, but unified actions certainly occur in nonunion settings. The threat or use of wildcat strikes, slowdowns, flooding the grievance procedure with complaints, and refusing overtime have all been described as part of the "fractional bargaining" process (Kuhn, 1961). It should be kept in mind that management is far from lacking in its own ability to use pressure tactics, possessing superior resources, the prerogative to set rules, and the ability to delay the appeal process. Pressure tactics can be difficult to distinguish from the third form of metamorphosis— retribution. When actions are taken to make management suffer with no real intention of altering a decision, then revenge appears as the sole motive. Sabotaging machines, turning the employer in for minor health and safety violations, and ridiculing promanagement employees can all be unilateral actions aimed at making the suffering mutual.

Compensatory acts, evident in many of our cases, appear to be an area deserving of discussion in greater detail. While effort reduction and theft have been alluded to in other literature, denigration and defiant acts are new and fertile ground. These unilateral actions include efforts to raise the employee's status or lower management's status, in the employee's mind, in order to restore an equitable balance. A material balance need not be struck; symbolic acts can carry great satisfaction for grievants, as two examples will illustrate.

The employees of a work group were tired of their autocratic supervisor. Upper-level management recognized the supervisor's people problems, but felt that matters would be worked out as the manager gained experience. One day, several of the group's members met in a storage area and began painting a picture of their supervisor on the wall with blue, yellow, and white Liquid Paper. Others soon joined in, adding some new colors with felt tip markers. The camaraderie and jovial atmosphere which appeared were in sharp contrast to the normally sullen tone. Underneath the portrait the title "Mis Management 19xx" was appended and a trophy was painted in her arms. A filing cabinet was moved to conceal the picture. When the painting was uncovered several months later, none of the employees were particularly interested in learning their supervisor's reaction. It was the social interaction and the defiant act itself that were paramount.

In another situation, a supervisor was viewed as lazy and incompetent. Frequent business trips were taken by the supervisor to a foreign country where her parents lived, but no sales were ever generated there. Rumors of a romantic involvement with one of the owners were frequently discussed as an explanation for recurrent three- and four-day weekends. Great resentment was expressed over their supervisor repeatedly meddling with documents generated by subordinates. Blocked by the romantic linkage from any direct appeal to top management, the employees responded by scrutinizing, characterizing, and criticizing every aspect of the supervisor's mannerisms, dress, and appearance. The group especially relished searching through the supervisor's office when she was away.

In both of these examples, the employees lowered the supervisor's status in their minds to rebalance the situation. When bilateral negotiations with the manager or a superior appeared fruitless, the grievants undertook compensatory acts on a unilateral basis. As is shown by the invasion of the second supervisor's privacy, when one or more of their rights have been denied, employees may rebalance the situation by denying a right to the opposing party.

The Incidence of Accumulation and Metamorphosis

In Chapter 8, supra, Alan Westin estimates that far less than 1 percent of those who feel unfairly treated pursue regulatory or legal action. Given the paucity of effective appeal systems in organizations, the inescapable implication is that there are many employees who feel that their conflict is unresolved. Our fifty cases were coded for evidence of accumulation and metamorphosis. Accumulation was found in 86 percent of the cases. Most of the grievances recounted to our interviewers were the result of a buildup of frustration over a substantial period of time. One grievant, while describing his grievance about a work assignment, unexpectedly offered the interviewer information about a prior and seemingly unrelated complaint involving a mode of dress required for safety reasons. This complaint had started two years earlier and was resolved in management's favor. However, it continued to bother the employee and evidently contributed to his filing of the work-assignment grievance.

Our cases showed ample evidence that employees feel they have the right to rebalance situations. If the rebalancing did not occur through negotiations with the other party, grievants frequently took it upon themselves to rebalance through one or another form of metamorphosis. Over one-half of the cases (58 percent) showed evidence of such metamorphosis: 14 percent showed restatement, 12 percent pressure tactics, 10 percent revenge, and fully 38 percent evidenced one or more forms of compensatory acts. Compensatory acts broke down as follows: denigration or defiant acts—16 percent; effort reduction—28 percent; and theft—6 percent.

These results suggest that no single form of metamorphosis dominates grievance cases, and that employees are creative in finding ways to rebalance their situations. All these forms of metamorphosis can be costly to organizations. For example, revenge can be devastating, as when one especially disgruntled engineer decided to sabotage a group project over a lengthy period of time, with nobody realizing that he had done so. Some acts of defiance and denigration can appear to be harmless, yet acts such as going through a supervisor's office when she is out of town reflect a lack of respect and a reduced willingness to accept a manager's directives or to put in extra effort for the good of the organization. With any form of metamophoris, the organization's "goodwill" among its own employees is eroded.

IMPLICATIONS FOR LEGAL ACTION

The Gap between Employee and Employer Expectations

A key question for organizations is "Why is there so much accumulation?" Our interviewers reported that at least one of every two people they interviewed could recount a serious problem they had personally experienced in the work environment within the last few years. Further, our results show that metamorphosis harmful to the organization occurs in a large percentage of these grievances. In the face of costs imposed by metamorphosis, many rights perceived by employees are still not being recognized by their employers.

In this volume's first chapter, Chimezie A. B. Osigweh, Yg., and Marcia P. Miceli argue that a recent and dramatic increase in employees' concern for workplace rights has occurred. When these concerns are unmatched by employer responses, a high incidence of accumulation is the result. If there is a wave of concern for employee rights, why have many employers not responded effectively? We offer two possible answers. One is that employers do not take into account the costs of unsatisfactory grievance outcomes. The second, which will be addressed in the section below, is that laws and court precedents are not sufficiently broad or pervasive to encourage managerial attention to true organizational justice.

Concerning employers' perceptions, we have conducted interviews with superiors involved in grievance situations. While these cases are not reported here, it appears from some of the interviews that many managers are not aware, until it is too late to prevent them, of the costs of employees getting even. Often, the costs are relatively intangible, untraceable, and spread over a lengthy period of time. Such was the case in our "Mis Management" grievance, where the gradual deterioration in a superior-subordinate relationship resulted from accumulation and denigration. When subordinates engage in covert, unilateral rebalancing, it is difficult for management to realize the costs or to attribute the costs to their own unresponsiveness.

The difficulty of perceiving the costs and attributing their causes is not the entire problem. Subordinates often give direct signals to superiors, which the superiors largely ignore or label as normal griping. One reason for the indifference is that managers do not *want* to perceive activities that collectively subvert organizational procedures (Dalton, 1959) or restrict output (Mathewson, 1969). In Mathewson's work, many managers reported that output restriction had been a problem in the past but was not at present, due to new procedures that had been instituted. Mathewson's own interviews with workers proved the managers wrong. While Melville Dalton and Mathewson are not explicit on managers' reasons for denying counterproductive activities, it appears that managers want to believe that they are in control of the work situations for which they are personally responsible. Some means must be found to make such unwilling observers aware of the costs of grievance accumulation.

The Limited Potential of Legal Action

The grievance cases analyzed for this study make clear that, in many cases, current laws are not causing managers to meet employees' expectations of their rights. Why is this, and how far could strengthened laws and court precedents go toward meeting employees' expectations? In some of our cases in which managers were interviewed, managers whose general tendency was to be unresponsive to employee complaints went to great lengths to settle cases in which they feared equal employment opportunity (EEO) risks. In certain cases, then, the threat of legal action can motivate employers toward greater concern for employee rights. Much depends on the particular nature of the legislation, as the earlier chapters by Jack Steiber (Chapter 3), Henry Perritt (Chapter 4), and Rebecca A. (Baysinger) Thacker and Stuart A. Youngblood (Chapter 5) demonstrate.

Experience with previous legislation bearing on the employment relationship suggests that managerial action does not always follow the intent of legal action. When employers feel that it is not in their interest—economic or personal—to adopt the spirit of legislation, they frequently find a means to bypass the law and avoid legal sanctions. The employment-at-will area provides the latest example of such organizational tendencies. While management has taken notice of some of the large unjust-dismissal awards, only a very select group of companies has decided to reform their personnel policies to provide better employee protection. Rather, the predominant reaction has been to withdraw possibly troublesome phrases from personnel manuals or to require employees to sign agreements stating that they may be terminated at will (Stieber, 1985). In some cases, terminated employees are offered severance benefits contingent on the waiver of future legal claims over the discharge (St. Antoine, 1985).

This defensive reaction is historically predictable. When *Griggs* v. *Duke Power Company* (1971) and its subsequent applications held that employers must validate selection criteria if adverse impact exists, many employers responded by discarding selection tests and making sure that their equal employment opportunity (EEO) numbers came out right. The alternative would have been to adopt personnel procedures, such as valid selection tests, that would have improved individual justice and EEO. The numbers-oriented response by employers saved money and avoided legal costs in the short run, but at the expense of decreased efficiency and poorer EEO attainment in the long run (Salipante and Aram, 1978; Schmidt and Hunter, 1980).

In the labor relations area, much the same picture of limited legal effectiveness has emerged. From both the legal and the moral perspectives, one would expect that employers would recognize the unfair labor practices set forth in the National Labor Relations Act, causing charges and violations to fall over time. However, the number of unfair labor practice charges has risen fourfold between 1960 and 1980. With a relatively constant level of union representation election activity over this twenty-year period, the number of employees awarded back pay or ordered reinstated rose fivefold (Freeman and Medoff, 1984). Some companies have repeatedly violated the law with threats, wiretapping, and discharges in order to intimidate employees (Kovach, 1979). While raising the penalties might reduce some of the more blatant violations, obstinate employers could still frustrate the intent of the law. For example, although yellow-dog contracts are illegal, employers can attempt to select antiunion employees through psychological profiles and background information, then watch them closely for danger signs during their probationary periods (Lagerfeld, 1981).

The implication of the above is that employee rights legislation, even if it were much stronger than appears likely in the foreseeable future, will produce defensive responses on the part of organizations and, at best, move only partially toward improved organizational justice.

Dealing with Expansive Expectations

The picture that emerges from grievance cases is that some employees have an extremely broad view of their rights in the workplace, despite the fact that many of their expectations are not met. From what sources do these expansive, if unmet, expectations arise? While Osigweh and Miceli's chapter points to many of the causes of an increase in expectations over the last several years, our view is that expansive expectations are more than a recent phenomenon. One possibility is that the expectations are the result of psychological processes, in particular the blaming of others for what has happened to oneself. Neither external legal standards nor well-developed organizational systems for due process could eliminate this source of unmet expectations. Other sources are the broad concepts of justice in our society's civil and criminal justice systems. Individuals carry these concepts with them into the work setting. Some of these concepts can be and have been mirrored in organizations' internal justice systems, such as the use of an impartial judge in the final (arbitration) stage of unionized grievance systems. Ironically, a final source of broad expectations may be the growing adoption by organizations of participative management policies. As the character of the superior-subordinate relationship improves, more conflict may surface as employees develop higher expectations of managerial treatment (Fortado, 1985).

The results from our fifty cases indicate that many employee expectations seem to spring from moral rather than legal sources. Note in Table 13.1 the number of cases in which the morally derived rights of responsiveness, autonomy, and reciprocal commitment were expected but deemed to be lacking. Laws are not likely to attend to such rights, especially since legislation must be concerned with employers' prerogatives (Perritt, Chapter 4, supra). Even strong union contracts, which go further in securing employee rights than any legal action is likely to, cannot assure proper attention to morally derived issues. The adversarial relationship typically found in union-management situations creates a zero-sum game outlook which impedes the granting of autonomy and makes reciprocal commitment a point of argument rather than of collaboration.

In sum, legal action cannot approach the breadth or depth of employees' expectations of their rights. Even when more than the basic rights are guaranteed in law, employee expectations will far outstrip those rights.

IMPLICATIONS FOR ORGANIZATIONAL ACTION

To the degree that employees' expectations of their rights are not respected by organizations, accumulation and metamorphosis will take place. Metamorphosis is not desired by employers, to whom it is costly, nor by employees, who resort to it primarily because the original or root issue has not been addressed. The unsatisfactory nature of metamorphosis to both employer and employee provides an opportunity for everyone involved to gain through development of effective due process within the organization. That is, it is in the best interests of grievants and organizations to develop approaches that ensure a high standard of organizational justice.

There is indeed much incentive for organizations to engage in voluntarism, as Alan Westin has argued in Chapter 8, supra. The question that remains is how to help organizations and their operating managers move toward a higher standard. Westin has indicated that the movement toward a different, more participative style of management facilitates managerial concern with organizational justice. Part and parcel of the new organizational philosophies and cultures that are slowly being developed should be a high valuation of effective conflict management. Organizational philosophies and procedures can create incentives for individual managers to seriously examine individual grievance cases according to expansive standards of fairness that are broadly accepted by the organization's members. The discussion in Chapter 7, supra, by Richard W. Humphreys, Frederick A. Zeller, and Sarah S. Etherton concerning the lack of impact of a positive discipline procedure demonstrates the fallacy of instituting new employee rights procedures without commensurate changes in managerial values. A growing literature discusses organizational culture and socialization processes for all levels of employees.

A complementary approach, consistent with this study, is for academics and expert practitioners to perform research that makes visible the economic costs to organizations of poor attention to employees' perceptions of their rights. Such studies may encourage organizations that are leaning toward a philosophy that embraces effective conflict management. Similarly, researchers and organizations can create measurement tools that make more visible the costs of metamorphosis. With the expanded scope of human resource data bases, the basis for such tools is already at hand in many organizations. Once the measures are available, the indicators of ineffective conflict management should be tied to individual organizational subunits. For example, rates of turnover, absenteeism, transfers into and out of a unit, and the step at which formal grievances are settled can serve as indicators of effective or ineffective conflict management (Aram, Salipante, and Knauf, 1987). By examining trends in these indicators over time for particular organizational units, feedback can be provided to managers about some of the consequences of their attention to subordinate complaints.

In terms of managerial response to specific complaints, the complexity of the cases in our sample suggests that each issue should be carefully defined and distinctly addressed by the organization. Otherwise, portions of the problem will continue to fester and become part of an ongoing accumulation of frustrations. As depicted in Figure 13.1, current organizational practices (broken ellipse in the figure) may address many legally derived rights, but relatively few of the rights proposed by the moral and practical perspective. Managers should aspire to cover a broader range of rights. While a significant zone of unattainable expectations will always exist, employer practices could be greatly expanded to dramatically reduce accumulation and metamorphosis.

A final suggestion is that organizations provide a budget for the adjustment of meritorious grievances. Mistakes in the distribution of rewards and sanctions are inevitable in human systems. By providing a contingency fund, organizations can more easily enact needed remedies. Such a fund also signals to all levels of managers that attention to organizational justice (and the remedying of occasional lapses in providing justice) is expected.

Acceding to all employees' expectations of their rights is unrealistic

Figure 13.1
Actual Employer Practices and the Zone of Unfulfilled Expectations

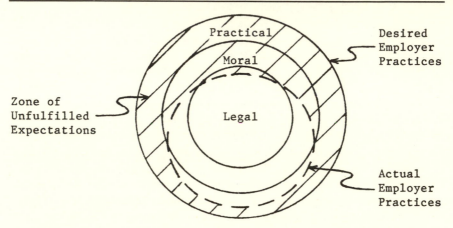

for organizations. Nevertheless, even those expectations that appear highly unreasonable to management must be addressed in order to reduce accumulation and metamorphosis. Our cases indicate that it would be in their own interests for organizations to pay greater attention to the eight rights we have outlined, and to inculcate in their managers a readiness to respond to grievants' demands for those rights. Otherwise, many employees will continue to feel that they are treated unjustly, and their organizations will continue to bear costs of which they are largely unaware.

14

A Social Constructionist and Political Economic Perspective of Employee Rights

_____ WALTER R. NORD

Books by David W. Ewing (1977) and Alan F. Westin and Stephen Salisbury (1980) have played an important role in placing employee rights on the academic agenda in the management discipline. For the most part, these treatments focus attention on important matters of the macrosocial context such as law, property rights, and national policy. This approach—which I call the contextual view—has already contributed much.

As others in this volume (e.g., Osigweh and Miceli, Chapter 1; Gordon and Coulson, Chapter 2; and Scott, Chapter 12) have observed, however, the agenda is incomplete and needs to be expanded. To suggest that the established approach is incomplete does not deny its continuing importance. The contextual variables it treats are crucial in the quest for employee rights. However, I believe the approach is insensitive to social processes that influence the creation and exercise of rights. The process elements I will address are central to achieving what Jurgen Habermas (1971) termed "emancipation"—the ability of people to exercise self-conscious control over their own outcomes.

Among other things, these processes affect the real rights people have—rights are forged and destroyed through social action. As Eric Hobsbawm (1984) observed: "Rights don't exist in the abstract, but only where people demand them or may be assumed to be aware of their

*Insightful comments on earlier drafts of this chapter from Elizabeth Doherty, Patrick Keleher, Jr., and Ann Nord are gratefully acknowledged.

lack" (p. 298). Moreover, rights "are not abstract, universal and unchanging. They exist as parts of particular sets of beliefs in the minds of men and women about the nature of human society and the ordering of relations between human beings within it" (p. 299). For the present chapter, "beliefs" is a very important word, because it directs our attention to the mutual influence of beliefs and the social processes that help to create them.

Given this view of rights and the goal of emancipation, the major thesis of this chapter can be summarized as follows: Traditionally, academics who have treated employee rights have tended to focus on law, philosophy, ethics, etc. While these are vital topics, such treatments are often broad and abstract. As Henry H. Perritt, Jr. (Chapter 4, supra) argued, the history of employment law in the United States has been characterized by the struggle of various interests to have their agendas recognized legally. Even more important, such treatments overlook the microlevel events that determine de facto rights. More specifically, even when laws are written, the laws are not automatically enforceable; even when policies and guidelines are issued, they do not thereby become *priorities* in day-to-day human activities. In fact, even when procedures are developed and signed into contracts, the procedures do not automatically get activated. In reality their activation is influenced by what individuals pay attention to, and most individuals have a variety of priorities and responsibilities in a milieu of organizational routines and partially conflicting objectives.

A particular aspect of exercising one's rights is what economists have called the agency problem. Even when enforcement of a person's rights is the formal responsibility of one's agent, such as a union official who is charged with representing the interests of union members, the agent usually has a number of other interests to attend to. The agent is constantly called on to make tradeoffs. Such tradeoffs are realities in all human organizations—the control of agents (the central problem addressed by agency theorists) is not limited to owners of capital. Managing one's agents is simply one component of the social processes that affect the de facto rights experienced in a social system—even a social system where such contextual factors as laws have been constructed in a manner that supports employee rights.

In short, the contextual factors cannot guarantee rights in a complex institution. Ultimately, even in a favorable institutional context, employee rights depend on the ability of individuals to take advantage of what the context provides—to be effective actors in complex social systems. Even if all the problems of context were to be resolved in favor of individual rights, the efficacy of individuals would still play a crucial role. Even if laws were readily enforceable, policies somehow did translate automatically into priorities, procedures were easily activated, and the agency problem did not exist, the detection of violation would still often be left to the individual. He/she would need to be aware of what rights truly prevail and to recognize the mismatch between these rights and what was happening at his/her workplace.

If these microlevel processes are so important in determining experienced rights, a number of questions emerge. For example: What are the characteristics of individuals who are effective in advancing their own interests and exercising their rights? What attributes of context might be important for the effective exercise of rights at the micro- as well as at the macrolevel of analysis?

I propose that an *interpretive/critical political economic perspective* can provide some useful guidance for answering these and related questions. In this chapter, I will describe this perspective and show how it can serve as a useful complement to the usual contextual approach to employee rights.

THE INTERPRETIVE/CRITICAL POLITICAL ECONOMIC PERSPECTIVE

The interpretive/critical political economic perspective combines three major intellectual themes: (1) the role of interpretation in the construction of social reality, (2) the goal of increasing the degree to which human beings control their own lives, and (3) the influence of macrolevel political/economic events on behavior at microlevels. In essence, it has two components. One component consists of what Linda L. Putnam (1983) called the *interpretative* approach, which focuses mainly on subjective social reality. As we will see, this first component consists of two schools of the interpretive approach—the naturalistic and the critical interpretivists. The second component can best be labeled as a *critical political/ economic* approach. It is concerned with objective social reality and emphasizes changing objective conditions so as to increase the chances for individuals to exercise conscious self-control over significant aspects of their lives. The two components overlap in that the critical interpretivists are also committed to the emancipatory goal.

The Interpretive Approach

During the last decade or so, organizational theorists have come to view organizations quite differently than before. This change in perception owes much to what Putnam (1983) described as the interpretive perspective. For interpretivists, the meanings that people give to their ongoing experiences constitute the operating reality of social systems, including organizations. Of particular interest are the processes through which members of a social system create social reality and function within it.

As Putnam noted, the interpretive perspective contains two related schools of thought. Members of both schools of the interpretive approach assume that human subjective experience plays a dominant role in creating social and organizational reality. However, the two schools differ in their major objectives.

The Naturalistic-Interpretive View

The more influential of these two schools, at least in the United States, has been what Putnam called the naturalists. In her words, the naturalists "aim to generate insights, to explain events, and to seek understanding" (p. 47). Leaders in developing this approach have been David Silverman (1970) and Karl E. Weick (1979). The essential features of the naturalist view that are central to this chapter can be highlighted by quoting a few key ideas of these two scholars. Silverman (1970) wrote:

Action arises out of meanings which define social reality. . . . Meanings are given to men by their society. Shared orientations become institutionalized and are experienced as social facts. . . . Particular constellations of meaning are only sustained by continual reaffirmation in everyday actions. . . . Through their interaction men also modify, change and transform social meanings. . . . It follows that explanations of human actions must take account of the meanings which those concerned assign to their acts; the manner in which the everyday world is socially constructed yet perceived as real and routine becomes a crucial concern for sociological analysis (p. 127).

Weick (1979) provided a series of creative insights about the *process* through which these meanings get constructed in organizations. (The word process is highlighted to reflect Weick's interest in organizing rather than organizations per se.) Selected key elements for understanding Weick's view of the relationship between the creation of meaning and organizing include:

Equivocal information triggers organizing. Efforts to stabilize meanings for equivocal displays typically involve the efforts of two or more people. Most efforts at sensemaking involve interpretation of previous happenings and of writing plausible histories that link these previous happenings with current outcomes. . . . Organizations have a major hand in creating the realities which they then view as "facts" to which they must accommodate. . . . Events in organizations are held together and regulated by dense, circular, lengthy strands of causality perceived by members (p. 13).

In short, individuals are constantly attempting to know what the stimuli they encounter "mean"—to make sense out of them (see Kavanagh,

Chapter 10, supra). People's own actions and those of others become stimuli that contribute to the emergence of a shared set of beliefs. The fact that these shared beliefs (social reality) were created by actors in the system does not, under most circumstances, make it easy for the participants to free themselves from its effects. (As Humphreys, Zeller, and Etherton noted in Chapter 7, supra, beliefs people have held in the past can impact how they implement procedures—such as a program of positive discipline—in such a way that they often see little or no change). The institutions, the language, and the interaction patterns that emerge out of social exchange are accepted as given and therefore are as controlling as they would be if they were absolute.

Interpretive-Critical View

The critical school, which Putnam (1983, p. 47) described as aiming "to free individuals from sources of domination and repression," is the second, and to date less influential component of the interpretative view. The critical writers have discussed a number of assumptions about organizations that previously were latent in the mainstream of inquiry. Their primary concerns have been the roles organizations play in social control and the liberative role that social science could play in modern society.

In comparison to the naturalists, the critical writers are more likely to take the influence of some macrosocial and institutional factors on the creation of meaning as problematic. Whereas the naturalists tend to focus mainly on how organizing builds upward from the individual and interpersonal relationships, the critical writers are more apt to discuss the downward effects of larger social units (e.g., society). Moreover, the liberative goal that underlies the critical school is associated with a pejorative view of the institutions that shape the current construction of social reality. Existing institutions are seen as interfering with the ability of people to exercise conscious self-control over their personal and collective outcomes. The concerns of these writers are closely related to Antonio Gramsci's (1971) treatment of hegemony. For example, the critical writers devote a great deal of attention to ideology as a mechanism of social control. As Stanley Deetz and Astrid Kersten (1983) observed, the critical writers see ideology as stabilizing and legitimating of the existing social order. Ideology is a source of social control that obscures contradictions in the social order and as Deetz and Kersten wrote, "mystifies the nature of the existing order either by covering up motives and interests or through reification and alienation" (p. 164).

Members of the critical school also maintain that social construction is affected by an assumed social conflict and that any given definition of reality benefits some people more than others. (For example, if trade restrictions are defined as necessary for future national defense, those who benefit from the restrictions have a much easier time gaining and maintaining them than if the restrictions are defined as profiteering.)

Beyond the Interpretative View

It is unlikely that one committed to emancipating people from all the forces that constrain their abilities to control their own outcomes will stay within the bounds of a purely interpretive approach. At some point, attention would likely shift to matters of political economy that influence what might be called objective social reality such as certain components of power and dependence.

Power and dependency are at the core of political economy, and since the net power of an actor in a social system is a function of the number of alternative sources of resources that he/she has to choose from, opportunities for choice become a central concern. If, for instance, the unemployment rate increases, the typical worker has fewer alternative employers. Consequently, he/she is more dependent on any particular employer, and is relatively less powerful than when jobs are more readily available. Thus, any realistic approach to issues of emancipation (such as work rights), even an approach that attaches substantial importance to the interpretative perspective, must be more than just interpretive. The second component of the framework advanced in this chapter emphasizes the importance of adding "objective elements" to the interpretative perspective.

Combining "objective" elements and a subjective view in the same framework raises a thorny philosophical issue. Why are some things assumed to be real and others not? This question cannot be addressed here except to note that there is some basis for such an integration in the realist view of science (see W.G. Scott's treatment in Chapter 12, supra). Stewart Clegg (1983), drawing heavily on the philosophical work of Roy Bhaskar, described the realist position as recognizing that while knowledge is a social product by antecedent social products, the objects from which knowledge is produced exist and act independently of people. The perspective advanced in this chapter rests on such a premise— it is assumed that both objective and subjective realities play important roles in social behavior and that the importance of each varies across events, conditions, and phenomena being taken as problematic. Having already explored the subjective aspect of rights, I turn to the objective elements highlighted by political economics.

The Critical Political Economic Component

This component is rooted in Karl Marx's famous statement in his "Theses on Feuerbach" (Easton and Guddat, 1967): "The philosophers have only *interpreted* the world in various ways; the point is, to *change* it" (p. 402). In seeking to change the real conditions of existence, the thrust of the political economic component parallels the emphasis the contextual approach gives to advancing rights by intervention through laws, national policy, and other macrolevel changes. While it parallels the work of the critical interpretivists in their pursuit of human emancipation, its macrofocus leads to the consideration of how aspects of the larger political and economic system affect the substance, process, means, and outcomes of the struggle over employee rights. Thus, it complements the interpretive component by stressing that politics, economics, and law do indeed make a difference. A synthesis of the interpretive component and the political economic component provides a useful perspective for examining employee rights.

AN INTERPRETIVE/CRITICAL POLITICAL ECONOMIC PERSPECTIVE ON EMPLOYEE RIGHTS

The interpretive/critical political economic approach directs attention to the dynamic interaction of micro- and macrolevel factors that contribute to both social stability and change. Moreover, it argues that both objective and subjective elements contribute to interpretation of micro- and macrolevel conditions. Finally, it is committed to emancipation or self-conscious control. In applying this perspective to employee rights, analysis of the social constructions and reifications surrounding some fundamental words and concepts is a logical starting point.

Social Construction and Reification of Basic Concepts

The interpretive/critical perspective attempts to uncover socially constructed, reified, and hegemonic features in social discourse. In particular, it analyzes how the words or labels that are applied to a stimulus or process contribute to meaning. Discussions of employee rights contain a number of concepts/words/labels that are prime candidates for such analysis. Here I will examine three illustrative ones—the concepts of rights and employees and the basic distinctions between government and nongovernment.

Rights

The interpretive/critical approach calls attention to the historical relativity of the substance of rights and reveals the use of the word "rights" as a political tool. Consistent with Hobsbawm's (1984) view of rights as beliefs that order social relationships, a right is seen as a special type of claim that some set of individuals can make in a particular social system at a given time. In this view, almost anything can be stipulated as a right for almost any reason. People can be said to have a right to live and a right to die, or a right to take the life of someone else who also has a right to live. There can be "absolute" rights and rights that exist under only some conditions. However, even an *absolute* right that all people may be said to have can become a *relative* right by defining some people as "nonpeople" (e.g., slaves), or by appealing to some other right. Obviously, any particular rights will be unique to certain historical circumstances. As Eugene Kamenka (1978) observed: "The concept of human rights is an historical product which evolved in Europe, out of foundations in Christianity, Stoicism and Roman law, . . . but which gains force and direction only with the contractual and pluralist nature of European feudalism, church struggles and the rise of Protestantism and of cities" (p. 6).

In this sense, rights may be viewed as firmly rooted social norms. Although rights are "only" social norms, they are especially potent norms—they are accorded a high degree of explicit legitimacy. Because they are so potent, social actors have incentives to have norms that reflect their interests accepted as rights by significant social actors, since in James W. Nickel's (1978–79) words: "Rights generally involve high-powered norms that can trump other value considerations" (p. 151). It is clearly to a person's advantage if he/she can justify a claim to something by labeling it in a way that induces others to accept the claim without dispute. As Mary Gibson (1983) put it:

Rights, in our world, are important as tools or handles for people to grasp in pressing their needs as these take shape and manifest themselves in the face of existing and changing circumstances. This is partly because the language of rights is the language most people speak in these contexts. There are reasons for that, too. One of the places people must fight out conflicts in our society is the courts. . . . Since the courts are the primary upholders of legal rights, and rights are the primary legal tools or weapons of self-defense, the rights-oriented perspective is very influential in the way people perceive and define their situations. . . . If one can get one's position hooked securely to a right, one has something relatively firm to hang on to (pp. 134–35).

Rights, seen in this way, have mixed consequences for increasing the conscious control that human beings exercise over their own outcomes. On the one hand, they are means for instituting very strong pressures for actualizing certain central values, such as when the rights of free speech and press protect society against actions that could constrain the pursuit of self-direction. On the other hand, rights can serve to reify certain social relationships. Gibson (1983) argued this point insightfully: "There are some ways in which the appeal to rights may circumscribe our thinking and have a conservative influence. Often when complex social issues are cast in terms of competing or conflicting rights, the question becomes simply which right outweighs the other. This can distort the issue and deflect attention from other relevant factors and important questions" (p. 136).

Gibson also asserted that the language of rights is, in fact, used by people to help divide and conquer opposition in the workplace. To illustrate, Gibson observed how in dealing with striking hospital employees, hospital administrators often find it useful to frame discussion in terms of competing rights—the right to strike versus the right of patients to medical care. Such a tactic can shift attention away from the essence of the dispute between the employees and the administration. Moreover, by emphasizing the conflicting rights between two relatively powerless groups (in this case the patients and the workers), the focus on rights can reduce the chances that these groups will discover areas where they have common interests vis-à-vis the administration. Consequently, they are less apt to act in concert against the administration.

From these examples, it is clear that the language of rights has important political uses. In fact, there is a very close relationship between rights and interests. In essence, rights are norms that are given a special label—rights. People whose interests are furthered by the special recognition given by this label strive for this advantage. From the critical perspective, such labels are in conflict with the exercise of conscious control because they make it appear that the norm represents something more than the underlying interests. Therefore, in attempting to advance emancipation, use of words such as "claims" or "interests" that avoid the mystifying and reifying entailment of the word "rights" are advocated.

Finally, the interpretive/critical view sensitizes one to the reactionary, nonemancipatory outcomes of some rights in a given social system. As Hobsbawm (1984) argued, the classical concept of rights has usually meant freedom from interference and therefore has often been much more useful to opponents than to advocates of social change. In other words, rights are constraints on the state that prevent it from limiting the ability of an individual to behave in a certain way. Often, however, actions of the state that limit the actions of some individuals advance the interests of some disadvantaged groups. For example, when an employer's rights to hire and fire are unconstrained, he/she is free to use criteria that are sexist or racist. In such cases, the employer's rights can be construed as in conflict with the rights of others. In short, constraining the rights of some may enhance the rights of others; increasing rights of some does not always lead to greater rights for the collectivity.

Employee

Like "rights," the word "employee" also describes a social relationship—a relationship that is paramount in the daily lives of most adults in our society. As with rights, the meaning of employee—the actual experience of the employment relationship—is, to a large degree, the outcome of an interpretive process.

An important part of this social construction emerges through anticipatory socialization. Through families, schools, churches, and other social institutions, as well as through observation and informal interactions, individuals learn what to expect in the world of work, including what behaviors will be rewarded, punished, ignored, etc. In an organizational society such as ours, people learn about hierarchy, rules, and what will be expected of them in an organization. While some commonalities are created, the process is not completely determined or fixed; all individuals do not learn exactly the same things. Moreover, expectations change over time (Yankelovich, 1981) as reality and interpretations of reality change. Nevertheless, people come to share many beliefs about what it means to be an employee.

These shared understandings often have a built-in potential to victimize those who hold them. The ethnomethodologist Harold Garfinkel's (1967) discussion of the "cultural dope" illustrates this process well. Garfinkel found, for example, that people can often gain lower prices through bargaining in such settings as department stores. However, people seldom bargain in these settings because they have been socialized to view such behavior as inappropriate.

Socialization into the role of employee could have analogous dysfunctional side effects. Numerous social critics (e.g., Pope, 1942; Bowles and Gintis, 1976) have argued that churches and schools have socialized people to accept a variety of constraints on their behavior that make them "better" employees, when better is defined as complying with the routines of organizations. In this manner, the label "employee" is associated with inclinations to accept limits imposed by an employer as legitimate and to reify them. These limits could well be arbitrary and unnecessary. The interpretive/critical view is concerned with elucidating the social construction of these meanings and enabling individuals to avoid arbitrary constraints that limit human choices.

It is worth noting that not only does the socially constructed meaning of "employee" have implications for the exercise of choice, but that labels used to classify employees have direct, legal consequences. An example—one that is currently very important with the increased hiring of part-time employees—is the distinction between full- and part-timers. Part-time employees have far more limited protections than do their full-time counterparts. The ability of employers to "assign" people to one of these categories has significant consequences on the quality and quantity of rights people have in the workplace. In short, labels have direct consequences upon employee rights.

Governments: Public and Private

The types and degrees of control organizations have exercised over members of society change over time. When one considers the existence of company towns in the not-too-distant past, the conventional wisdom that work organizations exert more influence on people's lives today than in the past may not be totally accurate. Nevertheless, some writers (e.g., Nord, 1983) have commented on the influence organizations exercise on our daily lives. Others have pointed to their macrolevel power; Robert A. Dahl (1970) and Charles E. Lindblom (1977) have discussed the enormous de facto influence that corporations have on government decisions. Some others, including Charles E. Merriam (1944) and Sanford A. Lakoff and Daniel Rich (1973), have gone so far as to say that many large organizations function as private governments—exercising enormous power with little accountability. Such unconstrained organizational influence led David W. Ewing (1977) to describe employee rights as a "black hole" in human rights.

While Ewing's position is well recognized in the rights literature, the interpretive/critical perspective gives it a new twist by emphasizing that the distinction between what is believed to be the province of government and what is believed to be private is, in large measure, socially constructed. Moreover, the social construction is neither random nor neutral with respect to the satisfaction of interests. The labels function as tools in the struggle for influence by obscuring the underlying social processes.

The outcomes of contests to frame things as private matters (and therefore not susceptible to influence by parties outside a given exchange) or as public (and therefore subject to more general influence) play a major role in determining whose interests *are* dominant. Although there are some benefits from distinguishing between what is government and what is private, to the degree that the distinction becomes reified and obscures the social dynamics, it reduces the opportunity for conscious self-control. Again, the critical perspective pushes for recognition that the frames are tools in the struggle of conflicting interests.

Summary and Conclusions

The interpretive/critical political economic perspective assumes that human action is in large measure a function of the meaning that people give to stimuli in their environment and that these meanings are influenced by the labels that are assigned to stimuli. Consequently, it leads to consideration of why the socially constructed meaning of terms in discussions of employee rights has important consequences and rec-

ognition of how words and labels become tools in the contest for influence, often by obscuring the concrete and specific interests under more
abstract and general concepts or labels. The labels influence how things
are framed and hence how they are interpreted. The labels induce attention to some things and inattention to others. They influence actions
and decisions by affecting perceptions—perceptions of what is figure
(and hence attended to) and what is ground (and hence left unattended).
Seldom are the labels neutral consequences of the various interpretations
equally favorable to conflicting interests. Therefore, social actors have
incentives to impose labels that favor their interests—to construct social
reality in their favor. Clearly these processes of social construction must
be central to inquiry and intervention concerning any social issue; here
our attention is limited to the workplace.

THE EXERCISE OF RIGHTS AND PURSUIT OF INTERESTS AT WORK

One consequence of, in fact I believe one of the important contributions of, the interpretive/critical perspective is a blurring of the distinction between rights and interests. The perspective, as I have suggested,
views a right as a label assigned to an interest that has achieved the
legitimacy of an explicit social norm. In this sense, rights are a special
class of interests. In addition, there is a second source of blurring from
the tendency of people who, in attempting to advance their interests,
refer to these interests as rights before they are acknowledged as rights
by the rest of the collectivity. Because of these types of blurring, there
is a problem in discussing how the interpretive/critical political economic
perspective may inform discussions of employee rights.

The problem stems from the fact that people with whom one is discussing use the term rights in a more absolutistic sense and have a
definite list of interests in mind. Because the discussion of a current
issue—such as employee rights—is framed by this more absolutistic
usage, and a definite list of interests, it is difficult to apply the interpre-
tive/critical view without either being inconsistent with the essence of
the perspective or taking the matters others call "rights" and relabeling
them as interests. To do the latter in the concluding chapter of a book
on employee rights would sacrifice coherence. As a result, I simply
accept the conventional use of the term rights and address the particular
interests that have achieved the label of rights in the literature on employee rights.

These topics are considered in two major sections. The first treats the
processes of social construction at the microlevel. These processes affect
the meaning that people individually and collectively give the stimuli
in their immediate environment. These meanings are important because

they affect the recognition of the relationship between ongoing events and interests and the manner in which interests can be defended and advanced. The second section discusses the objective conditions, many of which are operating at the level of the national and world political economy, that affect the costs of pursuing one's rights or interests.

Social Construction and Exercise of Rights at Microlevels

The exercise of rights at the microlevel depends on the meaning that participants in a social setting (such as employees in a work group) assign to the stimuli they encounter. Such meaning is affected by many elements, including personal attributes of people, formal structure and unobtrusive control in organizations, and technology and physical conditions.

Personal Attributes

A great deal is known about the attributes of individuals that influence their abilities to control their own destinies. Quite likely, these attributes will affect how effective people are in winning and exercising rights. For present purposes, the major attributes are divided into personality characteristics and social skills.

Personality characteristics. Much has been written about the attributes of individuals that are apt to be associated with behaviors that will shape and reshape objective and subjective social realities. Martin E. P. Seligman's (1975) work on learned helplessness, Richard de Charms' (1968, 1976) research on personal causation, and Ellen Langer's (1983) investigations of the perception of control are but three of the major research programs in mainstream psychology that have focused on the acquisition and consequences of beliefs about the ability to influence one's outcomes. From this body of research it is safe to conclude that individuals' perceptions about control have a major impact on their behavior. This research also indicates that these perceptions can be altered in ways that increase the propensity of individuals to exercise control. Similarly, techniques in psychotherapy (e.g., Ellis and Harper, 1970) are known to increase the influence that people exercise over their lives by changing how they think about the consequences of their actions. It can be concluded that (1) there are individual differences in the inclination to attempt to influence organization outcomes, (2) that these inclinations can be changed, and (3) that changes in the inclinations will be associated with actual changes in the quality of one's existence. In short, people can be taught to exercise control.

On the other hand, more sociologically oriented research has suggested that existing institutions teach large numbers of individuals *not* to exercise control over their own lives. For example, Richard Sennett and Jonathan Cobb (1972) and Sennett (1980) have demonstrated that a class-linked socialization process produces a working class whose members lack self-esteem and are psychologically unable to challenge authority. Based on extensive interviews with working-class people, Sennett and Cobb (1972) concluded that

> society injures human dignity in order to weaken people's ability to fight against the limits class imposes on their freedom . . . the use of badges of ability or of sacrifices is to divert men from challenging the limits on their freedom by convincing them that they must *first* become legitimate, must achieve dignity on a class society's terms, in order to have the right to challenge the terms themselves (p. 153).

Other scholars have come to parallel conclusions. L. Richard Della Fave (1980) asserted that the willingness to challenge the legitimacy of a social order is a positive function of one's self-evaluation and that existing social institutions induce individuals located at low levels in the social hierarchy to evaluate themselves negatively. Finally, Robert E. Lane (1979) argued that the minimal number of attempts to withhold legitimacy in modern society is due to an overdeveloped agentic capacity (i.e., an unquestioning obedience to authority figures) which is produced by existing market and governance processes.

Overall, then, individuals differ in their willingness to attempt to delegitimate an existing set of social relationships, and there is reason to believe that such a "powerlessness syndrome" may be overly represented in lower socioeconomic groups. To the degree that this is true, individuals whose interests are apt to be underrepresented in the existing definition of rights are the ones least prepared to address such matters. Accordingly, since the effective exercise of rights depends upon those whose interests are being sacrificed realigning the prevailing social reality, massive resocialization may be necessary.

Social skills. Individuals, even within a social stratum, have unequal abilities to influence a social system. Much research about individual differences in these skills exists, mostly under the heading of leadership. Despite the volume of research, however, the modern study of leadership may have bypassed certain skills that are essential in the struggle for rights.

Most recent treatments of leadership in social science have centered on what Edwin P. Hollander (1985) called "positional leadership"—the study of people who are assigned to established roles to direct the activities of others. Such research contributes to our knowledge of individuals who mobilize effort to achieve goals within existing systems with structures already in place, but does not inform us about individuals who play important roles in mobilizing efforts in unstructured situations by helping to *articulate* the ends. In short, we may have studied managers more than leaders.

Although there may be considerable overlap in substance between the skills that make one an effective manager/supervisor and those that would help one successfully orchestrate a process for lower-level participants to express their interests effectively, Abraham Zaleznik (1977) has argued persuasively that the attributes of leaders and managers may be quite different. In any case, there has been relatively little attention given to the understanding and cultivation of the skills that might make one an effective *insurgent leader*—a person who delegitimates and relegitimates social relationships in ways that advance the rights/interests of individuals and groups who may not be well represented by existing institutions.

Some preliminary insights into these skills can be found in discussions of consciousness-raising and empowerment. The creative research of Samuel A. Culbert (1974) and Culbert and John J. McDonough (1980) is particularly insightful. Their work, although directed mainly at managers, is based on an interpretive foundation. It describes a variety of ways that individuals can present themselves to others in order to "survive" and to pursue self-interest. For example, Culbert (1974) provided a series of tips on how to get out of the "organizational trap." Among other things he stressed the need to (1) recognize one's feelings of incoherence, signals that something is "off," (2) build mechanisms for social support and consciousness-raising, (3) develop divergent problem-solving skills that help the person to focus on the meanings of events, rather than just the events themselves, and (4) become more aware of a person's relationship with the organization, beginning with the analysis of his/her assumptions about the relationship. In other words, awareness of the need for building social support systems and the skills to build them are essential for the exercise of control.

An excellent example of the type of process that I have in mind is the scene in the movie *The Right Stuff,* where astronaut John Glenn has, contrary to the wishes of one of his superiors, just told his wife that if she did not want Vice-President Lyndon Johnson to come in their house, she should keep him out. Glenn's superior attempted to change Glenn's mind by threatening to reorder the assignment of astronauts to flights, with the clear implication that Glenn would suffer. This threat to Glenn's interest in protecting his "private life" evaporated when Glenn's fellow astronauts asked the superior who he was going to get to fly, with the clear implication that they would not. Although not all groups have such "objective" power, the point is that the exercise of rights often requires the support of one's peers. In the case of the astronauts, perhaps because of a long-standing infrastructure of military people sticking together against civilian interference, such support did not seem to require deliberate efforts on their part. In other cases, deliberate and skillful efforts will be needed to build such protective (or assertive) infrastructures. Here, the effective exercise of rights depends upon people recognizing the value of bulding such infrastructures and upon their skills to do so.

In essence, we are talking about the skills required to build collective action. Unfortunately, our preoccupation with positional leadership has not prepared us for this complex task. Human efforts at collective action are hampered by the free-rider problem and by the fact that seldom do two or more individuals have exactly the same set of preferences. Therefore, efforts at collective action are often rather easy to subvert through divide-and-conquer tactics. In large measure then, the effective exercise of rights depends on the existence of infrastructures at the "grass-roots" level that can resist such centrifugal forces—infrastructures that supply support and definitions of reality that aid collective action. However, building such structures often requires long-term efforts, and motivating people to pay the short-run costs to build them is a difficult problem. Finding ways to facilitate the development of such infrastructures is a major problem that needs to be solved in the struggle for employee rights. (See Axelrod [1984], especially Chapters 6 and 7 for some interesting ideas.)

As I suggested earlier in discussing the agency problem, the need for social influence skills may be essential even when organizations (e.g., unions) explicitly founded to help individuals advance and exercise their rights exist. Leaders of these organizations, like leaders of most formal organizations, are faced with managing competing goals and interests and often will neglect the least powerful and/or least visible interests. For example, Bruce Partridge's (1978) analysis of shop stewards revealed how their conflicting priorities could lead them not to fight for a particular grievant. In fact, rather than represent the grievant's interests (at least as the grievant defines them) the agent may attempt to quell the grievant—the "cooling out" process that Erving Goffman (1952) described. Consequently, exercise of one's rights may depend on the skill to avoid being "cooled out" by one's own formal agents, or upon insurgent leadership that challenges the formal agents.

Formal Structure and Unobtrusive Control in Organizations

Some of the forces that limit effective pursuit of employee rights (and other interests) are a function of the formal hierarchies that affect access to key physical and social resources. Such processes are well known to students of organizations, but are often subtle in reality.

For the sake of illustration, assume an organization where certain members have long possessed the rights to make certain decisions. The rights of faculty members at universities to control the curricula, faculty appointments, and tenure are good examples. Even if no changes are made in the formal rights, their exercise is always problematic. Through control of the agendas of meetings, even a moderately skillful administrator can influence not only the outcomes, but whether something is even considered. In addition, because choice is often exercised by selecting among viable or existing alternatives, those who shape the alternatives exercise considerable influence. Thus, administrators or others with formal authority can control the expression of interests by appointing and charging committees to develop the alternatives from which the final decision will be chosen. Similarly, the information available and the amount of critical attention devoted to some matters and not to others shapes outcomes. Moreover, the nature of information that the organization collects and selectively disseminates is influenced by the distribution of formal power in the organization. Clearly, the actual ability of the faculty to exercise its rights can be changed quite unobtrusively.

Although such processes may be most clear in organizations such as universities, they illustrate how structure is often used to curtail the effective exercise of rights through influencing the interpretation of reality. (For more complete accounts of these processes, see Pfeffer [1981], Edelman [1977], Cohen and March [1974], and McNeil [1978].) The exercise of rights by employees demands may be enhanced if they understand these unobtrusive events.

Distribution of Economic and Social Resources

Organizational hierarchies affect the relative control that people have over economic and social resources that help individuals to construct social reality in their favor. Leading students of management, including Karl Weick (1979), Jeffrey Pfeffer (1981), James G. March (1981), Linda A. Krefting and Peter J. Frost (1985), Joanne Martin, Sim B. Sitkin, and Michael Boehm (1985), Caren Siehl (1985), Chimezie A. B. Osigweh (1989), and Thomas Peters and Robert Waterman (1982), have suggested that the role of manager requires involvement in constructing and orchestrating social reality.

Not only are managers apt to be selected for their abilities to shape the definitions of reality, but they are groomed and provided the tools for doing so. Organizations invest substantial amounts of resources to develop relevant "human relations" skills in their managers. Likewise, managers are selected and trained to be able to create, interpret, and use the organization's accounting, technical, and other information resources. Moreover, their jobs are structured so as to allow managers to devote substantial time and resources to collect, understand, and disseminate information.

Managers can use their control of information to counter the interests and rights of employees. An executive's description of a company's response to union organizing efforts provides a concrete example. The executive reported that management developed a film about the history of the firm that stressed "one big happy family" aspects and showed it to employees at strategic times—such as when a union organizing attempt was in process. Similarly, information about the dire economic straits of a plant, firm, or industry can also be used by managers to influence the struggle over rights and interests. I am not suggesting that most of the outcomes of such information control are "bad" or that managers are the only actors able and willing to manage information in a self-serving way. The point is that, to the degree that recognition and exercise of rights are influenced by social construction, lower-level participants may be at a considerable disadvantage. Those who wish to be effective in gaining and exercising rights that conflict with the preferences of management are often facing a steep incline.

Technology and Physical Conditions

Technology. Most analysts, whether part of the interpretive/critical movement or not, would agree that by affecting the demand for various skills, technology has had a major impact on the distribution of power. Of course, as the distribution of power changes, so do the abilities of individuals and groups to press their claims. Thus, by altering the relative power of social actors, technology affects the exercise of rights. What the interpretive/critical perspective adds to this general view is attention to the role of social construction in the development of technology.

David Noble (1984) and Charles Perrow (1983) have contributed important insights into the role social construction has played in the evolution of technology and the deliberate cultivation of certain forms of technology in the contest for social power. Noble (1984) advanced the view that the push for automatic control was part of a long-standing fantasy of managers to have a completely automatic factory, freeing them from the need to deal with recalcitrant workers to advance management's rights. In Noble's words: "The new computer-based ideology of total control proved contagious. . . . It was coupled with both the traditional belief that superior efficiency resulted from work simplification, the substitution of capital for labor, . . . and to the postwar preoccupation with controlling labor as an end in itself, in order to safeguard and extend management 'rights' " (p. 57).

At the plant level, Noble continued, technologies changed the skill requirements of the jobs and hence the power of those who did them. Under such conditions, most employee job rights are ephemeral. Since, as Noble noted, the idea of progress through technology has become dominant in our society, the power of those who would seek to protect the "rights" they had under an existing technology was undermined by labeling them as enemies of progress.

Perrow (1983) advanced a similar argument, observing that often those who designed jobs and technology are heavily influenced by management's inclinations not to trust lower-level participants and hence management's preferences for building in ways to monitor employees closely. Elimination of unfavorable effects (e.g., fatigue, boredom, isolation, health and possible disability) on people who operate the technology has not been given priority in design. There is costly neglect of ergonomics: "Costs include excessive fatigue, boredom, excessive workload, isolation, frustration, and above all disability and death for hapless operators and innocent bystanders" (Perrow, 1983, p. 528). Perrow concluded that choices about technology are taken for granted "because they are a part of a largely unquestioned social construction of reality" (p. 540).

The arguments of Noble and Perrow are important in the interpretive/critical perspective. Both are suggesting that usually there are a variety of ways to design technology to accomplish a given task. From this feasible set, the form technology actually takes is often influenced by prevailing social interests. Moreover, both are suggesting that a widespread socially constructed reality obscures a number of important issues involved in alternative technologies, including job rights, safety, and the intrinsic nature of work itself. To the degree they are correct, the design of technology must be near the core of analysis of employee rights.

Physical conditions and the structure of work. Physical conditions can have a variety of effects on the likelihood that people will be motivated and able to exercise their rights. For example, objectively poor conditions might stimulate organizing to assert interests. Likewise, objectively good conditions could lead people to be apathetic or to develop higher expectations. My concern here, however, is not with how pleasant or unpleasant they are, but with how physical conditions influence the capacity of people to detect violations of their interests and to mobilize accordingly.

Classical social psychological studies (e.g., Newcomb, 1961; Homans, 1950) documented how physical and psychological proximity affect interaction among people. The quantity and quality of interpersonal interaction influences the likelihood that people will develop, recognize, and organize around common interests. A useful example of how the structure and physical conditions of work can influence the chances that people will be in a position to detect and address violations of their interests and act as insurgent leaders can be found in Hobsbawm's (1984) effort to account for the political radicalism of the nineteenth-century shoemakers. Among other things, Hobsbawm observed that the nature of their work permitted shoemakers to think and converse while working. Moreover, the shoemaker was less dependent on wealthy patrons than were other tradesmen (e.g., the blacksmith) and his most frequent customers were poor people. Finally, he was usually located in the center of things; not only did he work in town, but he interacted frequently with a wide variety of people who were his customers. Hobsbawm concluded: "Whether this is sufficient explanation for his frequently attested role as crowd-leader is not so clear. Under the circumstances, however, we are hardly surprised to find him on occasion in such a role" (p. 121).

Although such analysis leaves us a long way from knowing all we might like to about the relationship between the structure of work and assertion of rights, it does illustrate the role that such "background" factors might play and hence the need to include them in analysis of factors that will influence the exercise of employee rights.

Overview

In this section I have suggested a number of factors at the microlevel that affect the ability to pursue a number of interests that have been central in treatments of employee rights. These features are all influenced by a variety of societal forces. Any effort to advance a particular set of interests must alter the microlevel behaviors, but must be cognizant of the larger system in which the microlevel events are embedded. A few of these macrolevel elements are discussed in the next section.

The Political Economy of the Acquisition and Exercise of Rights: Some Macrolevel Factors

As I suggested earlier, existing discussions of employee rights have centered primarily on macro- or contextual topics such as legal and constitutional issues. Here, I will only discuss briefly three topics highlighted most directly by a political economic stance, which so far have received surprisingly little attention in the existing literature on employee rights. These include the availability of alternatives to permit choice, ideologies and social assumptions, and the ease of organizing protests.

Existence of Alternatives

It is widely accepted (see, e.g., Thibaut and Kelley, 1959) that the availability and value of alternatives to one's current conditions influence behavior. A major principle on which both our market economy and democracy are based is the ability to choose among alternatives. The greater the number and value of alternatives (where the value of the alternative is the difference between the benefits one gains from the alternative minus the costs of getting it) from which a person can choose, the less dependent he/she is on any one relationship and the more able he/she will be to exercise rights and pursue interests by threatening to and/or actually leaving a current relationship. As Albert O. Hirschman (1970) described it, "exit" is an alternative to voice in exercising control.

On the other side of the coin, an employer who can find an adequate replacement for a given worker at little or no cost has little incentive to worry about the possibility the worker will leave. (Note in the example of the astronauts cited earlier, it was because Glenn's superior lacked alternatives that he had to back down.) In this context, two macrolevel conditions are directly relevant to the exercise of rights: unemployment and the nature of alternative jobs.

Unemployment. As the radical economists put it, unemployment acts to discipline the work force. If, other things being equal, employees know that other workers (Marx's reserve army of the unemployed) are ready and able to assume their jobs and the employees perceive they have few alternative employment opportunities, they will be far less likely to take the risks that may be involved in seeking and/or asserting rights than when the employer is more dependent upon them (i.e., few substitutes are available) or when the employees themselves have more alternative employers. In short, unemployment is a constraint on the effective exercise of employee rights. Employer rights are, of course, enhanced by opposite circumstances—by conditions that make them less dependent on employees.

Nature of alternative jobs. Harry Braverman (1974) observed that Taylorism and modern employment practices have made most jobs very similar to each other. Consequently, workers have little to choose from if the absence of true alternatives reduces the value of exit in asserting one's interests. Since there may be much more to choose from with respect to organization policies that influence one's rights than with respect to jobs, how far Braverman's example can be extended to the matter of rights is unclear. Nevertheless, the principle is quite generalizeable. The fewer the employers who provide any particular employee right, the more difficult it will be for employees in general to gain and to exercise that right.

Ideologies/assumptions

Beliefs about work and organizations will have a great deal of influence on the acquisition and exercise of rights. To the degree that existing organizational forms are granted social legitimacy, those who control the organizations will find it easier to establish and sustain their interests as rights and thereby fend off challenges by those with other preferences. Lindblom (1977) has argued that such is very much the case in our society because the interests of business (especially larger corporations) have become such a central component of contemporary American ideology that their interests are, almost unconsciously, accorded substantial weight in most decisions. For example, the ideas of efficiency and the importance of technology to progress are so widely accepted that successfully linking one's interests to them can yield a considerable advantage over one's rivals.

Other ideologies, such as those about work itself, can also play an important role in the struggle to determine whose interests are given priority. Daniel Rodgers (1974), for example, argued persuasively that the work ethic was in large measure a socially constructed set of beliefs that served to rconcile a highly coercive system of work with democratic values. So powerful was this set of beliefs, Rodgers pointed out, that even those who sought to reform work were apt to overlook the real conditions in the factories and ground their arguments in a conservative set of assumptions: "Even for those who chafed at labor, the appeal to the moral centrality of work was too useful to resist" (p. 181).

Ease of Organizing Protest

Concrete social and economic conditions, such as the labor market conditions noted earlier, influence the capacities of people to assert themselves. In addition, certain demographic factors such as the physical concentrations of people can affect the chances that they will develop what is often referred to as a collective consciousness. For example, Herbert G. Gutman (1977) observed that successive waves of immigrants, with each wave consisting of people who had widely different languages and cultures, severely constrained worker protest in the United States during industrialization. Finally, social traditions for resolving social conflict can have a significant effect on the costs and benefits of expressing interests or exercising rights.

Overview

This brief discussion attempted to call attention to the role that macropolitical and macroeconomic forces play in the quest for employee rights. It is important to recognize the interaction between the micro- and macrolevels. First, the conditions created by political economic realities (e.g., the level of unemployment) have direct and substantial effects on the costs and benefits of devoting one's resources to asserting one's interests. Second, general social assumptions influence the social construction of reality at the microlevel. They influence people's perceptions of what is right and just and of what are the appropriate means to respond to perceived violations of their rights. These perceptions influence behavior at the microlevel, and in so doing, over time, influence the political economic conditions—the social traditions and beliefs and the nature of alternative jobs and organizations. After all, the day-to-

day behaviors of individuals are the building blocks of macrosocial structures.

CONCLUSIONS

Barrington Moore, Jr. (1978) suggested that it is as important to ask
why, when faced with objective conditions of injustice, people do not
revolt, as it is to ask why they do. Although the issues addressed here
are less extreme than the social revolutions addressed by Moore, his
emphasis on accounting for the failure of people who are somehow
disadvantaged in a system to attempt and to succeed in exercising their
current rights and in establishing new ones, helps to summarize the
major theme of this chapter. I have tried to show that employee rights
are not abstract and unchanging, but rather are won and sustained by
people in pursuit of their interests. These pursuits are affected by a
combination of subjective and objective forces that operate at micro-and
macrolevels. We must examine the construction of social reality at the
microlevel—what it is and how it emerges. Further, we must also look
at macroconditions that affect the costs and benefits of attempting to
pursue one's interests, as well as consider how macrolevel elements
(e.g., ideologies) influence the process and substance of interpretations
of stimuli at the microlevel. Moreover, my analysis has been motivated
by the critical writers' objectives of emancipation and demystification
and the assumption that the more disadvantaged members of society
have the most to gain from such emancipation and demystification.
Together, these three foci constitute the type of interpretive/critical political economic perspective that I believe needs to become a central part
of discussions of employee rights.

Finally, I believe the emancipation/demystification objective has a special meassage for those of us who might be tempted to try to advance
the interests of employees by invoking the concept of rights to gain
rhetorical advantage by adding "surplus" meaning to our arguments by
labeling our preferences as "rights." Such a tactic is every bit as inconsistent with the exercise of self-conscious control whether it is used by
us or by those on some other side. The negotiation of the allocation of
our planet's finite resources among conflicting interests is apt to yield
the greatest overall benefits through commitment to a process that takes
interests for what they are—that is, preferences—rather than making
them appear to be something else—that is, rights.

Bibliography

COURT CASES

Alexander v. Gardner-Denver, Co., 415 U.S. 36 (1974).

Allis-Chalmers Corp. v. Lueck, 105 S. Ct. 1904 (1985).

American Trucking Association v. United States, 627 F. 2d 1313, 1321 (D.C. Cir. 1980).

Atonio v. Wards Cove Packing Co., 38 FEP Cases 1170 (1985).

Bauer v. Bailar, 647 F. 2d 1037 (1981).

Belknap, Inc. v. Hale, 463 U.S. 491 (1983).

Beller v. Middendorf, 413 F. Supp. 66, 69 (1986, E.D. La). Also 632 F. 2d 788 (9th Cir. 1980).

Bibbs v. Block, 747 F. 2d 508 (1984).

Board of Regents v. Roth, 408 U.S. 564 (1972).

Bottini v. Sadore Management Corp., 746 F. 2d 116, 120 (2d Cir. 1985).

Brockmeyer v. Dun & Bradstreet, 113 Wis. 2d 561, 573, 335 N.W. 2d 834, 840–41 (1983).

Buckhalter v. Pepsi-Cola General Bottlers, 768 F. 2d 842 (7th Cir. 1985).

Burkhart v. Mobil Oil Corp., 143 Vt. 123, 463 A. 2d 226 (1983).

Burns v. United Telephone Co. of Kansas, Inc., 683 F. 2d 339 (1982).

Burrows v. Chemed Corp., 567 F. Supp. 978 (1983).

Camp v. Pitts, 411 U.S. 138 (1973).

Carroll v. Sears, Roebuck & Co., 708 F. 2d 183 (1983).

Carpenter v. Stephen F. Austin Univ., 06 F. 2d 608 (1983).

Catlett v. Missouri Highway & Transportation Comm., 589 F. Supp. 929 (1983).

Chisholm v. U.S. Postal Service, 665 F. 2d 482 (1981).

Cleveland Board of Education v. Loudermill, U.S. 105 S. Ct. 1487 (1985).
Coe v. Yellow Freight System, Inc., 646 F. 2d 444 (1981).
Colon-Sanchez v. Marsh, 733 F. 2d 78 (1984).
Connick v. Meyers, 461 U.S. 138 (1983).
Conner v. Fort Gordon Bus Co., 761 F. 2d 1495 (1985).
Craik v. Minnesota State University Board, 731 F. 2d 465 (1984).
Crawford v. Western Electric Co., Inc., 614 F. 2d 1300 (1980).
Cuthbertson v. Biggers Bros., Inc., 707 F. 2d 454 (1983).
Dickerson v. Metropolitan Dade County, 659 F. 2d 574 (1981).
Eastland v. Tennessee Valley Authority, 704 F. 2d 613 (1983).
EEOC v. Korn Industries, Inc., 662 F. 2d 265 (1981).
Ellison v. Best Foods, 598 F. Supp. 159 (1984).
Eubanks v. Pickens-Bond Const. Co., 635 F. 2d 1341 (1980).
Falcon v. General Telephone Co. of the Southwest, 626 F. 2d 369 (1980).
Farrakhan v. Sears, Roebuck, & Co., 511 F. Supp. 893 (1980).
Fell v. Bolger, 708 F. 2d 1312 (1983).
Firefighters Local 1784 v. Stotts, 467 U.S. 561 (1984).
Fisher v. Procter & Gamble Mfg. Co., 613 F. 2d 527 (1980).
Fortune v. National Cash Register Co., 373 Mass. 96, 104, 364 N.E. 2d 1251 (1977).
Foster v. MCI Telecommunications Corp., 555 F. Supp. 330 (1983).
Garibaldi v. Lucky Food Stores, Inc., 726 F. 2d 1367 (1984).
Gates v. Life of Montana Insurance Co., 196 Mont. 178, 368 P. 2d 1063 (1982).
Gilchrist v. Bolger, 733 F. 2d 1551 (1984).
Gorin v. Osborne, 756 F. 2d 834, 836 (11th Cir. 1985).
Goss v. Lopez, 419 U.S. 545, 581 (1975).
Grano v. Dept. of Development of City of Columbus, 699 F. 2d 836 (1983).
Griffen v. Big Spring Independent School District, 706 F. 2d 645, 655 (5th Cir. 1983).
Griggs v. Duke Power Co., 401 S. Ct. 424 (1971).
Harris v. Group Health Assn., Inc., 662 F. 2d 869 (1981).
Hawkins v. Bounds, 752 F. 2d 500 (1985).
Health v. John Morrell & Co., 768 F. 2d 245, 248 (8th Cir. 1985).
Hearn v. R. R. Donnelly & Sons Co., 739 F. 2d 304 (1984).
Hebert v. Monsanto Co., 682 F. 2d 1111 (1982).
Hill v. K-Mart Corp., 699 F. 2d 776 (1983).
Holsey v. Armur & Co., 743 F. 2d 199 (1984).
Jackson v. Seaboard Coast Line Railroad Co., 678 F. 2d 992 (1982).
Jayasinghe v. Bethlemen Steel Corp., 760 F. 2d 132 (1985).
Johnson v. General Tire & Rubber Co., 652 F. 2d 574 (1981).
Johnson v. Railway Express Agency, Inc., 421 U.S. 454 (1975).
Kelly v. Mississippi Valley Gas Co., 397 So. 2d 874 (Miss. 1981).
Knight v. Nassau County, 649 F. 2d 461 (1982).
Lewis v. N.L.R.B., 750 F. 2d 1266 (1985).
Lewis v. St. Louis University, 573 F. Supp. 300 (1983).
Lewis v. Univ. of Pittsburgh, 725 F. 2d 910 (1983).
Lilly v. Harris-Teeter Supermarket, 545 F. Supp. 686 (1982).
Local 28, Sheet Metal Workers' Intl. Assoc. v. EEOC, 41 FEP 139 (1986).
Local 93, Intl. Assoc. of Firefighters v. City of Cleveland, 41 FEP 107 (1986).

Loehr v. Ventura County Community College District, 743 F. 2d 1210, 1317 (9th Cir. 1984).

Major v. Hampton, 413 F. Supp. 66, 69, E.D. La (1976).

Mason v. Continental Illinois Natl. Bank, 704 F. 2d 361 (1983).

Mathews v. Eldridge, 424 U.S. 319 (1976).

McDonald v. City of West Branch, 466 U.S. 284, 291 N. 10 (1984).

McDonald v. Penn Central Transportation Co., 337 F. Supp. 803, 805–806 (D. Mass. 1972).

McDonald v. Sante Fe Trail Transportation Co., 427 U.S. 273 (1976).

McKenzie v. Sawyer, 684 F. 2d 62 (1982).

McNulty v. Borden, Inc., 474 F. Supp. 1111 (1979).

Merritor Savings Bank, FSB v. Michelle Vinson et al., U.S. 106 S. Ct. 2399, 91 L. Ed. 2d 49 (June 1986).

Milton v. Wienberger, 696 F. 2d 94 (1982).

Mohammed v. Callaway, 698 F. 2d 395 (1983).

Monge v. Beebe Rubber Co., 114 N.H. 130, 316 A. 2d 549 (1974).

Murphy v. American Home Products Corp., 461 N.Y.S. 2d 232, 58 N.Y. 2d 293, 448 N.E. 2d 86 (1983).

Murphy v. Middletown Enlarged City School Dist., 525 F. Supp. 678 (1981).

Movement for Opportunity, Etc. v. General Motors, 622 F. 2d 1235 (1980).

Nanty v. Barrows Co., 660 F. 2d 1327 (1983).

Nees v. Hocks, 272 Or. 210, 536 P. 2d 512 (1975).

Nieves v. Metropolitan Dade Co., 598 F. Supp. 955 (1984).

NRLB v. Borg-Warner Corp., 42 LRRM 2034 (1958).

NLRB v. Plasterers Local 79, 404 U.S. 116, 136 (1971).

Nord v. United States Steel Corp., 758 F. 2d 1462 (1985).

Norton v. Macy, 417 F. 2d 1161 (D.C. Cir. 1969).

Novosel v. Nationwide Insurance Co., 721 F. 2d 894 (3d Cir. 1984).

O'Sullivan v. Mallon et al., 390 A. 2d 149 (1978).

Olguin v. Inspiration Consolidated Copper Co., 740 F. 2d 1468 (9th Cir. 1984).

Page v. Bolger, 645 F. 2d 227 (1981).

Page v. U.S. Industries, Inc., 726 F. 2d 1038 (1984).

Parker v. Board of School Commissioners of the City of Indianapolis, 729 F. 2d 524 (1984).

Patton v. J.C. Penney Co., Inc., 719 P. 2d 854 (Ore. 1986).

Payne v. Western & Atlantic R.R., 81 Tenn. 507, 519–520 (1884).

Paxton v. Union Natl. Bank, 688 F. 2d 552 (1982).

Perry v. Sindermann, 408 U.S. 593 (1972).

Petermann v. Teamsters, 174 Cal. App. 2d 184, 344 P. 2d 25 (1959).

Peters v. Lieuallen, 568 F. Supp. 261 (1983).

Phillips v. Goodyear Tire & Rubber Co., 651 F. 2d 1051, 1056–57 (5th Cir. 1981).

Pickering v. Board of Education, 391 U.S. 563 (1968).

Pine River State Bank v. Mettille, cited in H. H. Perritt (1984), *Employee dismissal law and practice.* N.Y.: John Wiley & Sons, section 7.20.

Pouncy v. Prudential Ins. Co. of America, 668 F. 2d 795 (1982).

Ramirez v. Hoffeinz, 619 F. 2d 442 (1980).

Reynolds v. Sheet Metal Workers Local 102, 498 F. Supp. 952 (1980).

Richardson v. Perales, 402 U.S. 389, 409–410 (1971).

Robinson v. Polaroid Corp., 732 F. 2d 1010 (1984).

Rossini v. Ogilvy & Mather, Inc., 597 F. Supp. 1120 (1984).

Rowe v. Cleveland Pneumatic Co., Numerical Control, 690 F. 2d 88 (1982).

Rowe v. General Motors, 457 F. 2d 348 (1972).

Royal v. Missouri Highway & Transportation Comm., 655 F. 2d 159 (1981).

Sabine Pilot Services, Inc. v. Hauck, 687 S.W. 2d 733 (Tex. 1985).

Schweiker v. McClure, 456 U.S. 188, 102 S. Ct. 1665 (1982).

Sessions v. Rusk State Hospital, 658 F. 2d 1066 (1981).

Sheets v. Teddy's Frosted Foods, Inc., 179 Conn. 471, 427 A. 2d 385 (1980).

Simpson v. Western Graphics Corp., 613 P. 2d 1276, 1278 (1982).

Sklenar v. Central Board of Education of the School District of the City of Detroit, 497
    F. Supp. 1154 (1980).

Slohoda v. United Parcel, Inc., 475 A. 2d 618, 622 (N.J. Super. App. Div. 1984).

Smith v. St. of Georgia, 749 F. 2d 683 (1985).

Smith v. Univ. of North Carolina, 632 F. 2d 316 (1980).

Spearmon v. Southwestern Bell, 506 F. Supp. 761 (1980).

St. Peter v. Secretary of the Army, 659 F. 2d 1133 (1981).

Stastny v. Southern Bell Telephone & Telegraph Co., 628 F. 2d 267 (1980).

*State of Illinois v. Film Recovery Systems, Metallic Marketing, Kirschbaum, Rodriguez,
    O'Neil*, Cook County Circuit Court, case number 83 C 110 91 (June 1985).

Stinson v. Tennessee Dept. of Mental Health & Mental Education, 553 F. Supp. 454
    (1982).

Stones v. Los Angeles Community College Dist., 572 F. Supp. 1072 (1983).

Tameny v. Atlantic Richfield Co., 164 Cal. Reporter 839 (1980).

Texas Dept. of Community Affairs v. Burdine, 101 S. Ct. 1089 (1981).

Thompson v. Sawyer, 678 F. 2d 257 (1982).

Thompson v. St. Regis Paper Co., 102 Wash. 2d 219, 685 P. 2d 1081, 1086 (1984).

Tompkins v. Public Service Electric & Gas Co., 16 FEP Cases 22 (1977).

Toussaint v. Blue Cross and Blue Shield of Michigan, 408 Mich. 579, 292 N.W. 2d
    880 (1980).

United Steelworkers v. Warrior & Gulf Navigation Company, 363 U.S. 574, 46 LRRM
    2416 (1960).

Universal Camera v. NLRB, 340 U.S. 474 (1951).

Valentino v. U.S. Postal Service, 511 F. Supp. 917 (1981).

Verniero v. Air Force Academy School District, 705 F. 2d 338 (1983).

W. R. Grace & Co. v. Rubber Workers Local 759, 461 U.S. 757 (1983).

Wadeson v. American Family Mutual Insurance Co., 343 N.W. 2d 367 (N.D. 1984).

Wagenseller v. Scottsdale Memorial Hospital, 147 Ariz. 370, 710 P. 2d 1025 (1985).

Walker v. Jefferson Co. Home, 726 F. 2d 1554 (1984).

Walls v. Mississippi St. Dept. of Public Welfare, 730 F. 2d 306 (1984).

Whatley v. Skaggs Companies, Inc., 707 F. 2d 1129 (1983).

Whittaker v. Care-More, Inc., 621 S.W. 2d 395, 397 (Tenn. App. 1981).

Williams v. Colorado Springs, Colorado School District, 641 F. 2d 835 (1981).

Wilmore v. City of Wilmington, 533 F. Supp. 844 (1982).

Woolley v. Hoffman-LaRoche, Inc., 99 N.J. 284, 491 A. 2d 1257, modified, 101 N.J.
    10, 499 A. 2d 515 (1985).

Womack Shell Chemical Co., 514 F. Supp. 1062 (1981).

Wygant v. Jackson Bd. of Education, 40 FEP 1321 (1986).

FORMAL AND INFORMAL PUBLICATIONS

AAUP support offered to Kemp. (1986, March/April). *Academe*, 73–74.

Adams, J. S. (1963). Toward an understanding of inequity. *Journal of Abnormal and Social Psychology, 67*, 422–24.

Adams, J. S. (1965). Inequity in social exchange. In L. Berkowitz (Ed.), *Advances in experimental social psychology*. Vol. 2 (pp. 267–299). New York: Academic Press.

Ad Hoc Committee on Termination at Will and Wrongful Discharge, Appointed by the Labor and Employment Law Section of the State Bar of California. (1984). *To Strike a New Balance*. Report, February 8.

AFL-CIO Committee on the Evolution of Work. (1985). *The changing situation of workers and their unions*. Washington, D.C.: AFL-CIO.

AFL-CIO. (1987, February). The employment-at-will doctrine. Statements adopted by the AFL-CIO Executive Council, Bal Harbour, Florida.

Agee, Philip. (1976). *Inside the company*. New York: Bantam Books.

Ahrons, C. R. (1976). Counselors' perceptions of career images of women. *Journal of Vocational Behavior, 8*, 197–207.

Almquist, E. M, and Angrist, S. S. (1971). Role model influence on college women's career aspirations. *Merrill-Palmer Quarterly, 17*, 263–79.

American Bar Association, Labor and Employment Section. (1985). Report of the committee on individual rights and responsibilities in the workplace. *The Labor Lawyer, 1*, 777, 783.

Anderson, Jack, and Van Atta, Dale. (1986, May 21). Whistleblowing can prove to be job hazard. Daily Chronicle. Dekalb/Sycamore, Ill.

Anderson, Robert M. et al. (1980). *Divided loyalties: Whistleblowing at BART*. West Layfayette, Ind.: Purdue Research Foundation.

Anderson, Susan Saiter. (1981, August 30). Hamburger U. offers a break. *New York Times*, Survey of Continuing Education section, 27–28.

Antiunion grievance ploy, The. (1979, February 12). *Business Week,* 117, 120.

Aram, J. D., and Salipante, P. F. (1981). An evaluation of organizational due process in the resolution of employee/employer conflict. *Academy of Management Review, 6* (2), 197–204.

Aram, J. D., Salipante, P. F., and Knauf, J. (1987). Human resource indicators for hospital managers. *Health Care Management Review, 12* (2), 15–22.

Arendt, H. (1965). *Eichmann in Jerusalem*. New York: Viking Press.

Arvey, Richard D., and Jones, Allen P. (1985). The use of discipline in organizational settings: A framework for future research. *Research in Organizational Behavior, 7*, 389.

Axelrod, R. (1984). *The evolution of cooperation*. New York: Basic Books.

Baer, Walter E. (1972). *Discipline and discharge under the labor agreement*. New York: American Management Association.

Baldwin, Deborah. (1985, January/February). The loneliness of the government whistleblower. *Common Cause Magazine, 11*, 32–34.

Baritz, L. (1960). *The servants of power*. Middletown, Conn.: Wesleyan University Press.

Barnard, C. I. (1938). *The functions of the executive*. Cambridge, Mass.: Harvard University Press.

Barrett, R. S. (1966). *Performance rating*. Chicago: Science Research Associates.

Barrows, S. D. (1986). *Mayflower madam*. New York: Arbor House.

Bartholet, E. (1982). Application of Title VII to jobs in high places. *Harvard Law Review, 95,* 947–1027.

Baucus, M., Near, J. P., and Miceli, M. P. (1985, August). Organizational culture and whistleblowing. Paper presented at the 45th annual meeting of the Academy of Management.

Beam, Alex. (1986, March 24). This dean doesn't practice what his school preaches. *Business Week,* 58.

Beer, M., Ruh, R., Dawson, J. A., McCaa, B. B., and Kavanagh, M. J. (1978). A performance measurement system: Research, design, introduction and evaluation. *Personnel Psychology, 62,* 422–27.

Belohav, James, A. (1985, Fall). A comparative view of employee disciplinary practices. *Public Personnel Management, 14* (3), 245.

Bentham, J. (1948/1780). *An introduction to the principles of morals and legislation.* New York: Hafner Publishing Co. Originally printed in 1780 and published in 1789 in Oxford, England.

Berenbeim, R. (1980). *Non-union complaint systems: A corporate appraisal.* New York: The Conference Board, Report No. 770.

Beyer, Janice, M., and Trice, Harrison M. (1984). A field study of the use and perceived effects of discipline in controlling work performance. *Academy of Management Journal, 27* (4), 745.

Bierhoff, H. W., Cohen, R. L., and Greenberg, J. (Eds.) (1986). *Justice in social relations.* New York: Plenum Press.

Bierman, L., and Youngblood, S. A. (1984). Employment-at-will and the South Carolina experiment. *Industrial Relations Research Association, Proceedings of the 37th Annual Meeting,* 242–49.

Blades, Lawrence E. (1967). Employment at will v. individual freedom: On limiting the abusive exercise of employer power. *Columbia Law Review, 67,* 1404–35.

Blau, F. D. (1984). Occupational segregation and labor market discrimination. In B. F. Reskin (Ed.), *Sex segregation in the workplace.* Washington, D.C.: National Academy Press.

Blowing the whistle on Georgia. (1986, February 24). *Time,* 65.

Blumberg, Phillip. (1971). Corporate responsibility and the employee's duty of loyalty and obedience: A preliminary inquiry. *Oklahoma Law Review, 24,* 278–318.

Blumrosen, Alfred. (1978). Strangers no more: All workers entitled to just cause protection under Title VII. *Industrial Relations Law Review, 2,* 517.

Bok, Sissela. (1982). *Secrets: On the ethics of concealment and practice.* New York: Pantheon Books.

Borman, W. C. (1978). Exploring the upper limits of reliability and validity in job performance ratings. *Journal of Applied Psychology, 63,* 135–44.

Bormann, Ernest G. (1975). *Discussion and group methods: Theory and practice,* 2nd ed. New York: Harper & Row, Chapter 3.

Borsay, H. A., and Leff, A. M. (1977). Physician drug addiction—a challenge to medical educators. *Ohio State Medical Journal, 73,* 740–42.

Bouwen, R., and Salipante, P. F. (1986). The kaleidoscope model of grievance formulation. Working paper, Weatherhead School of Management, Case Western Reserve University.

Bowles, S., and Gintis, H. (1976). *Schooling in capitalist America.* New York: Basic Books.

Braverman, H. (1974). *Labor and monopoly capital.* New York: Monthly Review Press.

Brett, J. M. (1983, August). Procedural justice. Paper presented at a symposium on *Justice: Beyond equity theory* at the Academy of Management, Dallas, Tex.

Brett, J. M. (1986). Commentary on procedural justice papers. In R. J. Lewicki, B. H. Sheppard, and M. H. Bazerman (Eds.), *Research on negotiation in organizations.* Vol. 1 (pp. 81–90). Greenwich, Conn.: JAI Press.

Brief, Arthur P. (1982, September). Methods for reducing conflicts in expectations: Undoing the educational process of the newly hired professional. *Personnel Administrator,* 55–58.

British Government. (1978). Employment Protection (Consolidated) Act 1978 (1978, c. 44). *Halisbury's Statutes, 48* (1978 cont. vol.), p. 452, as amended by Sections 6–10, Employment Act 1980, 50 (1) *Halisbury's Statutes, 387* (1980 cont. vol.).

Bruner, J. S. (1958). Social psychology and perception. In E. Maccoby, T. Newcomb, and E. Hartley (Eds.), *Readings in social psychology,* 3rd ed. (pp. 85–94). New York: Holt, Rinehart.

Bruner, J. S. (1961). The act of discovery. *Harvard Educational Review, 31,* 21–32.

Bureau of Labor Statistics. (1979). *U.S. Bureau of Labor Statistics News.* September 3.

Bureau of National Affairs. (1979, April). *Policies for Unorganized Employees.* PPF Survey No. 125. Washingtron, D.C.: BNA.

Bureau of National Affairs. (1982). *The employment-at-will issue.* A BNA Special Report (p. 23). Washington, D.C.: BNA.

Bureau of National Affairs. (1985). *Employee discipline and discharge.* Personnel Policies Forum, Survey No. 139. Washington, D.C.: BNA.

Bureau of National Affairs (1986). *Basic patterns in union contracts,* 11th ed. Washington, D.C.: BNA.

Business Publications. (1978). Punishment and discipline in organizations. *Organizational behavior: An applied psychological approach.* Dallas, Tex.: Business Publications, Inc.

Byrne, John A. (1986, March 24). Twenty leading business schools—by the numbers. *Business Week,* 67–70.

California General Assembly Bill, No. 3017. (1984, February). Cited in Job security and the role of law: An economic analysis of employment-at-will (1984). *Stanford Journal of International Law, 20,* 353–55.

California Labor Code, 1102.5 (1986 Supp.) .

California Labor Federation, AFL:CIO. Resolution No. 34. Adopted by the 15th Biennial Convention of the California Labor Federation, AFL-CIO.

Campbell, David N., Fleming, R. L., and Grote, Richard C. (1985, July/August). Discipline without punishment—at last: Why and how you should implement a nonpunitive approach to discipline. *Harvard Business Review,* 1–8.

Canadian Government. (1978). Section 21 of the 1987 Act to Amend the Labour
    Code, 26–27 Eliz. II c. 27, 1977–78 Canadian Statute 614, added a new
    Division V.7, Section 61.5, to the Canadian Labor Code, 5 *Can. Rev. Stat.*
    L–1.

Cascio, W. F., and Bernardin, H. J. (1981). Implications of performance appraisal
    litigation for personnel decisions. *Personnel Psychology, 34,* 211–26.

Cathcart, David A., and Dichter, Mark S. (1985). Employment-at-will: A 1985
    state-by-state survey. Larkspur, Calif.: National Employment Law Insti-
    tute.

Cavanagh, G. H., Moberg, D. J., and Velasquez, M. (1981). The ethics of or-
    ganizational politics. *Academy of Management Review, 6,* 363–74.

Clegg, S. (1983). Phenomenology and formal organizations: A realist critique.
    In S. B. Bacharach (Ed.), *Research in the sociology of organization.* Vol. 2
    (pp. 109.–52). Greenwich, Conn.: JAI Press.

Clinard, M. B. (1983). *Corporate ethics and crime: The role of middle management.*
    Beverly Hills, Calif.: Sage Publications.

Cohen, M. D., and March, J. G. (1974). *Leadership and ambiguity.* New York:
    McGraw-Hill.

Coke, Simon. (1983, February). Putting professionalism in its place. *Personnel*
    Management, 15, 44–46.

Colorado House Bill, No. 1485. (1981).

Committee on Labor and Employment Law, Bar Association of the City of New
    York. (1981). At-will employment and the problem of unjust dismissal.
    Report. *Record of Association of the Bar of the City of New York, 36,* 170.

Condon, Thomas J. (1984). *Fire me and I'll sue! A manager's survival guide to*
    employees rights. New York: Alexander Hamilton Institute.

Conference on Employee Responsibilities and Rights, Session on Labor-Man-
    agement Cooperation, Kirksville, Missouri, May 2–3, 1985. Transcript
    available from the Council on Employee Responsibilities and Rights, P.O.
    Box 61411, Virginia Beach, VA 23462.

Connecticut General Statute, 31–51m (1985 Supp.).

Copeland, Jeff B., Turque, Bill, Wright, Lynda, and Shapiro, Daniel. (1987,
    February 16). The revenge of the fired. *Newsweek,* 46–47.

Coulson, Robert. (1981). *The termination handbook.* New York: Free Press.

Culbert, S. A. (1974). *The organization trap and how to get out of it.* New York:
    Basic Books.

Culbert, S. A., and McDonough, J. J. (1980). *The invisible war.* New York: Wiley
    and Sons.

Cyert, R. M., and March, J. G. (1963). *A behavioral theory of the firm.* Englewood
    Cliffs, N.J.: Prentice-Hall.

Dahl, R. A. (1970). *After the revolution? Authority in a good society.* New Haven:
    Yale University Press.

Dalton, G. (1971). Motivation and control in organizations. In G. Dalton and
    P. R. Lawrence (Eds.), *Motivation and control in organizations.* Homewood,
    Ill.: Richard D. Irwin.

Dalton, M. (1959). *Men who manage.* New York: Wiley & Sons.

Darr, K. (1987, July 29). White males corner top federal jobs, study shows.
    Columbus Dispatch, 2D.

Dean, Malcom. (1985, June). Man who blew the whistle on firm demands £ 1/ 2m. *Manchester Guardian Weekly*, 5.

DeBiasi, G. L., and Kavanagh, M. J. (1984, August). Use and acceptability of a state-of-the-art performance appraisal system in a multi-hospital organization. Paper presented at the annual meeting of the Academy of Management, Boston.

de Charms, R. (1968). *Personal causation*. New York: Academic Press.

de Charms, R. (1976). *Enhancing motivation: Change in the classroom*. New York: Irvington.

Deetz, S. A., and Kersten, A. (1983). Critical models of interpretive research. In L. L. Putnam and M. E. Pacanowsky (Eds.), *Communicaton and organizations: An interpretive approach* (pp. 147–71). Beverly Hills, Calif.: Sage Publications.

DeGeorge, Richard T. (1982). *Business Ethics* (pp. 157–65). New York: Macmillan.

DeGeorge, Richard T. (1985, Fall). Ethical responsibilities of engineers in large organizations: The Pinto case. *Business Professional Ethics Journal*, *1*, 1–17. Reprinted in Richard A. Wassertstrom (Ed.) (1985). *Today's Moral Problems*, 3rd ed. (pp. 292–304). New York: Macmillan.

Della Fave, L. R. (1980). The meek shall not inherit the earth: Self-evaluation and the legitimacy of stratification. *American Sociological Review*, *45*, 955–71.

De Pree, Max (1984). Theory fastball. *New Management*, *1* (4), 29–36.

Deutsch, M. (1975). Equity, equality, and need: What determines which value will be used as the basis of distributive justice? *Journal of Social Issues*, *31*, 137–49.

Deutsch, M. (1986). Cooperation, conflict, and justice. In H. W. Bierhoff, R. L. Cohen, and J. Greenberg (Eds.), *Justice in social relations* (pp. 3–18). New York: Plenum Press.

DeVries, D. L., and McCall, M. M. (1976, January). Performance appraisal: Is it tax time again? Paper presented at the Managerial Performance Appraisal Conference, Center for Creative Leadership, Greensboro, N.C.

Dickson, Wiliam, J., and Roethlisberger, F. J. (1966). *Counseling in an organization: A sequel to the Hawthorne researches*. Boston: Division of Research, Graduate School of Business Administration, Harvard University.

Dingwall, Robert, and Lewis, Philip. (1983). *The sociology of the professions*. New York: St. Martin's.

Donaldson, T. (1982). *Corporations and morality*. Englewood Cliffs, N.J.: Prentice-Hall.

Donnelly, J. C. (1983). Coping and development during internship. In J. P. Callan (Ed.), *The physician: A professional under stress* (pp. 46–80). Norwalk, Conn.: Appleton-Century-Crofts.

Dotson, Donald. (1986, May 30). Letter from Donald Dotson, Chairman, NLRB, to representative Hoyer. *Daily Labor Reporter* (Washington, D.C.: Bureau of National Affairs), A6.

Drucker, Peter F. (1954). *The practice of management*. New York: Harper & Row.

Drucker, Peter F. (1981). What is "business ethics"? *The Public Interest*, *63*, 18–36.

Dunlop, John T. (1976). The limits of legal compulsion. *Labor Law Journal, 27,* 67.

Easton, L. D., and Guddat, K. H. (Trans. and Eds.). (1967). *Writings of the young Marx on philosophy and society.* Garden City, N.Y.: Anchor.

Eddy, J. P. (1968). Campus ombudsmen in American higher education. *Kappa Delta Pi Record, 5,* 34–35.

Edelman, M. (1977). *Political language: Words that succeed and policies that fail.* New York: Academic Press.

Elkouri, Frank, and Elkouri, Edna A. (1985). How arbitration works, 4th ed. (pp. 692–707). Washington, D.C.: Bureau of National Affairs.

Ellis, A., and Harper, R. A. (1970). *A guide to rational living.* North Hollywood, Calif.: Wilshire.

Elliston, Frederick A. (1982, February). Civil disobedience and whistleblowing: A comparative appraisal of two forms of dissent. *Journal of Business Ethics, 1,* 23–28.

Elliston, Frederick A. (1982, August). Anonymity and whistleblowing. *Journal of Business Ethics, 1,* 167–77.

Elliston, Frederick, Keenan, J., Lockhart, P., and Van Schaick, J. (1985). *Whistleblowing: Managing dissent in the workplace.* New York: Praeger.

Employee discipline and discharge. (1985). Personnel Policy Forum, Survey Number 139. Washington, D.C.: Bureau of National Affairs, 2.

Equal Employment Opportunity Commission. (1981, September). *Fair Employment Guidelines, 194,* 1–8.

Estreicher, Samuel. (1982). At-will employment and the problem of unjust dismissal: The appropriate judicial response. *New York State Bar Journal, 54,* 146–49, 170–75.

Eveland, Wilbur Crane. (1980). *Ropes of sand: America's failure in the Middle East.* London: W. W. Norton.

Ewing, David W. (1977). *Freedom inside the organization.* New York: McGraw-Hill.

Ewing, David W. (1983). *Do it my way or you're fired: Employee rights and the changing role of managerial prerogatives.* New York: Wiley & Sons.

Ewing, David W. (1984, September/October). What business thinks about employee rights. *Harvard Business Review, 55,* 81–94.

Executive Order 12044. (1978, March 23). Promulgated by President Jimmy Carter. *Federal Register, 43,* 12661.

Executive Order 12291. (1981, February 17). Promulgated by President Ronald Reagan. *Federal Register, 46,* 13193.

Feinstein, Selwyn. (1988, May 31). A special news report on people and their jobs in offices, fields, and factories. *The Wall Street Journal,* 1.

Ferguson, Linda J. (1987, October). Corporate and legal response to whistleblowers. *Proceedings of the 1987 Annual National Conference of the Council on Employee Responsibilities and Rights* (pp. 101–5). Virginia Beach, Va.: CERR.

Festinger, L. A. (1954). A theory of social comparison processes. *Human Relations, 7,* 117–40.

Finney, H. C., and Lesieur, H. C. (1982). A contingency theory of organizational crime. *Research in the Sociology of Organizations.* Vol. 1 (pp. 225–99). Greenwich, Conn.: JAI Press.

Flaim, Paul O., and Fullerton, Howard N. (1978, December). Labor force participation in 1990: Three possible paths. *Monthly Labor Review*, 25–36.

Flippo, E. B. (1980). *Personnel management*. New York: McGraw-Hill.

Folger, R. (1986). Mediation, arbitration, and the psychology of procedural justice. In R. J. Lewicki, B. H. Sheppard, and M. H. Bazerman (Eds.), *Research on negotiation in organizations*, Vol. 1 (pp. 57–79). Greenwich, Conn.: JAI Press.

Folger, R., and Greenberg, J. (1985). Procedural justice: An interpretive analysis of personnel systems. In K. Rowland and G. Ferris (Eds.), *Research in personnel and human resources management*. Vol. 3 (pp. 141–83). Greenwich, Conn.: JAI Press.

Fortado, B. (1985). The cooperation-conflict conundrum. *Proceedings of the 28th Annual Conference of the Midwest Academy of Management, 17*, 4–178.

Foulkes, F. K. (1980). *Personnel policies in large nonunion companies*. Englewood Cliffs, N.J.: Prentice-Hall.

Freedman, A. (1985). *The new look in wage policy and employee relations*. New York: The Conference Board, Report No. 865.

Freeman, R. B. (1985). Why are unions faring poorly in NLRB representation elections? In Thomas A. Kochan (Ed.), *Challenges and choices facing American labor* (pp. 45–64). Cambridge, Mass.: MIT Press.

Freeman, R. B., and Medoff, J. L. (1984). *What do unions do?* New York: Basic Books.

Friedman, R. C. (1971). The intern and sleep loss. *New England Journal of Medicine, 285*, 201–3.

Fritzsche, D. J., and Becker, H. (1984). Linking management behavior to ethical philosophy: An empirical investigation. *Academy of Management Journal, 27*, 166–75.

Fullerton, H. N. (1980, December). The 1995 labor force: A first look. *Monthly Labor Review, 103*, 15.

Fulmer, William. (1986). How do you say you're fired? *Business Horizons, 29* (1), 31–38.

Gackenbach, J. I., and Auerbach, S. M. (1980, January/February). One-the-job sex discrimination. *Business*, 24–30.

Garfinkel, H. (1967). *Studies in ethnomethodology*. Englewood Cliffs, N.J.: Prentice-Hall.

Garrison, Lloyd K. (1937, February). The national railroad adjustment board: A unique administrative agency. *Yale Law Review, 46*, 567.

Getman, J. G., Goldberg, S. B., and Herman, J. B. (1976). *Union representation elections: Law and reality*. New York: Basic Books.

Gibson, M. (1983). *Workers' rights*. Totowa, N.J.: Rowman and Allanheld.

Glazer, Myron. (1983, December). Ten whistleblowers and how they fared. *The Hastings Center Report, 13*, 33–41.

Goffman, E. (1952). On cooling the markout. *Psychiatry, 15*, 451–63.

Goldberg, J. P., Ahern, E., Haber, W., and Oswald, R. A. (1977). *Federal policies and worker status since the thirties*. Madison, Wis.: Industrial Relations Research Association.

Goodale, J. G., and Hall, D. T. (1976). Inheriting a career: The influence of sex, values, and parents. *Journal of Vocational Behavior, 8*, 19–30.

Goodman, Ellen. (1984, September 25). It's hard work spending all that money. *Minneapolis Tribune,* p. 10A.

Goodman, Ellen. (1986, October 20). Forget sex, think about business. *Seattle Times.*

Goodpaster, K., and Mathews, J. B. (1982, January/February). Can a corporation have a conscience? *Harvard Business Reviews,* 132–41.

Gorden, William I., and Infante, Dominic A. (1987). Employee rights: Content, argumentativeness, verbal aggressiveness and career satisfaction. In Chimezie A. B. Osigweh, Yg. (Ed.), *Communicating employee responsibilities and rights: A modern management mandate* (pp. 149–64). Westport, Conn.: Quorum Books.

Gordon, M. E. (1987, December 29). Grievance systems and workplace justice: Tests of behavioral propositions about procedural and distributive justice. Paper presented at the Annual Meeting of the Industrial Relations Research Association, Chicago.

Gordon, M. E., and Bowlby, R. L. (1988). Propositions about grievance settlements: Finally, consultation with grievants. *Personnel Psychology, 41* (1), 107–24.

Gordon, M. E., and Long, L. N. (1981). Demographic and attitudinal correlates of union joining. *Industrial Relations, 20,* 306–11.

Gordon, M. E., and Miller, S. J. (1984). Grievances: A review of research and practice. *Personnel Psychology, 37,* 117–46.

Gordon, M. E., and Nurick, A. J. (1981). Psychological approaches to the study of unions and union-management relations. *Psychological Bulletin, 90,* 293–306.

Gordon, M. E., Schmitt, N., and Schneider, W. G. (1984). An evaluation of laboratory research on bargaining and negotiations. *Industrial Relations, 23,* 218–33.

Gordon, M. E., Slade, L. A., and Schmitt, N. (1986). The "science of the sophomore" revisited: From conjecture to empiricism. *Academy of Management Review, 11,* 191–207.

Gottschalk, E. C., Jr. (1981, October 22). Promotions grow few as "baby boom" group eyes managers' jobs. *Wall Street Journal,* 1.

Graen, G. (1976). Role-making processes within complex organizations. In M. D. Dunnette (Ed.), *Handbook of industrial and organizational psychology* (pp. 1201–45). Chicago: Rand McNally.

Graham, J. W. (1983). *Principled organizational dissent.* Ph.D. diss., Northwestern University.

Graham, J. W. (1986). Principled organizational dissent: A theoretical essay. In B. M. Staw and L. L. Cummings (Eds.), *Research in organizational behavior.* Vol. 8 (pp. 1–52). Greenwich, Conn.: JAI Press.

Gramsci, A. (1971). *Selections from the prison notebooks.* New York: International.

Green, Mark, et al. (1979). The case for a corporate democracy act of 1980. Sec. 403. Mimeo.

Greenberg, J. (1983). Overcoming egocentric bias in perceived fairness through self-awareness. *Social Psychology Quarterly, 46,* 152–56.

Greenberg, J. (1986). Determinants of perceived fairness of performance evaluations. *Journal of Applied Psychology, 71,* 340–42.

Greenberg, J. (1987). A taxonomy of organizational justice theories. *Academy of Management Review, 12,* 9–22.

Greenberg, J. (1988). Cultivating an image of justice: Looking fair on the job. *Academy of Management Executive, 2* (2), 155–58.

Greenberg, J., and Cohen, R. L. (Eds.). (1982). *Equity and justice in social behavior.* New York: Academic Press.

Grote, Richard C. (1979). Employee discipline: A positive approach. *Industrial Relations Guide Service.* Englewood Cliffs, N.J.: Prentice-Hall.

Gutman, H. G. (1977). *Work, culture and society in industrializing America.* New York: Vintage Books.

Habermas, J. (1971). *Knowledge and human interests.* Boston: Beacon.

Hall, L. (1986). *Report card on Canadian MBA programs.* Kingston, Ontario: School of Business, Queens University.

Hall, Richard H. (1986). Professionalization and bureaucratization. *American Sociological Review, 33* (1), 92–104.

Hammer, T. H., and Bacharach, S. B. (1977). Overview: The search for solutions to ever-present problems of life in organizations. In T. H. Hammer and S. B. Bacharach (Eds.), *Reward systems and power distributions* (pp. 1–7). Ithaca, N.Y.: New York State School of Industrial and Labor Relations.

Hamner, W. C. (1975). Reinforcement theory and contingency management in organizational settings. In H. Tosi and W. C. Hamner (Eds.), *Organizational behavior: A contingency approach.* Chicago: St. Clair Press.

Hauserman, Nancy R. (1986a, October). Whistleblowing: Reasserting individual and community morality beyond the corporation. *Proceedings of the 1986 Annual National Conference of the Council on Employee Responsibilities and Rights* (pp. 63–67). Virginia Beach, Va.: CERR.

Hauserman, Nancy R. (1986b). Whistleblowing: Individual morality in a corporate society. *Business Horizons, 29* (2), 4–9.

Hayes, Robert H., and Abernathy, William T. (1980). Managing our way to economic decline. *Harvard Business Review, 58* (4), 67–76.

Henderson, L. J. (1935). *Pareto's General Sociology.* Cambridge, Mass.: Harvard University Press.

Herzberg, F. (1966). *Work and the nature of man.* Cleveland, Ohio: World Publishing.

Herzberg, F., Mausner, B., and Snyderman, B. (1959). *The motivation to work,* 2nd ed. New York: Wiley & Sons.

Heuer, L., and Penrod, S. (1987). The effect of third-party behavior on disputant satisfaction: Implications for a theory of procedural justice. Working Paper No. 19. Northwestern University: Dispute Resolution Research Center.

Hiers, Richard H. (1982). Section 1985 (3) employment discrimination litigation: Progress and confusion in judicial construction and policy-making, 1971–1981. *The Cumberland Law Review, 12,* 562–631.

Hiley, David R. (1984, Fall). Employee rights and the doctrine of at-will employment. *Business & Professional Ethics Journal, 4,* 1–10. "Commentary" by Robert Sass, pp. 11–16.

Hirschman, A. O. (1970). *Exit, voice and loyalty.* Cambridge, Mass.: Harvard University Press.

Hobsbawm, E. (1984). *Workers: Worlds of labor.* New York: Pantheon Books.

Hoerr, John, Glaberson, W. G., Moskowitz, D. B., Cahan, V., Pollock, M. A., and Tasini, J. (1985, July 8). Beyond unions: A revolution in employee rights is in the making. *Business Week*, 72–77.

Hollander, E. P. (1985). Leadership and power. In G. Lindzey and E. Aronson (Eds.), *Handbook of social psychology: Vol. 2. Special fields and applications*, 3rd ed. (pp. 485–537). New York: Random House.

Hollander, E. P., and Julian, J. W. (1970). Studies in legitimacy, influence, and innovation. In L. Berkowitz (Ed.), *Advances in experimental social psychology*. Vol. 5 (pp. 33–69). New York: Acdemic Press.

Homans, G. C. (1950). *The human group*. New York: Harcourt, Brace and World.

Homans, G. C. (1961). *Social behavior: Its elementary forms*. New York: Harcourt, Brace and World.

Hutchison, W. R. (1986, October). Positive discipline. *Proceedings of the 1986 Annual National Conference of the Council on Employee Responsibilities and Rights* (pp. 205–8). Virginia Beach, Va.: CERR.

Ichniowski, C. (1986). The effects of grievance activity on productivity. *Industrial and Labor Relations Review, 40*, 75–89.

Ichniowski, C., and Lewin, D. (1987). Grievance procedures and firm performance. In M. N. Kleiner, R. N. Block, M. Roomkin, and S. W. Salsburg (Eds.), *Human resources and the performance of the firm* (pp. 159–93). Madison, Wis.: Industrial Relations Research Association.

Ilgen, D. R., Fisher, C. D., and Taylor, M. S. (1979). Consequences of individual feedback on behavior in organizations. *Journal of Applied Psychology 64*, 349–71.

Jahoda, M. A. (1961). A social psychological approach to the study of culture. *Human Relations, 14*, 23–30.

James, Gene G. (1983). Whistleblowing: Its nature and justification. In Wade L. Robison et al. (Eds.), *Profits and professions: Essays in business and professional ethics* (pp. 287–303). Clifton, N.J.: Humana Press.

Jansen, E., and Von Glinow, M. A. (1985). Ethical ambivalence and organizational reward systems. *Academy of Management Review, 10*, 814–22.

Jaksa, James A., Pritchard, Michael S., and Kramer, Ronald C. (1988). Ethics in organizations: The *Challenger* explosion. In J. A. Jaksa and M. S. Pritchard (Eds.), *Communication Ethics: Methods of Analysis* (Chapter 8). Belmont, Calif.: Wadsworth.

Jenkins, R. L., and Reizenstein, R. C. (1984, Spring). Insights into the MBA: Its content, output, and relevance. *Selections: The Magazine of the Graduate Management Admission Council, 1*, 19–24.

Jensen, J. Vernon. (1986, October). The communicative act of whistleblowing. (Abridged version). *Proceedings of the 1986 Annual National Conference of the Council on Employee Responsibilities and Rights* (pp. 175–79). Virginia Beach, Va.: CERR.

Jensen, J. Vernon. (1987). Ethical tension points in whistleblowing. *Journal of Business Ethics, 6*, 321–28.

Job redesign on the assembly line: Farewell to blue-collar blues. (1973). *Organizational Dynamics, 2*, 51–67.

Kafka, F. (1976). *Franz Kafka: The complete stories*. Edited by N. N. Slatzer. New York: Schocken Books.

Kamenka, E. (1978). The anatomy of an idea. In E. and A. Erh-Tay Soon (Eds.), *Human rights*. London: Edward Arnold.

Kaplan, L. (1980, April). Sexual harassment: A commentary. *Stanford Campus Report*, 12–13.

Katz, D., and Kahn, R. L. (1978). *The social psychology of organizations*, 2nd ed. New York: Wiley & Sons.

Kavanagh, M. J. (1982). Evaluating performance. In K. M. Rowland and G. R. Ferris (Eds.), *Personnel management* (pp. 187–226). Boston: Allyn and Bacon.

Kavanagh, M. J., Hedge, J. W., and DeBiasi, G. (1983, August). An empirically based, multiple criteria approach to the design, development, and implementation of a performance measurement system. Symposium presented at the annual meeting of the Academy of Management, Dallas, Texas.

Kavanagh, M. J., Hedge, J., Ree, M., Earles, J., and DeBiasi, G. (1985, May). Clarification of some empirical issues in regard to employee acceptability of performance appraisal: Results from five samples. Paper presented at the meeting of the Eastern Academy of Management, Albany, New York.

Kleinfield, N. R. (1986, November 9). The whistle blowers' morning after. *The New York Times*, sec. 3, 1, 9, 11.

Kochan, T. A. (1979). How American workers view labor unions. *Monthly Labor Review, 102* (4), 23–31.

Kosterlitz, Julie, and Norrgard, Lee. (1984, November/December). The selling of the pentagon. *Common Cause Magazine, 10*, 14–18.

Kovach, K. A. (1979). J. P. Stevens and the struggle for union organization. *Labor Law Journal, 29*, 300–308.

Krefting, L. A., and Frost, P. J. (1985). Untangling webs, surfing waves, and wildcatting: A multiple-metaphor perspective on managing organizational culture. In P. J. Frost, L. F. Moore, M. R. Louis, C. C. Lundberg, and J. Martin (Eds.), *Organizational culture* (pp. 155–68). Beverly Hills, Calif.: Sage Publications.

Kuhn, J. W. (1961). *Bargaining in grievance settlement*. New York: Columbia University Press.

Kuhn, J. W. (1980). Electrical products. In *Collective bargaining: Contemporary American experience*. Madison, Wis.: Industrial Relations Research Association.

LaCroix, Wilfred L. (1979). *Principles for ethics in business*, rev. ed. (pp. 118–20). Washington, D.C.: University Press of America.

Ladenson, Robert F. (1983). Freedom of expression in the corporate workplace: A philosophical inquiry. In *Profits and professions: Essays in business and professional ethics*. Edited by Wade L. Robinson et al. (pp. 275–86). Clifton, N.J.: Humana Press.

Lagerfeld, S. (1981, November). The pop psychologist as union buster. *AFL-CIO American Federationists*, 6–12.

Lakoff, S. A., and Rich, D. (Eds.). (1973). *Private government: Introductory readings*. Glenview, Ill.: Scott Foresman.

Landy, F., Barnes-Farrell, J., and Cleveland, J. (1980). Perceived fairness and accuracy of performance evaluation: A follow-up. *Journal of Applied Psychology, 65*, 355–56.

Landy, F., Barnes, J. L., and Murphy, K. R. (1978). Correlates of perceived fairness and accuracy of performance evaluation. *Journal of Applied Psychology, 63,* 751–54.

Lane, R. E. (1979). The legitimacy bias: Conservative man in market and state. In B. Denitch (Ed.), *Legitimation of regimes* (pp. 55–79). Beverly Hills, Calif.: Sage Publications.

Langer, E. J. (1983). *The psychology of control.* Beverly Hills, Calif.: Sage Publications.

Latham, G. P., Wexley, K. N., and Pursell, E. D. (1975). Training managers to minimize rating errors in the observation of behavior. *Journal of Applied Psychology, 60,* 550–55.

Laurendeau, Normand M. (1982, Fall). Engineering professionalism: The case for corporate ombudsmen. *Business & Professional Ethics Journal, 2,* 35–45. "Commentary" by Michael R. Rion, pp. 47–48.

Lawler, E. E. (1969). Job design and employee motivation. *Personnel Psychology, 22,* 4226–35.

Lawler, E. E., and Mohrman, S. A. (1985, January/February). Quality circles after the fad. *Harvard Business Review,* 65–71.

Lawshe, C. H., and Guion, R. M. (1951). A comparison of management-labor attitudes toward grievance procedures. *Personnel Psychology, 4,* 3–17.

Lerner, M. J., and Lerner, S. C. (Eds.) (1981). *The justice motive in social behavior.* New York: Plenum Press.

Leventhal, G. S. (1976). Fairness in social relationships. In J. W. Thibaut, J. T. Spence, and R. C. Carson (Eds.), *Contemporary topics in social psychology* (pp. 211–39). Morristown, N.J.: General Learning Press.

Leventhal, G. S., Karuza, J., and Fry, W. R. (1980). Beyond fairness: A theory of allocation preferences. In G. Mikula (Ed.), *Justice and social interaction* (pp. 167–218). New York: Springer-Verlag.

Levi, B. H. (1979). *Barbarism with a human face.* New York: Harper & Row.

Lewin, D. (1987). Dispute resolution in the nonunion firm. *Journal of Conflict Resolution, 31,* 465–502.

Lindblom, C. E. (1977). *Politics and markets.* New York: Basic Books.

Lipset, S. M., and Schneider, W. (1983). *The confidence gap.* New York: Free Press.

Lochner, A. H., and Teel, K. S. (1977). Performance appraisal—a survey of current practices. *Personnel Journal, 56,* 245–47; 254.

Lofland, J., and Lofland, L. (1984). *Analyzing social settings.* Belmont, Calif.: Wadsworth.

MacIntyre, Alasdair. (1981). *After virtue.* Notre Dame, Ind.: University of Notre Dame Press.

Magnuson, Ed. (1988, February 1). Putting schedule over safety. *Time,* 20–21.

Maine Revised Statutes Ann., Title 26, Section 821.30. The whistleblower's protection act, 1983, is described in *Maine Legislative Review* (1985), ch. 452.

Malin, Martin H. (1983). Protecting the whistleblower from retaliatory discharge. *University of Michigan Journal of Law Reform, 16,* 277–318.

March, J. G. (1981). Decisions in organizations and theories of choice. In A. H. Van De Ven and W. F. Joyce (Eds.), *Perspectives on organization design and behavior* (pp. 205–44). New York: Wiley and Sons.

Martin, J. (1986). When expectations and justice do not coincide: Blue-collar visions of a just world. In H. W. Bierhoff, R. L. Cohen, and J. Greenberg (Eds.), *Justice in social relations* (pp. 317–35). New York: Plenum Press.

Martin, J. E., and Peterson, M. M. (1987). Two-tier wage structures: Implications for equity theory. *Academy of Management Journal, 30,* 297–315.

Martin, J., Sitkin, S. B., and Boehm, M. (1985). Founders and the elusiveness of a cultural legacy. In P. J. Frost, L. F. Moore, M. R. Louis, C. C. Lundberg, and J. Martin (Eds.), *Organizational culture* (pp. 99–124), Beverly Hills, Calif.: Sage Publications.

Mathewson, S. B. (1969). *Restriction of output among unorganized workers.* Carbondale, Ill.: Southern Illinois University Press.

Maslow, A. H. (1943). A theory of human motivation. *Psychological Review, 50,* 370–96.

Maslow, A. H. (1965). *Eupsychian management.* Homewood, Ill.: Dorsey Press.

McClintock, C. G., and Keil, L. L. (1982). Equity and social exchange. In J. Greenberg and R. L. Cohen (Eds.), *Equity and justice in social behavior* (pp. 337–87). New York: Academic Press.

McCurdy, H. E. (1977). *Public administration: A synthesis.* Menlo Park, Calif.: Cummings.

McEwen, C. A., and Maiman, R. J. (1981). Small claims mediation in Maine: An empirical assessment. *Maine Law Review, 33,* 237–68.

McKelvey, J. T. (1985). Introduction. In J. T. McKelvey (Ed.), *The changing law of fair representation* (pp. 1–12). Ithaca, N.Y.: ILR Press.

McKersie, R. B., and Shropshire, W. W. (1962). Avoiding written grievances: A succesful program. *The Journal of Business, 35,* 135–52.

McMillen, E. (1987, April 1). With 25 complaints filed in 3 years, the faculty joke about "lawsuit of the week" doesn't seem very funny. *The Chronicle of Higher Education,* 12–13.

McNeil, K. (1978). Understanding organizational power: Building of the Weberian legacy. *Administrative Science Quarterly, 23,* 65–90.

Mennemeier, Kenneth C. (1982). Protection from unjust discharges: An arbitration scheme. *Harvard Journal of Legislation, 19,* 49–96.

Mennemeier, Kenneth C. (1983). Reforming at-will employment law: A model statute. *Journal of Law Reform, 16,* 389.

Merriam, C. E. (1944). *Public and private government.* New Haven, Conn.: Yale University Press.

Miceli, M. P., and Near, J. P. (1985). Characteristics of organizational climate and perceived wrongdoing associated with whistle-blowing decisions. *Personnel Psychology, 38,* 525–44.

Miceli, M. P., and Near, J. P. (1988a). Individual and situational correlates of whistle-blowing. *Personnel Psychology, 41,* 267–81.

Miceli, M. P., and Near, J. P. (1988b, August). Predictors and outcomes of pay satisfaction in pay-for-performance plans. Paper presented at the 48th Annual Meeting of the Academy of Management, Anaheim, Calif.

Michener, H. A., and Lawler, E. J. (1975). The endorsement of formal leaders: An integrative model. *Journal of Personality and Social Psychology, 31,* 216–33.

Michigan Comprehensive Laws Ann., Section 15.362 (prohibition), Section 15.363 (civil action for injunctive relief or damages).

Michigan House Bill, No. 4665. (1979).

Michigan House Bill, No. 5892. (1982). Representative Perry Bullard has rein-
troduced this bill and Bill No. 4665 since 1982.

Michigan, House of Representatives. (1983). House Bill No. 5155.

Mincer, J., and Polachek, S. (1974). Family investments in human capital: earnings of women. *Journal of Political Economy, 82,* 576–80.

Minneapolis Star Tribune. (1985, June 14).

Mishler, E. G. (1986). *Research interviewing: Context and narrative.* Cambridge,
Mass.: Harvard University Press.

Missouri Revised Statute, Section 290.140 (1986 Supp.).

Mitroff, I. I. (1983). *Stakeholders of the organizational mind.* San Francisco: Jossey-
Bass.

Montana (1987). Wrongful Discharge from Employment Act, HB 241, L. 1987,
effective July 1, 1987, tit. 39, ch. 2, part 9, Montana Code Ann. Also
reprinted in *Individual Employee Rights Manual.* Washington, D.C.: BNA,
July 1987.

Moore, B., Jr. (1978). *Injustice: The social bases of obedience and revolt.* White Plains,
N.Y.: M. E. Sharpe.

Mumford, E. (1980). *Interns: From students to physicians.* Cambridge, Mass.: Harvard University Press.

Munchus, George. (1987). Battle of the ban on smoking in the workplace. In
C.A.B. Osigweh, Yg. (Ed.), *Communicating employee resonsibilities and rights:
A modern management mandate* (pp. 87–98). Westport, Conn.: Quorum
Books.

Mundinger, D. (1967). The university ombudsman—his place on the campus.
Journal of Higher Education, 38, 493–99.

Nader, Ralph, Green, Mark, and Seligman, Joel. (1976). *Taming the giant corporation.* New York: W. W. Norton.

Nader, Ralph, Petkas, Peter J., and Blackwell, Kate (Eds.). (1972). *Whistle Blowing:
The report of the conference on professional responsibility.* New York: Gross-
man.

Near, J. P., and Miceli, M. P. (1985). Organizational dissidence: The case of
whistle-blowing. *Journal of Business Ethics, 4,* 1–16.

Near, J. P., and Miceli, M. P. (1987a). Whistle-blowers in organizations: Dissi-
dents or reformers? In B. Staw and L. Cummings (Eds.), *Research in organizational behavior,* Vol. 9 (pp. 321–68). Greenwich, Conn.: JAI Press.

Near, J. P., and Miceli, M. P. (1987b, October). Predictors of retaliation against
whistle-blowers. *Proceedings of the 1987 Annual National Conference of the
Council on Employee Responsibilities and Rights* (pp. 37–41). Virginia Beach,
Va.: CERR.

Newcomb, T. M. (1961). *The acquaintance process.* New York: Holt, Rinehart, &
Winston.

New Jersey General Assembly Bill, No. 1832. (1980).

Newman, B. (1986, February 24). Fired and furious, many Britons insist on a
second opinion. *Wall Street Journal,* 1, 8.

Newman, R. A. (1973). *Equity in the world's legal systems.* Brussels, Belgium:
Establishments Emile Bruylant.

New York Labor Law, Ch. 660, L. 1984 (1984, September—effective date), adding Sections 740.1 to 740.7 to N.Y. labor law.

Nickel, J. W. (1978–79). Is there a human right to employment? *The Philosophical Forum, 10,* 149–70.

Nilsen, Thomas R. (1979, Winter). Confidentiality and morality. *Western Journal of Speech Communication, 43,* 38–47.

Noble, D. F. (1984). *Forces of production.* New York: Alfred A. Knopf.

Nord, W. R. (1983). A political-economic perspective on organizational effectiveness. In K. S. Cameron and D. A. Whetten (Eds.), *Organizational effectiveness* (pp. 95–133). New York: Academic Press.

Norwood, Janet L. (1982, September). *The male-female earning gap: A review of employment and earning issues.* Report 673. Washington, D.C.: U.S. Department of Labor.

Nova Scotia Statute, c. 10, sec. 68 (1972).

Nowak, J., Rotunda, R., and Young, J. (1978). *Constitutional law,* 402.

Nussbaum, Bruce, and Beam, Alex. (1986, March 24). Remaking the Harvard b-school. *Business Week,* 54–58.

O'Neil, Robert. (1978). *The rights of government employees.* New York: Avon Books.

Oberdorfer, Dan. (1984, September 15). Editorial. *Minneapolis Star and Tribune,* 18A.

Ontario Revised Statute, C. 137, Secs. 4, 40.

Organ, D. W., and Bateman, Thomas. (1986). *Organizational behavior: An applied psychological approach,* 3rd ed. Plano, Tex.: Business Publications.

Orr, Leonard H. (1981, Fall). Is whistle-blowing the same as informing? *Business and Society Review,* 4–18.

Osigweh, Chimezie A. B. (1983). *Improving problem-solving participation: The case of local transnational voluntary organizations.* Lanham, Md.: University Press of America.

Osigweh, Chimezie A. B. (1985a). *Professional management: An evolutionary perspective.* Dubuque, Iowa: Kendall/Hunt Division, Wm. C. Brown.

Osigweh, Chimezie A. B. (1985b, Spring). Collective bargaining and public-sector union power. *Public Personnel Management Journal, 14* (1), 75–84.

Osigweh, Chimezie A. B. (1985c, Spring). Public-sector union power and the economic, financial, and political contexts of collective bargaining. *Akron Business and Economic Reviews, 16* (1), 24–30.

Osigweh, Chimezie A. B. (1986, Summer). Management and professionalism. *The Mid-Atlantic Journal of Business* (formerly *The Journal of Business), 24* (2), 1–20.

Osigweh, Chimezie A. B. (1987a, Fall). Management campaigns and union organizing in a multifacility organization: Learning from KCOM-KOHC Medical, Inc. Prepared for the *Journal of Management Case Studies, 3.* Also available from Norfolk, Va.: Norfolk State University, School of Business.

Osigweh, Chimezie A. B. (1987b). Communication, responsibilities, and pro-rights revolution in the industrial workplace. In Chimezie A. B. Osigweh (Ed.), *Communicating employee responsibilities and rights: A modern management mandate* (pp. 3–40). Westport, Conn.: Quorum books.

Osigweh, Chimezie A. B. (1988a, March). The challenge of responsibilities: Confronting the revolution in workplace rights in modern organizations. *The Employee Responsibilities and Rights Journal, 1* (1), 5–25.

Osigweh, Chimezie A. B. (1988b). Management as if rights mattered: The challenge of employee rights and management responsibilities. Paper presented to the First Industrial Relations Congress of the Americas, Quebec, Canada, August 24–27.

Osigweh, Chimezie A. B. (1989). The myth of universality in transnational organizational science. In C.A.B. Osigweh, Yg. (Ed.), *Organizational science abroad: Constraints and perspectives* (pp. 3–26). New York: Plenum Press.

Pareto, V. (1935). *The mind and society.* New York: Harcourt, Brace & Company.

Parmerlee, Marcia, Near, Janet, and Jensen, Tamila. (1982). Correlates of whistleblowers' perceptions of organizational retaliation. *Administrative Science Quarterly, 27,* 17–34.

Pasztor, Andy, and McMurray, Scott. (1985, May 5). E. F. Hutton scheme involved more cash than disclosed, U.S. prosecutor says. *Wall Street Journal,* 3, 24.

Pasztor, A., Ingersoll, B., and Hertzberg, D. (1985, May 3). Hutton unit pleads guilty in fraud case. *Wall Street Journal,* 1, 3, 9.

Patridge, Bruce. (1978). The process of leadership on the shop floor. In B. King, S. Streaufret, and F. E. Fielder (Eds.), *Managerial control and organizational democracy* (pp. 187–200). New York: Wiley & Sons.

Peach, D., and Livernash, E. R. (1974). *Grievance initiation and resolution: A study in basic steel.* Boston: Graduate School of Business, Harvard University.

Pearson, Drew, and Anderson, Jack. (1968). *The case against Congress,* Part I. New York: Simon & Schuster.

Peck, C. J. (1979). Unjust discharge from employment: A necessary change in the law. *Ohio State Law Journal, 40* (1), 13–38.

Pennsylvania House Bill, No. 1742. (1981).

Pentagon told to fire auditor, demote two. (1985, June 14). *Minneapolis Star Tribune,* 19A.

Perlman, S. (1928). *A theory of the labor movement.* New York: A. M. Kelley.

Perritt, Henry H., Jr. (1984a). *Employee dismissal law and practice.* New York: Wiley & Sons. See also, 2nd edition, 1987.

Perritt, Henry H., Jr. (1984b). Employee dismissals: An opportunity for legal simplification. *Labor Law Journal, 35,* 407.

Perritt, Henry H., Jr. (1984c). And the whole earth was of one language: A broad view of dispute resolution. *Villanova Law Review, 29,* 1049.

Perritt, Henry H., Jr. (1987). Wrongful dismissal legislation. *UCLA Law Review, 35,* 65.

Perrow, C. (1983). The organizational context of human factors engineering. *Administrative Science Quarterly, 28,* 521–41.

Perrucci, R. M., Anderson, R. M., Schendel, D. E., and Trachtman, L. E. (1980). Whistle-blowing: Professionals' resistance to organizational authority. *Social Problems, 28,* 149–64.

Peters, Charles, and Branch, Taylor. (1972). *Blowing the whistle: Dissent in the public interest.* New York: Praeger.

Peters. T. J., and Waterman, R. H., Jr. (1982). *In search of excellence: Lessons from America's best-run companies.* New York: Harper & Row.

Pfeffer, J. (1981). *Power in organizations.* Marshfield, Mass.: Pitman.

Pfeffer, J., and Salancik, G. R. (1978). *The external control of organizations.* New York: Harper and Row.

Phelps, Orme W. (1959). *Discipline and discharge in the unionized firm.* Berkeley and Los Angeles: University of California Press.

Pierce, Ellen R., Mann, Richard A., and Roberts, Barry S. (1982–83). Employee termination at-will: A principled approach. *Villanova Law Review, 28* (1), 46.

Ploscowe, Stephen A., and Goldstein, Marvin M. (1987, March). Trouble on the firing line. *Nation's Business,* 36–37.

Pope, K. (1942). *Millhands and preachers: A study of Gastonia.* New Haven: Yale University Press.

Potter, R. L. (1983). Resident, woman, wife, mother: issues for women in training. *Journal of American Women's Association, 38,* 98–102.

Powell, G. N. (1980, May/June). Career development and the woman manager— a social power perspective. *Personnel,* 22–32.

Pulakos, E. D. (1984). A comparison of rater training programs: Error training and accuracy training. *Journal of Applied Psychology, 69,* 581–88.

Putnam, L. L. (1983). The interpretive perspective: An alternative to functionalism. In L. L. Putnam and M. E. Pacanowsky (Eds.), *Communication and organizations: An interpretive approach* (pp. 31–54). Beverly Hills, Calif.: Sage Publications.

Quebec Statute, C. 45, Section 124 (1979).

Rafaeli, A. (1985). Quality circles and employees' attitudes. *Personnel Psychology, 38,* 603–15.

Ramos, A. G. (1981). *The new science of organizations.* Toronto: University of Toronto Press.

Rasor, Dina. (1985). *The Pentagon underground.* New York: Times Books.

Redding, Charles W. (1985, July). Rocking boats, blowing whistles, and teaching speech communication. *Communication Education, 34,* 245–58.

Redeker, James R. (1988). *Discipline: Policies and procedures.* 2nd ed. Washington, D.C.: Bureau of National Affairs.

Reis, H. T. (1986). Levels of interest in the study of interpersonal justice. In H. W. Bierhoff, R. L. Cohen, and J. Greenberg (Eds.), *Justice in social relations* (pp. 187–209). New York: Plenum Press.

Restatement (Second) of Torts, Section 870 (1979).

Revising the U.S. Senate Code of Ethics. (1981, February). *The Hastings Center Report, 11,* 1–28.

Rinke, C. M. (1981). The professional identities of women physicians. *Journal of American Medical Association, 245,* 2419–21.

Ritzenthaler, Rob. (1986, February 6). Agriculture Department whistleblowers awarded damages. *The Daily Cardinal* (Madison, Wis.), 4.

Robison, Wade L. et al. (Eds.). (1983). *Profits and professions: Essay in business and professional ethics.* Clifton, N.J.: Humana Press.

Rodgers, D. T. (1974). *The work ethic in industrial America: 1850–1920.* Chicago: University of Chicago Press.

Roethlisberger, F. J., and Dickson, W. J. (1939). *Management and the worker.* Cambridge, Mass.: Harvard University Press.

Rosenberg, J. M. (1988, February 14). Retailers search for more workers. *Bloomington Herald-Times*, Fl.

Rowe, M. P. (1984). The non-union complaint system at M.I.T.: An upward-feedback mediation model. *Alternative to the High Cost of Litigation, 2*, 10–18.

Rowe, M., and Baker, M. (1984, May-June). Are you hearing enough employee complaints? *Harvard Business Review, 62* (3), 127–36.

Ryan, Michael. (1985, April 1). The whistle-blower. *New York Magazine, 52,* 54, 56–59.

Salipante, P. F., and Aram, J. D. (1984). The role of organizational procedures in the resolution of social conflict. *Human Organization, 43* (1), 9–15.

Salipante, P. F., and Aram, J. D. (1978). The role of special grievance systems in furthering equal employment opportunities. *Industrial Relations Research Association, Proceedings of the 31st Annual Meeting,* 299–307.

Salipante, P., F., and Bouwen, R. (1985). A model of grievance formulation and its consequencs. *Proceedings of the 28th Annual Conference of the Midwest Academy of Management,* 102–6.

Salipante, Paul, and Fortado, Bruce. (1986, October). Employee rights: Required v. desired. Abridged version. *Proceedings of the 1986 Annual National Conference of the Council on Employee Responsibilities and Rights* (pp. 102–6). Virginia Beach, Va.: CERR.

Sampson, E. E. (1983). *Justice and the critique of pure psychology.* New York: Plenum Press.

Sanders, Wayne. (1981, Summer). Free speech for the private employee: Will state action rulings bring the Constitution to the workplace? *Southern Speech communication Journal, 46,* 397–410.

Sanders, Wayne. (1983, Summer). The first amendment and the government workplace: Has the Constitution fallen down on the job? *Western Journal of Speech Communication, 46,* 253–76.

Sanders, Wayne, (1987). Freedom of speech and private sector at-will employment: Implications for society, the individual, and management. In Chimezie A. B. Osigweh, Yg. (Ed.), *Communicating employee responsibilities and rights: A modern management mandate* (pp. 63–71). Westport, Conn.: Quorum Books.

Sashkin, Marshall. (1984, Spring). Participative management is an ethical imperative. *Organizational Dynamics, 12* (2), 5–22.

Sashkin, Marshall. (1986, Summer). Participative management remains an ethical imperative. *Organizational Dynamics, 14* (3), 62–75.

Sashkin, Marshall, and Morris, William C. (1987). Communicating employee responsibilities and rights: The medium and the message. In Chimezie A. B. Osigweh, Yg. (Ed.), *Communicating employee responsibilities and rights: A modern management mandate* (pp. 113–18). Westport, Conn.: Quorum Books.

Sayles, L. R. (1958). *The behavior of industrial work groups.* New York: Wiley & Sons.

Schein, E. G. (1965). *Organizational psychology.* Englewood Cliffs, N.J.: Prentice-Hall. See also, 3rd edition, 1980.

Schmidt, F. L., and Hunter, J. E. (1980). The future of criterion-related validity. *Personnel Psychology, 33*, 41–60.

Schriesheim, C. A. (1978). Job satisfaction, attitudes toward unions, and voting in a union representation election. *Journal of Applied Psychology, 63*, 548–52.

Schumacher, E. F. (1973). *Small is beautiful: A study of economics as if people mattered.* London and New York: Harper & Row.

Schutt, S. R. (1982). White collar crime: The nation's largest growth industry. *The Accountants Digest, 47* (3), 18–20.

Scott, William, G. (1985). Organizational revolution: An end to managerial orthodoxy. *Administration and Society, 17* (2), 149–70.

Scott, William G., and Mitchell, Terence R. (1985, December 11). The moral failure of management education. *The Chronicle of Higher Education, 35*.

Scott, W. G., and Mitchell, T. C. (1986, Fall). Markets and morals in management education. *Selections, 3* (2), 3–8.

Sears, D. O., and Whitney, R. E. (1973). Political persuasion. In I. S. Pool, F. W. Frey, W. Schramm, N. Maccoby, and E. B. Parker (Eds.), *Handbook of communications.* Chicago: Rand McNally.

Seligman, M.E.P. (1975). *Helplessness: On depression, development, and death.* San Francisco: W. H. Freeman.

Selznick, P. (1969). *Law, society, and industrial justice.* New York: Russell Sage Foundation.

Sennett, R. (1980). *Authority.* New York: Vintage Books.

Sennett, R., and Cobb, J. (1972). *The hidden injuries of class.* New York: Vintage Books.

Shapiro, E., and Lowenstein, L. (Eds.). (1979). *Becoming a physician: Development of values and attitudes in medicine.* Cambridge, Mass.: Ballinger.

Sheppard, B. H. (1983). Managers as inquisitors: Some lessons from the laws. In M. H. Bazerman and R. J. Lewicki (Eds.)., *Negotiating in organizations* (pp. 193–213). Beverly Hills, Calif.: Sage Publications.

Sheppard, B. H. (1984). Third-party conflict intervention: A procedural framework. In B. M. Staw and L. L. Cummings (Eds.), *Research in organizational behavior.* Vol. 6 (pp. 141–190). Greenwich, Conn.: JAI Press.

Sheppard, B. H., and Lewicki, R. J. (1987). Toward general principles of managerial fairness. *Social Justice Research, 1*, 161–76.

Siegel, B., and Donnelly, J. C. (1978). Enriching personal and professional development: The experience of a support group for interns. *Journal of Medical Education 53*, 908–14.

Siehl, C. (1985). After the founder: An opportunity to manage culture. In P. J. Frost, L. F. Moore, M. R. Louis, C. C. Lundberg, and J. Martin (Eds.), *Organizational culture* (pp. 125–140). Beverly Hills, Calif.: Sage Publications.

Silverman, D. (1970). *The theory of organizations.* New York: Basic Books.

Simon, H. (1947). *Administrative behavior.* New York: Macmillan.

Sinclair, Ward. (1986, January 15). USDA whistleblower will argue case in court. *Minneapolis Star Tribune*, 3A.

Small, G. W. (1981). House officer stress syndrome. *Psychosomatics, 22*, 860–69.

Smith, Stephen A. (1983). The uncivil servants: Public employees and political expression. *Free Speech Yearbook, 51*–61.

Some kind of hearing. (1975). *Pennsylvania Law Review, 123,* 1267–94.

South Dakota Code, Section 60.1.1 (1978). Establishes a presumption that employment is to continue for a period of time defined by the pay interval.

St. Antoine, J. J. (1985). The revision of employment-at-will enters a new phase. *Industrial Relations Research Association, Proceedings of the 1985 Spring Meeting,* 563–67.

Staw, B. M., and Szwajkowski, E. (1975). The scarcity-munificence component of organizational environments and the commission of illegal acts. *Administrative Science Quarterly, 20,* 345–54.

Stengel, Richard, and Constable, Anne. (1987, April 6). Balancing act: In a sweeping decision, the high court expands affirmative action. *Time,* 18–20.

Stessin, Lawrence. (1960). *Employee discipline.* Washington, D.C.: Bureau of National Affairs.

Stewart, Lea P. (1980, May). Whistleblowing: Implications for organizational communication scholars. Paper presented at the International Communication Association Convention, Acapulco, Mexico.

Stewart, Lea P. (1987, November). Where were the whistleblowers? The case of Allan McDonald and Roger Boisjoly. Paper presented at the Annual Meeting of the Speech Communication Association, Boston, Mass.

Stieber, Jack. (1983). Employment-at-will: An issue for the 1980s. Presidential Address, Industrial Relations Research Association, 1.

Stieber, Jack. (1984). Employment-at-will: An issue for the 1980s. *Industrial Relations Research Association, 36th Annual Proceedings,* 1–13.

Stieber J. (1985). Recent developments in employment-at-will. *Industrial Relations Research Association, Proceedings of the 1985 Spring Meeting,* 557–63.

Stieber, Jack. (1986, October). Legislation: The best approach to unjust dismissal. *Proceedings of the 1986 Annual National Conference of the Council on Employee Responsibilities and Rights* (pp. 92–95). Virginia Beach, Va.: CERR.

Stieber, J., and Block, R. (1983). *Discharged workers and the labor market.* U.S. Department of Labor, Employment and Training Administration Grant 21–26–80–11.

Stieber, Jack, Block, R., and Corbitt, L. (1985). How representative are published decisions? In W. J. Gershenfeld (Ed.), *Arbitration 1984: absenteeism, recent law, panels, and published decisions.* Proceedings of the 37th Annual Meeting, National Academy of Arbitrators (p. 176, Table 1). Washington, D.C.: Bureau of National Affairs.

Stieber, Jack, and Murray, Michael. (1983). Protection against unjust discharge: The need for a federal statute. *Journal of Law Reform, 16* (2), 336–41.

Stouffer, S. A., Lumsdaine, A. A., Lumsdaine, M. H., Williams, R. M., Smith, M. B., Janis, I. L., Star, S. A., and Cottrell, L. S. (1949). *The American soldier.* Vol. 2. Princeton, N.J.: Princeton University Press.

Stouffer, S. A., Suchman, E. A., DeVinney, L. C., Star, S. A., and Wiliams, R. N. (1949). *The American soldier.* Vol. 1. Princeton, N.J.: Princeton University Press.

Summers, Clyde B. (1976). Individual protection against unjust dismissal: Time for a statute. *Virginia Law Review, 58* (1), 481–532.

Summers, Clyde B. (1980). Protecting *all* employees against unjust dismissal. *Harvard Business Review, 58* (1), 132–39.

Tang, T. L., Tollison, P. S., and Whiteside, H. D. (1987). The effect of quality circle initiation on motivation to attend quality circle meetings and on task performance. *Personnel Psychology, 40,* 799–814.

Tangney, J. P. (1987, August). Factors inhibiting self-correction in science. Paper presented at the Annual Meeting of the American Psychological Association, New York, New York.

Tannenbaum, S. I., Kavanagh, M. J. (1984, August). Rater-ratee differences, interview processes, and acceptance of performance evaluations. Paper presented at the Annual Meeting of the American Psychological Association, Toronto.

Taylor, S. M., and Walther, F. (1981). The relationship of feedback dimensions to work attitudes and behavior: Process and practical implications. *Proceedings of the Midwest Academy of Management,* 347–60.

Terborg, J. R. (1977). Women in management: A research review. *Journal of Applied Psychology, 62,* 647–64.

The Conference Board. (1980). *Nonunion complaint systems: A corporate appraisal.* Washington, D.C.: The Conference Board.

Thibaut, J., and Walker, L. (1975). *Procedural justice: A psychological analysis.* Hillside, N.J.: Lawrence Erlbaum Associates.

Thibaut, J., and Walker, L. (1978). A theory of prcedures. *California Law Review, 66,* 541–66.

Thibaut, S. W., and Kelley, H. H. (1959). *The social psychology of groups.* New York: Wiley & Sons.

Title VII of the Civil Rights Act (1964). Section 703 (e).

Thompson, J. D. (1967). *Organizations in action.* New York: McGraw-Hill.

Thomson, A.W.J., and Murray, V. V. (1976). *Grievance procedures.* Lexington, Mass.: Lexington Books.

Throdahl, Monte. (1981). Anyone can whistle. *Business and Society Review, 39,* 16–17.

Thurow, L. C. (1975). *Generating inequality.* New York: Basic Books.

Tobias, P. H. (1985). The plaintiff's perception of litigation. In J. T. McKelvey (Ed.), *The changing law of fair representation* (pp. 128–44). Ithaca, N.Y.: ILR Press.

Towne, H. R. (1886). The engineer as economist. *Transactions of the American Society of Mechanical Engineers, 7,* 428–32.

Townsend, Robert. (1984). *Further up the organization.* New York: Alfred A. Knopf.

Trice, H. M., and Beyer, J. M. (1984, October). Studying organizational cultures through rites and ceremonials. *Academy of Management Review,* 653–69.

Tyler, T. R. (1986). The psychology of leadership evaluation. In H. W. Bierhoff, R. L. Cohen, and J. Greenberg (Eds.), *Justice in social relations* (pp. 299–316). New York: Plenum Press.

Unger, R. (1976). Law in modern society. Mimeo, 193–97.

United States Bureau of Labor Statistics. (1981). *BLS earnings and other characteristics of organized workers, May, 1980.*

United States Code Ann., 5, Sections 553 note, 501 note, 556–57 (1983 Supp.).

United States Code, *29*, Section 623 [f] (1984), Age Discrimination in Employment Act, Section 623 (f).

United States Code, *42* (1981).

United States Code, *42*, Section 20003.2 [e] (1984). Title VII of the Civil Rights Act, Section 703 (e).

United States Department of Labor, Bureau of Labor Statistics. (1986a, June). *The Employment Situation: May 1986.* Document Number USDL 86–226. Washington, D.C.: Government Printing Office.

United States Department of Labor, Bureau of Labor Statistics. (1986b, May). *Employment and Earnings, 33* (5). Washington, D.C.: Bureau of Labor Statistics.

United States Merit Systems Protection Board, Office of Merit Systems Review and Studies. (1981). *Whistleblowing and the federal employee: Blowing the whistle on fraud, waste, and mismanagement—who does it and what happens.* Washington, D.C.: U.S. Merit Systems Protection Board.

United States Merit Systems Protection Board, Office of Merit Systems Review and Studies. (1984). *Blowing the whistle in the federal government: A comparative analysis of 1980 and 1983 survey findings.* Washington, D.C.: U.S. Merit Systems Protection Board.

Valko, R. J., and Clayton, P. J. (1975). Depression in the internship. *Diseases of the Nervous System, 36*, 26–29.

Vaughn, Robert G. (1984). *Merit systems protection board: Rights and remedies.* New York: Law Journal Seminars Press.

Verkuil, Paul R. (1978). The emerging concept of administrative procedure. *Columbia Law Review, 78*, 258–329.

Waite, L. J., and Berryman, S. (1985). *Women in nontraditional occupations.* Santa Monica, Calif.: The Rand Corporation.

Waldo, D. (1980). *The enterprise of public administration.* Novato, Calif.: Chandler and Sharp.

Waley, Arthur. Trans. (1938). *The analects of Confucius.* New York: Vintage Books.

Walster, E., Berscheid, E., and Walster, G. W. (1973). New directions in equity research. *Journal of Personality and Social Psychology, 25*, 151–76.

Walster, E., and Walster, G. W. (1975). Equity and social justice. *Journal of Social Issues, 31* (3), 21–43.

Walster, E., Walster, G. W., and Berscheid, E. (1978). *Equity: Theory and research.* Boston: Allyn & Bacon.

Walton, R. E. (1969). *Interpersonal peacemaking: Confrontations and third-party consultations.* Reading, Mass.: Addison-Wesley.

Waxman, M. (1986). Ecology of educational institutions: The teaching hospital as a model. *The Campus Ecologist, 4*, 2–3.

Waxman, M., Vosti, K. L., and Barbour, A. B. (1986a). Use of a medical center ombudsman's office by medical students. *Journal of Medical Education, 61*, 62–64.

Waxman, M., Vosti, K. L., and Barbour, A. B. (1986b). Role of the ombudsman in the modern medical center. *Western Journal of Medicine, 144* (5), 627–30.

Weber, M. (1947). *The theory of social and economic organization.* Translated by

A. M. Henderson and T. Persons, and edited by T. Parsons. Glencoe, Ill.: Free Press.

Weick, K. E. (1979). *The social psychology of organizing,* 2nd ed. Reading, Mass.: Addison-Wesley.

Weisman, C. S., Morlock, L. L., Sack, D. G., and Levine, D. M. (1976). Sex differences in response to a blocked career pathway among unaccepted medical school applicants. *Sociology of Work and Occupations, 3,* 187–208.

Werhane, Patricia H. (1985). *Persons, rights, and corporations.* Englewood Cliffs, N.J.: Prentice-Hall.

Werhane, Patricia H. (1987). Defining and communicating employee and employer rights in an institutional context. In Chimezie A. B. Osigweh, Yg. (Ed.), *Communicating employee responsibilities and rights: A modern management mandate* (pp. 41–54). Westport, Conn.: Quorum Books.

Werhane, Patricia H., and D'Andrade, Kendal (Eds.) (1985). *Profit and responsibility: Issues in business and professional ethics.* New York: Edwin Mellen Press.

Westin, Alan F. (1979). *Computers, personnel administration, and citizen rights.* National Bureau of Standards, Special Publication 500–50, U.S. Department of Commerce. Washington, D.C.: Government Printing Office.

Westin, Alan F. (1980). *Whistle blowing!* New York: McGraw-Hill.

Westin, Alan F. (1983). Employer responses to new judicial rulings on at-will employment: A warning about the "legal armorplate" approach. *Proceedings of the New York University 36th Annual National Conference on Labor.* Albany, N.Y.: Mathew Bender.

Westin, Alan F. (1988). Past and future in employment testing: A socio-political overview. *University of Chicago Legal Forum, 1,* 93–111.

Westin, Alan F. (Ed.). (1981). *Whistle blowing: Loyalty and dissent in the corporation.* New York: McGraw-Hill.

Westin, Alan F., and Feliu, Alfred G. (1988). *Resolving employment disputes without litigation.* Washington, D.C.: Bureau of National Affairs.

Westin, Alan F., and Salisbury, Stephen (Eds.). (1980). *Individual rights in the corporation.* New York: Edwin Mellen Press.

Westin, Alan F., Schweder, Heather A., Baker, Michael A., and Lehman, Sheila. (1985). *The changing workplace.* White Plains, N.Y.: Knowledge Industries.

"Whistleblower" gets poor job rating. (1985, August 1). *The New York Times,* 12A.

Whistleblower wins promotion, legal fees. (1982, June 16). *Minneapolis Star Tribune,* 12A.

Whyte, William F. (1987, July). From human relations to organizational behavior: Reflections on the changing scene. *Industrial and Labor Relations Review, 40* (4), 487–500.

Wiebe, R. H. (1975). *The segmented society: An introduction to the meaning of America.* New York: Oxford University Press.

Wilensky, Harold L. (1964). The professionalization of everyone? *American Journal of Sociology, 70* (1), 137–58.

Wilson, W. (1887). The study of administration. *Political Science Quarterly, 2,* 197–222.

Winslow, Gerald R. (1984, June). From loyalty to advocacy: A new metaphor for nursing. *The Hastings Center Report, 14,* 32–40.

Wright, Peter. (1987). *Spycatcher.* New York: Viking Penguin.

Yankelovich, D. (1981). *New rules: Searching for self-fulfillment in a world turned upside down.* New York: Random House.

Yin, R. K. (1984). *Case study research: Design and methods.* Beverly Hills, Calif.: Sage Publications.

Youngblood, S.A., and Bierman, L. (1985). Due process and employment-at-will. In K. M. Rowland and G. R. Ferris (Eds.), *Research in personnel and human resources management,* Vol. 3 (pp. 185–230). Greenwich, Conn.: JAI Press.

Youngblood, Stuart A., and Tidwell, Gary L. (1981, May/June). Termination at will: Some changes in the wind. *Personnel,* 22–33.

Zaleznik, A. (1977). Managers and leaders: Are they different? *Harvard Business Review, 55* (3), 67–78.

Zalusky, J. (1976). Arbitration: Updating a vital process. *AFL-CIO American Federationist, 83* (11), 1–8.

Index

Absenteeism, 110, 114
Academic lawyers, and wrongful discharge legislation, 63, 65
Actual effectiveness, 28
Adams, J. S., 180
Adams, Stacy, 26, 29
Adjudicative system. *See* Grievance system
Administrative state, 199, 200
Advocacy, 46
Age Discrimination in Employment Act (1967), 119
Agency problem, 244; and rights, 230
Alexander v. *Gardner-Denver Co.*, 43
Allis-Chalmers Corp. v. *Lueck*, 43–44
Allocation decisions, rules for, 28–29
Alternatives, 8, 248–49
American Federation of Labor and Congress of Industrial Organizations (AFL-CIO), 46
Appeal, 28; in nonunion firms, 36–37
Aram, John, 36
Arbitration, 28, 37; challenge to, 46; evaluation of, 30–31; for wrongful dismissal, 73–74. *See also* Grievance system

Arendt, Hannah, 202
Authority, consent theory of, 205–6

Baby boomers, 10
Baritz, Loren, 200, 206, 207
Barnard, Chester I., 200, 203, 205–6, 207
Barrett, Richard S., 176
Barrows, Sidney Biddle, *Mayflower Madam*, 202
Beliefs, 230
Blackmun, William, 44
Black population, socialization of, 90
Blumberg, Phillip, 197
Boesky, Ivan, xxii
Bok, Derek, 8
Branch, Taylor, 189, 193
Braverman, Harry, 249
Brett, Jeanne, 30
Brockmeyer v. *Dun & Bradstreet*, 61
Bruner, Jerome S., 176, 177
Bureaucracy, versus flexibility, 10–12
Business education, 18; moral void in, 14–16. *See also* Management education

California, wrongful discharge legis-
lation in, 56–57, 65
Canada, 65
Civil Rights Act (1964), 84, 119
Civil rights movement, 10
Civil Service Reform Act (CSRA), 196
Clegg, Stewart, 234
Coaching, 102
Cobb, Jonathan, 242
Cognitive politics, 205
Collective action, obstacles to, 244
Collective bargaining: encouragement
of, 119; rejection of, 16–17; roots
of, 118. *See also* Unions
Commitment, employee, 102, 103,
105, 108
Communication, employee, 112–13,
156, 158
Compensatory acts, 221–22
Complexity, in organizations, xv
Conflict: and accumulation, 222, 223,
226; growth and expression of,
219–22; metamorphosis of, 220–22,
223, 226; and ombudsman role,
168–72
Consciousness-raising, 243
Context, and rights, 230–31
Corporatism, emergence of, 199
Corruption, 13–14, 200
Counseling, 102, 125
Courts: climate of, 16; and disparate-
treatment theory, 92; and em-
ployee interests, 67–68; and unjust
discharge, 51–54, 55, 73; on whis-
tleblowing, 195. *See also* Law;
United States Supreme Court
Critical political economic compo-
nent, 234–35
Culbert, Samuel A., 243
Culture, diversity of, 9–10

Dahl, Robert A., 239
Dalton, Melville, 223
de Charms, Richard, 241
Decision-making: control of, 30–31,
34; ethical, 14, 15; participatory, 8
Decision-making leave, 105, 126;
paid/unpaid, 105–7

Deetz, Stanley, 233
Defense bar, and wrongful discharge
legislation, 62, 63, 64
Della Fave, L. Richard, 242
Dependency, and political economy,
234
Deutsch, Morton, 31, 32
DeVries, David L., 176
Dialogue, 108
Discharge. *See* Termination; Wrongful
dismissal
Discipline: employee recommendations, 137–39; functions of, 123–24;
juridicial view of, 119–20, 122–23;
organizational behavior view of,
123–24; philosophies of, 119–20. *See
also* Positive discipline; Progressive
discipline
Discrimination, xviii-xix, 84; intentional v. benign, 85, 86, 87; proving, 92; root causes of, 89–91
Dismissal. *See* Termination; Wrongful
dismissal
Disparate-impact theory: advantages
of, 84; application of, 92, 93; claims
statistics on, 88; defined, 84; reliance on, 88; requirements under,
91; and work force composition, 89
Disparate treatment theory: advantages of, 92, 93; claims statistics on,
88; claims suitable for, 89, 90, 91;
criticism of, 84, 90; defined, 83–84;
reliance on, 88
Distributive justice, 26–27; and grievance system, 38, 39; recommendations about, 31–32. *See also* Justice;
Procedural justice
Do no harm principle, 11, 13
Drucker, Peter, 200

Economic resources, distribution of,
245–46
Edwards, Harry T., 46
E. F. Hutton & Company, xxii
Elite: administrative, 199–200; author-
ity of, 205; myth systems of, 204
Emancipation, 234, 251; and rights,
230

Employee: concept of, 237–38; demographics of, 9–10; desired rights of,
214–15; emancipation of, 230, 234,
251; interdependency of, 8–9; interests of, 70–71; and job alternatives,
8, 248–49; mobility of, 9. *See also*
Nonunion employee; Organized
employee; Work force
Employee attitude surveys, 113–14,
158
Employee rights: conceptions of, 211–
14; forces in, 250; and grievance
case studies, 215–16; grievance
study methodology, 216–18; in-
terpretive/critical political economic
perspective on, 235–39; legal conceptions of, 212; legal efforts for,
41–47; moral perspective of, 212–
13; practical perspective of, 213–14
Employee rights and responsibilities,
109–10; defining, 4–5; examination
framework, 17–18; importance of,
xv–xvi; viewpoints of, xvi
Employer: autonomy, 59; interests of,
68–69; procedural voluntarism by,
74–77; and wrongful discharge legislation, 62, 63, 64
Employer-employee relations: adversarial, 100–101; new issues in, 3;
reciprocal character of, 4; transformation factors of, 5, 8–17
Employer rights and responsibilities,
109–10
Employment, alternative, 8, 248–49
Employment-at-will (EAW) doctrine,
xviii, xix-xx; background, 118–19;
employees subject to, 53; erosion
of, 16, 51; exceptions to, 51–53; status of, 212; union challenge to,
120, 122–23
Employment law, employer prerogative era of, 151–52
Empowerment, 243
Equal Employment Opportunity
(EEO), 152
Equal Pay Act (1963), 119
Equity: obstacles to, 34–35; restoration of, 26

Equity theory, 11–12, 26; classification of, 29; and pay fairness, 27
Ethics, 200–201; codes of, 8; study of,
14–16, 208
Ewing, David W., 35, 229, 239
Excellence, 102
Expectations: communication about,
110; employee, 26, 218–19, 225–26;
employee/employer, 23–24, 223–24

Fair Labor Standards Act, 119
Fairness: complexity of, 11; per-
ceived, 23, 28; principles of, 33; re-
source allocation decisions, 26–27
Ferguson, Linda, 198
Festinger, Leon A., 176, 177
Fifth Circuit Court of Appeals, 53
Firefighters Local 1784 v. *Stotts*, 84
Firing. *See* Termination; Wrongful
dismissal
Flexibility, versus bureaucracy, 10–12
Folger, Robert, 31, 33–34
Fortune v. *National Cash Register Co.*,
61
Foulkes, Fred, 35
Free speech, 3
Fulmer, William, 101

Garfinkel, Harold, 238
Garibaldi v. *Lucky Food Stores, Inc.*, 42–
43, 45
Gibson, Mary, 236–37
Goffman, Erving, 244
Gordon, Michael, 38, 39
Goss v. *Lopez*, 75
Government: public/private, 239;
worker protection role of, xviii, 41–
42; wrongdoing in, 14
Gramsci, Antonio, 233
Great Britain, 41, 65
Great Depression, 212
Greenberg, Jerald, 29, 33–34
Grievances, decline in, 114
Grievance system: attitudes toward,
40–41; behavioral research on, 39–
41; benefits of, 37, 47–48; empirical
research into, 153; employee repre-
sentation in, 158; future of, 159–60;

issues involved in, 40–41; and justice, 38, 39; primacy of, 45; requirements for, 153–59. *See also* Arbitration
Griggs v. *Duke Power Company*, 224
Guion, Robert, 38
Guohland, Amy, 8
Gutman, Herbert G., 250

Habermas, Jurgen, 229
Hauserman, Nancy, 198
Hawthorne studies, 25
Heuer, Larry, 30–31
Hirschman, Albert O., 249
Hobsbawm, Eric, 229–30, 235, 237, 247–48
Hollander, Edwin P., 242
Homans, George, 26
Huberman, John, 126

Ideologies, and work, 249–50
Inequity, 26
Information, managing, 246
Instrumental problems, 201
Interest, rights, 240–51
Interest groups, and wrongful discharge legislation, 62–65
International Association of Firefighters, AFL-CIO v. *City of Cleveland*, 85, 86, 89, 92
Interpretive approach, 231, 232, 234
Interpretive/critical political economic perspective, 231–35
Interpretive-critical view, 233–34

Justice, xvii; as behavioral science issue, 22; defined, 22–25; and expectations, 24; organizational action for, 226–28; psychological study of, 24; research on, 11–12; scholarship, on, 21; as socially comparative, 25–26; study background, 25–29; subjective conceptualizations of, 24–25; taxonomy of theories on, 29. *See also* Distributive justice; Procedural justice

Kahn, Robert, 32, 33
Kamenka, Eugene, 236

Katz, Daniel, 32, 33
Kavanagh, M. J., 176
Keil, Linda, 23
Kersten, Astrid, 233
Kochan, Thomas, 38
Kuhn, J. W., 213

Labor-Management Relations Act (1947), 119
Lakoff, Sanford A., 239
Landy, Frank, 32
Lane, Robert E., 242
Langer, Ellen, 241
Language, of rights, 237
Law: challenges to unions, 42–47; climate of, 16; and employee expectations, 224–25; and employee rights, 17–18; and legislatures, 67–68; limitations of, 46; and nonunion workers, 41–42; and workplace justice, xviii; for wrongful discharge, 55–58, 59–60. *See also* Courts
Lawler, Edward E., 10
Lawshe, Charles, 38
Lawyers, xvii, 63, 65
Leadership, 242–43; and justice, 32–33
Legislatures, and employee interests, 67–68
Leventhal, Gerald, 28, 33
Levi, Barnard-Henri, 208
Lewicki, Roy, 33
Lewin, David, 36–37, 39
Lindblom, Charles E., 239, 249–50
Lipset, Seymour, 200
Litigation, xvii; effect of, 46–47; frequency of, 16; and nonunion worker, 35, 42; and organized labor, 45–46
Local 28 of the Sheet Metal Workers' International Association v. *Equal Employment Opportunity Commission*, 84–86, 89, 92
Lockouts, 37

McCall, Morgan M., 176
McClintock, Charles, 23
McCurdy, H. E., 206

McDonough, John J., 243
MacIntyre, Alasdair, 207, 208
Malin, Martin H., 196, 198
Management: corruption in, 200; de-
    mystification of, 251; and ethics,
    208; and manipulation, 207; moral
    decay in, 201; paradox in, 201–6;
    power of, 203
Management by objectives (MBO),
    177
Management education, xxii-xxiii,
    200, 208. *See also* Business educa-
    tion
Managers: as disciplinarians, 101;
    goodwill of, 157; and grievance
    systems, 155; removal of, 157–58
Manipulation, 207
Market, as supreme, 12
Martin, Joanne, 24
Marx, Karl, 234–35
Mathewson, Stanley B., 213, 223
Mathews v. *Eldridge*, 73
Mayflower Madam (Barrows), 202
Mediation, evaluation of, 30–31
Merriam, Charles E., 239
Miceli, Marcia P., 5
Michigan, wrongful discharge statute
    in, 56, 57
Minority groups, 84, 90
Mississippi Supreme Court, 52–53
Mitchell, Terence, 200
Mobility, 9
Mohrman, S. A., 10
Monge v. *Beebe Rubber Co.*, 61
Montana, wrongful dismissal statute
    in, 56, 76–77, 78, 80–81
Moore, Barrington, Jr., 251
Morality, xxii
Murphy v. *American Home Products
    Corp.*, 55
Myth, in orthodox management, 204–
    5

National Association of Manufactur-
    ers, 118
National Labor Relations Act (NLRA,
    1935), 42, 54, 119, 225; proposed
    amendment to, 55

Naturalistic-interpretive view, 232–33
Near, Janet P., 5
Nees v. *Hocks*, 60–61
Newman, Ralph, 22
Nickel, James W., 236
Noble, David, 246
Nonunion employee: due process
    for, 35–37; justice for, 47; protec-
    tion of, 157; resources to, 156; se-
    curity of, xvii-xviii; and wrongful
    discharge legislation, 63, 64. *See
    also* Employee; Organized em-
    ployee; Work force
Nonunion employer, rule structures
    for, 152–53

Olguin v. *Inspiration Consolidated Cop-
    per Co.*, 77
Ombudsman, xx-xxi; within academic
    institutions, 161–62; and institu-
    tional disequilibrium, 169–70; and
    proactive problem-solving, 172; re-
    sistance to, 161
Ombudsman office: and conflict reso-
    lution modes, 170–72; issues for,
    168–69; for medical center, 166; ori-
    gin of, 162–63; structure of, 166–67
Oral reminder, 103–4, 126
Oregon Supreme Court, 52
Organizations: changes in, 10–12;
    corruption in, 13–14; formal struc-
    ture in, 244–48; unobtrusive control
    in, 244–48
Organized employee: due process
    for, 37–41; and grievance system
    use, 39; justice for, 47. *See also* Em-
    ployee; Nonunion employee; Work
    force
Orthodoxy: managerial, 12–13; of
    modern administration, 200
Osigweh, Chimezie A. B., 5

Pareto, Vilfredo, 203–4
Partridge, Bruce, 244
Patton v. *J. C. Penney Co., Inc.*, 52
Penrod, Steven, 30–31
Performance appraisal process, xxi;
    accuracy in, 179; basis of, 180–81;

comprehension of, 184; employee need for, 176–77; employee rights in, 178–84; and employer competence, 183; fairness of, 179–80, 183–84; function of, 175–76; and justice, 32; literature on, 177–78; performance/reward relationship, 180; privacy of, 181; and right to appeal, 181–82; structure of, 184–85; and supervisor-employee counseling relationship, 182–83
Perritt, Henry H., Jr., 230
Perrow, Charles, 246
Personal attributes, and rights, 241–44
Personality characteristics, and rights, 241–42
Personnel policy, merit-oriented, 155
Petermann v. *Teamsters*, 61
Peters, Charles, 189, 193
Peters, Thomas, 99, 200, 206
Pickering v. *Board of Education*, 195
Plaintiff bar, and wrongful discharge legislation, 63–64
Positive discipline, xix, xx; adult-to-adult precepts of, 102; assumptions of, 103; background, 139; choice of, 101–2; defined, 99–100; empirical analysis of, 127–29, 131–33; employee communication about, 112–13; employee complaints about, 132–33; and employee/employer rights and responsibilities, 109–10; employee evaluation of, 138; as good faith dealing, 107; implementation of, 110–11; implementation team, 110–11; maintenance of, 113; managerial requirements for, 115; manager training in, 112; results of, 113–14; as soft approach, 107–9; structure of, 102–5, 126–27. *See also* Discipline
Positive science, 201
Power, 234; differential, 22; managerial, 206; and political economy, 234; and technology, 246–47
Prima facie tort concept, 67
Privacy, 3

Problem-solving, participatory, 5
Procedural justice: concerns about, 32; and grievance system, 38, 39; research on, 27–29; and resource allocation fairness, 27; techniques for, 30–31. *See also* Distributive justice; Justice
Professionalization, and awareness, 5, 8
Professoriate, responsibilities of, 207–8
Progress, through technology, 246–47
Progressive discipline, xx, 125, 126; characteristics and effects of, 100–101; disadvantages of, 107–8; empirical analysis of, 133–34, 136–37; as poor management, 99. *See also* Discipline
Prospect theory, 24
Protest, ease of organizing, 250
Psychological contract, 23–24, 37
Punishment: as dysfunctional, xix; effects of, 123, 124; emphasis on, 99, 100. *See also* Progressive discipline
Punitive system. *See* Progressive discipline
Putnam, Linda L., 231–32

Quality circle programs, 10
Quality of Work Life (QWL), 177

Ramos, A. G., 203, 205, 208
Reality, constructing, 245
Redding, Charles W., 188
Redeker, James, 109–10
Reinstatement, 79–80
Reis, Harry, 27
Relative deprivation, 25
Research, wrongdoing in, 14
Responsibility, xvii; individual, 103, 108, 114–15
Rich, Daniel, 239
Rights: concept of, 235–37; defining, xvii; and emancipation, 230; existence of, 229–30; and interests, 240–51; language of, 237; micro-level exercise of, 241–44; and per-

sonality, 241–44; political economy of, 248–51; surplus meaning to, 251
Rodgers, Daniel, 250
Rules: allocation, 28–29; application of, 12; function of, 11; for nonunion employers, 152–53; utilitarian, 13

Sabine Pilot Services, Inc. v. *Hauck*, 52
Salipante, Paul, 36
Salisbury, Stephen, 229
Sampson, Edward, 24
Sanders, Wayne, 195
Schein, Edgar, 23
Schneider, William, 200
Scott, William, 12, 200
Selection of agents, 28
Self-awareness, 199–200
Self-discipline, 114–15
Seligman, Martin E.P., 241
Sennett, Richard, 241
Service ethic, 8
Sex-role stereotyping, 90
Sheets v. *Teddy's Frosted Foods, Inc.*, 61
Sheppard, Blair, 33
Silverman, David, 232
Simon, Herbert, 200, 203, 207; *Administrative Behavior*, 205
Simpson v. *Western Graphics Corp.*, 52
Social dynamics, analytical categories for, 203–4
Social exchange: defined, 22, 24; expectations, 23; and justice, 25; scientific study of, 23
Socialization: anticipatory, 238; and legal theories, 93; of minority population, 90; of working class, 242
Social reality, construction of, 251
Social resources, distribution of, 245–46
Social Security, 119
Social skills, and rights, 242–44
Specialization, 8–9
Stanford University Medical Center, 161, 165, 168
Stewart, Lea P., 187
Strikes, 37

Substantive due process analysis, 67
Summers, Clyde, 59

Taylor, Frederick W., 118
Technology, and power distribution, 246–47
Tennessee Court of Appeals, 53
Termination: after decision-making leave, 105; after unpaid suspension, 108. *See also* Wrongful dismissal
Texas Supreme Court, 51
Thibaut, John, 27, 28, 29, 30, 33
Thompson v. *St. Regis Paper Co.*, 61
Title VII litigation, 86–88, 91–92
Toussaint v. *Blue Cross and Blue Shield of Michigan*, 61
Towne, Henry, 200
Toxic Substances Control Act (1977), 195–96
Tribunals, 41–42, 78–79
Tyler, Tom, 33

Unemployment, as discipline, 249
Uniform Guidelines on Employee Selection, 11
Union Arbitration Act, 76
Union Carbide Corporation, 99; positive discipline at, 101–2, 110–11, 113–14
Unions: advocacy function of, 45–46; disciplinary efforts of, 120, 122–23; economic power of, 17; factors for, 21; legal challenges to, 42–47; need for, 36; and nonunion employees, 46; rejection of, 16–17; responsibilities of, 131–32; satisfaction with, 37–39; and wrongful dismissal, 54, 62–63, 64, 77. *See also* Collective bargaining
United States Merit Systems Protection Board (MSPB), 196–97
United States Supreme Court: on arbitration, 44–45; discrimination cases, 84–86; on employment-at-will doctrine, 118–19; on whistleblowing, 195; on wrongful discharge, 43

United Steelworkers v. *Warrior & Gulf Navigation Company*, 44–45
University, dual function of, 207–8
Unjust discharge. *See* Wrongful dismissal
Unorganized worker. *See* Nonunion employee

Values, 10; deobjectification of, 201–2; manipulation of, 12–13; study of, 15, 208; utilitarian, 15

Waldo, Dwight, 199–200
Walker, Laurens, 27–28, 29, 30, 33
Walster, Elaine, 26
Walster, G. William, 26
Waterman, Robert, 200, 206
Weick, Karl E., 232
Werhane, Patricia, 195
Westin, Alan F., 178, 226, 229
Whistleblower: characteristics of, 191–94; protection of, 16, 65, 66, 194–97, 198
Whistleblowers Protection Act (Michigan), 196
Whistleblowing, 5, 68; as communicative act, xxi, 188–91; complexity of, 197–98; current status of, 194–97; increase in, 187

Wilson, Woodrow, 200
Women, 9–10; socialization of, 90
Work, beliefs about, 249
Workers. *See* Employee
Workers' compensation, 119
Work force: aging of, 10; changing characteristics of, 5, 8–9; size of, 9
Work structure, and power distribution, 247–48
Written reminder, 104–5, 126
Wrongful dismissal, 42–43; actions against, 54–55; case volume estimate, 80; doctrines of, 60–62; and forum selection, 73–80; simple proposals against, 69–70; single proceeding for, 77–78
Wrongful dismissal legislation: in California, 56–57, 65; just-cause, 65, 66; in Michigan, 56, 57; in Montana, 56, 76–77, 78, 80–81; procedural fairness, 72–73; proposal for, 71–72; and substantive fairness, 66–72
Wygant v. *Jackson Board of Education*, 84

Zaleznik, Abraham, 243

Contributors

ROBERT COULSON is present of the American Arbitration Association (AAA). He is a member of the New York Bar, and Certified Association Executive (CAE) of the American Society of Association Executives, and a director of the New York Society of Association Executives. He is chairman of the Federation of Protestant Welfare Agencies and a director of the Fund for Modern Courts. Formerly secretary of the Association of the Bar of the City of New York (1961–1963), before joining the AAA in 1963, he practiced law in New York City. He is a member of the International Council for Commercial Arbitration and the London Panel of International Arbitrators, an honorary fellow of Arbitrators' Institute of Canada, and an honorary member of the American Society of Appraisers. Coulson is the author of *How to Stay Out of Court*, *Labor Arbitration*, *Business Arbitration*, *The Termination Handbook*, *Fighting Fair: Family Mediation Will Work for You*, and *Professional Mediation of Civil Disputes*. He has written and lectured extensively on the settlement of disputes. Coulson is a graduate of Yale University and Harvard Law School and holds an honorary degree of Doctor of Science in Business Administration from Bryant College.

SARAH S. ETHERTON is a research assistant in applied research, evaluation and planning at West Virginia University. A former newspaper journalist-editor, she developed an interest in industrial relations as a result of her experiences with the Newspaper Guild. She is in the dissertation stage of the requirements for a Ph.D. degree in economics with a specialty in industrial relations. Her research interests focus on labor-management cooperation, labor market economics, and human resource development. Currently, the impact of plant-closings and the part that worksite labor-management cooperation can play in the economic viability of industry are her primary research efforts. She has coauthored research reports and papers in applied social and economic research and evaluation.

BRUCE FORTADO is assistant professor of management at the University of North Florida. Fortado received a B.S. in economics (magna cum laude) from the Wharton School, University of Pennsylvania (1980) and an M.A. in business administration (1981) and a Ph.D. in management (1986) from the Weatherhead School of Management, Case Western Reserve University. Fortado is conducting in-depth interviews of employees and personnel managers to identify the roots and manifestations of conflict in the workplace as well as unusual organizational programs that address these issues.

MICHAEL E. GORDON (Ph.D., University of California, Berkeley, 1969, psychology) is a professor at the Institute of Management and Labor Relations at Rutgers University. He has studied workplace justice, union commitment, and a variety of methodological issues inherent in research on organizational behavior and industrial relations. His work has been published in journals of organizational behavior (*Academy of Management Review, Academy of Management Journal*), industrial psychology (*Journal of Applied Psychology, Personnel Psychology*), and industrial relations (*Industrial and Labor Relations Review, Industrial Relations*). He currently serves on the editorial boards of the *Journal of Applied Psychology* and the *Employee Responsibilities and Rights Journal*.

RICHARD W. HUMPHREYS is the director of the Institute for Labor Studies at West Virginia University. He also serves as director of the Institute of Industrial and Labor Relations and is professor of industrial and labor relations in the College of Business and Economics. He is the author of *Work Measurement: A Review and Analysis*. He has also published articles in the area of negotiated and legislated employee benefits and serves as a consultant in the area of design and installation of employee benefit programs. His research interests include various aspects of labor-management cooperation both at the legislative level and the collective bargaining level. He is a charter member of the International Society of Employee Benefit Specialists, was president (1987) of the West Virginia chapter of the Industrial Relations Research Association, and is editor of the *Labor Studies Journal*. He is a labor economist and received his undergraduate and graduate degrees from Hamline University (1948) and the University of Wisconsin (1949–1958).

WILLIAM R. HUTCHISON is director of corporate employee relations and personnel program at Union Carbide Corporation. He holds a B.S. degree in business administration and an M.S. in industrial relations from West Virginia University. Results of some of Hutchison's innovative employee relations programs in the responsibilities-rights area at Union Carbide have been the subject of articles appearing in scholarly and practitioner outlets such as the *Harvard Business Review*.

J. VERNON JENSEN is professor of speech communication at the University of Minnesota where he teaches courses in argumentation, ethics, rhetorical criticism, British public address, and Asian rhetoric. The author of two books, *Perspectives on Oral Communication* (1970) and *Argumentation: Reasoning in Communication* (1981), he has just completed a book on Thomas Henry Huxley as a communicator. Two articles on Huxley were published in 1988 in the *British Journal for the History of Science* and *Notes and Records of the Royal Society of London*. He has published numerous book reviews and over thirty-five articles in various communication, history, political science, and English journals in the United States, Great Britain, Ireland, Canada, Burma, and Australia. His recent articles on ethics include "Ethical Tension Points in Whistleblowing" (*Journal of Business Ethics*, 6, 1987) and "Teaching Ethics in Speech Communication" (*Communication Education*, 34, 1985). He is currently working on a textbook on ethics in communication. He has been a Fulbright Lecturer in Burma and has traveled widely, researching in Asia and Western Europe. In June 1988 he was one of ten scholars from the United States selected to participate with ten Asian scholars in a conference on "Rhetoric: East and West," sponsored by the National Endowment for the Humanities, held at the East-West Center in Honolulu.

MICHAEL J. KAVANAGH is associate dean of the School of Business and professor of management at the State University of New York, Albany. His articles have appeared in publications such as the *Administrative Science Quarterly, Academy of Management Journal, Journal of Applied Psychology, Journal of Conflict Resolution, Journal of Management, Organizational Behavior and Human Performance, Personnel Psychology,* and *Supervisory Management*. Kavanagh received his B.A. (psychology) from Duquesne University and an M.A. and Ph.D. (industrial-organizational psychology, 1969) from Iowa State University. He was formerly editor of *Industrial-Organizational Psychologist* (1976–1979) and has served as an expert witness in many litigation cases involving employee and employer responsibilities and rights issues. He is a fellow of the American Psychological Association and has done extensive consulting with a variety of public- and private-sector organizations involving all aspects of human resources management. He has helped develop and implement performance appraisal systems in a number of organizations and is currently involved in a major research project with the U.S. Air Force on performance appraisal. Kavanagh has published over one hundred articles in the fields of management and industrial-organizational psychology on a variety of topics. His major fields of interest are performance appraisal, applied research methodology, technology and organizational change, job-related stress, and labor relations.

MARCIA P. MICELI is currently associate professor of management and human resources at Ohio State University. She earned a D.B.A. from Indiana University. Her teaching and research interests include employee rights, particularly whistleblowing and compensation systems. Miceli's articles have previously appeared in such journals as the *Academy of Management Review*, *Academy of Management Journal*, *Administrative Science Quarterly*, and *Personnel Psychology*.

WALTER NORD is professor of organizational psychology in the School of Business, Washington University (St. Louis). He is coauthor (with Peter Frost and Vance Mitchell) of the well-received book *Organizational Reality: Reports from the Firing Line* (Goodyear, 1982). He is also author or coauthor of three other books including *Implementing Routine and Radical Innovations* (with Sharon Tucker). His articles have appeared in numerous major practitioner and scholarly journals such as the *Administrative Science Quarterly*, *Academy of Management Journal*, *Academy of Management Review*, *American Journal of Economics and Sociology*, *Group and Organization Studies*, *Journal of Applied Behavioral Science*, *Journal of Applied Psychology*, and *Organizational Dynamics*. He holds a B.A. (economics) from Williams College, an M.S. (organizational behavior) from Cornell University, and a Ph.D. (social psychology) from Washington University. Nord is on the editorial board of the *Journal of Management* and is coeditor of the *Employee Responsibilities and Rights Journal*.

CHIMEZIE ANTHONY-BAYLON-PASCAL OSIGWEH received his M.A., M.L.H.R. (Master of Labor Relations and Human Resource Management), and Ph.D. (1982) from Ohio State University. He earned his B.S. degree (magna cum laude) in 1978 from East Tennessee State University after completing the four-year undergraduate program in two years. Osigweh is currently executive president, The Council on Employee Responsibilities and Rights (CERR), Virginia Beach, Virginia. He is also professor of management and director of personnel and industrial relations research at Norfolk State University. He was a research associate at the Mershon Center and has also taught at Northeast Missouri State University (the arts and sciences university of the state of Missouri) and Ohio State University. In addition, Osigweh has served as a consultant to a number of business organizations in the United States and abroad. His interests and publications extend to areas as diverse as management, international business, labor relations, organizational communication, problem-solving, international relations, and poetry. His recent research and consulting activities have focused on training and development, participative organizational strategies, effective interviewing systems and skills, workplace communication effectiveness, labor-management relations, and problem diagnosis and solving. Osigweh has served as an occasional reviewer and on editorial review boards for a number of scholarly publications, such as the *Journal of Voluntary Action Research* and the international *Journal of Economic Development*. He is also editor in chief of the interdisciplinary research and practice quarterly, *The Employee Responsibilities and Rights Journal*. His research in the last six years has resulted in the publication of more than forty learned articles. He is published in more than eighteen different journals and is the author of a number of books, including, *Improving Problem-Solving Participation: The Case of Local Transnational Voluntary Organizations* (1983), *Petals of Fire* (poems, 1984), *Professional Management: An Evolutionary Perspective* (1985), *Communicating Employee Responsibilities and Rights: A Modern Management Mandate* (1987), *Organizational Science Abroad* (1989), and *The Divided Organization* (1990, with P. F. Salipante and B. Fortado). Osigweh received the Outstanding Virginia Faculty Award in 1989, from the Virginia State Council for Higher Education.

HENRY H. PERRITT, JR., is professor of law at Villanova University. He is the author of *Employee Dismissal Law and Practice* and *Labor Injunctions*, both of which were published by John Wiley and Sons. He is also the management cochairman of the American Bar Association, Committee on Railway and Airline Labor Law. His articles have appeared in many journals such as the *American University Law Review, Georgetown Law Review, Transportation Law Journal, Villanova Law Review, Labor Law Journal*, and *Journal of Political Analysis and Management*. He has served as a consultant to the U.S. Department of Labor and other private- and public-sector organizations. Perritt holds an S.B. from the Massachusetts Institute of Technology, an S.M. from Sloan School of Management at MIT, and a J.D. from Georgetown University.

PAUL F. SALIPANTE, JR., is associate professor of industrial relations at Case Western Reserve University. He is coauthor of *Job Satisfaction and Productivity: An Evaluation of Policy-Related Research* (1977), with Shrivastva, Cummings, and others. His articles have appeared in many journals such as *Human Organization, Monthly Labor Law, Human Relations, Human Resource Management, Academy of Management Review, Journal of Applied Psychology,* and *Organization and Administrative Sciences.* Salipante has served as a consultant to many major organizations. He obtained an S.B.E.R. (electrical engineering) from MIT (1966), and an M.B.A. (1971) and Ph.D. (1975) from the University of Chicago. His recent research emphasizes the handling of day-to-day conflict in employment settings. This stream of research has focused upon issues of due process and organizational procedures for resolving employer-employee conflict, and upon employees' perceptions of conflict, rights, and managerial responses to claims of injustice. He served as the president and program chairperson of the 1988 Annual National Conference on the Council on Employee Responsibilities and Rights.

WILLIAM G. SCOTT is affiliate program professor of management and organization, University of Washington (Seattle). He was formerly editor of the *Academy of Management Journal* (1969–1972) and associate editor of *Administration and Society* (1979–1984). Scott has held many endowed chairs and distinguished lectureships and fellowships at various points in his career (e.g., at Syracuse University, University of Missouri, Battelle Memorial Institute, University of Santa Clara). He was winner of both the Chester I. Barnard Award for outstanding article of the year in the *Southern Review of Public Administration* (1983) and the Dimock Award for distinguished contribution to the *Public Administration Review* in 1983. Scott is author or coauthor of about sixteen books, several of which are also available in French, Spanish, Chinese, and Japanese translations. His numerous articles have appeared in almost every major scholarly and practitioner journal in management and public administration, as well as in other disciplines (e.g., *Journal of Communication*). Scott received an A.B. (sociology) from DePaul University, an M.S.I.R. (industrial relations) from Loyola University, and a D.B.A. (management) from Indiana University. Scott is a fellow of the Academy of Management.

JACK STIEBER is professor of labor and industrial relations and economics at Michigan State University. He is a graduate of the City College of New York, earned his master's degree at the University of Minnesota where he was a Littauer and a Wertheim Fellow. Stieber served as director of the Michigan State School of Labor and Industrial Relations from 1956 to 1985 and associate director for research and planning from 1956 to 1959. He received the Distinguished Faculty Award at Michigan State University in 1974. Before coming to MSU, Stieber served as research associate, Harvard Business School, 1954–56; executive assistant to the CIO members of the Wage Stabilization Board during the Korean War, 1951–52; economist, United Steelworkers of America, 1948–50; and labor specialist in the National Housing Agency, 1946–47. In 1962 Stieber was executive secretary to President Kennedy's Advisory Committee on Labor-Management Policy. He was research consultant in the International Labour Organization in 1963–64. Stieber has taught and lectured abroad in Great Britain, Belgium, Japan, India, Iran, Israel, New Zealand, and Australia. He was an overseas fellow at Churchill College, Cambridge University, in 1978. In 1983 he served as president of the Industrial Relations Research Association. Stieber has authored or edited eleven books and many articles in professional journals. His most recent books are *Protecting Unorganized Employees against Unjust Discharge* (1983), *U.S. Industrial Relations 1950–1980: A Critical Assessment* (1981), *Multinationals, Unions and Industrial Relations in Industrialized Countries* (1977), and *Public Employee Unionism* (1973). He is on the editorial review board of the *Employee Responsibilities and Rights Journal*, has served as a labor arbitrator since 1956, and is a member of the National Academy of Arbitrators.

REBECCA A. (BAYSINGER) THACKER is an assistant professor of management at the University of Louisville, Kentucky. She recently served as a visiting assistant professor of management at Texas A&M University and has taught at the University of Houston, Clear Lake. She received her Ph.D. from Texas A&M University in management. Her area of specialization is human resource management. Thacker's background includes several years as a personnel manager for financial institutions, and her research interests include the role of public policy in human resource management, human resource management and the law, labor market differences between the sexes, and strategic human resource management.

MERLE WAXMAN is director of the Office for Women in Medicine at Yale University. She was formerly associate ombudsman at the Stanford University Medical Center (1982–1985). Her research articles have appeared in publications such as the *Journal of Medical Education*, *Neuroscience Letters*, and the *Western Journal of Medicine*. She received a B.S. (1968) from Boston University and an M.A. (1972) from City University of New York.

ALAN F. WESTIN is president of the Educational Fund for Individual Rights, and professor of public law and government at Columbia University. He is also president of Changing Workplaces (a management information consulting organization). Westin is an internationally recognized expert on the organizational, social, and legal implications of emerging information technologies. He has written or coauthored over thirty books on law, politics and technology, including *Freedom Now: The*

Civil Rights Struggle in America (1964), *Privacy and Freedom* (1967), *Banks in a Free Society* (1972), *The Trial of Martin Luther King* (1975), *Individual Rights in the Corporation* (1980), *Whistle Blowing* (1980), *The Changing Workplaces* (1985), *Privacy Issues in the Monitoring of Employee Work on VDTs in the Office Environment* (1985), and *Fair Process at Work* (1986). Westin has directed studies of more than one hundred mechanisms by corporate, government, and nonprofit organizations under the sponsorship of the Russell Sage, Ford, and Rockefeller foundations. He has identified issues and recommended approaches that have become cornerstones of U.S. information privacy policies to the present day. His articles have appeared in *The Personnel Administrator, Business Week, Wall Street Journal, New York Times Magazine,* and *Fortune,* as well as in many scholarly journals and other leading periodicals. He has been a consultant to more than one hundred companies, government agencies, and foundations. Westin received his law degree and a Ph.D. in political science from Harvard University.

STUART A. YOUNGBLOOD is currently associate professor of management at Texas A&M University. He received his Ph.D. in administrative sciences from Purdue University and taught at the University of South Carolina prior to joining the faculty at Texas A&M. His research interests include absenteeism and turnover, unjust dismissal disputes, and legal issues related to human resources practices. He has coauthored a textbook with Randall Schuler and coedited a readings book and a case book with Schuler. His articles have appeared in such periodicals as *Journal of Applied Psychology, Journal of Occupational Medicine, Personnel, Industrial Relations Law Journal, Business and Economic Review, Personnel Administrator,* and *Arbitration Journal.*

FREDERICK A. ZELLER is managing editor of the *Employee Responsibilities and Rights Journal.* He is also director of the Institute of Industrial and Labor Relations, president of the board of trustees of the Frankel Foundation, and research professor of industrial relations and program leader for applied research evaluation and planning at West Virginia University. Zeller is the author or coauthor of four books and monographs, including *The Practice of Local Union Leaders: A Study of Five Local Unions* (1965) and *Manpower Development* (1969). Zeller has presented or published more than eighty-three learned papers in such leading journals as *Industrial and Labor Relations Review, Labor Law Journal, Monthly Labor Review, Industrial Relations,* and the *Journal of Industrial Arts Education.* He received his B.Sc. (industrial management) and M.A. (economics) from the University of North Dakota and his Ph.D. (labor economics, 1963) from Ohio State University. Zeller has served as a consultant to various corporations and state government agencies in North Dakota, Ohio, and West Virginia. He was associate director of the national Surveys of Labor Force Behavior at Ohio State University during 1969–1970.